Modern and Contemporary Poetry and Poetics

Series Editor
David Herd
University of Kent
Canterbury, UK

Founded by Rachel Blau DuPlessis and continued by David Herd, *Modern and Contemporary Poetry and Poetics* promotes and pursues topics in the burgeoning field of 20th and 21st century poetics. Critical and scholarly work on poetry and poetics of interest to the series includes: social location in its relationships to subjectivity, to the construction of authorship, to oeuvres, and to careers; poetic reception and dissemination (groups, movements, formations, institutions); the intersection of poetry and theory; questions about language, poetic authority, and the goals of writing; claims in poetics, impacts of social life, and the dynamics of the poetic career as these are staged and debated by poets and inside poems. Since its inception, the series has been distinguished by its tilt toward experimental work – intellectually, politically, aesthetically. It has consistently published work on Anglophone poetry in the broadest sense and has featured critical work studying literatures of the UK, of the US, of Canada, and Australia, as well as eclectic mixes of work from other social and poetic communities. As poetry and poetics form a crucial response to contemporary social and political conditions, under David Herd's editorship the series will continue to broaden understanding of the field and its significance.

More information about this series at
http://www.palgrave.com/gp/series/14799

Jo Lindsay Walton · Ed Luker
Editors

Poetry and Work

Work in Modern and Contemporary
Anglophone Poetry

Editors
Jo Lindsay Walton
Bath Spa University
Bath, UK

Ed Luker
University of Surrey
Guildford, UK

Modern and Contemporary Poetry and Poetics
ISBN 978-3-030-26124-5   ISBN 978-3-030-26125-2   (eBook)
https://doi.org/10.1007/978-3-030-26125-2

Cover credit: The Picture Art Collection/Alamy Stock Photo

This Palgrave Macmillan imprint is published by the registered company Springer Nature Switzerland AG
The registered company address is: Gewerbestrasse 11, 6330 Cham, Switzerland

ACKNOWLEDGEMENTS

Jo Lindsay Walton acknowledges the support of the Institute of the Advanced Studies in the Humanities, University of Edinburgh, and the Sussex Humanities Lab, University of Sussex, for part of the time spent preparing this collection. Both Jo and Ed would like to thank our families and friends, as also to express our gratitude to Rachel Blau Duplessis, Robert Hampson, Rodrigo Toscano, Juliana Spahr, Anne Boyer, Samantha Walton, Lila Matsumoto, Nat Raha, Eleanor Careless, Sara Crangle, David Herd, Surya Sekaran, Preetha Kuttiappan, and Allie Troyanos for their contributions and enthusiasm, and to Rachel Jacobe at Palgrave for her patience, encouragement, and scrupulousness. And we'd both like to give special thanks to Ian Davidson for all his support and guidance.

PRAISE FOR *POETRY AND WORK*

"This volume represents an outstanding contribution to current debates in contemporary poetry. It examines the poetry of work and the work that poetry does in a highly original, theoretically sophisticated and analytically nuanced manner. The essays engage with work and labour across a range of poetries and constituencies and provide a timely address to the place of work in the context of a post-work future and the privatised digital market. It is likely to be seen as a major, paradigm-shifting work in relation to contemporary poetry."

—Robert Hampson, *Professor of English, Royal Holloway, University of London, UK, and author of* Seaport *(2008)*

"To think poetry and work together is to question poetry's standing both against and as work, to hypothesize what poetry itself might be in the world of those who wish to end all we have hitherto known as labor. The essays in this collection engage fearlessly with the permutations, consequences and destructive capacities of this questioning. They represent a new generation—perhaps, we hope, the last generation—of those who will even speak the words poetry and work as if they were commensurate. That the book speaks to such a hope is the highest possible form of recommendation."

—Anne Boyer, *Associate Professor, Kansas City Art Institute, USA, and author of* A Handbook of Disappointed Fate *(2018) and* Garments Against Women *(2015)*

"In a time when there is virtually no subjectivity that hasn't found its 'voice,' no 'topic' that hasn't been duly treated, no 'issue' that's not been confronted, the concept and reality of *work* in poetics remains elusive at best; at worst, a near censorship of it reigns. But upon close examination, it becomes clear that overtly flushing out the phenomenon of work from aesthetic acts, *embarrasses* aesthetic discourse in general. Idealism collapses unto materialism. And it is from this humbling and renewed state of awareness that we must begin. In this riveting new collection, the three intertwined aspects of work—the symbolic, the productive, and the distributive—are explored thoroughly. The essays themselves stand as authentic poetic acts. Cultural archeologists of the future might well regard this volume as an essential guide to the ever expanding horizon of that strange human productive activity we call poetry."

—Rodrigo Toscano, *author of* Collapsible Poetics Theater *(2008) and* Explosion Rocks Springfield *(2016)*

"This collection of essays rigorously explores how capitalism, reproductive labor, the falling rate of profit, and acts of working are represented in post-war poetry. Poets are unacknowledged day job workers of the cultural production world. A significant part of post-war poetry is written during time stolen on the day job or late in the evening, after a long shift. As such, poems are full of theoretical possibilities for understanding how work has shaped the aesthetics, the affinities, and the utopian claims of contemporary literature. This book stands as a committed investigation into an array of affinities between the ordinary grounding of work and its utopian claims."

—Juliana Spahr, *Professor of English, Mills college, USA, and author of* That Winter the Wolf Came *(2015)*

CONTENTS

NOTES ON CONTRIBUTORS

Eleanor Careless completed her AHRC-funded Ph.D. *Serve Your Own Sentences: Incarceration in the Poetry* of Anna Mendelssohn at the University of Sussex in 2018. Her current research focuses on representations of imprisonment by women in the twentieth century. She is currently an Associate Tutor within the School of English at the University of Sussex. In 2016 she was the recipient of an AHRC International Placement Scheme research fellowship at the Library of Congress, Washington, DC, and in 2017 she was awarded a Literary Encyclopedia Travel Award which facilitated archival research at the Harry Ransom Centre in Austin, Texas. She won a British Association of Modernist Studies essay prize in 2018, and has publications forthcoming from Palgrave (2019), *Modernist Cultures* (2019) and *College Literature* (2020). She is the co-editor of a forthcoming special issue on Anna Mendelssohn for the *Journal of British and Irish Innovative Poetry*.

Amber DiPietra has worked as a community practice artist, poet, performer, disability rights advocate, intimacy coach, and a certified Sexological Bodyworker/Somatic Sex Educator. Since this piece was written in 2010, Amber DiPietra has left San Francisco and moved back to Florida due to health issues and increasing pain. Public transit as well as disability services and community are fairly non-existent in Florida, so she is now a sex worker and body worker, which is labor she can do from home. Her book *Waveform* (2011), in collaboration with Denise Leto, meditates on chronicity and floating. Her work has also been anthologized in *Beauty is a Verb: The New Poetry of Disability* (2011). Her first solo performance art piece The Opposite of Evolution Dance Studio premiered at the Tampa Fringe Festival in 2018. You can find her at thebodypoetik.com.

Annabel Haynes teaches poetry, modernism, creative writing and utopian fiction at the University of Sussex, where she is a Teaching Fellow in Modern and Contemporary English. Her thesis, *Making Beauty: Basil Bunting and the Work of Poetry* (Durham University), adopted a new critical focus on the British modernist by investigating the consistent attention his poetry pays to different kinds of labor. Bunting's ideas about alternative and ideal forms of creative work align with Annabel's further interests in utopian work societies, and utopian and dystopian writing. She is working on a book on Bunting, as well as writing about utopian fiction and Afrofuturism for the forthcoming *The Oxford Handbook of Thomas More's Utopia*. She continues to write on Bunting and other poets writing in the modernist tradition, and recently considered Bunting's translocal connection to objectivist, and fellow folk-interested poet, Lorine Niedecker in a chapter for *Navigating the Transnational in Modern American Literature and Culture*, eds. Tara Stubbs and Doug Haynes (Routledge, 2017).

Lisa Jeschke teaches at CAU Kiel and is a freelance translator. Both occupations are part-time. Publications include, with Adrian May (eds.), *Matters of Time: Material Temporalities in Twentieth-Century French Culture* (Oxford: Peter Lang, 2014), with Marina Vishmidt, "Work Breaks Us, We Break Work", in *365 Days of Invisible Work*, ed. domestic worker photographer network (Leipzig: spector books, 2017, n.p.) and, with Lucy Beynon, *The Tragedy of Theresa May* (Cambridge: Tipped Press, 2018).

Aimée Lê is an Associate Member of the Poetics Research Centre at Royal Holloway. She received her Ph.D. from Royal Holloway, University of London, on the national question in twentieth-century American literature. With Fiona Chamness, she is the author of a book of poetry, *Feral Citizens* (Red Beard Press, 2011). Recent projects include an EP of (mis)translated Greek pop songs, *Aliki in Saigon*, through Greek queer label Fytini, and publications in *Muzzle, Litmus Magazine,* and *The Journal of British and Irish Innovative Poetry.*

Ed Luker has recently finished a Ph.D. at Northumbria University on the politics of attention in the early poetry of J. H. Prynne and late modernism. He holds an M.A. in Critical Theory and a B.A. in Literature and Philosophy from the University of Sussex. He runs the RIVET. poetry series. He is the author of a handful of poetry collections, including *Peak Return* (2014), *Headlost* (2014), *The Sea Together* (2016), *Compound Out The Fractured World* (2017), and *Heavy Waters* (2019).

Lila Matsumoto received her Ph.D. from the University of Edinburgh, with a thesis on the Scottish-American transatlantic poetry connection as witnessed in the little magazines *Migrant* and *Poor.Old.Tired.Horse.* She currently lectures at the University of Nottingham. Her critical writing has been published in the *Journal of British and Irish Innovative Poetry* and *Shearsman Review* among other places. She co-edits the magazine *Front Horse* and her recent organizational work includes Modernist Art Writing/Writing Modernist Art; Outside-In/Inside-Out Festival of Outside and Subterranean Poetry, and an international symposium on artists' books at the Scottish National Gallery of Modern Art. Her first collection of poetry *Urn & Drum* was published by Shearsman in 2018. She collaborates widely with musicians, artists, and other poets.

Peter Middleton studied at Oxford, Sheffield and SUNY Buffalo, and is currently a Professor of English at the University of Southampton. His books include *Physics Envy: American Poetry and Science in the Cold War and After* (2015), *Distant Reading: Performance, Readership, and Consumption in Contemporary Poetry* (2005). With Nicky Marsh he edited *Teaching Modernist Poetry* (2010). His research interests include science and literature, modern and contemporary poetry, and autobiographical non-fiction. He has recently written essays on the role of analogy in literature and science studies, literary images of queer poetry communities, the history of science fiction, the poetry of Peter Gizzi, and the frontier trope in late twentieth-century sciences. Peter's poetry includes *Aftermath* (2003).

Jose-Luis Moctezuma received his Ph.D. from the University of Chicago in 2018. His poetry and criticism have been published in *Jacket2, Chicago Review, Big Bridge, MAKE Magazine, PALABRA, FlashPoint, Cerise Press,* and elsewhere. His chapbook, *Spring Tlaloc Seance,* was published by Projective Industries in 2016, and his first full-length book of poems, *Place-Discipline*, was published in 2018. *Place-Discipline* was selected by Myung Mi Kim as the winner of the 2017 Omnidawn 1st/2nd Poetry Book Prize. He teaches at Wilbur Wright College in Chicago.

Holly Pester is a Lecturer in Poetry and Performance at University of Essex, Department of Literature, Film and Theatre. Between 2014 and 2016 she was an associate researcher at the Wellcome Collection's Hub project, researching themes of rest and its opposites in neuroscience, social sciences and the arts. Her AHRC-funded doctoral research at Birkbeck, University of London led to a major AHRC Cultural Engagement Award in contemporary poetic research. Her current research seeks to develop innovative practice-led research methodologies in relation to feminist theory. Her book on gossip and anecdote as forms of archive enquiry was published by Book Works in 2015, and was developed through an Arts Council funded research at the Women's Art Library at Goldsmiths College's Special Collections. Other publications include book chapters in *Memory in the Twenty-First Century: Critical Perspectives from Sciences and Arts and Humanities*, ed. Sebastian Groes (London: Palgrave Macmillan and NESTA, 2015), and articles in *Feminist Review* (Vol. 115, Issue 1, 2017) and *Women: A Cultural Review* (Vol. 26, Issue 1, 2015).

Nat Raha is a poet, scholar and queer/trans activist. She is completing a Ph.D. thesis titled *Queer Capital: Marxism in Queer Theory and Post-1950 Poetics* at the University of Sussex. Her poetry includes the collections: *Of Sirens, Body & Faultlines* (Boiler House Press, 2018), *Countersonnets* (Contraband Books, 2013), and *Octet* (Veer Books, 2010), alongside numerous pamphlets. Nat's essay, "Transfeminine Brokeness, Radical Transfeminism," appears in the *South Atlantic Quarterly*, and she is the co-editor of the *Radical Transfeminism Zine*.

Lytton Smith is Associate Professor of English and Creative Writing and Director of the Center for Integrative Learning at SUNY Geneseo, having received his Ph.D. and M.F.A. from Columbia University. The author of two collections of poetry from Nightboat Books, most recently *While You Were Approaching the Spectacle But Before You Were Transformed By It*, his critical work on Craig Santos Perez and Peter Gizzi has appeared in *Literary Geographies* and *In the Air: The Poetry of Peter Gizzi* (Wesleyan UP). He is working on projects that explore the interaction between citizenship and poetic acts.

Catherine Wagner is a Professor at Miami University in Oxford, Ohio, where she directs the Creative Writing Program and is a founding member and president of the local chapter of the American Association of University Professors, which advocates for university labor. Full-length collections of her poetry include *Macular Hole* (Fence Books, 2004), *My New Job* (Fence Books, 2009), *Nervous Device* (City Lights Books, 2012) and *Of Course* (Fence Books, forthcoming). Her writing has been published widely in journals and in anthologies including the *Norton Anthology of Postmodern American Poetry* (Norton, 2014) and *Out of Everywhere 2: Linguistically Innovative Poetry by Women in North America & the UK* (Reality Street Editions, 2015). She has previously written on the subject of poetry and labor for the Anglophone poetics anthology *Toward. Some. Air* (Banff Centre Press, 2014) and *Poetic Labor Project* (July 2012).

Jo Lindsay Walton completed his Ph.D. at Northumbria University in 2016, and since then has been working at Surrey, Bath Spa, Leicester, Edinburgh, UEA, and Sussex. He is co-editor of a special issue of ASLE-UKI's *Green Letters* on crime fiction and the environment (2018); a special issue of *The Journal of British and Irish Innovative Poetry* on poetry and secrecy (2018); the poetry reviews journal *Hix Eros* (2013–); the British Science Fiction Association journal *Vector* (2018–); and the small poetry press Sad Press (2009–).

Samantha Walton is a Reader in Modern British Literature at Bath Spa University. Her research explores the intersection of mental health and ecology. In 2018–2019, she was a Writing Fellow at the Rachel Carson Center, Munich, and in 2016 held an Environmental Humanities Research Fellowship at IASH, University of Edinburgh. Samantha was funded by the British Academy in 2015–2017 for the project *Landscaping Change*, and the AHRC through their ECR Leadership Fellowship scheme for the project *Cultures of Nature and Wellbeing* (2016–2018). She co-edits the ASLE-UKI journal, *Green Letters: Studies in Ecocriticism* and the poetry publisher Sad Press. Her academic publications include *Guilty But Insane: Mind and Law in Golden Age Detective Fiction* (OUP, 2015) and *The Living World: Nan Shepherd and Environmental Thought* (Punctum, 2019). In 2018, she published her first full length poetry collection, *Self Heal*, from Boiler House Press.

Tyrone Williams is a Professor at Xavier University, Cincinnati, where he teaches literature and theory. He is the editor of *African American Literature: Revised Edition* (Salem Press, 2008) and has published widely in scholarly and literary journals. His full-length collections of poetry include *c.c.* (2002), *On Spec* (2008), *The Hero Project* (2009), *Adventures of Pi* (2011), *Howell* (2011) and *As Iz* (2018).

LIST OF FIGURES

CHAPTER 1

Introduction: Working Late

Jo Lindsay Walton and Ed Luker

This collection has a twofold purpose: both to present a breadth of scholarship on poetry in relation to work, and to stand testament to the work of scholarship itself, as one of the mediums within which poetry prospers and accomplishes a rich variety of significances and effects. The collection's contributors explore a range of post-war and contemporary poets writing in English, with some emphasis on modernist and avant-garde writing. Drawing on a variety of theoretical approaches, these essays address how work and labour manifest in and around such poetry.[1]

---

[1] Throughout the collection, the words *work* and *labour* are for the most part used interchangeably. However, many theorists do draw some distinction or other. For instance, sometimes *labour* is a large and inclusive category, whereas *work* is paid or otherwise formalised labour. That distinction more-or-less aligns with the Marxist tendency to treat *labour* as human creative power which is exploited and alienated by capital as *work*. Hannah Arendt divides things somewhat differently, with *labour* referring to the perpetual and necessary work of biological sustenance, associated with the *animal laborans*, beast of burden, or slave, and *work* referring to the artificing of a common world, associated with the maker, or *homo faber*; for Arendt, even work is still bound up with instrumentality, and is not the

J. L. Walton (✉)
Bath Spa University, Bath, UK

E. Luker
Northumbria University, Newcastle upon Tyne, UK

© The Author(s) 2019
J. L. Walton and E. Luker (eds.), *Poetry and Work*,
Modern and Contemporary Poetry and Poetics,
https://doi.org/10.1007/978-3-030-26125-2_1

1

They explore questions like: What can poetry tell us about work? What kind of work is poetry? What kind of workers are poets? What can the act of writing poetry tell us about other kinds of work? What kind of work do poets do when they're not writing poetry? How does poetry imagine 'better' work—work that is freer and more just, work that is less exploitative and less alienated?

If you start to look for references to work in modern and contemporary poetry, you'll find them everywhere. A line from George Oppen's *Of Being Numerous* (1968) evokes a perpetual busyness: "They will begin over, that is, / Over and over."[2] The poem "Money and Land" by Karen Brodine, from her collection *Illegal Assembly* (1980), lists the jobs she's had: "berry-picker, baby-sitter, dance-teacher, writer, secretary, bread-baker, art model, waitress, house-cleaner, old woman's companion, slide-mounter, writing teacher, dish-washer, paste-up person, typesetter, house-painter, inventory-taker, label-maker."[3] The first poem from Harryette Mullen's *S*PeRM**K*T* (1992) draws together the poet's work with that of a supermarket worker. "Lines assemble gutter and margin," and among these lines of commodities is "[h]er hand scanning throwaway lines."[4] While poetry booklets have gutters and margins, and lines of poetry are scanned for their metre, the "gutter" is also proverbially where you may end up if you have no work, and the word "lines" implies the taxonomising of commodities via barcodes. "Her hand," presumably that of a woman working on a checkout, becomes the labouring component. The focus on the hand alone suggests alienation, and the way capital disintegrates the worker into the components that create value and the components that don't matter; probably the "she" whom this hand belongs to would rather be elsewhere. These actions fit Oppen's description too: presumably they will occur "[o]ver and over" until the working day is done. And then the next day.

In *Poetic Artifice: A Theory of 20th-Century Poetry* (1978), Veronica Forrest-Thomson argues for poetry as a form where language is

realm of true human freedom; that is political life, for which she distinguishes a third term, *action*. See also the opening of Lytton Smith's chapter in this collection.

[2] George Oppen, *Of Being Numerous* (1968) in *New Collected Poems* (New York: New Directions, 2008), 170.

[3] Karen Brodine, *Illegal Assembly* (Brooklyn: Hanging Loose Press, 1980), 37–38.

[4] Harryette Mullen, *Recyclopedia* (Minneapolis, MN: Graywolf Press, 2006), 65.

inherently autonomous from its everyday use. Forrest-Thomson's argument confronts what she sees as the unambitious and impoverished spirit
of post-war British poetry, exemplified by Philip Larkin. At the same
time, we still find her own poetry inextricably bound to the everyday
world of work. For instance, Forrest-Thomson writes in "Strike," from
On The Periphery (1976), that "Jobs were scarce and someone with a
purple-point siamese to keep / In strawberries and cream has a certain
standard of living. When I sold my rings and stopped buying clothes I
knew / It was the end." These ironized references to recession and poverty inevitably also imply their de-ironized versions.[5] Even poetry that
seems to be determined not to be about work can be understood in the
shadow of work. One famous example is Frank O'Hara's "A Step Away
From Them," in *Lunch Poems* (1964), which Peter Middleton discusses
in the following chapter.

Within poetry, the theme of work can create a window onto much
wider views of self, society, and universe. Since the end of the nineteenth
century, the story of work in the West has, in its rough outlines, been the
story of Taylorism and Fordism, of the construction and partial disman-
tling of the welfare state, and of the rise of neoliberalism and post-Fordism; we also could identify a distinct recent phase characterised by the
growth of the gig economy and the use of digital platforms to organise
work. It has also been the story of the interaction between the labour
movement and new social movements, especially women's liberation and
feminism, and struggles for access to paid work and to careers, for more
just recognition of who is a worker and what should count as work, and
for the right to reject work. Finally, it has been the story of globalisation, and the intensifying connectivity and exploitation across the Global
North/South divide.

The poetry explored here does not provide any straightforward reflection or distillation of this history. In plenty of cases, events in the world
of work do emerge immediately and palpably in the poetry being written at the time. But poetry's untimeliness can be just as significant. For
instance, half a century ago, Language poetry aimed to subvert the hierarchy of author and reader, hoping to recruit the reader as a more active
meaning-maker. This avant-garde strategy now appears as a foreshadow-
ing of the dispersed digital labour of social media content, in which the

---

[5]Veronica Forrest-Thomson, *On the Periphery* (1976) in *Collected Poems* (Bristol:
Shearsman, 2008), 134.

roles of producer and consumer are likewise blurred. On the other hand, a long, complex backward glance can be discovered in relatively recent writing by J. H. Prynne, in its concern with a productivist ethos that does not merely romanticise pre-Taylorist craftwork. To take another example, Andrea Brady's *Wildfire: A Verse Essay On Obscurity And Illumination* (2010) actively positions itself within a very large history of incendiary devices, from Greek fire to IEDs. Brady has also tried to make the work of poetry-writing more visible and accountable, letting the poem take shape online, while minutely registering her sources and inspirations. In the following fragment she invokes complicity, consumerism, and the mundane condemnation to the labour of self-reproduction:

> The hope drunk in which we dress ourselves
> for a day labour gaming
> with maximum power and killer graphics
> taking it hard, the must-haves this autumn
> whinge at the prison of the veil.
> Secularism is another orthodoxy we can't shake,
> to recognise the politics in fancy dress
> also buries its charge under the base
> though the countdown is not due to start
> for you or your oldest child
> or for the slaves you inherit after that.[6]

Across the stanza a curious twist occurs between the pronouns "we" on the opening line and the "you" of the last two lines. The stanza starts with the kinds of internal fantasy people ("hope drunk") use to sustain their energy "for a day labour gaming." The word "gaming" might imply computer games (or gamification specifically[7]) and suggest how labour is mediated and transformed by technology. The word also brings to mind the labour of gendered and racialised performance in the workplace: that is, both submitting to 'playing the game,' and seeking where possible to 'game' your own domination. By the end of this stanza, what is really stressed is that capitalism is not a system where everyone equally suffers from "a day labour gaming." Some of the people included in

---

[6]Andrea Brady, *Wildfire: A Verse Essay on Obscurity and Illumination* (San Francisco: Krupskaya, 2010), 15.

[7]Gamification: the use of techniques and elements such as points, badges, leaderboards, to organise action in non-game contexts.

"we" are "you or your oldest child / or the slaves you inherit after that." These "slaves" must include the estimated forty million people, mostly women, in slavery today.[8] But Brady also, with deliberate crudeness, collapses distinctions between chattel slavery, indentured slavery, and wage slavery. Yes, there are many differences between inheriting human beings as property, and inheriting a position of structural privilege—but right now Brady's poem is more interested in the similarities. To live 'comfortably' in capitalism, it says, is to be a slave-owner.

This rest of this introductory chapter maps some of the major themes of the collection, identifying dialogues across chapters, and offering some basic context and definitions. It begins with feminist approaches to work, looking at a variety of key terms such as *reproductive labour*, *affective labour*, and *aesthetic labour*; then touches on Marxian alienation; craftwork; publics and the labour of activists and citizens; corporeality and transcorporeality, colonialism and postcolonialism; memory and performance; carceral labour; autoethnography; and precarity and postwork theory.

Manifold Labour

As Jane Commane writes, "work should be every bit as universal a theme as love, and yet too often it remains the unspoken, unsung business of our days."[9] The collection opens with Middleton's "Show Your Working," which mentions the "remarkable lack in modern and contemporary modernist poetry of explicit poetic treatments of contemporary labour conditions."[10] But there are plenty of exceptions. Middleton points to explicit accounts of industrial exploitation in Muriel Rukeyser's *US 1* (1938), Barry MacSweeney's *Black Torch* (1978), or Mark Nowak's

[8] International Labour Organization and Walk Free Foundation, "Global Estimates of Modern Slavery: Forced Labour and Forced Marriage" (Geneva, 2017). The 2017 estimated figure of 40.3 million people in slavery breaks down as 15.4 million in forced marriage, 4.8 million in forced sexual exploitation, 4.1 million in state-imposed labour (including prison labour which does not meet ILO standards), and 24.9 million in other forms of forced labour (including domestic work, construction, manufacturing, agriculture/fishing, and other kinds of work).

[9] Jane Commane, "Ideas Above Your Station: Eight Thoughts on Writing the Working Life," in *Magma* No. 74 (Summer 2019), ed. Benedict Newbery and Pauline Sewards, 20.

[10] Peter Middleton, "'Show Your Working': Other Forms of Labour in Recent Poetry," q.v.

Shut Up Shut Down (2004). To these we could add recent work in an investigative vein such as Alena Hairston's *The Logan Topographies* (2007), Rita Wong's *Forage* (2008), Frances Kruk's *Pin* (2014), and Anne Boyer's *Garments Against Women* (2015), as well as more autoethnographic work such as Leslie Kaplan's *L'excès-l'usine* (1982), translated by Julie Carr and Jennifer Pap as *Excess—The Factory* (2018), Catherine Wagner's *My New Job* (2009), or Karen Brodine's *Work Week* (1977), *Illegal Assembly* (1980), and *Woman Sitting at the Machine, Thinking* (1990). Some of these texts are addressed in later chapters. Looking beyond these overt accounts, however, Middleton also suggests we rethink what is often understood by poetic representation of work. First, choose any poem you like, and work is implicitly everywhere. Work is implied, for example, by everyday objects, by the built environment, and indeed by any landscape shaped by human deeds. Second, work must be understood as a large and nebulous category, extending well beyond the production of material things, and well beyond paid employment.[11]

"A Womans Work is never done" (c.1654) recounts a day of unremitting housewife's work, from the first moments of wakefulness ("Before that I my head with dressings adorn, / I sweep & cleanse the house as need doth require / Or if that it be cold, I make a fire") through to

---

[11] Just ranging across some uses of the word *work* conveys the concept's versatility. You work in an office. Or you are working from home. Or you work on the assembly line. Or you work for Bob. Or you work on a poem. Or you work on a new idea. You work all the time. You're working even when you're not working. You're out of work. You are worked up. You are working off whatever you did to hurt your friend, but you wish you could work out what it was. The two of you really need to work on your communication. You are working your way through those biscuits. You made quick work of them. You are working on the assumption that the bar is this way. You are working on your body positivity. You are working on your tan. You are working on your masterpiece. You are working on your imposter syndrome. You are working the room. You are working your ticket. You are working your way through the amusement park rides. You are on the dancefloor working your butt. You are at work working your butt off. You worked out what it is you love about her so much. You've had some work done. This is Moriarty's work! You aren't the person you want to be but you're working on it. Your splinter will work its way out. You are working through Season Six now. You are working on your wellbeing. You are working on your relationship. You don't think this is working anymore. You are working through the day in your dreams. Teamwork makes the dream work. You have back pain and you can't sleep—is what you're doing work? The popular or folk-theoretic understandings of work, as expressed in everyday idiomatic language, form a useful complement to the various theoretical taxonomies presented here.

a restless night interrupted by the work of breastfeeding and sex.[12] In *Women and Economics* (1898), Charlotte Perkins Gilman writes that women's labour "is neither given nor taken as a factor in economic exchange" and that it is rather "held to be their duty as women to do this work." Critiquing the fancy that a marriage is like a business partnership, with a wife's labour contribution recognised in her husband's earnings, Gilman adds that "whatever the economic value of the domestic industry of women is, they do not get it."[13] Gilman's novel *Herland* (1915) depicts a separatist feminist utopia, built around care, childraising, and education. Gilman's thought experiment reveals how the civic, artistic, cerebral, and spiritual dimensions of this kind of work might thrive when no longer delegitimised, marginalised, and smothered by patriarchy.[14]

The term *reproductive labour* emerges within feminist thought of the 1970s, against a background of many more women entering the labour market, the flourishing of second-wave feminism, and specifically the International Wages for Housework Campaign. The term primarily refers to unwaged domestic work including cleaning, cooking, shopping, home-making, and the care and socialisation of children. Such work is called *reproductive labour* because it reproduces the social order. So *reproductive labour* is also being tacitly distinguished from the paid *productive labour* which it enables.[15] Mariarosa Dalla Costa writes in 1972 how washing and cleaning "are social services inasmuch as they serve the reproduction of labor power," adding that "capital, precisely by instituting its family structure, has 'liberated' the man from these functions so that he is completely 'free' for direct exploitation; so that he is free

---

[12] "A VVomans VVork is never done / Here is a Song for Maids to sing, / Both in the Winter and the Spring; / It is such a pretty conceited thing, / Which will much pleasure to them bring. / Maids may sit still, go, or run, / But a Womans work is never done" (London: Printed for John Andrews, at the White Lion in Pye-Corner, [c.1654]).

[13] Charlotte Perkins Gilman, *Women and Economics: A Study of the Economic Relation Between Men and Women as a Factor in Social Evolution* (Berkeley: University of California Press, 1998 [1898]), ark.cdlib.org/ark:/13030/ft896nb5rd/, accessed 15 October 2018.

[14] Charlotte Perkins Gilman, *Herland* (New York: Pantheon Books, 1979 [1915]).

[15] While reproductive labour and productive labour are *distinguished*, they are also *combined*: the concept of reproductive labour is intended to widen thinking about what counts as production.

to 'earn' enough for a woman to reproduce him as labor power."[16] The term *reproductive labour* also links social reproduction with biological reproduction, with the work of creating humans through sex, pregnancy, labour, and feeding and caring for infants. Sometimes—for instance in Nat Raha's chapter in this collection—the term *socially reproductive labour* is used instead of *reproductive labour*.

The gendering of labour, paid or unpaid, whether productive and/or reproductive, is not just about the differentiation of 'men's work' from 'women's work'; nor is it really only about the distribution of compensation, status, and autonomy across those categories, nor even about the mechanisms which police and adjust their boundaries. As well as all this, the gendered division of labour implies gender-based differentiation of the apparatuses that define, motivate, monitor, recompense, and extract value from work. Unequal pay for equivalent work is one obvious aspect of this: that is, a given piece of work is often valued differently according to whether it is undertaken *as* 'men's work' or 'women's work.' A related aspect is how different gender identities are expected—and expect themselves—to undertake a given piece of work in different *ways*. For instance, Robin Leidner writes that "the degree to which workers accept the identity implied by a job is [...] determined in part by the degree to which they can interpret the job as expressing their gender in a satisfying way."[17] Leidner's point also extends to race, ability, sexuality, social class, and other identity characteristics: workers are encouraged to weave their own identities into the fabric of their working practices. Unpaid reproductive labour such as childcare and housework certainly interacts with more formal workplace contexts in complex and forcible ways. Or, to make this same point in terms familiar from Black feminist thought, intersections between different forms of work tend to be *transformative*, not merely *additive*. When two workers have separately undertaken a given piece of work, there are no guarantees of how much, if any, lived experience they share of it, since such work is highly sensitive

[16] Mariarosa Dalla Costa, "Women and the Subversion of the Community," in Mariarosa Dalla Costa and Selma James, *The Power of Women and the Subversion of the Community* (Falling Wall Press and a group of individuals from the Women's Movement in England and Italy, 1975 [1972]) 33–34.

[17] Robin Leidner, *Fast Food, Fast Talk: Service Work and the Routinization of Everyday Life* (Berkeley: University of California Press, 1993), 194.

to whatever other work they were carrying out alongside, around, and within that work.

It's worth noting that, while second-wave feminist theorisation of reproductive labour may often focus on activities like cleaning, cooking, and shopping, it also extends to acts of what we might today call *affective labour* (which we will get to in more detail in a moment). For instance, Dalla Costa writes, "Women, responsible for the reproduction of labor power, on the one hand discipline the children who will be workers tomorrow and on the other hand discipline the husband to work today, for only his wage can pay for labor power to be reproduced."[18] Rather more broadly defined, reproductive labour might include all kinds of activities that—whoever you are—are oriented towards performing your identity, rendering yourself intelligible, cultivating and patching the interdependencies of your social world, disciplining and socialising others, and furnishing others with spaces of security, freedom, and play. Roughly speaking, this is the work of being yourself, and facilitating others in being themselves.

Identity can certainly often be experienced as work: the work of maintaining your outward performance of self and inward sense of self, as well as the work of identifying the inner with the outer. For instance, in his chapter in this collection, Jose-Luis Moctezuma mentions "schizophrenogenic behaviors in subjects within workplace situations," and the labour of being self-identical.[19] But broadening our understanding of reproductive labour in this way, out from the traditional domestic sphere, may call for new term. So we could perhaps instead talk of the work of *self-fashioning*, or of *action* in Hannah Arendt's sense,[20] or even better, coin the term *identity labour*. The labour of holding yourself together has always arisen within hierarchical orders including race,

[18] Dalla Costa, "Women and the Subversion of the Community," 47–48.

[19] Jose-Luis Moctezuma, "'What Gives Pause or Impetus': The Double Bind of Labor in Rodrigo Toscano's Poetics," q.v.

[20] See Stephen Greenblatt, *Renaissance Self-Fashioning: From More to Shakespeare* (Chicago: University of Chicago Press, 1980). Another somewhat relevant term might be Hannah Arendt's category of *action*, "the only activity that goes on directly between men without the intermediary of things or matter." Arendt distinguishes action from other kinds of activity which do not allow people to disclose who they are (in her taxonomy labelled *work* and *labour*, which have loose affinities with productive labour and reproductive labour respectively). *The Human Condition* (Chicago: University of Chicago Press, 1958), 7.

gender, sexuality, social class, nationality, and ability and disability. Toni Morrison writes that "[t]he function, the very serious function, of racism is distraction. It keeps you from doing your work. It keeps you explaining, over and over again, your reason for being. Somebody says you have no language, so you spend twenty years proving that you do."[21] Identity labour is thus distributed within the differential affordances, platforms, obligations, pressures, obstacles, disturbances and threats that constitute such orders, that both keep you working and keep you from doing your work. In this sense, identity labour encompasses the work of self-restoration and self-preservation, while moving through environments of often violently contradictory imperatives, as well as the work of establishing solidarities and mounting challenges across those imperatives.

Both these terms, reproductive labour and identity labour, overlap with *intersubjective labour*,[22] another term used by Middleton in his chapter, and with the labour of *worldmaking*, a concept which Nat Raha invokes in her analysis of John Wieners' work. In this sense, they also interface with various theorisations of what it is to be a member of a polity or community. For instance, in Lytton Smith's chapter on Alena Hairston's poetry, he raises Charles T. Lee's notion of "ingenious citizenship," which challenges the pre-eminence of democratic agency as the only legitimate mode of political agency, and seeks to recognise many "surprising and even unthinkable ways to improvise and expand spaces of inclusion and belonging, thus obtaining 'citizenship' via nonlinear routes."[23]

Another closely related term is *affective labour*. Affective labour is labour that functions primarily to influence the affects of others. Affects may loosely be understood to mean feelings, emotions, moods, attitudes, and will (some theorists might challenge this description[24]). The term

---

[21] Toni Morrison, "Public Dialogue on the American Dream, Part 2" (1975), pdxscholar. library.pdx.edu/orspeakers/90/, accessed 5 June 2018.

[22] Middleton also develops the term *intersubjective labour*, which in his useage gathers a positive nuance: intersubjective labour "acts in and through a relationship with another person in which one person works on the mind and feelings of another to help the development of the recipient in some way." Peter Middleton, "'Show Your Working': Other Forms of Labour in Recent Poetry," q.v.

[23] Charles T. Lee, *Ingenious Citizenship: Recrafting Democracy for Social Change* (Durham: Duke University Press, 2016), 6.

[24] For example, for Phoebe V. Moore, "emotional labour is the visible production of affective labour. It can be as the correspondence between body and mind that is not

emotional labour is also used. As Arlie Hochschild influentially puts it in her 1983 book *The Managed Heart: Commercialization of Human Feeling*:

> The flight attendant does physical labor when she pushes heavy meal carts through the aisles, and she does mental work when she prepares for and actually organizes emergency landings and evacuations. But in the course of doing this physical and mental labor, she is also doing something more, something I define as *emotional labor*. [...] This labor requires one to induce or suppress feeling in order to sustain the outward countenance that produces the proper state of mind in others – in this case, the sense of being cared for in a convivial and safe place. This kind of labor calls for a coordination of mind and feeling, and it sometimes draws on a source of self that we honor as deep and integral to our individuality. [...] The workers I talked to often spoke of their smiles as being *on* them but not *of* them.[25]

Such affective or emotional labour may be more obvious in some areas of work—entertainment, education, healthcare, sex work, hospitality, sales, and marketing—than it is in others, but it is also deeply woven throughout all kinds of work. Even in sectors like agriculture, engineering, construction, or manufacturing, communicative coordination would be impossible without the capacity to kindle and modulate feelings in each other: to make each other feel curious, attentive, challenged, teased, safe, satisfied, esteemed, entitled, empowered, heeded, understood, comfortable, connected, indulged, ignored, patient, trusted, etc., as appropriate to the tasks at hand.

Affective labour is curiously placed vis-à-vis autonomy. On the one hand, the affective labourer may act as the avatar of some value-extracting imperative. If you are smiling at a customer and hoping they have

instantly knowable in the way that emotion and affections may be." Phoebe V. Moore, *The Quantified Self in Precarity: Work, Technology and What Counts* (London and New York: Routledge, 2017). Although authors often make clear and useful distinctions between emotion and affect—involving axes such as conscious/pre-conscious, apodictic/falsifiable, social/idiosyncratic, structured/formless, intersubjective/subjective—we haven't been able to find enough consistency in these distinctions to offer a reliable amalgamation. In this introduction *affective labour* and *emotional labour* get used interchangeably.

[25] Arlie Russell Hochschild, *The Managed Heart: Commercialization of Human Feeling* (Berkeley and Los Angeles: University of California Press, 2003 [1983]), 7–8.

a nice weekend, you may be genuinely rooting for their weekend, but you may also be carrying out a formal or informal company policy. But on the other hand, many acts of affective labour involve shielding somebody else from forces which would act on their subjectivity, and creating a space in which they can more freely express, explore, and process emotion. Affective labour is nodding. Affective labour is smiling, frowning, listening, comforting, caring, crying, reassuring, pausing, validating, respecting, mirroring, imagining, enduring, guessing, venturing, waiting, forbearing, rephrasing, empathising, enabling, empowering. Affective labour is, like the reproductive labour with which it overlaps, highly gendered, and intricately associated with constructions of the feminine and presuppositions about what women can or should do or be. The term affective labour is, finally, a perilously inclusive one. Since affects circulate and transform all the time, it becomes quite easy to frame any situation in terms of affective labour, potentially masking other important dynamics. But this is not to claim that the term is vague and obfuscatory—rather, it is testament to the omnipresence of patriarchal and capitalist demand for such labour. All poetry can certainly be thought of as affective labour.

Still another related term is *aesthetic labour*, which primarily refers to the self-disciplinary work of managing your appearance, involving exercise, diet, hair, skin, smell, make-up, clothing, posture, the extension of your appearance into your belongings and environments, the curation of your digital self, the cultivation of affective performances—extending even to the injunction to *authentic* feeling—as well as constant vigilance to the shifting qualities of the attention in which all this self-presentation occurs. Clearly such aesthetic labour overlaps substantially with self-fashioning or identity labour. As Alison Winch writes, "managing the body is [...] the means by which women acquire and display their cultural capital."[26] Elias, Gill and Scharff point out that there are "multiple

[26]Alison Winch, "Brand Intimacy, Female Friendship and Digital Surveillance Networks," *New Formations: A Journal of Culture/Theory/Politics*, vol. 84 (2015), 233. muse.jhu.edu/article/597741. Elias, Gill, and Scharff frame the politics of beauty as having been stuck in "an impasse between polarised positions, stressing—for example—oppression by beauty norms versus pleasure and playfulness, female agency versus cultural domination, entrenched suspicion of the beauty-industrial complex versus hopefulness about women's capacity to resist" (loc. 437). Their work hopes to budge this impasse by connecting the politics of beauty more explicitly with affective and other forms of labour,

labours" involved "in 'looking good'—labours that are simultaneously physical, cultural, technological and also psychological," and that there are "increasing entanglements of forms of visual appearing with rapidly changing digital technologies and social media."[27]

In the last part of his chapter, Middleton applies some of this theoretical matrix to poetry, tracing moments of aesthetic and affective labour at the heart of Simone White's poem "Lotion" from *Of Being Dispersed* (2016). Looking at Marcella Durand's *Traffic and Weather* (2008), Middleton also plays with understanding the agency of nonhuman matter as a kind of work. However, his focus settles on the invisible human labour which an ecopoetic approach can bring to light. Samantha Walton also picks up the ecopoetic thread in her later chapter, with her reading of the poetry of Rita Wong.

TRULY FREE LABOUR

The question of how to define work recurs in the chapter which follows: Lisa Jeschke moves through several prose texts by the poet J. H. Prynne, teasing out an argument about the commodification of poetry and labour-power. Jeschke echoes Middleton in emphasising the breadth and diversity of work. Work spills abundantly beyond the boundaries of paid employment. However, Jeschke also wants to complicate this point. First, we can say that, under capitalism, even waged labour is not *truly* waged, in the sense that workers are never completely compensated for what they do.[28] On the flip side, Jeschke suggests that even unwaged activities are not truly

---

as well as a renewed focus on subjectivity and on specifically neoliberal configurations of the politics of beauty. Ana Sofia Elias, Rosalind Gill, and Christina Scharff, "Introduction," in *Aesthetic Labour: Rethinking Beauty Politics in Neoliberalism* (London: Palgrave Macmillan, 2017).

[27] Elias, Gill, and Scharff, "Introduction," in *Aesthetic Labour*, loc. 437–439.

[28] In Karl Marx's analysis, capital coerces people into lending an increasingly large part of their very being to someone else. Our labour produces surplus value for those who own the means of production. Simply put, surplus value means that the sheer quantity of value that the worker produces is larger than the remuneration they receive in the form of wages. What this means is that society is fundamentally constructed around an economic principle that benefits a small number of property owners at the expense of the significantly larger amount of unpropertied workers, as well as domestic workers, or those excluded from work. Labouring in general, for the vast majority of people, is a situation in which their freedom is curtailed.

unwaged—at least, in the sense that they remain profoundly shaped by the primacy of the wage relation.[29]

Within capitalist society, the means of production are controlled by a few people, and everybody else is forced to commodify their labour-power. This is the basic principle of social alienation produced by capitalism. If you are like most people, capitalism forces you to convert a large chunk of your daily activities into a marketable product. Moreover, whatever you get paid to do will be primarily organised around creating exchange value—providing goods and services to sell—and not around knowledge of what would actually be useful or harmful for you to do. These are the arrangements Jeschke refers to when she talks about "the wage relationship." The implications of the wage relationship reach wide and deep. Within such a society, as Marx puts it in his influential account of commodity fetishism, social relationships among people take on "the fantastic form of a relation between things."[30] In a later chapter in this collection, Holly Pester even asks if it is possible for the human body "to express itself outside the currency of work?" Pester observes that we are "in a continuous state of producing data and value," and that this is true even when we

perform acts of leisure timewasting, creative practice, or therapeutic exercise. This a situation well understood as a facet of economic neoliberalism, where the body is a configuration of entangled acts of work and

---

[29] Jeschke's point might also be supported, for instance, by a glance into the sociology of leisure. In an influential 1962 article Harold Wilensky distinguishes two major ideas about how work shapes leisure: the *compensatory* hypothesis where leisure routines become "an explosive compensation for the deadening rhythms of factory life" and the *spillover* hypothesis where "alienation from work becomes alienation from life [...] 'killing time' at work can become 'killing time' in leisure, apathy in workplace can become apathy in politics." Harold Wilensky, "Labor and Leisure: Intellectual Traditions Industrial Relations," *A Journal of Economy and Society*, vol. 1, no. 2 (February 1962), 3–4. Silvia Federici, in her 1975 essay "Why Sexuality is Work," writes about "what comes out when we 'let go' is more often our repressed frustration and violence than our hidden self ready to be reborn in bed. [...] Among other things, we are always aware of the falseness of this spontaneity. No matter how many screams, sighs, and erotic exercises we make in bed, we know that it is a parenthesis and tomorrow both of us will be back in our civilized clothes (we will have coffee together as we get ready for work)." Silvia Federici, "Why Sexuality is Work" (1975) in Silvia Federici, *Revolution at Point Zero: Housework, Reproduction, and Feminist Struggle* (Brooklyn: Common Notions, 2012), 23–24.

[30] Holly Pester, "Distributed and Entangled Posture in Cathy Wagner's *My New Job* and *Nervous Device*," q.v.

productivity within effaced boundaries between work and life, biology and market economy.[31]

Jeschke explores how workplaces like "the office, the home in which unpaid domestic labour is performed, the cell in which a body is incarcerated," despite their many differences, all "stand in a relation to the institution of wage labour." For Jeschke, this necessitates a balancing act.[32] Capital remakes reality with a reach that must not be underestimated: creeping into every corner of our lives to reconfigure it, in some way or other, in accordance with the logic of exchange. However, even as we bear witness to this damaging logic, we'd better take care not to project it into *everything* in the world, let alone onto every possible world. Not everything is work, and not all work is capitalist work. Jeschke quotes Endnotes: "To the north, the woodless hills that roll either side were cleared not by capital, but by neolithic people. [...] To theoretically project capital's totalisation beyond what capital can legitimately explain is to make a false – merely imaginary – totalisation."[33]

The question for Jeschke is whether poetry-making might provide a model of an activity at the very edge of the wage relation, and a model of labour free of capitalist logic. In the *Grundrisse* (1857), Marx suggests that "*[t]ruly* free labouring, e.g. composing, is the most *damned* seriousness, the most intensive straining."[34] The German word which is translated as "composing," *Componiren*, is one that can be used to describe either the work of composing music, or, also, writing poetry. It may seem a strange choice. Marx's conception of freedom does not simply mean a situation where individuals do as they please. Rather, such freedom would have a social character, and an inbuilt tilting towards the common good. Being free would mean being intimately concerned with creating freedom for others, with the active sharing of a commons

---

[31] Pester, "Distributed and Entangled Posture," q.v.

[32] Or even perhaps a contradiction, a balancing act whose high wire has a span of less than zero.

[33] Endnotes, "Error," in *Bad Feelings*, ed. Arts Against Cuts (London: 2016), n.p. Perhaps non-capitalist work may even be found 'within,' or intimately alongside, capitalist extraction; cf. Nat Raha's chapter in this collection, which picks up on Matthew Tinkcom's theorisation of camp labour, the traces of queer subjectivity—including queer knowledge of capital—that may take refuge in the superficial homogeneity of the commodity form.

[34] Ed Luker's translation. Karl Marx, *Grundrisse*, in *Ökonomische Manuskripte 1857/58*, Teil 2 [MEGA: BAND 1] (Berlin: Dietz Verlag, 1981), 499.

which previously would have been parcelled out as private property. So an entire society based around truly free labour would certainly require the end of capitalism, and an end to any form of society where people are kept atomised and separated from one another. But this is not to say that there are not some bits of truly free labour even under capitalism.

One promising sign is that poetry is not economically rewarding. A commodity is something made primarily to be sold, and even if you really wanted to commodify poetry, you'd find it tough going. By and large, composing poems is an activity for which a very small number of people are financially remunerated. As Basil Bunting bitterly puts it, there is "no provision made for poets in this society." Nevertheless, there are poets.[35] Moving through Prynne's texts, Jeschke teases out a notion of a kind of *poiesis* that is not exactly work per se, and that also gestures towards a larger reconciliation of work and play beyond literary production. Jeschke emblematizes this reconciliation by invoking work-song and bird-song together. Such a reconciliation, in the account Jeschke reconstructs, turns upon the primacy of *production* over *transaction*. In other words, poetry that remains devoted to exchange value will be unlikely to give us any glimpse of truly free labour. We know poetry isn't very financially rewarding, so we probably don't want to be too strict in our understanding of 'exchange value' here. Where poetry is consumed in some sense *like* a commodity, even if it is not literally sold, that is enough to consider its creation as unfree labour.

In Jeschke's presentation, this linkage of poetry with the limits of the wage relation is a tentative, qualified, and deliberately optimistic idea. Even so, the idea may sound a bit self-aggrandising: probably an idea had by challenging poets and brilliant literary critics. To explore it further, it will be handy to sketch some of Marx's thoughts on *alienation*. Marx's argument here complements, though it is distinct from, his writing about surplus value. In various ways throughout his oeuvre, Marx describes a kind of structural exploitation whereby people who own

---

[35] Andrew McAllister and Sean Figgis, "Basil Bunting: The Last Interview [1984]," *Bete Noire*, vol. 2, no. 3 (1987), 127. Catherine Wagner's reflective chapter, "The Exploit," does complicate the truism that poetry doesn't pay at all, with a nuanced account of working as a salaried poet and creative writing academic. To commodify oneself as a poet within a mixed marketplace of social, cultural, and educational capital may be difficult, unpleasant, ethically problematic, and suffocating of poetic practice, but it is not categorically impossible.

capital feed off of people who don't.[36] He points out that in the capitalist mode of production, labour becomes a commodity—bought and sold in a market—but that it is a commodity like no other. How is it possible, Marx wonders, for new value to come into the world? Exchange by itself cannot explain the creation of new value, since exchange just moves value around. For Marx, under the influence of David Ricardo, the solution to the puzzle is labour. Although labour "is not the source of all wealth"[37]—since nature itself is useful and therefore valuable—the worker *is* the one ingredient in the production process who "materialises more labour-time in their product than is materialised in the product that keeps them in existence as a worker."[38]

However, in his writings on alienation, Marx is really conducting a different kind of attack on labour under capitalism, one more concerned with how this work feels and what it is like.[39] The term *alienation* implies separation, distance, and estrangement, and perhaps also

---

[36]A few recent statistics may be helpful context. Most people in the world are employed in some sense. The International Labour Office estimates that there are a little under 200 million unemployed people globally, an unemployment rate of around 5.5%. Many of those who are employed are nevertheless impoverished in terms of their local surroundings as well as the global context. Of workers in the *emerging countries* category, about 8% live on less than $1.90 a day. The ILO defines this as extreme working poverty. That estimate is based on purchasing power, rather than exchange rates; it also includes the strange assumption that each household shares its income equally. In the *developing countries* category, about 40% of workers are in extreme poverty. The next tier up, moderate working poverty ($1.90–$3.10 per day) is experienced by about 430 million workers in developing and emerging countries. Marx's argument, of course, is not just about empirical economic inequality: his critique is aimed at oppressive power relations, at the wrong of extracting surplus value, and at the alienations experienced by workers.

[37]Karl Marx, *Critique of the Gotha Programme* (1999 [1875]), www.marxists.org/archive/marx/works/1875/gotha/ch01.htm, accessed 5 June 2018, n.p.

[38]Karl Marx, *Theories of Surplus Value* (1863), www.marxists.org/archive/marx/works/1863/theories-surplus-value/ch04.htm, accessed 5 June 2018, n.p.

[39]Another term worth mentioning here, which offers ways of linking the critique of alienation with that of surplus value extraction, is *oppression*. As Abigail B. Bakan writes: "Both oppressor and oppressed suffer alienation, but the condition of oppression ensures that they do not experience their alienation as a common human condition. Rather, the experience of the alienation of the oppressor and the alienation of the oppressed is reinforced, codified, rendered 'rational,' and reified, as if to constitute a permanent condition of separation and distance." "Marxism and Anti-Racism: Rethinking the Politics of Difference," in *Theorizing Anti-Racism: Linkages in Marxism and Critical Race Theories* (Toronto: University of Toronto Press, 2014), loc. 2457–2460.

dissociation, discomfort, obstruction, confusion, corruption, and loss. In the *Economic and Philosophic Manuscripts of 1844*, Marx suggests four ways in which, as a worker in the capitalist system, you are alienated. First, you are alienated from the commodity that you produce. Marx writes that you confront product of your labour as "*something alien*, as a *power independent* of the producer."[40] Second, you are alienated from the act of production itself. For instance, you may have limited control over your working conditions and the techniques you must use. Third, you are alienated from other workers, who are in direct competition with you. Fourth, you are alienated from your *Gattungswesen*—from your species-being, species-essence, or loosely speaking, from your human nature.

This last idea can be a slippery one. Marxist theory, after all, is one space in which the concept of 'human nature' gets thoroughly critiqued, historicised, and recognised as an ideological construct. Marx is a forerunner of both critical humanisms and posthumanisms. Someone telling you that they know your 'true essence,' even better than you know it yourself, should put you on red alert, and Marxist thought offers many ways to combat or securely ignore such a claim. But in that case, what on earth is this nature or essence from which we are supposedly alienated? While Marx is careful to maintain that human nature always manifests in some specific historical configuration, he is also trying to understand the commodification of labour as specifically *dehumanising*. As it happens, the nature that Marx evokes in the *Economic and Philosophic Manuscripts* is definitely not a sort of static biological reality, sitting outside of history, waiting to explain what we are doing or should be doing. Nor is it exactly a standard kernel that is repeated again and again within each individual. It is more like the sum of various needs, drives, instincts, and powers that is spread across everybody. Becoming a commodity that can only produce other commodities, Marx thinks, tends to tear us out of this mesh, and suppresses and degrades our human creativity, our expressivity, our deep connectivity with the needs, hopes, and experience of others, and—crucially—our capacity to picture and to pursue alternative realities.

---

[40] *Economic and Philosophical Manuscripts of 1844*, translation 1932 by Martin Mulligan. MEA, 2009 [1844], www.marxists.org/archive/marx/works/1844/manuscripts/preface. htm, accessed 5 June 2018.

So how can composing poetry exemplify work that is unalienated or less alienated? Autonomy is part of the story. As a private, and arguably bourgeois activity, composing may represent a relatively secluded kind of labour. Making poems, making music, making art: while these *can* be social activities, they are also certainly activities that are often sequestered in spaces in-between the drudgeries of the working day, spaces of relative secrecy and security. Theodor Adorno—quoted by Annabel Haynes in her chapter—describes how

> poetic subjectivity is itself indebted to privilege: the pressures of struggle for survival allow only a few human beings to grasp the universal through immersion in the self or to develop as autonomous subjects capable of freely expressing themselves.[41]

Or, to put it another way, people write poetry because they want to and they can, rather than because someone is telling them to, or watching them, or because they know they have to write poetry to pay the bills. And yet, because poetry is constituted in language and culture, it is necessarily produced with an inbuilt consideration for the lives of others. So poetry is both intensely private and intensely social. Unalienated labour of *all* kinds would imply a world where everyone would be labouring because they wanted to do so, rather than because they were being forced to do so ... but also a world where everyone's labour involved a strong consideration for the lives of others.

And we can come at the question another way, by trying to describe what this 'good' labour—unalienated, truly free, truly human labour—would actually feel like. Marx has a stab at this in "Comments on James Mill" (written 1844).[42] Essentially, Marx guesses that truly human labour would be enjoyable, expressive, unselfish, and in some sense spontaneous and uninhibited. It is also clear that Marx isn't endorsing the democratic subjugation of the individual. He is not restaging Rousseau's notorious shrug, the confession that, in the last instance, whoever can't abide by the general will must be "forced to be free."[43] More specifically, the labour that

[41] Theodor Adorno, "On Lyric Poetry and Society," in *Notes to Literature Volume One,* ed. Rolf Tiedemann (New York: Columbia University Press, 1991), 45.

[42] Karl Marx, "Comments on James Mill" (1844), trans. Clemens Dutt, in *Collected Works,* www.marxists.org/archive/marx/works/1844/james-mill/, accessed 5 June 2018, n.p.

[43] Jean-Jacques Rousseau, *On the Social Contract* (Mineola: Dover Thrift, 2003 [1762]), 11.

Marx imagines would be woven into the ways people affirm and love one another and themselves. "Our products would be so many mirrors in which we saw reflected our essential nature."[44] For your work to be truly human, you have to be able to trace your own individuality in whatever it is that you make or do. You have to also be able to experience expressive happiness within deeds that are lucid, within works can be recognised and enjoyed by others. Marx's slightly more elusive and vague proposition is that this relationship goes both ways, that these others must likewise encounter *their* individuality and *their* collective belonging affirmed in the work that *you* do.[45] There are links to be drawn with the labour of worldmaking (see "Worldmaking and Worldbreaking" below).

What this means is that in a truly free society, people might feel themselves to be working in the same way that they do when they write poetry (if that isn't too scary a thought). Immanuel Kant may also hover faintly in the background here, at least informing the structure of Marx's instincts. One of Kant's most lasting insights is his use of *aesthetic judgments*—which are awkwardly balanced on the threshold between the objective and the subjective, between the universally communicable and the fundamentally private—to adduce a way beyond the deadlock between rationalist dogmatism (philosophy which stakes too much on the objective and a priori) and empiricist scepticism (philosophy which stakes too much on the subjective and a posteriori). That is, for Kant, the very possibility of making judgements of taste—judgements that are both completely personal and yet universally communicable—presupposes a *sensus communis*, something we all share and which knits us all together.[46] Likewise, Marx's account of making things "as humans," rather than as capitalism's alienated and isolated workers, suggests aspects of literary or artistic experience. It is also, as the next section explores, resonant with aspects of craftwork … although we shouldn't

---

[44] Marx, "Comments on James Mill," 1844.

[45] "I would have been for you the *mediator* between you and the species, and therefore would become recognised and felt by you yourself as a completion of your own essential nature and as a necessary part of yourself, and consequently would know myself to be confirmed both in your thought and your love. […] In the individual expression of my life I would have directly created your expression of your life, and therefore in my individual activity I would have directly *confirmed* and *realised* my true nature, my *human* nature, my *communal nature*." Marx, "Comments on James Mill," (1844).

[46] Kant understands this as being generated in the interplay of different powers without which mental reality would be completely impossible.

assume that it is *only* because of their affiliation with craft that poetry, music, and art offer themselves as an alternative model of less-alienated labour.

CRAFT

Clearly connections could be drawn here not only with artistic or literary composition, but also with *craft*. That is, craft could also offer a model of work that is more free and less alienated. Unsurprisingly, craft plays a key role in this collection, especially in Annabel Haynes's chapter on Basil Bunting, and Lila Matsumoto's chapter on Pamela Campion and Ian Hamilton Finlay.

Craft can be defined in many ways, but it will be helpful to create a provisional sketch. Above all, we might say that the minute division of labour is inimical to craft. The crafter's productive activity takes place at a similar scale and granularity to the way things are actually used in society. However, although craft resists the dissolution of work into minute, highly specialised tasks, craft doesn't really offer any resistance to the sexual division of labour. Reproductive labour undertaken by women, whether it's craft or not, has historically been concealed, devalorised, and figured as 'natural' or inevitable. Secondly, organising work as craft means accepting that the ability to do or make something may not necessarily be communicable through instructions. Because of this, craftwork tends to be deferent to traditions and institutions where various kinds of tacit knowledge or *savoir faire* might feasibly flourish. In this respect, craft is also fairly tolerant of mystery and numinousness. It is happy to dwell in Max Weber's notional "great enchanted garden," prior to the rationalisation, secularisation, and bureaucratization of modernity.[47] Third, craftwork tends to treat quality as a function of distinctiveness rather than one of sameness. For instance, quality may be manifest in the ways an object embodies the skill and judgement of its crafter, rather than its conformity with a generic template.[48] Finally, we would suggest that there isn't really

---

[47] Max Weber, *The Sociology of Religion* (1920), translated 1963 by Ephraim Fischoff (London: Methuen, 1971), 270.

[48] There is a narrow view of poetic craft, manifest in formally conservative lyric free verse that is carefully polished through workshopping. Well-crafted poetry in this narrow sense is often especially vigilant against cliché, bathos, and catachresis. It is often organised around the virtues of succinctness and plainspokenness, livened up a bit by precise musicality, by

a strong distinction between art and craft, and that craft often emerges as a category when some practice that might otherwise be considered art has limited access to certain kinds of cultural prestige.

This way of looking at craft is really a way of looking *back* at craft, an understanding generated within the modernizations that displaced craft. Taylorism, also known as scientific management, constitutes a significant shift in the working practices beginning in the late nineteenth century. Techniques of measurement, analysis, and standardisation are introduced, in order to define and eliminate waste, and establish greater economic efficiency. Fordism, though it evolves later and somewhat separately from Taylorism, extends this same pattern of rationalisation. Fordism has two very prominent features. First, there is the mass production of inexpensive, standardised consumer goods. Second, there is the factory assembly line, which is archetypally a moving conveyor belt lined with workers, each of whom repeats the same small task again and again.[49] Together Taylorism and Fordism complete a shift from craft production to mass production. Compared with Taylorism or Fordism, post-Fordism is a more contentious term, and it probably encompasses a wider variety of things. There is broad agreement, however, that most Fordist societies transition to post-Fordism in the 1970s, and loosely, post-Fordism can be thought of as deindustrialisation and a refocusing on white collar jobs, together with a shift away from mass production, not back towards craft methods, but towards 'flexible production.'[50]

moderately interesting imagery, by temperate estrangements, and by usually well-demarcated ambiguities or points to ponder.

[49] Fordism also has a variety of secondary associations, such as the pursuit of economies of scope (cost savings gained by producing certain related products) and economies of scale (per unit cost savings gained by producing in greater bulk), and a paternalistic attitude to workers (manifest in the de-skilling of work, the guarantee of relatively high wages—at least while times were good—and the suppression of unions). More generally, it signifies the wide penumbra of state and civil society institutions characteristic of rich countries during the forties, fifties and sixties. Introducing his discussion of Lyn Hejinian in this collection, Peter Middleton uses the term slightly more broadly: signifying a range of possible alienating and objectifying modes of production, distinguished from 'intersubjective' labour.

[50] Some of the more important developments may include the extension of the commodification of women's labour; the expansion and deregulation of financial markets; the shrinkage of welfare states; the erosion of worker rights; the intensification of precarity; the decline of manufacturing sectors; the growth in service jobs, with 'service' being very broadly understood to include clerical, administrative, managerial, retail, marketing, sales, accounting, legal, etc.; the emergence of 'just-in-time' or 'lean' manufacturing methods

However, while craft may have been diminished, displaced, and redistributed by the new regime, it hasn't disappeared. Writing poetry certainly still seems, with interesting exceptions, to be more closely related to craft than it is to mass production.[51] This is certainly true in the case of Basil Bunting. In her chapter Annabel Haynes makes the case that work is *the* central theme of Basil Bunting's poetry. She traces the interplay between overt representations of making and doing and Bunting's understanding of poetry-making as craft. Haynes here draws on Richard Sennett's somewhat provocatively inclusive construal of craft. She also connects craft with craftiness. Picking up on Bunting's use of the word "sleights" in his preface to his *Collected Poems*, Haynes comments:

> In bringing to mind hands and handiwork, dexterity and skilled manual work, Bunting's definitive "sleights" indicate the uniting concern of Bunting's life works: the link between the hand and the head forged by wholesome work, or craft.

The notions that craft might be not only tricky but tricksy, that it might be agile and evasive, and that this might let it be "wholesome," echo what was discussed in the last section: work that can perhaps slip

---

aimed at keeping inventories low and thus having implications for economies of scope and scale (see previous footnote); the more extensive monitoring and responsivity to consumer markets; the emergence of new techniques for targeting and shaping consumer markets; and the growing significance of information technology.

[51] Computer-generated poetry might be one exception. Furthermore, the production of a novel might involve, for example, a first draft of 50,000 words written during National Novel Writing Month (NaNoWriMo) through meeting daily word targets, supported by a website that awards badges upon meeting milestones, and informal support and rivalry from fellow NaNoWriMo participants, followed by the purchase of several phases of specialised editorial services, and a mixture of paid and unpaid consultation and focus grouping with beta readers, sensitivity readers, and subject specialists. The relationship between handicraft and poetry might also be a complicated one as demonstrated, for example, by the use of work-songs and chants to regularise and measure out labour. Fiona McNeil gives the example of early modern bonelacemaking: "Lacemakers used work songs not only to keep count of the pins as they put them into the pillow, but also to maintain the rapid pace of their work without making mistakes. Their chants were knows as 'tells,' from the word 'tally,' meaning 'to count.'" "Free and Bound Maids: Women's Work Songs and Industrial Change in the Age of Shakespeare," in *Oral Traditions and Gender in Early Modern Literary Texts*, ed. Mary Ellen Lamb and Karen Bamford (London and New York: Routledge, 2016), 102.

away from capitalism long enough to flourish as truly free or unalienated labour. But wait. It's also worth drawing some distinctions here. In particular, if the craft-impulse is mainly about—as it is in Sennett's view, invoked by Haynes—doing "a job well for its own sake," then this doesn't really match Marx's focus on individuality achieved through communality, and communality through individuality.[52] As Marx puts it, "This relationship would moreover be reciprocal; what occurs on my side has also to occur on yours." So if we do want to claim that Marx is alluding to craft in his "Notes on Mill," we'd have to say it's not *just* the craft of making for its own sake or for the maker's own satisfaction, but also the craft of making for and from others, and the craft of enjoying for and from others.

A somewhat more recent account of unalienated labour could be excavated from Mihaly Csikszentmihalyi's analysis of intrinsically motivating tasks and the experience of "flow."[53] For Csikszentmihalyi, flow occurs when there is complete absorption in a task, a proportionality between challenge and skill, and a merging of action and awareness such that all ruminative thought evaporates. Although flow may well be a feasible account of what is pleasant about a lot of crafting (and perhaps some poetry-writing too), Csikszentmihalyi is again at odds with Marx. For starters, flow contradicts Marx's romantic and somewhat Faustian wish for "the most *damned* seriousness, the most intensive straining." But more importantly, Csikszentmihalyi's account again leaves no room for sociality. There is no collective, there is only the individual and the task. In fact, it might not even leave much room for the individual, since there is a suggestion that when you experience flow you are miraculously automated, right down to your desires, in service of the task at hand.[54] So maybe there is not even the individual and the task. There is only the task.

Nevertheless, even if these construals of craft experience don't dovetail with the Marxian understanding of truly human labour, they may still have

---

[52]Richard Sennett, *The Craftsman* (New Haven and London: Yale University Press, 2008), 10.

[53]Mihaly Csikszentmihalyi, *Flow: The Psychology of Optimal Experience* (New York: Harper & Row, 1990).

[54]We might compare Jose-Luis Moctezuma's comment on "labor at its finest or highest intensity" in his chapter on Rodrigo Toscano. "For instance, the self-regulating or automatic machine, well-built or well-trained, organic or inorganic, seems to function seamlessly once inserted into the site of operations: this might describe labor at its finest or highest intensity."

a critical and even revolutionary potential of their own. To be utterly capti-
vated by autotelic craftwork, so much so that you forget yourself, might be
to enter "a space of discourse organized by nothing other than discourse
itself," to appropriate one of Michael Warner's characterizations of what a
public is.[55] That is, the sublation of crafter and beneficiary into the craftwork could be thought of not as *erasure* but as a kind of integration or
even *unity*. It could be interesting to try to understand sex, dancing, taking
entactogenic drugs, crowd psychology, and Dionysian euphoria, through
the lens of craftwork.

Furthermore, Haynes points out how rather than "turning to established forms, Bunting's sounds and rhythms are derived from nature,
and from humans' interaction with nature." Not every undertaking is
reducible to the forms which capital establishes within it, and absorption
in the undertaking can bring to light that which exceeds those forms.
Insofar as Bunting's poetry is craft, it is a sustained musical confrontation with the "[s]ocial and economic conditions" that both enable and
restrain it.[56] A more recent and explicit illustration of the same principle
might be found in Verity Spott's long poem *Click Away Close Door Say*
(2017), which engages with Spott's job in a care unit for young adults
with autism. The premise of the book is that this work is entirely necessary: labour worth doing. However, as the care unit suffers from cuts to
its budget, increasing pressure on frontline staff, the poet finds the job
increasingly challenging. She feels she can't provide support to people
in the way that they need. The opening lines of the poem are "I used
to love to work; to come inside / here every day, begin to move." The
opening section of the poem describes the poet's experience of entering
the workplace through a series of doors that utilise a complex system of
codes and locking mechanisms. In a sort of capitalist diurnal, reading this
opening of the poem, like the opening of the day, becomes a pained and
humorous reminder of the intractable difficulty of getting into work, and
the strange convoluted configurations that being at work can put you in.
It is not only people, but also things, tasks, materials, can be intractable, prickly, weird, curious, ungainly, unaccountably abundant or resonant, and one-of-a-kind. Absorbed in the craft of your work, you may
find yourself painfully at odds with the otherwise undetectable ideologies

---

[55] Michael Warner, "Publics and Counterpublics," *Public Culture*, vol. 14, no. 1 (2002), 50.
[56] Sennett, *The Craftsman*, 10.

that enforce certain values at the expense of others. You may even gain a special critical purchase on such ideologies. As Sennett writes, "craftsmanship focuses on objective standards, on the thing in itself. Social and economic conditions, however, often stand in the way of the craftsman's discipline and commitment."[57]

Craft also has a central role in Lila Matsumoto's chapter, on Pamela Campion and Ian Hamilton Finlay's poem-embroidery pieces. Matsumoto quotes Susan Stewart: "In handicrafts that are two-sided, such as embroidery or rug making, there is often a front for viewing and a back that shows evidence of touching and making."[58] Matsumoto's chapter is concerned with both sides, aiming to redress a familiar pattern where the work of a female collaborator is both occluded and devalued. For instance, in Finlay's wider practice, things and spaces not conventionally understood as art can easily slip into aesthetic and morally weighty categories. By contrast, several of Campion's contributions to exhibitions get marginalised as 'pleasing extras' unworthy of accreditation. In Finlay's delighted dismissal of Campion's creations, we can read a larger history of work which could easily be considered productive being framed as reproductive, elements of an ephemeral ambience, oriented to generating and modulating affect.

Within the poem-embroideries themselves, Campion's needlework is consistently figured as craft, rather than as art. Her work also remains associated with domestic busywork, in contrast to high-status masculine craft. In snippets of correspondence, laden with charm and admiration, Finlay locates Campion's aesthetic labour among acts of gendered reproductive labour such as childcare and cooking. These hierarchies of masculine versus feminine and art versus craft are also conducted within the reinforcing hierarchies of Finlay as creator versus Campion as interpreter or translator, and Finlay as boss versus Campion as a talented but ultimately replaceable employee. Through archival research, Matsumoto is able to reconstruct some of the pair's working arrangements, in order to more accurately weigh Campion's creative agency. Campion does not only contribute brow-sweat and expertise as a manual worker, or sensitivity and skill as an interpreter. She is involved in imaginatively generating and shaping the project on multiple levels. Finlay's correspondence is

[57] Sennett, *The Craftsman*, 10.

[58] Susan Stewart, *Poetry and the Fate of the Senses* (Chicago and London: University of Chicago Press, 2002), 162.

available for inspection, and Campion's is not. Yet even from the halved conversation, the picture which emerges is of Campion contributing affectively and cognitively to the conceptualization and curation of their collaborative practice. It's especially striking that Campion and Finlay's poem-embroideries specifically and consciously thematise homespun domesticity. These works engage critically and transformatively with attitudes of nostalgia and sentimentality surrounding domesticity and craft. Nevertheless, the discourse underpinning their creation is entangled with these very attitudes.

In the last section, we touched on poetry's capacity to emphasise the logic of production above the logic of transaction. We wondered whether some poetry could even demarcate a fragile and contested zone where moments of truly free or unalienated labour might exist. Jeschke is certainly alive to the strong possibility that even winning such a zone, arduous as that task may be, might not do any good in the end. Any haven in which appear "glimpses of a better life" may do no more than "distract from the struggle to turn a better life for all into a reality." As for Marx, a more sceptical take on his "truly free labour" might say that it really is stuck in the image of the lone creative genius, despite his best efforts to bring in everybody else. Evidence might be found where Marx calls Milton a silkworm; unlike "the Leipzig literary proletarian" who produces work in exchange for pay, John Milton is not required to be a productive worker: "Milton produced *Paradise Lost* in the way that a silkworm produces silk, as the expression of *his own* nature."[59] It is identity between the creative act of writing and an expression of Milton's internal and self-possessed nature that grounds the possibility of creative freedom. Another way of phrasing this problem is, hypothetically, why would it not be possible for the literary proletarian, writing for money, to be able to write a work as significant as *Paradise Lost*, if they are not selling their labour-power doing something else? Is aesthetic freedom an element that can only be grasped from the activities of the wills of those who are not forced to sell their labour-power?

The questions around freedom and aesthetic autonomy in relation to the histories of German philosophy are continually in the background of the theoretical writings of Fred Moten. In an essay entitled "Blackness

---

[59] Karl Marx and Frederick Engels, *Collected Works*, Vol. 34 (Electronic Book: Lawrence and Wishart, 2010), 136.

and Poetry," he writes that poetry, as an artistic activity, constantly over-rides and spills out beyond the legislative attempts to delineate and contain it. It is therefore a powerfully generative art. He states that:

> Poetry is the highest verbal art, the place where this interplay of creativity and rule manifests itself in such a way as to prove, more or less constantly, the capacity for the supersensual to assert itself, after all, in triumph over the tumultuous derangements of original folly, of this constant tendency for unruly materialization and differing.[60]

Part of what Moten means by the "supersensual" may be all those elements of feeling and existing that are curtailed by the legislative reign of labouring and commodity production within capitalism (alongside all its antecedent elements of exploitation, such as the histories of slavery that characterise modernity).[61] Poetry becomes a site where all those elements of the human, especially of those whose humanity is continually denied, are allowed to flourish. In his argument, poetry is an endlessly expansive disproof of attempts to fix and control identity and meaning as those projects are undertaken in the histories of bourgeois philosophy (and their attendant histories of violence). Poetry exemplifies a kind of non-identical freedom from conceptual meaning, and this freedom has no dependence on any particular kind of subject for its production.

Moten's stress on aesthetic freedom as immanent to certain kinds of creative activity, transcendent of the subjugations of race or class, can be seen in the same essay in an argument about the technique of the jazz piano player Thelonious Monk:

> What if we refuse the distinction between fine art and handiwork, [Thelonious] Monk's dissident elbow work, the imposition of position in his halting dance, its extended recursion and still moving? What if practicing, what if the practice of art, is improvisation's continual breaking and

---

[60] Fred Moten, "Blackness and Poetry," in *Evening Will Come* 55 (1 July 2015), arcade. stanford.edu/content/blackness-and-poetry-0, accessed 3 June 2018, n.p.

[61] In *In The Break: The Aesthetics of the Black Radical Tradition*, Moten writes that "the specific conditions of the possibility modernity […] [are] namely, European colonialism […] and chattel slavery." Fred Moten, *In The Break: The Aesthetic of the Black Radical Tradition* (Minneapolis: University of Minnesota Press, 2003), 32.

making of the rule of art, in jurisgenerative refusal, in unofficial recusal, in the continual putting into play, of the very idea of the work of art?[62]

As her safeguard, Jeschke insists on cultivating a historical conscious-ness, including vigilant attention to the voices of the most silenced, exploited, and vulnerable. Matsumoto's contribution acts as a further reminder that in the tussle between productive and transactional logics, there remains the risk of sidelining reproductive labour, and reproduc-tive labour's own radical potentials, including that of "jurisgenerative refusal": the cultivation of new rules and norms through improvisational acts of resistance. Such radical potentials come to the fore, in particu-lar, in Nat Raha's chapter on John Wieners, and Jose-Luis Moctezuma's chapter on Rodrigo Toscano, discussed in the next section.

WORLDMAKING AND WORLDBREAKING

For the Earl of Shaftesbury in 1709, "All Politeness is owing to Liberty." He is writing at a moment when the medieval European understanding of socialisation through 'life cycle' service—for instance as apprentice, page, lady-in-waiting, etc.—is being turned on its head. Instead of the autonomous individual who emerges after years and years of labouring for their betters, Shaftesbury posits the autonomous individual as what is needed *in the first place* for socialisation to occur; socialisation must therefore also become a perpetual process, something without clear beginnings and endings, and something primarily located in a discur-sive space somewhat distinct from state authority and private commerce. This is Shaftesbury's sense of a *sensus communis*—a common sense, a folk wisdom, something we all share, that knits us together. "We polish one another, and rub off our Corners and rough Sides by a sort of *amicable Collision*."[63] To think of a public this way is to think of it as a self-creat-ing, autopoietic phenomenon and—speaking roughly—as a market, albeit one that is ambiguously distributed across work and leisure activities.

---

[62] Moten, "Blackness and Poetry," n.p.

[63] Anthony Ashley Cooper, Earl of Shaftesbury, "*Sensus Communis*: An Essay on the Freedom of Wit and Humour – in a letter to a friend" (1709) in Anthony Ashley Cooper, Earl of Shaftesbury, *Characteristics of Men, Manners, Opinions, Times*, Vol. 1 (Indianapolis: Liberty Fund, 2001 [1737]), 64.

Nancy Fraser, writing in 1992, develops the notion of subaltern counterpublics, that is, "parallel discursive arenas where members of subordinated social groups invent and circulate counterdiscourses to formulate
oppositional interpretations of their identities, interests, and needs."[64]
These counterpublics are constituted more in the work of protecting,
sustaining, and elaborating differences than in the work of smoothing
differences away. Fraser is responding in part to the somewhat idealised
picture of the public sphere elaborated by Jürgen Habermas (and later
enlarged and transformed into his theory of communicative action).
There is some suggestion, in Fraser's account, of the improvisational and
fugitive character of public-constituting labour.

Michael Warner follows Fraser in recognising a complex manifold
of overlapping publics, but questions whether her analysis has really set
enough distance from its Habermasian point of departure. For Warner,
public discourse is not a matter of reasoning and persuasion conducted among different pre-formed interlocutors, not even allowing
for Shaftesburian "*amicable Collisions*" that could slowly reform these
interlocutors. No: public discourse "is poetic." By this Warner means
that "all discourse or performance addressed to a public must char-
acterize the world in which it attempts to circulate, projecting for that
world a concrete and livable shape, and attempting to realize that world
through address."[65] Warner's terminology also seems to be influenced
by his sense of the poetic as characterised by unparaphrasable somatic,
affective, and ludic qualities, qualities which are discarded within a more
Habermasian view of the public sphere as a realm of rational–critical
discourse:

> Public discourse imposes a field of tensions within which any world-mak-
> ing project must articulate itself. To the extent that I want that world to
> be one in which embodied sociability, affect, and play have a more defining
> role than they do in the opinion-transposing frame of rational-critical dia-
> logue, those tensions will be acutely felt.[66]

[64] Nancy Fraser, "Rethinking the Public Sphere: A Contribution to the Critique of
Actually Existing Democracy," in *Habermas and the Public Sphere*, ed. Craig Calhoun
(Cambridge: MIT Press, 1992), 122–123.

[65] Warner, "Publics and Counterpublics," 81.

[66] Warner, "Publics and Counterpublics," 88.

In his chapter in this collection, Jose-Luis Moctezuma explores the work of the contemporary poet Rodrigo Toscano in relation to grassroots political activism, and theorises the "poetic act" as the projection of a public, or of a counterpublic, that would be capable of enacting radical social change. He starts with Occupy. The global Occupy movement, whose chief catalyst and focal point was the 2011 Occupy Wall Street occupation in Zuccotti Park, was incarnated in a public or set of publics. These publics were primarily held together by quasi-arbitrary geographies; by broad commitment to social justice, inclusivity, and the enrichment of social ties through mutual aid; by a dominant ethos of consensus decision-making (as often pointed out, a relatively labour-intensive form of self-governance); and of course by the enemies it produced from an analysis of global economic inequality. These enemies were, in particular, tax-evading multinational corporations, as well as investment banks and other financial institutions. But would that be enough? Occupy also engendered fierce controversies around what else might be necessary to constitute it both as a public and as an actor. This is the historical background for Moctezuma's exploration of how Toscano's work both addresses and imagines publics.

As in previous chapters, we see a concern with those capitalist forms of collectivity that fail to transcend their status as aggregations of private individuals. "No commune," Moctezuma writes, "only disparities, in the plural. Under such conditions, the question of labor remains a question of redefining the self in its relation to the public, to work, and to the cultural apparatus."[67] In Moctezuma's account, Toscano sees the poetic act as the moment when the private self is indeed dissolved. However, there are limits to how the self can be redefined "in its relation to the public, to work, and to the cultural apparatus."[68] In the absence of the material conditions necessary for meaningful and lasting solidarity and other 'truly' political action, the only thing this dissolved self can do is circulate through a set of "uninhabitabilities," addressing a public that does not exist. In this sense Moctezuma is in dialogue with Jeschke, via the delicate and volatile synthesis of work and play confined to certain acts of poetic production, and the concern with forms of autonomy that can evade or resist the transactional order; he is also in dialogue with Haynes

---

[67] Jose-Luis Moctezuma, "'What Gives Pause or Impetus': The Double Bind of Labor in Rodrigo Toscano's Poetics," q.v.

[68] Moctezuma, "What Gives Pause or Impetus,'" q.v.

and Matsumoto, via the possibility of craftwork as a lens on restrictive economic and social conditions.

But in comparison with all the chapters mentioned so far, we see a subtle and significant shift of emphasis here. Moctezuma is a bit less interested in the work of making poetry or the kinds of work represented or embodied in poetry, and a bit more interested in the work that poetry can do. Paraphrasing Toscano's own ambivalence, Moctezuma raises the possibility that the very best political work by poetry communities may "remain frivolous or woefully behind the corporeal immediacy and policy-oriented politics" that radical grassroots movements such as Occupy require. To put it another way, if the poetic act *does* culminate in the inhabitation of uninhabitabilities, should we understand this as some kind of advance or accomplishment? Or does it just confirm that poetry has nothing to do with social change? Or that poetry is only connected to social change through its vanishingly small involvement in what Asef Bayat calls *social nonmovements*, "large numbers of ordinary people whose fragmented but similar activities trigger much social change, even though these practices are rarely guided by an ideology or recognizable leaderships and organizations"?[69] Are we perhaps just dealing with a mildly interesting piece of trivia, a kind of life-hack: the fact that attempting to do politics through poetry (a) doesn't work and (b) spawns some epistemological benefits as a consolation prize?

In short, what poetic acts if any do any worthwhile political work? Moctezuma doesn't offer a straightforward answer. He seeks to creatively reframe the question, first, by playing on the dual sense of *occupation*.[70] "On the one hand, to occupy a site or situation [...] is to fill it with the '*stuff*' of history. It is to fill it with bodies that generate,

---

[69] Asef Bayat, *Life as Politics: How Ordinary People Change the Middle East*, 2nd ed. (Stanford: Stanford University Press, 2013 [2010]), 15.

[70] *Occupation* may mean a profession, livelihood, or task, and/or some kind of politicised seizure of place: 'occupying' in this second sense is also something done by both armies and peace activists. The word is given further theoretical valence by Gilles Deleuze's "Boulez, Proust, and Time, 'Occupying Without Counting,'" which first appeared in French in 1986. This brief, intricate essay takes as its starting point questions of influence—specifically the composer Pierre Boulez's 'occupation' of Marcel Proust—to explore a dialectic between "blocks of duration" (striated, pulsed space-time, defined by "divisibilities, commensurabilities, and proportionalities") and "time bubbles" (smooth, non-pulsed space-time of "undecomposable distances and proximities"). Gilles Deleuze, "Boulez, Proust, and Time: 'Occupying Without Counting,'" translated and introduced by

interrogate, remix, and rewrite the functions of history." But the stuff of history is liable to melt into air if it is not supported by the other sense of *occupation* as work, that is, if such work "isn't sufficiently defined, demarcated, and distributed across a feasible plan of longevity that transcends the basic requirements of visible action and enunciation." For example, what if committing to an Occupy occupation means that you lose your normal job? Moctezuma is also innovatively renovating a long-standing problematic, one which may also appear in the guise of words versus deeds, or immaterial versus material labour, or representation versus praxis, or talk versus action. As political actors, poets may be all talk and no action. Usually they work on their poetry when they could be working on social change. Those activities may overlap sometimes— poets may be occupied in both at once—but poets do have an interest in exaggerating and disguising the extent to which those activities really do overlap. Still, just because the poets are overconfident, it doesn't follow that those activities *never* overlap. Moreover, the confidence itself, whatever its knowledgeable status, is potentially a valuable resource within political struggle. As Warner writes:

> In the idea of a public, political confidence is committed to a strange and uncertain destination. Sometimes it can seem too strange. Often, one cannot imagine addressing a public capable of comprehension or action. This is especially true for people in minor or marginal positions, or people distributed across political systems. The result can be a kind of political depressiveness, a blockage in activity and optimism – a disintegration of politics toward isolation, frustration, anomie, forgetfulness. This possibility, never far out of the picture, reveals by contrast how much ordinary belonging requires confidence in a public.[71]

To elaborate how poetry does and doesn't fulfil the dual obligations of occupation, Moctezuma draws out from Toscano the notion of the "double bind." A double bind is a bit like a dilemma: It's something you

---

Timothy S. Murphy, *Angelaki: Journal of the Theoretical Humanities*, vol. 3, no. 2 (1998), 71. In Rick Dolphijn's account, "the occupation is not directed towards a presence but is equally interested in those things that are not there (yet)." Rick Dolphijn, "The Revelation of a World That was Always Already There: The Creative Act as an Occupation," in *This Deleuzian Century: Art, Activism, Life*, ed. Rosi Braidotti and Rick Dolphijn (Leiden and Boston: Brill and Rodopi, 2014), 191.

[71]Warner, "Publics and Counterpublics," 52.

get stuck in because you are required to do two incompatible things, meaning that you probably end up standing there doing neither of them. Moctezuma's version could even be called (if you prefer) a quadruple bind: It's when you are faced with the obligation to do A rather than B, and to do B rather than A, *and* with the obligation to do not-A rather than not-B, and to do not-B rather than not-A. Is that just two different ways of saying the same thing? Maybe, or maybe it brings some interesting nuance. For example, perhaps capital catches all of its workers in a double bind: your labour must be chosen and not forced (you are a worker not a slave); your labour must be forced and not chosen (you are a slave to the market); *and* you must force yourself to labour so no other force can work through you (you must enslave yourself); you must choose to labour so no other choice can work through you (you must free yourself). Perhaps Occupy's politics of presence, its insistence on *being there* to participate in an evolving, self-governing spectacle, weaves a double bind of its own. You must work within the event, and not just do your normal job; you must not ask this event to sustain you, so you must just do your normal job; *and* you must work within this event just as if doing your normal job; you must go away and do your normal job just as if you were working within this event.[72] Being a poet faced with a situation which promises radical social transformation may certainly impose a double bind:

> [...] yes, poetry is an occupation that can and must speak for other occupations (representation); and yes, poetry is without occupation because it presumably does nothing practical or efficient (praxis) and elaborates space in a nondirective ways. Poetry is simultaneously caught in the reverse dilemma: it cannot sufficiently represent the unrepresentable qualities and stages of labor, but poetry is an occupation that can and must, at least, enact forms of practice that resonate at some level with those who labor, even if particular laborers do not really compute the 'difficult' vernaculars of poetic form.

At certain points in Moctezuma's contribution—as in chapters by Jeschke, Pester, Raha, and others, including this introductory chapter!—there are tactical equivocations, which reject the obligation to specify exactly how much poetry, *poiesis*, or the "poetic act" is literally about

---

[72]This is not to imply of course that your job actually was sustaining you.

poetry in some obvious way, and how much these words allude myste-
riously to something else. Are we really talking about printing ragged
blocks of words in stapled pamphlets, or uploading them to blogs and
Instagram, and reading these out at literary gatherings, or maybe on rare
occasions through a megaphone? A cynical interpreter may see the equiv-
ocation as an attempt to gerrymander a little political cachet for poetry—
and for literary criticism—by unconvincingly stretching the definition of
what poetry is. A more generous or gullible interpreter may point out
the need to preserve the conditions of possibility for radical praxis wher-
ever possible, and to ignore the demand to minutely specify materials,
methods, and aims, a demand which so often does no more than quell
hopes, sow discord, and drain and disperse transformative energy.

Another approach, somewhere between the cynical and the generous
or gullible, is to situate poetry-writing within networks of other things
poets do, especially the work of political activism. In her chapter on John
Wieners, Nat Raha adopts this approach to Wieners' work in the 1970s.
Raha examines Wieners' writing, his participation in the *Fag Rag* publishing collective, and his involvement with Gay Liberation and Boston's
Mental Patients' Liberation Front. She frames this work as *queer world-
making*: that is, she is interested in how Wieners' activity enables and
supports queer subjectivities and queer lives. Queer worldmaking—an
idea theorised by Berlant, Warner, and Muñoz, among others—might be
loosely thought of as a kind of reproductive labour.[73] While being alive
to "the ways in which the worlds produced by the work of gay liberation reproduced hierarchies of sexism, racism, classism, transmisogyny,
ableism and ageism," Raha also states:

> The labour of queer cultural production, the circulation of newspapers,
> the spread of poetry like that of Wieners, enables the political, social, intel-
> lectual, creative, sexual and affective realisation of a world that held the
> promise of Liberation [...] This was work largely unwaged, performed
> outside the reproduction of capital within heterosexist society; but by no
> means entirely outside, as writing, typesetting, printing and distributing
> newspapers required money and physical labour.

---

[73]José E. Muñoz, *Cruising Utopia: The Then and There of Queer Futurity* (New York:
New York University Press, 2009). Lauren Berlant and Michael Warner, "Sex in Public,"
Critical Inquiry, vol. 24, no. 2 (1998), 547–566.

However, to classify queer worldmaking as reproductive labour may create a bit of a misnomer. Queer worldmaking certainly foregrounds a tension that is present in much of the writing of reproductive labour. This tension is the fact that reproductive labour is transformative and oppositional as well as conservative. While reproductive labour may be devoted to reproducing the social order, it is also devoted to destroying it. The values implied by the continuous work of care and replenishment are *not* the values of the social order that is actually being cared for and replenished. This dynamic is intensified in queer worldmaking; queer worldmaking is not only making queer worlds in the spaces afforded by dominant normativity. Queer worldmaking is also straight worldbreaking. This critical and oppositional character of queer worldmaking comes out in José E. Muñoz's *Cruising Utopia*, which theorises queerness as an affective "ideality" that "lets us feel that this world is not enough." This affective ideality asks that we both "dream and enact new and better pleasures, other ways of being in the world, and ultimately new worlds." In this sense, queer worldmaking, and the other queer labour with which it is implicated, constitute "a doing for and toward the future."[74]

Raha's exploration of John Wieners' queer worldmaking resonates with Lytton Smith's use of citizenship in his chapter, a close reading and contextualisation of the first collection by Alena Hairston, *The Logan Topologies* (2007). Hairston's book follows in the tradition of Whitmanesque poetics of the American landscape; as Smith outlines, it is a historical and spatial examination of the development of Logan, West Virginia, through an exploration of the labouring relations of the people who live there. In this, it could suggest works such as William Carlos William s's *Paterson* (1946) and Charles Olson's invocation of Gloucester in *The Maximus Poems* (1953). However, unlike these great American masculinist epics, Hairston's work "takes place somewhere between a particular historical experience of place and an experience of repetitions of the same in which minority experience in America can be mapped."[75] As Chris Green notes, the stylistic influences on Hairston's work include the documentary poetics of Muriel Rukeyser, alongside

---

[74] Muñoz, *Cruising Utopia*, 1.

[75] Lytton Smith, "'Because We Love Wrong': Citizenship and Labour in Alena Hairston's *The Logan Topographies*," q.v.

work by Quince Troupe and Lucille Clifton.[76] In this sense the book can be seen as a rerendering (as well as a regendering) of the experimental American landscape epic; like Olson and Rukeyser, Hairston engages in a simultaneously microscopic and expanded macro-topological view of the particularities of Logan, focusing and refocusing on life and labour in West Virginia, originally part of the British Virginia Colony established by settlers in 1607.

Smith draws upon the repeated images of physical and manual labouring processes in the book, such as coal mining, and explores their tensions with images of the vernal regeneration of nature. These tensions call into question the relation between natural processes of reproduction and the unnecessary expenditure of human toil in the capitalist development of the United States. *The Logan Topographies*, Smith suggests, draws the reader's attention to how these labour processes, stratified along class lines, are implicated in the occlusion of the labour of Black workers, who are shunted to the edges of the town, kept out of sight and in poverty while the development of the city is dependent on their life-blood. (It is significant for Hairston that, as is true of many places in the Appalachian region of the United States, Black people in Logan live in 'Black Bottom'). Furthermore, Smith explores how Hairston repeatedly draws connections between the labouring of motherhood as another obscured form of work—stratified along lines of race, gender, and class—and images of natural regeneration. As Smith argues, by placing the "spasms" and "jolts" of maternal labour alongside images of the geographical and natural origins of Logan as a landscape (where the rock face is striated like the historical sedimentations of race, class, and gender), Hairston calls into question the origins of extant American society and its dependency upon subordination.[77] Logan becomes a model for exploring the country as a whole.

As Smith also notes, Hairston's experimental lyric mode, through its use of inference and allusion, allows the work to vocalise the intractable difficulties of identity as they are experienced within capitalist social relations. Smith argues that the exploration of the lived experience of race and gender within a set of geographically and historically localised particularities allows for the work to be a living-breathing aesthetic topology

[76]Chris Green, "Reviewed Work: *The Logan Topographies: Poems* by Alena Hairston," *Journal of Appalachian Studies*, vol. 13, no. 1/2 (Spring/Fall, 2007), 255.

[77]Smith, "'Because We Love Wrong," q.v.

of Kimberlé Crenshaw's influential concept of intersectionality.[78] What intersectionality means here is not, of course, that the concepts of race, gender, or class become homogenous and oppositional blocks (each with its own internal coherency), but that different communities, neighbour-hoods, and social relations within the town are fraught by the damage of exploitative labour relations, impoverishment, and capitalist modes of competition. Poetry like Hairston's demands a particular kind of reading, one that requires the work of elaborating, extrapolating, interpolating, and drawing connections both within the work and outward into history and practice. It is work that demands a return to distinct and disparate elements. In this sense the work is a poetic map, one drenched in the documentation of history. Smith's chapter seeks to reflect the dynamism of Hairston's book, drawing it alongside contemporary debates on capi-talism and subjective identity, as well as theoretical concerns around ecol-ogy and place. It shows how poetry, through its attention to particulars, can aid our understanding of how work (re)produces the social antago-nisms of subjective experience.

CORPOREALITY AND CATASTROPHE

In "In the Morning" from *On the Imperial Highway* (2009), Jayne Cortez describes the aftermath of the transatlantic slave trade like this: "Disguised in my mouth as a swampland / nailed to my teeth like a ris-ing sun." The aftermath of slavery is a nail in the mouth. Within these degraded conditions, the very work of existence and speech can become a ferocious, repetitive, humdrum toil: "In the morning in the morning in the morning / gonna kill me a rooster."[79] Edward Kamau Brathwaite's poem sequence *X/Self* (1987) opens "Rome burns / and our slavery begins."[80] The sequence takes up poetic fragments of the West which can only be read through this fact of origin: the development of a civili-sation that is dependent on the labour of chattel and indentured slaves.

---

[78] Cf. e.g. Kimberlé Crenshaw, "Demarginalizing the Intersection of Race and Sex: A Black Feminist Critique of Antidiscrimination Doctrine, Feminist Theory and Antiracist Politics," *University of Chicago Legal Forum*, no. 1 (1998).

[79] Jayne Cortez, *On the Imperial Highway: New and Selected Poems* (Hanging Loose Press, 2009).

[80] Edward Kamau Brathwaite's poem sequence *X/Self* (London: Oxford University Press, 1987), 5.

Brathwaite's sequence weaves together economies and ecologies to bear witness to this history. The second poem in his sequence, "Salt," perhaps alludes to the use of the substance as a medium of exchange, as well as its heavy presence in seawater. In "Mont Blanc,"[81] Brathwaite writes through Percy Bysshe Shelley's meditation on imagination, sublimity, and the possibility of reconciliation with awful nature,[82] in order to figure the catastrophic energy of European "industry." In "Mont Blanc," the braided history of racialised slavery and capitalism becomes a kind of apocalyptic hyperobject, a dynamic that is indescribable, and yet seems to hover at higher order of magnitude than the many other indescribable horrors—the atom bomb, the Nazi death camp—which it spawns and contains; this white mountain is something whose "unships" sail "the black sea dead to the world to the red sea of isaias."[83]

To write within the momenta of postcolonialism is to be bombarded with demands to describe the indescribable. One response may be to place priority on the work of cultural memorisation. If no literary production can hope to be equal to the complexity and scale of colonial injustice, then perhaps textuality that is embodied and ensouled in human practice can, instead, discover a generative friction with the history it can never entirely recount. Incommensurability can then, instead of acting as an impediment, start to activate, fuel, and variegate the work of decolonisation. Or to put this another way: fighting to decolonise society involves reconstructing and publicising past acts of violence that are irreversible and irreparable, while nevertheless constantly inventing reparative orientations and driving reparative projects. Randal Robinson, for instance, even writes that "the issue here is not whether or not we can, or will, win reparations. The issue rather is whether we will fight for reparations, because we have decided for ourselves that they are our

---

[81] "Mont Blanc" is later retitled "The Sahell of Donatello."

[82] In "Mont Blanc: Lines Written in the Vales of Chamouni" (1817), Shelley addresses the mountain: "Thou hast a voice, great Mountain, to repeal / Large codes of fraud and woe; not understood / By all, but which the wise, and great, and good / Interpret, or make felt, or deeply feel."

[83] We're using the term *hyperobject* somewhat loosely. It comes from Timothy Morton, who identifies global warming as one hyperobject to watch; in *Hyperobjects: Philosophy and Ecology after the End of the World* (Minneapolis: University of Minnesota Press, 2013) he characterises these vast, distributed 'objects' by their viscosity, nonlocality, temporal undulation, phasing, and interobjectivity.

due."[84] Memory is one way to structure such necessarily preservative and creative work. It can be the work of memorising, of remembering, and of communicating memories, vigilant to the ways in which past violence is inscribed into the operation of ongoing violence.

Aimée Lê's contribution to this collection, "Without the Text at Hand: Postcolonial Writing and the Work of Memorisation," explores a series of questions around labour, performance, and memory, in relation to race and colonial violence. Lê's chapter centres on memorisation as a poetic practice, but it also offers connections with embodied memory, with cultural memory, and with transgenerational indebtedness. Lê makes her argument with special reference to Kei Miller, M. NourbeSe Philip, and Derek Walcott. Drawing on Ron Silliman's remarks on performance, Lê suggests that the divide between 'stage' and 'page' which can frequently be found in avant-garde poetry scenes—where there is often an implicit common-sense valorisation of fidelity to the work on the page—is symptomatic of a separation from performance poetry cultures. In performance poetry cultures, Lê suggests, these questions have often been more fully explored and interrogated, and there is often a less dogmatic adherence to a sense of 'correct' ways of performing.

What is key for Lê is that within the labour of performing, there will always be something new wrought by the moment of performance, as "the spoken text will always be distinct from the read text."[85] Her exploration of performance becomes a way into thinking about suppressed histories of colonial labour. Lê argues that due to the racialisation of labour, poets of colour are forced to engage with performance in ways white writers are not. In the work she examines, Lê finds unique models mediating poetry on the page with the labour of performance,[86] and seeks to understand "the ways in which abstract and occasionally even mundane

[84] Randall Robinson, *The Debt: What America Owes to Blacks* (New York: Penguin, 2000), 206.

[85] Aimée Lê, "Without the Text at Hand: Postcolonial Writing and the Work of Memorisation," q.v.

[86] For example, in her reading of M. NourbeSe Philip's *Zong!* (2008), Lê argues that the poem on the page can be read as a script intended for a variegated and instantaneously differential set of performances; each vocalisation of this script would be a different historical intervention into the record and materials that Philip's book explores. In the process of composing the work Philip was working with a set of self-imposed restrictions, and Lê describes this script, and the labour of inscription, as a double form of bondage for

procedures, such as a manner of reading from the page, might have an operant presence,"[87] as well as the relationship of this operant presence to different kinds of labour that raced subjects are required to perform. Themes of corporeality, performativity, racialization, and the mystification of systemic violence, also arise in Rita Wong's *forage*, which Samantha Walton explores in her chapter. Wong's work bears witness to specific experiences of exploitation and injury, and specific points of culpability, in particular in the Chinese manufacture of American-bought goods. At the same time, Wong attempts to give some account of the systemic nature of these injustices. The capitalist organisation of the world—if that is even the right way to put it—is difficult to represent and know in any sustained way. The problem of adequately representing capitalism is also the problem of adequately representing its most innovative and disruptive product yet, the Anthropocene. As McKenzie Wark puts it:

> The unspeakable secret about climate change is that nobody really wants to think about it for too long. […] It's just too depressing! Reading about it sometimes seems like helplessly watching some awful train derailment careen in slow motion. Rather, let's take this world-historical moment to be one in which to reimagine what the collective efforts of everyone who labors could make of the world, and as a world.[88]

Within avant-garde writing, one locus of representational experiment is the deployment of form to convey the ways in which capital spreads, mystifies, connects, fragments, and transforms. Walton uses an ecocritical approach, illuminating Wong's work through concepts such as slow violence and transcorporeality. Walton's approach is also Marxist, in its concern with recovering a mystified materiality, as well as the subsumption of the labour process by economic relations. Marx distinguishes between the 'formal' subsumption and the 'real' subsumption of labour. Formal subsumption is the first stage; capital takes over existing production

Philip. The poet is attentive to histories of Black suffering and thinks about how to make visible the submerged and lost voices of history from the documents of brutality which are their only record (in this case the insurance papers of the slave ship 'Zong' from which 133 African slaves were thrown overboard to drown in 1781).

[87] Lê, "Without the Text at Hand," q.v.

[88] McKenzie Wark, *Molecular Red: Theory for the Anthropocene* (London: Verso, 2015), loc. 159–162.

arrangements, such as equipment, technologies, working practices, means of distribution, etc. In real subsumption, capital not only extracts value from these resources, but thoroughly transforms them, and continues to transform them, to suit its purposes. In the acute kinds of subsumption adduced by Walton and Wong, humans and other living beings become conduits and sinks for toxins, as their bodies are indistinguishably assimilated into the material from which capital works its value.

Corporeality and performativity are also key concerns in Holly Pester's chapter on Catherine Wagner. Pester begins with posture. Posture is both the result of work and a form of work itself. Often posture is affective labour. It is the activity of holding the body up to achieve social effects: to enact productive spells on others, on circumstances, and on ourselves. Posturing is also how we position our abstract selves within a public; our bodies blur into active metaphors for our personae. This is where a posture becomes a performance, and a performative configuration of identity and body-matter. Posture often becomes known through its pathologies. Normally posture goes unnoticed unless it is 'bad' posture. Here again, the compulsion to work to be self-identical within interlocking matrices of domination is evident.[89] That is not how a 'man' holds his chest; that is not how a 'good girl' sits. Even good posture, when it becomes flagrant, appears faintly suspect. What lurking impulse to crookedness could have provoked such thorough training in the first place? Bad posture may include failure to hold yourself up against the rhythms of work, with the situation of deskwork returning to the scene of the body, and the tasks accomplished or deferred returning to the body as slouch. Posture is, finally, expressive. 'Body language' is spoken and heard through the medium of posture. Posture is a medium of expressions about work, as well as through and because of work. Pester ties her dialectical understanding of posture to Bertolt Brecht's neologism *Gestus*, a word suggesting both 'gesture' and 'gist,' which seeks to capture everything that is expressed in a person's entire social physicality. The dejection or the euphoria expressed in a body's posture cannot quite be dismissed as illusory simply because it does not correlate with the current affect of the body so configured; the utterance is not speaker-less simply because the utterance cannot be attributed to the first obvious speaker.

---

[89] Patricia Hill Collins, *Black Feminist Thought: Knowledge, Consciousness, and the Politics of Empowerment* (Boston: Unwin Hyman, 1990), 221–238

The chapter goes on to examine the intersection of gendered embodiment and performativity with capital, through the work of Catherine Wagner's *My New Job* and *Nervous Device*. Marx scrutinised how human labour is congealed and jellied in the commodity; he also investigated the commodification of the human as a worker on the labour market. Pester illuminatingly unites these two concepts, in an account of the human labour that is sedimented and mystified within the human commodity. In this case, that commodity is the poet Catherine Wagner. Pester's account broadly portrays a worker-subject who is lodged in an extraordinarily energetic, mercurial, and violent milieu, made of complex flows of imperatives: extractive, disciplinary, generative, sensuous, administrative. Wagner's work, Pester claims, contains

> all the actual disintegration, dislocation and indeterminacy suffered by this figure, yet embodies them as infinite possibilities to resist capital and orders of patriarchy as systems of domination, which offer destructive ways for things to be in common where everything is related primarily by value.[90]

What does it mean to approach this figure through her work? Pester gives the concept of posture a phenomenological inflection, describing it as the "meaningful signification of a body, which is a combination of matter and form, and through which we can read a politics of work-time in correlation with performances of gendered subjectivity."[91] This means that posture also becomes, for Pester, the constantly deleted and redrawn defining line between worker-subject and milieu; posture becomes the body as a "configuration of entangled acts of work and productivity within effaced boundaries between work and life, biology and market economy."[92] In this sense, perhaps posture can offer a kind of provisional solidity or stability within this flux, "a spatial politics, where the past and future are in erotic and syntactic tension as historicity."[93] Again, Brecht provides useful material for comparison. Walter Benjamin refers to the gesture as the "raw material" of Brecht's epic theatre, a raw material with "two advantages over the highly deceptive statements and

---

[90] Pester, "Distributed and Entangled Posture," q.v.

[91] Pester, "Distributed and Entangled Posture," q.v.

[92] Pester, "Distributed and Entangled Posture," q.v.

[93] Pester, "Distributed and Entangled Posture," q.v.

assertions normally made by people and their many-layered and opaque actions": the gesture is "falsifiable only up to a point" and has "a definable beginning and a definable end."[94] Like gesture, perhaps posture offers us certain talismans against deception, and certain finitudes, which can be imposed on the baffling flows of capital without reifying or otherwise oversimplifying those flows (as certain new materialist approaches have often felt previous materialisms are prone to do). If so, then perhaps posture can become the raw material of an interpretative methodology, one which accommodates (and even makes use of) the paradox that "the more specifically the body is defined, the more vulnerable it appears to manipulation as mere value, and therefore the more de-specified and ill-defined it becomes,"[95] so as to confront capital's mystification of life as exchange and circulation. Pester uses posture, and vice versa, to trace the distribution of these poems' production across multiple contexts and scales, and the distinct logics each implies: "sexual encounter, at work in the office, on the yoga mat, or at the point of composing and performing poetry" and others.[96] In the final part of her chapter, Pester also connects posture with the Blakean "bounding line," that which "works within the world to crucially discriminate one thing from another."[97]

CARCERAL LABOUR

Jackie Wang's *Carceral Capitalism* (2018) explores the deeply embedded logic of punitive incarceration within American society. In her acknowledgements, Wang mentions a poetry workshop at The Harvard Divinity School which helped her to refine "The Prison Abolitionist Imagination," the book's seventh chapter.[98] In this chapter Wang gathers an array of poetic fragments from those who have been imprisoned—including Mahmoud Darwish, George Jackson, and Rosa Luxemburg—seeking the possibility of freedom from the carceral state in the context of maximum unfreedom. Writing by George Jackson and Frank Hampton is described as containing a suppressed "divine spark,"

---

[94] Walter Benjamin, *Understanding Brecht*, trans. Anna Bostock (London: NLB, 1973), 4.

[95] Pester, "Distributed and Entangled Posture," q.v.

[96] Pester, "Distributed and Entangled Posture," q.v.

[97] Pester, "Distributed and Entangled Posture," q.v.

[98] Jackie Wang, *Carceral Capitalism* (South Pasadena, CA: Semiotext(e), 2018), 358.

which were it to be free, "would spread until the world as we know it would be upended."[99] There is a utopian impulse in the writing and poetry of imprisoned revolutionaries. It holds a secret that the world cannot bear, one that could also 'upend' the world.

In Eleanor Careless's chapter, "Work in the Poetry and Prison Correspondence of Anna Mendelssohn," Careless intervenes inventively into discussions around the social value of prison writing. Utilising the theoretical work of the post-autonomist feminist Leopoldina Fortunati, Careless considers work usually given to women in British prisons as extended forms of domestic and reproductive labour. She contextualises the poetry of Anna Mendelssohn, written mostly across the eighties and nineties, in relation to her period of incarceration in Holloway Women's Prison in London during the seventies. In 1971, Mendelssohn was arrested for conspiracy to cause explosions and received a ten-year sentence for her association with the anarchist group The Angry Brigade (she was released on parole in 1976). In opposition to the image of the imprisoned male genius (Ezra Pound, Oscar Wilde, George Jackson), Careless recounts—with close attention to archival material recently made available—how Mendelssohn's incarceration can be characterised through a stultifying absence of the creative impulse. For Mendelssohn, as for other female writers such as Angela Davis and Ulrike Meinhof, prison was a place where writing became incredibly difficult. Careless associates this suppression with the gruelling feminised labour regimes that Mendelssohn would have been put through while in the women's prison.

While the piece also looks at how physical labour and incarceration can destroy the creative impulse, Careless's chapter is an example of what the work of poetry scholarship can reveal. Through scrupulous attention to the surface of Mendelssohn's poetry, in combination with a ventilation of the poetry through its historical context, Careless shows how the existence of carceral punishment can be deeply traumatic and damaging to those who are made to bear it. Fundamental to Careless's argument is that the time of carceral punishment has a 'before' and an 'after' that can be read through the surface of Mendelssohn's dense and fragmentary

---

[99] Wang, *Carceral Capitalism*, 307.

lyric work. Because the time of the composition of poetry is intimately related to the subjectivity that exists within language, reading poetry can expand our conceptions of how social forces are suffered. Careless also articulates how "the political constitution of the subject," and especially the subject as one who is made to bear race or gender, is a labouring subject that is forced to submit to the law.[100] Her careful close readings of Mendelssohn's poetry explore the juridical role of the reader, how the logic of the law is reproduced on an intra-subjective level, through what she terms "granular inscriptions."[101]

In *The Time That Remains: A Commentary on The Letters to the Romans*, Giorgio Agamben makes the theological claim that there is a "kind of eschatology [that] occurs within the poem itself."[102] He asserts that the poem as such "has its own *time*."[103] In distinction to this rather generalising philosophical claim about the relation between poetry and time, Careless shows that in the particular case of Mendelssohn, her poetry is inflected by the damage and subjective experience of the sentence of imprisoned labour time, which all her writing came to be *after*. Such scholarship brings to light how textual interrogation of poetry may deepen and broaden understanding of lived experiences of prison. In Michel Foucault's extremely influential formulation, our society operates through regimes of discipline and punishment that emerge through the bourgeois form of the judiciary; Careless's essay helps us to understand how this punishment comes to impact most heavily on certain subjects and irreparably damages their psychic relations with the world. Her careful readings of this difficult body of poetry illuminate how imprisonment marks the body and how regimes of coercive labour are part of "the long-lasting trauma of incarceration as a form of debilitation."[104]

[100] Eleanor Careless, "Work in the Poetry and Prison Correspondence of Anna Mendelssohn," q.v.

[101] Careless, "Work in the Poetry and Prison Correspondence of Anna Mendelssohn," q.v.

[102] Giorgio Agamben, *The Time That Remains: A Commentary on the Letter to the Romans* (Stanford, CA: Stanford University Press, 2005), 79.

[103] Agamben, *The Time That Remains*, 79.

[104] Careless, "Work in the Poetry and Prison Correspondence of Anna Mendelssohn," q.v.

Reflections

What kind of work do poets do? Since we first came up with the idea of this collection, it was important to us we include some autobiographical or autoethnographic contributions, written in the first person by poet-scholars. The larger, first part of the book collects essays about representations of work in poetry, about the work of poetry, and about how theories of work and labour can be used to generate new understandings of poetry. The second part consists of three such critical-creative reflections by Amber DiPietra, Tyrone Williams, and Catherine Wagner.

As Holly Pester explores in her essay on Wagner, the status and power available to a poet is of a curious kind. On the one hand, the poet could be well known within certain academic, artistic, or intellectual circles, such that they could travel to many cities around the world and find generous audiences. People might even *have read* the poet's work. It is even possible that it could have been acknowledged in whatever passes for the public sphere or mainstream media. However, unlike, say, successful novelists, filmmakers or visual artists, it is not really possible to make a living just from selling poetry. This is what Pester describes in relation to the poetry of Wagner as "the albeit limited capital and measures of employability and social reputation in recompense for the poem's production."[105] However, while poetry pays out very little hard cash, its institutional prestige means that some poets can monetize their labour in indirect ways. As the white male poet Joshua Clover candidly writes, despite his public expression of radical sentiments on many political issues, as a poet he "got hired for writing a book of poetry with some sort of prestige," and "got hired for all the demographic unfairnesses," and now he gets "paid on the last of the month."[106]

A fair few of the poets in this collection may at one point or another have benefitted from institutional prestige. Others have not—or not sufficiently to get by without conducting other forms of work. But a poet from either set may approach the work of poetry with a strange kind of seriousness. On the one hand, they often appear highly committed, finding the time in-between all their other kinds of work to write and share their poems. On the other hand, they may have a sneaking

---

[105] Pester, "Distributed and Entangled Posture," q.v.

[106] Joshua Clover, "Unfree Verse," *Poetry Foundation Blog*, 15 April 2016, www.poetry-foundation.org/harriet/2016/04/unfree-verse, accessed 1 June 2018, n.p.

suspicion that poetry is entirely useless. Does anyone ever read poetry, they may wonder, or really listen to it? If contemporary society is filled, as David Graeber argues, with "bullshit jobs," could poetry be a bullshit hobby?[107]

Ben Lerner articulates some of this apathy and hostility in *The Hatred of Poetry* (2016), while also hoping to convince "the haters" that poetry is important work. He concludes by imploring those who hate poetry to work on their relationship with it. They can begin by bringing that hatred to their reading, "where it will be deepened, not dispelled, and where, by creating a place for possibility and present absences (like unheard melodies), it might come to resemble love."[108] Perhaps Lerner is being coy, and hinting that hatred *will* turn into love. But perhaps he really means it about hatred that resembles love, and offers this as a legitimate way of engaging with the poetry's volatile and ambivalent value— or perhaps, its stubborn lack of value.

In Alli Warren's poem "Protect Me From What I Want," this uncertainty about poetry's social status is both seriously embraced and playfully ironized. Warren's poem is built around refrains in the structure of "I did it to [X]" or "I did it for [Y]." The verb *to do* is typically transitive, that is, you do *something*. The something you do is often some kind of work. But the poem never reveals what kind of work "it" is:

> I did it to carry my propriety into property
> I did it for the things that resonate around me
> I did it for the archaic loss I did it for the clustering
> I did it for the rope chain I did it for the many
> I did it for the thousands of unknown civilians their
>   disappearance their unsteady accounting.

So what kind of work is this? Is it 'real' work? It is difficult to imagine a work that could accommodate all these claims, other than the work of the poem itself. Perhaps Warren's poem is a retort to the unheard interrogation which brings it into being: 'Why does this poem exist? Why did you write it? Why did you become the poet who could and did write it? What did you do it *for*? What did you do it in order *to* do?' As one line puts it: "I did it to learn my handicraft in the daytime." In this sense, the

---

[107] See the section on "Platforms, Precarity, Pointlessness, and Postwork" in this introduction.

[108] Ben Lerner, *Hatred of Poetry* (London: Fitzcarraldo Editions, 2016), 86.

poem could be taken as an elaborate series of considerations around the status of poetry as real work.

Real work is, at least *partly*, whatever you think of as real work. So far this book has mentioned various species of labour, including productive labour and reproductive labour, 'identity' labour, affective labour and emotional labour, aesthetic labour, intersubjective labour and worldmaking, carceral labour, craftwork, unalienated or 'truly free' labour, and of course the labour of poetry—and there are still more varieties in store later. Diverse distinctions like these are, of course, needed to understand and participate in scholarly and political debates about work.[109] But as they multiply, the idea that we'll ever develop any *final* taxonomy of labour—one that is equal to the complex flux of our collective experience, and one that honours both particularity *and* solidarity—does start to look pretty far-fetched. Does that matter? Perhaps it does. On one hand, it means there's a risk that we may reject the mess of classification altogether, in favour of some kind of cursory nominalism (*'everything* is labour, when you think about it!'). On the other hand, we may be tempted to fetishize classification, treating each refinement to how we recognise 'real work' as a magical talisman, to be brandished against exploitation, oppression, and alienation, but without ever asking whether the magic itself is real.

Another option, adopted by Amber DiPietra in her chapter, is to articulate a highly situated and personal classification of work forms. This more phenomenological approach allows DiPietra to emphasise significant distinctions and interdependencies among different kinds of work, without any pretension that they are (or should be) universal. DiPietra's chapter is based on her contribution to The Poetic Labor Project, an online blog that contains, at present, around eighty responses from poets about the jobs and general labour they have to do to sustain their writing process. Most of the contributions are from poets from the West Coast of the United States, however there are contributions from all over the country and a sizable number from Chile. The project emerged out of a Bay Area gathering in Oakland 2010—a gathering that was a conference

---

[109] For example, such distinctions help us to make sense of our own experience; to shine light on experience and events that might be otherwise shoved into the shadows; to evolve our discursive practices to accommodate ongoing ecological and technological transformation; to de-naturalise the division of labour which patriarchal capitalism confronts us with; and of course to place poetry somewhere within all this.

in some ways, although very deliberately not a conference in others—concerned with how poets earn a living.

DiPietra explores the various interconnected forms of work she undertakes. For instance, DiPietra has worked as a community practice artist, poet, performer, disability rights advocate. She also describes her extremely disciplined and rigorous health regime, which she names "body-work." DiPietra has a disability that means she has barely any cartilage between her bones, and "body-work" is the continual physical labour that she performs, including exercises to move and to rest her joints throughout her body so that they don't seize up. DiPietra describes carrying out this labour of self-maintenance alongside advocacy and activist work supporting people with disabilities, including leading writing classes.

Body-work is one key component of DiPietra's elegant micro-catalogue of her personal work forms: alongside body-work, she also contemplates freelance-work, social- and domestic-work, poetry- and sleep-work, and work-work. One key theme of her chapter is encapsulated in her beautifully succinct phrase, the "labor it takes for things to elapse in time."[110] Through description of the rigorous physical labour of constituting the body with which she identifies, woven with acknowledgement of the importance of reflecting on her experience of such labour, DiPietra's chapter allows for a sharper conception of the spaces in-between creative activity. The labour that is hidden within any body of poetry, in the lines on the surface of any poem, or in the oeuvre of any writer, includes the "labor it takes for things to elapse in time" (q.v.). It includes some uneven distribution of getting *back* to work, of distraction and interruption, of feelings of protracted unhappiness or discomfort, of feeling 'not yourself,' and of all the working-through of difficult experience that may have structured the time in which the poet could have been writing. Likewise, on a slightly different timescale, it may be a helpful exercise to look at the time elapsed between the publication of one text and the next, and to reflect on all the alienated labour accumulated in-between.

Distraction from writing is also one theme of Catherine Wagner's contribution, "The Exploit: Affective Labor and Poetry at the University." Wagner's chapter is also the story of a poetic experiment,

---

[110]Amber DiPietra, "Extract from the Poetic Labor Project," q.v.

and a critique of the political economy of poetry in North America, especially in relation to the university, and its many forms of affective, administrative, and other kinds of labour. Wagner's critique engages with the corporatisation of the academy. She looks at changes in employment structures in US universities due to funding cuts, examining how academics have been forced into taking up increased administrative and entrepreneurial labour alongside teaching and research, and the expansion of academics' pastoral roles as students themselves come under great pressures.

In part, these changes reflect the loss of administrative and specialist pastoral staff, but they may also relate to what is being done, as well as who is being asked to do it. For instance, David Graeber comments on the growth within universities of data gathering and quality assurance procedures, and other administrative tasks, of dubious usefulness:

> I suspect that bullshitization has been so severe because academe is a kind of meeting place of the caring sector — defined in its broadest sense, as an occupation that involves looking after, nurturing, or furthering the health, well-being, or development of other human beings — and the creative sector. These are, certainly, the two sectors of undeniably valuable work that have been most plagued by bullshitization.[111]

Wagner reads changes such as these alongside the expansion and exploitation of the adjunct labour force. Wagner writes, "I found myself, even before becoming director of creative writing, spending minimal time on teaching and writing in comparison to time spent on public relations and marketing, filling out spreadsheets, and doing various assessments and metrics tasks to help administrators figure out how to reallocate resources."[112] What is equally important is that the non-salaried adjuncts that are also required to do this work are paid at a much lower rate than the poet.

Wagner describes her project, the Exploit, as a 'hack' of this political economy. Wagner plays on the senses of *exploit* as a hack, an abuse, or a deed or adventure. This word *hack* can also be taken in at least

---

[111] David Graeber, "Are You in a BS Job? In Academe, You're Hardly Alone," 6 May 2018, *The Chronicle of Higher Education*, www.chronicle.com/article/Are-You-in-a-BS-Job-In/243318, accessed 5 June 2018.

[112] Cathy Wagner, "The Exploit: Affective Labor and Poetry at the University," q.v.

two senses. It can be taken to mean a breach of the structures of the circulation of poetry by reusing content or by using content produced by others (typically Wagner's graduate students) under the placeholder "Catherine Wagner." Another sense might be that of the hack writer, the hack job, or hackneyed writing, implying a conceptual ploy whereby the work submitted by "Catherine Wagner" is produced to standards different to those usually required by these structures. "The Exploit" highlights the sheer amount of unpaid labour conducted by career academics and career poets. Importantly, poetry's lack of wholesale value, as Wagner argues, means "it sanctions the exploitation of workers' commitments to poetry."[113] The Exploit also confronts the bizarre and brutal differences in the treatment of senior versus junior university staff, the laughably illogical efforts to treat different workers as fungible, and the ways institutional prestige allows well-known writers to get away with things that early career academics and less established poets would not.

Wagner's piece acknowledges a broad array of collaborators as co-authors, some of whom were conducting teaching on Wagner's courses while she was on research leave. The list is long, but probably not long enough: it dramatises the difficulty—or the impossibility—of really giving credit where credit is due. Whose labour has really made this chapter possible? A notional 'perfect' set of acknowledgements might take us into the realm of reparative justice.

Questions of indebtedness are also at the heart of "Floating On—if not Up—ward," in which the poet Tyrone Williams recounts his upbringing in Detroit in a Black working-class family in the sixties, and reflects on social mobility, and the relationship between his own work and his father's work. The key words *debt, sacrifice,* and *choice* have an elliptical, lyrical, and fruitful quality in this memoir. Williams considers how his parents' hard work when he was a child may have meant they sacrificed the creative activities they most loved. Williams contrasts this with how, as an adult, he composed music and wrote, and later taught. Williams reflects on how his own priorities, choices, and gambles, suggest that he will never be able to support his parents as they supported him. "I was devastated because I knew I'd never make enough money for him and my mother to retire on with ease."[114]

---

[113] Cathy Wagner, "The Exploit: Affective Labor and Poetry at the University," q.v.

[114] Tyrone Williams, "Floating On—if not Up—ward," q.v.

It is tempting to think of all debt as financial debt, and in fact Williams—probably a bit tongue-in-cheek—calls on financial metaphors to articulate what he feels he owes his family. But his memoir also lucidly shows that relationships of debt exceed financial expression. Debt relations can be social ties, ways of knowing each other, and relations of power. (Or perhaps it would better to be a bit Foucauldian, and say that debt relations are fields of power-knowledge). Even though the possibility of repayment seems to be inherent in the nature of a debt, it also seems feasible that debts exist "that *cannot* be paid."[115] When two people are close, they usually owe each other a million little things that don't cancel out.

In the final part of this introduction, we look briefly at postwork discourse, and its challenge to the work ethic. Why do so many of us punish ourselves and each other with work? How has the world of work become a means to *prevent* our societies from enjoying their relative material abundance and communicative sophistication? Postwork theory suggests various reasons, but perhaps Williams' memoir highlights one reason which deserves a bit more attention. That is, perhaps the work ethic is a space where we process and transform debt relations that are generated within the family, and within other intimate networks. Shakespeare's wanton Prince Hal could be taken as embodying an antiwork ethic; at one point Hal—fresh from a rumination on the relations between work and sport, and between abundance and scarcity—claims he's going to eventually throw off his "loose behaviour" and thereby "pay the debt [he] never promised."[116] Here Hal is restaging his dissolute leisure as the active management of expectations, and as the repression of a debt which would otherwise arise of its own accord … a debt Hal is happy to pay so long as he does not owe it. Could Hal be using his leisure ethic the way many of us use the work ethic: to erode the legitimacy of the nonfinancial debts we owe, not because we *don't* want to pay them, but because we *do*?

Williams's piece can, finally, also be read as an oblique commentary on *opportunity cost*, a foundational concept in mainstream economics and its understanding of scarcity and efficiency. It's just one story, but

---

[115]David Graeber, *Debt: The First 5,000 Years* (Brooklyn: Melville House, 2011), loc. 2710–2711.

[116]William Shakespeare, *The Complete Works of William Shakespeare*, ed. W. J. Craig (London: Oxford University Press, 1943), 412.

it brings to the surface all the kinds of sacrifices that poets may make, the debts they may incur, and even the damages that they may do, when they commit to writing in the face of other expectations and obligations. The tone steers clear of regretful, but it has a candid, troubled quality. It thinks about what might get lost in translation from one generation to the next; about the mutual unintelligibilities that are manufactured through the division of labour; and about the conflict one generation may feel, between its aspirations that the next generation recreate its world, redeem its world, transcend its world, or become altogether unintelligible or free.

For a period, Eddie Lee Williams floated—'upward'?—towards white collar work but then, for reasons that must be complex and opaque, and must certainly be entangled with Tyrone Williams' own life, he settled back into blue-collar work, especially truck driving. For economists, opportunity cost is the cost of forgoing the second-best choice. It is the value of whatever you almost did, but did not. But when opportunity cost is construed narratively, rather than within mathematical modelling, it is clear that the value of what-might-have-been has no objective reality; in Williams' memoir, the valuation of what-might-have-been is an effect generated by coming to terms with what-is.[117]

> Did he stop attending night school simply because he lost interest in architectural design? Was driving a truck – which he still does today even though he is 'officially' retired – his way to have a career he could prosper at and enjoy?[118]

Platforms, Precarity, Pointlessness and Postwork

The post-Fordist transformation of societies can be crudely divided into three phases: the first Thatcherite wave of neoliberalism; the second Blairite wave, rebooting neoliberalism as an alleged 'Third Way' between Keynesian embedded liberalism and free market fundamentalism; plus a more recent, unnamed and volatile mix, existing for the last decade, in

---

[117] Opportunity cost asks us to specify what someone would have done, had they not done what they did. But from a narrative perspective, this may threaten to begin an endless fractal line of enquiry: what would the opportunity cost have been, were it not the opportunity cost that it is?

[118] Williams, "Floating On—if not Up—ward," q.v.

which the violence of high-tech neoliberalism jostles with the violence of resurgent ethnic nationalisms. This most recent phase might especially be characterised by the emergence of the digital platform as a way of organising labour.

A platform may loosely be understood as a privatised digital market, whose operations are often relatively insulated from legal and regulatory inspection and intervention. The platform is unlike most traditional markets in the sense that it is far more inspectable and manipulable by whoever owns it. Particularly emblematic and influential platform corporations include eBay (established 1995); Airbnb (2008), and Uber (2009), and platforms very directly associated with work include those such as Upwork (established 2003), Amazon's Mechanical Turk (2005), TaskRabbit (2008), and Fiverr (2010). There are a cluster of overlapping buzzwords and ideas associated with the platform, including the sharing economy, the gig economy, online marketplaces, peer-to-peer networking, prosumption, co-production, collaborative consumption, crowdfunding, crowdsourcing, e-lancing, unbundling, gamification, the prefix micro-, and even perhaps social media per se. Insofar as the platform business model has inherent interests in building vast data sets and in tying together the material world with data networks, it also has less visible but equally significant affiliations with infrastructure development through Quantified Self technologies and 'sousveillance,' smart cities and smart homes, and the Internet of Things.

But the platform is a misleading metaphor. The platform may suggest the studied neutrality of a theatrical stage, designed to host a great diversity of activities, without predetermining the nature of those activities. It may suggest 'giving a platform' and 'sharing a platform': furnishing people an empty open space, so they can meet more-or-less as equals and get on with more-or-less whatever business or leisure they want together. Platform companies have tended to encourage this perception, presenting themselves as disintermediators, who merely clear away the clutter among pre-formed actors, enabling and facilitating their interactions. Unsurprisingly, not only because they are mostly *not* neutral disintermediators, but also in their limited capacity *as* neutral disintermediators, platforms have been doing much more than this. The transformation of housing markets by Airbnb is one visible example. Platforms can profoundly reconfigure social ontologies, actively generating new practices, forms of knowledge, subjectivities, and spatialities. Karen Gregory, for instance, draws attention to the greater role that tech corporations and platforms are playing in the ways that cities are thinking about the future of their infrastructures, and about how public goods and services will be distributed and accessed.[119] As Andrew Spragg suggests, platforms appear to be spreading features of creative labour—particularly downsides—into new domains. In Rosalind Gill and Andy Pratt's account, such creative labour is characterised by

> a preponderance of temporary, intermittent and precarious jobs; long hours and bulimic patterns of working; the collapse or erasure of the boundaries between work and play; poor pay; high levels of mobility; passionate attachment to the work and to the identity of creative labourer (e.g. web designer, artist, fashion designer); an attitudinal mindset that is a blend of bohemianism and entrepreneurialism; informal work environments and distinctive forms of sociality; and profound experiences of insecurity and anxiety about finding work, earning enough money and 'keeping up' in rapidly changing fields.[120]

[119] Karen Gregory, "Karen Gregory Talks About the Negatives and Positives of Computer Platform Capitalism," RadioLabour, 2 November 2017, congress.world-psi.org/karen-gregory-talks-about-the-negatives-and-positives-of-computer-platform-capitalism, accessed 5 June 2018.

[120] Rosalind Gill and Andy Pratt, "Precarity and Cultural Work in the Social Factory? Immaterial Labour, Precariousness and Cultural Work." Andrew Spragg invokes Gill and Pratt as part of a critique of J. T. Welsch's conciliatory engagement with 'the occupational turn.' In a 2018 article, Welsch identifies an atmosphere of greater openness, within UK poetry communities, to the language and ideology of business and marketing. Welsch entertains the idea that scorn for such 'professionalisation' has functioned in the past as a gatekeeping practice. He suggests "we might come to view poetry's occupational turn as less a threat to creative integrity than a reflection of the need to widen its opportunities." However, he does remain uneasy with the business-entrepreneurial spirit in its raw form, and suggests that some reimagining will be necessary to complete the occupational turn: "In a relatively short period, we have gone from [Salt co-director Chris Hamilton-Emery's] provocation that 'the world of poetry can be a bear pit' (and Salt's subsequent retreat from poetry hustling) to [Jo Bell and Jane Commane's] *How to Be a Poet*'s emphasis on 'sharing your work with a wider community.'" J. T. Welsch, "Audit: The Promise of Professionalism," 2018, poetrysociety.org.uk/audit-the-promise-of-professionalism-by-j-t-welsch, accessed 5 January 2019. By contrast, Spragg does not see much point in welcoming neoliberal rationality—with or without local customizations—into one of the few domains that has up till now proved a partial refuge against it. He briefly pulls Welsch up for dislocating poetry from its larger social and economic context, for forgetting poetry's duty to hold power accountable and bear witness to suffering, and for fudging the issue of poetry's commercial viability: though Welsch may go as far as saying that "Teaching people to write a cover letter, book proposal, or event budget […] needn't be

But if poets and artists are providing models for the labour of platform workers, their own working lives are also being reshaped by platforms. For example, Gregory notes the desire of unsecure young artists to acquire tech and data skills to support their creative practice, the permeation of their practice by such skills, and the reconfiguring of networks of solidarity and artistic affiliation around these skills.[121] We might also point to the emergence of platform poets such as Rupi Kaur, whose labour is conducted within the affordances of network connectivity and virality. More generally, the platform is also reshaping the available forms of penurious bohemianism. That is, one characteristic of platform capitalism is the new forms and intensities of precarity which it brings about.

Broadly speaking, precarious work means any work that is unreliable, unpredictable, and unsustaining in various ways: temporary work, day labour and other contingent and casual work, flexible work, work without sick pay, ununionized work, work inadequately protected by law and regulations, or where the worker cannot access enforcement of notional rights, etc. Platform precarity implies the precarity of working within a network market owned and controlled by a company with no democratic accountability, and organised according to opaque proprietary algorithms. *Precarity* recently entered English from the French *précarité*. In its early usage, the term tended to refer to labour conditions of acute vulnerability and exploitation; generally it meant workers without access to formal labour markets. The term has since widened considerably. In

---

entirely disconnected from writing poems," he sensibly stops short of claiming that there are any livelihoods in poetry, even for the most ruthless and innovative go-getter. Spragg and Welsch do both readily endorse creative and professional development initiatives for underrepresented groups, but Spragg adds that "one does not solve inequality by aggressively pursuing a form of self-exploitation, or embracing the language that enables it. We should be resisting at all points the professionalism of anything as gloriously unauditable as writing, embracing instead all its radical possibilities. Leave fame for the arseholes. The best way to be a writer in real life is to be in real life." "Response: Andrew Spragg on J. T. Welsch's 'The Promise of Professionalism,'" 2018, poetrysociety.org.uk/response-andrew-spragg-on-j-t-welschs-the-promise-of-professionalism, accessed 5 January 2019. See also Alison Gerber, *The Work of Art: Value in Creative Careers* (Palo Alto, CA: Stanford University Press, 2017); Jo Bell and Jane Commane's, *How to Be a Poet: A Twenty-First Century Guide to Writing Well* (Rugby: Nine Arches Press, 2017); Chris Hamilton-Emery, *101 Ways to Make a Poem Sell* (Cromer: Salt, 2006).

[121] Karen Gregory, "Is the Public a 'Market'?" Paper at Exploring Digital Publics symposium, Institute for Advanced Studies in the Humanities, Edinburgh. 1 June 2018.

its current usage, it might awkwardly encompass the experience of both undocumented workers in low paid informal work and creative professionals for whom self-employment and irregular short term contracts are an industry norm. Precarity "has provided a rallying call and connecting device for struggles surrounding citizenship, labour rights, the social wage, and migration."[122]

However, if we construe precarity as a lack of something, we need to recognise that that 'something' has only ever existed for a short time and in quite limited regions, roughly speaking as a function of Fordism. To some extent, anti-precarity movements remain rooted in a broadly Fordist imaginary. Precarity is in a vexed relationship with autonomy. Unpredictable income, unpredictable work obligations, a lack of job security—in the sense that the precarious worker may be quickly and inexpensively 'fired,' whether or not it takes the legal form of termination of employment—can be variously correlated with dubious freedoms. The flexibility to work when you choose and how you choose. The freedom to shape a skillset, a personal brand, and a network. A lack of stable housing is the opportunity to travel and explore. The gig economy's promises of flexibility, variety, and autonomy in work, however bogus and brutal, point to real needs which were not met by the Fordist form of labour organisation. For most, the classic 'job for life' was an intricate prison. *Postwork* represents one kind of opposition to precarity which attempts to move outside of this imaginary. Instead of demanding the renewal of security eroded by post-Fordism, postwork and antiwork discourse challenges the central role work plays in our collective life. Kathi Weeks, for example, proposes to "counter the power of the work ethic with a postwork politics."[123]

Precarity and exhausting and dangerous overwork have also, strangely, become entwined with a celebratory discourse. In 2016, a cute story appeared on the publicity blog of the ridesharing corporation Lyft. Mary, "[l]ong-time Lyft driver and mentor" continued to work while, having

---

[122] Brett Neilson and Ned Rossiter, "FCJ-022 From Precarity to Precariousness and Back Again: Labour, Life and Unstable Networks," 2015, five.fibreculturejournal.org/fcj-022-from-precarity-to-precariousness-and-back-again-labour-life-and-unstable-networks/, accessed 5 June 2018.

[123] Kathi Weeks, *The Problem with Work* (Durham and London: Duke University Press), 228.

gone into labour, she drove herself to the hospital. An advertisement for the digital labour platform Fiverr runs:

> You eat a coffee for lunch. You follow through on your follow through. Sleep deprivation is your drug of choice. You might be a doer.

In smaller lettering below, the tag exalts, "In Doers We Trust." The word 'God' is rather ostentatiously replaced with "Doers"—who are simultaneously the bearers of a specific temperament, plus anybody who happens to work for Fiverr—perhaps to disguise the other words that might have been replaced, such as 'Workers,' 'Employees,' 'the Precariat,' 'Indentured Labourers,' or—who knows?—'Slaves.' The slogan is balanced between blasphemy and devotion. There is a trace here of Algernon Sidney's "God helps those who help themselves," albeit conflated with a stab at hedonism that is cringe-inducing in its own right.[124] The image is a photograph of a "Doer." Deeply shaded cheekbones and thick eyeliner are redolent of 90s heroin chic: this is what it's like when you work yourself to the bone. In most adverts in the same series, eyelids narrow in focused resolve, but this model's eyelids are minimal. The expression suggests the repressed gurns and torrential pupils of a postclub, pre-comedown wander. Writing in summer 2018, we note that this same image forms the banner of the Twitter account of Micha Kaufman, Fiverr CEO, who—in another context—makes this commitment:

> to continue building a marketplace that will enable lean entrepreneurship so that all of you, and anyone else who is willing to pour sweat and tears into their work, can thrive in this new economy. [...] But it's a two-way street. As a community, don't ever stop pushing, growing, and evolving. Keep hustling and keep grinding each day to make it more productive than the last.

He summarises: "Wake up every day to get shit done. [...] We'll help you do it."[125] Do we have to? Is it okay if you don't help? To conclude

---

[124] See Algernon Sidney, *Discourses Concerning Government*, ed. Thomas G. West (Indianapolis: Liberty Fund, 1996 [1698]), 210. (The sentiment appears in works by Sophocles, Euripides, Aesop and others; Sidney's wording seems to have been popularised by Benjamin Franklin's 1736 *Poor Richard's Almanack*).

[125] Micha Kaufman, "In Doers We Trust: From an Ideal to a Movement," 9 January 2017, blog.fiverr.com/doers-trust-ideal-movement/, accessed 5 June 2018.

this introduction, let's turn briefly to antiwork and postwork dis-course,[126] and other attempts to theorise and challenge the celebration of activities degrading, exhausting, dehumanising and unjust. In *Bullshit Jobs: A Theory* (2018), David Graeber distinguishes *shit jobs*, whose workers are badly treated and poorly paid (occupying jobs that "are in no sense inherently degrading, but they can easily be made so"[127]) from *bullshit jobs*, which are of little or no social value.[128] A job may be either one of these things, or both, or neither; the latter are Graeber's focus. Graeber suggests that identifying a bullshit job is primarily a subjective matter, insofar as any worker is probably best-placed to know if they do little or no work all day, or if the work which they do is mostly point-less. Graeber does qualify this self-reporting approach, claiming that sometimes "managers intentionally break up tasks in such a way that the workers don't really understand how their efforts contribute to the over-all enterprise,"[129] and also gesturing towards structural incentives which may influence the upper echelons to perceive their jobs as non-bullshit. Graeber also suggests five broad categories of bullshit jobs: flunkies (who do little except increase the status of their bosses), goons (who convince people to buy things they don't want), duct tapers (who fix the mistakes of senior people who could have just done the things themselves), box tickers (who allow organisations to claim they're doing something that they aren't really), and taskmasters (who create and supervise bullshit tasks and bullshit work).

William Rowe's poem "bullshit jobs" engages with Graeber's the-ory. Within the developed economies of contemporary capitalism a large number of people are engaged in labour which they—presumably correctly—perceive to be pointless. But Rowe brings a little more of a

---

[126] One possible distinction between antiwork and postwork is that the former is about challenging the existing work ethic, and the latter is about looking beyond it to something that it would be unwise to fully plan in advance. Or we could even say: work is the thesis, antiwork the antithesis, and postwork the synthesis.

[127] David Graeber, *Bullshit Jobs: A Theory* (Allen Lane, 2018), 14.

[128] Or more specifically: "a bullshit job is a form of paid employment that is so completely pointless, unnecessary, or pernicious that even the employee cannot justify its existence even though, as part of the conditions of employment, the employee feels obliged to pretend that this is not the case."

[129] Graeber, *Bullshit Jobs*, 11.

notion of false consciousness into this account, suggesting that perhaps *all* forms of work under capitalism may fall into this category:

> working time
> working work
> working not working
> working death
> the factory is everywhere.[130]

What this poem might imply is, if Graeber wants to claim that a large number of jobs are not socially necessary, what forms of work are indeed 'necessary'? What can it mean for a job to *not* be 'bullshit'? But Graeber's intent here is probably to support (in Weeks's words) "reformist projects with revolutionary aspirations."[131] That is, Graeber is a bit more interested in really spotting the most pointless jobs than he is in large, stirring indictments of the system as a whole; however, this is not because he would ultimately like to settle for getting rid of these bullshit jobs, and just leaving it at that. He is interested in why our societies tolerate work of this kind, and in the possibility of creating societies that do not.[132] Why has the world of work become an impediment to happiness, rather than a means of realising it? That is, he interested in the *work ethic*, the broader matrix from which the exhortation can emerge to "[w]ake up every day to get shit done" (q.v.).

Weeks elaborates and refines Max Weber's seminal account of the protestant work ethic, at whose heart is "the command to approach

---

[130] "Bullshit jobs" in Will Rowe, *Collected Poems* (London and Barcelona: Crater, 2016), 21.

[131] Weeks, *The Problem With Work*, 229.

[132] "We are, as the existentialists liked to put it, condemned to be free, forced to wield the divine power of creation against our will, since most of us would really rather be naming the animals in Eden, dining on nectar and ambrosia at feasts on Mount Olympus, or watching cooked geese fly into our waiting gullets in the Land of Cockaygne, than having to cover ourselves with cuts and calluses to coax sustenance from the soil. [...] Now, one could argue that this is simply in each case a poetic extrapolation of the two key aspects of what has become our common definition of work: first, that it is something no one would ordinarily wish to be doing for its own sake (hence, punishment); second, that we do it anyway to accomplish something beyond the work itself (hence, creation). But the fact that this 'something beyond' should be conceived as 'creation' is not self-evident. In fact, it's somewhat odd. After all, most work can't be said to 'create' anything; most of it is a matter of maintaining and rearranging things." Graeber, *Bullshit Jobs*, 221.

one's work as if it were a calling,"[133] exploring how the ethic "extended its reach beyond the bourgeois class of the industrial period and today's professional and managerial class [...] by means of its exclusions based on race and gender."[134] Graeber suggests that we have come to believe that people "who do not work harder than they wish at jobs they do not particularly enjoy are bad people unworthy of love, care, or assistance from their communities."[135] This belief is also profoundly internalised, so that many people who hate their jobs, and don't believe they are worthwhile, would nevertheless feel worthless if they stopped doing them.

So work is undertaken with—to borrow Ben Lerner's apology for poetry—hatred that has come to resemble love. The core of postwork theory and activism is its challenge to this work ethic, to these dominant cultural attitudes to work. Weeks is clear that to call the work ethic into question "is not to deny the necessity of productive activity" but rather "to insist that there are other ways to organize and distribute that activity and to remind us that it is also possible to be creative outside the boundaries of work" and "to suggest that there might be a variety of ways to experience the pleasure that we may now find in work, as well as other pleasures that we may wish to discover, cultivate, and enjoy."[136]

This does place postwork in some tension—although not irresolvably so—with political projects that seek to win autonomy, security, and recompense for undervalued and marginalised work. Weeks suggests that by and large, "feminists who address questions of work today focus on the struggle for more and better work and tend to neglect the possibility of struggling also for less work."[137] In fact, a similar tension probably exists *within* many such projects themselves. Elizabeth Simins's website 'The Womansplainer' offers "Got a question for a feminist? I would be happy to educate you! Below are my rates"; services range from "Let Me Google That For You" ($50) to a forty-minute Twitter conversation ($200), and the drop-down menu of queries include, "Aren't you worried about alienating potential allies?", "What about male victims of domestic violence / sexual assault / etc.?" and "What does 'cis' mean?"; Simin describes this

---

[133] Weeks, *The Problem With Work*, 42.
[134] Weeks, *The Problem With Work*, 63.
[135] Graeber, *Bullshit Jobs*, xxiv–xxv.
[136] Weeks, *The Problem With Work*, 12.
[137] Weeks, *The Problem With Work*, 152.

site as "part performance art, part (ironic but also not) business opportunity."[138] These services are quite seriously for sale, but by commodifying her participation in such exchanges, Simin is not seeking to legitimate them, but rather to highlight their illegitimacy, and to challenge the structures which extract affective labour from feminist women. Similarly as Weeks also points out, the Wages for Housework movement sought to differentiate itself both from the capitalist and the Marxist valorisations of work, demanding wages for housework as a step towards refusing housework. Nicole Cox and Silvia Federici write, "Wages for Housework, then, is not a demand, one among others, but a political perspective which opens a new ground of struggle, beginning with women, for the entire working class."[139] The contemporary postwork perspective does not only focus on cultural shifts through cultural means, but also on legal, economic, and regulatory reform. Questions around the strategic significance of 'concrete demands'—especially in the context of Occupy—may have put Graeber at odds with the more accelerationist strand of postwork theory.[140] Nevertheless, his theory of bullshit jobs broadly aligns with the postwork programme's efforts to seek both short-term and long-term possibilities for change.

For some postwork thinkers, a key proposal is the provision of universal basic income (UBI) on top of traditional welfare state services. There are strong proponents and opponents of UBI on both ends of the political spectrum, and a variety of views on the affordability of different levels of UBI. Some of the deeper problems around UBI include how to define who is entitled; how to safeguard the unconditional character of such income; how to ensure its purchasing power is not eroded by (for instance) rent inflation; the risk it will contribute to the inappropriate privatisation of public services; the use of UBI to punish, discipline, and divide; and the ways it might play with regard to gender, race, and

---

[138] The Womansplainer, hellogiggles.com/lifestyle/womansplainer, accessed 15 April 2018.

[139] Nicole Cox and Silvia Federici, "Counter-Planning from the Kitchen," in *Counter-Planning from the Kitchen: Wages for Housework, a Perspective on Capital and the Left*, ed. Nicole Cox and Silvia Federici (New York: New York Wages for Housework Committee and Falling Wall Press, 1975), 3.

[140] See the 'folk politics' touched on by Moctezuma in his chapter in this collection. "These critics often claim that making a demand means giving into the existing order of things by asking, and therefore legitimating, an authority. But these accounts miss the antagonism at the heart of making demands, and the ways in which they are essential for constituting an active agent of change." Nick Srnicek and Alex Williams, *Inventing the Future: Postcapitalism and a World Without Work* (London: Verso, 2015), 107.

those with and without legal status. Proponents of UBI tend to emphasise its potential to alleviate poverty; to strengthen individual independence while at the same time strengthening civil society; to provide
workers with a stronger negotiating position; to redeploy resources currently caught up in means-testing and other assessment procedures; and
to push back against the weaponisation of such procedures within the
punitive and disciplinary welfare state. They also emphasize, of course,
the potential of UBI—and indeed the project of demanding UBI itself—
to initiate a shift in cultural conceptions of work.[141] "Rather than preach
the ethics of thrift and savings, the politics of concession, or the economics of sacrifice," says Kathi Weeks, "the demand for basic income invites
the expansion of our needs and desires." Other elements of a broad postwork programme include reducing the hours of the working week; better recognising and compensating care work; democratising workplaces;
challenging perpetual GDP growth from postgrowth and degrowth perspectives; prioritising investment in automation; and rethinking of the
role that technology, including digital networks and platforms and artificial intelligence, can play in releasing humans from toil and enlivening
our experience of economic life.

Works Cited

Adorno, Theodor. "On Lyric Poetry and Society." In *Notes to Literature Volume One*, edited by Rolf Tiedemann. New York: Columbia University Press, 1991.
Agamben, Giorgio. *The Time That Remains: A Commentary on the Letter to the Romans*. Stanford, CA: Stanford University Press, 2005.
Arendt, Hannah. *The Human Condition*. Chicago: University of Chicago Press, 1958.
Bayat, Asef. *Life as Politics: How Ordinary People Change the Middle East, Second Edition*. Stanford: Stanford University Press, 2013 [2010].
Bell, Jo, and Jane Commane. *How to Be a Poet: A Twenty-First Century Guide to Writing Well*. Rugby: Nine Arches Press, 2017.
Benjamin, Walter. *Understanding Brecht*. Translated by Anna Bostock. London: NLB, 1973.

---

[141] Srnicek and Williams emphasize that legitimate UBI "must provide a *sufficient* amount of income to live on; it must be *universal*, provided to everyone unconditionally; and it must be a *supplement* to the welfare state rather than a replacement of it." *Inventing the Future*, 119.

Berlant, Lauren, and Michael Warner. "Sex in Public." *Critical Inquiry*, vol. 24, no. 2 (1998): 547–566.

Brady, Andrea. *Wildfire: A Verse Essay on Obscurity and Illumination*. San Francisco: Krupskaya, 2010.

Brathwaite, Edward Kamau. *X/Self*. Oxford: Oxford University Press, 1987.

Brodine, Karen. *Illegal Assembly*. Brooklyn: Hanging Loose Press, 1980.

Clover, Joshua. "Unfree Verse." Poetry Foundation Blog, 15 April 2016. www. poetryfoundation.org/harriet/2016/04/unfree-verse. Accessed 1 June 2018.

Collins, Patricia Hill. *Black Feminist Thought: Knowledge, Consciousness, and the Politics of Empowerment*. Boston: Unwin Hyman, 1990.

Commane, Jane. "Ideas Above Your Station: Eight Thoughts on Writing the Working Life." Edited by Benedict Newbery and Pauline Sewards. *Magma*, no. 74 (Summer 2019), 20–22.

Cox, Nicole, and Silvia Federici. "Counter-Planning from the Kitchen." In *Counter-Planning from the Kitchen: Wages for Housework, a Perspective on Capital and the Left*, edited by Nicole Cox and Silvia Federici. New York: New York Wages for Housework Committee and Falling Wall Press, 1975.

Crenshaw, Kimberlé. "Demarginalizing the Intersection of Race and Sex: A Black Feminist Critique of Antidiscrimination Doctrine, Feminist Theory and Antiracist Politics." *University of Chicago Legal Forum*, no. 1 (1998).

Csikszentmihalyi, Mihaly. *Flow: The Psychology of Optimal Experience*. New York: Harper & Row, 1990.

Dalla Costa, Mariarosa. "Women and the Subversion of the Community." In *The Power of Women and the Subversion of the Community*, by Mariarosa Dalla Costa and Selma James. Falling Wall Press and a Group of Individuals from the Women's Movement in England and Italy, 1975 [1972].

Deleuze, Gilles. "Boulez, Proust, and Time: 'Occupying Without Counting.'" Translated and Introduced by Timothy S. Murphy. *Angelaki: Journal of the Theoretical Humanities*, vol. 3, no. 2 (1998), 69–74. https://doi. org/10.1080/09697259808571985.

Dolphijn, Rick. "The Revelation of a World That Was Always Already There: The Creative Act as an Occupation." In *This Deleuzian Century: Art, Activism, Life*, edited by Rosi Braidotti and Rick Dolphijn. Leiden and Boston: Brill and Rodopi, 2014.

Elias, Ana Sofia, Rosalind Gill, and Christina Scharff. "Introduction." In *Aesthetic Labour: Rethinking Beauty Politics in Neoliberalism*. London: Palgrave Macmillan, 2017.

Endnotes. "Error." In *Bad Feelings*, edited by Arts Against Cuts. London: 2016.

Federici, Silvia. "Why Sexuality is Work" (1975) in Silvia Federici, *Revolution at Point Zero: Housework, Reproduction, and Feminist Struggle*. Brooklyn: Common Notions, 2012.

Forrest-Thomson, Veronica. *On the Periphery* (1976) in Veronica Forrest-Thomson, *Collected Poems*. Bristol: Shearsman, 2008.

Fraser, Nancy. "Rethinking the Public Sphere: A Contribution to the Critique of Actually Existing Democracy." In *Habermas and the Public Sphere*, edited by Craig Calhoun. Cambridge: MIT Press, 1992.

Gerber, Alison. *The Work of Art: Value in Creative Careers*. Palo Alto: Stanford University Press, 2017.

Gilman, Charlotte Perkins. *Herland*. New York: Pantheon Books, 1979 [1915].

———. *Women and Economics: A Study of the Economic Relation Between Men and Women as a Factor in Social Evolution*. Berkeley: University of California Press, 1998 [1898]. ark.cdlib.org/ark:/13030/ft896nb5rd/. Accessed 15 October 2018.

Graeber, David. "Are You in a BS Job? In Academe, You're Hardly Alone." *The Chronicle of Higher Education*, 6 May 2018. www.chronicle.com/article/Are-You-in-a-BS-Job-In/243318. Accessed 5 June 2018.

———. *Bullshit Jobs: A Theory*. London: Allen Lane, 2018.

———. *Debt: The First 5,000 Years*. Brooklyn: Melville House, 2011.

Green, Chris. "Reviewed Work: The Logan Topographies: Poems by Alena Hairston." *Journal of Appalachian Studies*, vol. 13, no. 1/2 (Spring/Fall, 2007): 255–257.

Greenblatt, Stephen. *Renaissance Self-Fashioning: From More to Shakespeare*. Chicago: University of Chicago Press, 1980.

Gregory, Karen. "Is the Public a 'Market'?" Paper at Exploring Digital Publics symposium. Institute for Advanced Studies in the Humanities, Edinburgh, 1 June 2018.

———. "Karen Gregory Talks About the Negatives and Positives of Computer Platform Capitalism." RadioLabour, 2 November 2017. congress.world-psi.org/karen-gregory-talks-about-the-negatives-and-positives-of-computer-platform-capitalism. Accessed 5 June 2018.

Hamilton-Emery, Chris. *101 Ways to Make a Poem Sell*. Cromer: Salt, 2006.

Hochschild, Arlie Russell. *The Managed Heart: Commercialization of Human Feeling*. Berkeley and Los Angeles: University of California Press, 2003 [1983].

International Labour Organization and Walk Free Foundation. "Global Estimates of Modern Slavery: Forced Labour and Forced Marriage." Geneva, 2017.

Kaufman, Micha. "In Doers We Trust: From an Ideal to a Movement," 9 January 2017. blog.fiverr.com/doers-trust-ideal-movement/. Accessed 5 June 2018.

Lee, Charles T. *Ingenious Citizenship: Recrafting Democracy for Social Change*. Durham: Duke University Press, 2016.

Leidner, Robin. *Fast Food, Fast Talk: Service Work and the Routinization of Everyday Life*. Berkeley: University of California Press, 1993.

Lerner, Ben. *Hatred of Poetry*. London: Fitzcarraldo Editions, 2016.

Marx, Karl. *Grundrisse der Kritik der Politischen Ökonomie*, in *Ökonomische Manuskripte 1857/58*, Teil 2 [MEGA: BAND 1]. Berlin: Dietz Verlag, 1981.

Marx, Karl. "Comments on James Mill, *Éléments D'économie Politique*." Translation 1932 by Clemens Dutt. MEA, Undated [1844]. www.marxists. org/archive/marx/works/1844/james-mill/. Accessed 5 June 2018.

———. *Critique of the Gotha Programme*. Translator Unlisted. MEA, 1999 [1875/1891]. www.marxists.org/archive/marx/works/1875/gotha/ch01. htm. Accessed 5 June 2018.

———. *Economic and Philosophical Manuscripts of 1844*. Translation 1932 by Martin Mulligan. MEA, 2009 [1844]. www.marxists.org/archive/marx/ works/1844/manuscripts/preface.htm. Accessed 5 June 2018.

———. *Grundrisse*. Translation 1939–1941 by Martin Nicolaus. MEA, 2015 [1857–1861]. www.marxists.org/archive/marx/works/1857/grundrisse/. Accessed 5 June 2018.

———. *Theories of Surplus Value*. Translation by Renate Simpson et al. MEA, Undated [1863]. www.marxists.org/archive/marx/works/1863/theories-surplus-value/ch04.htm. Accessed 5 June 2018.

Marx, Karl, and Frederick Engels. *Collected Works*. Vol. 34. Electronic Book: Lawrence and Wishart, 2010.

McAllister, Andrew, and Sean Figgis. "Basil Bunting: The Last Interview [1984]." *Bete Noire*, vol. 2, no. 3, (1987): 22–50.

McNeill, Fiona. "Free and Bound Maids: Women's Work Songs and Industrial Change in the Age of Shakespeare." In *Oral Traditions and Gender in Early Modern Literary Texts*, edited by Mary Ellen Lamb and Karen Bamford. London and New York: Routledge, 2016 [2008].

Moore, Phoebe V. *The Quantified Self in Precarity: Work, Technology and What Counts*. London and New York: Routledge, 2017.

Morrison, Toni. "Public Dialogue on the American Dream, Part 2." Portland State Black Studies Center, 1975. pdxscholar.library.pdx.edu/orspeakers/90/. Accessed 5 June 2018.

Morton, Timothy. *Hyperobjects: Philosophy and Ecology After the End of the World*. Minneapolis: University of Minnesota Press, 2013.

Moten, Fred. "Blackness and Poetry." In *Evening Will Come 55*, 1 July 2015. arcade.stanford.edu/content/blackness-and-poetry-0. Accessed 3 June 2018.

———. *In The Break: The Aesthetic of the Black Radical Tradition*. Minneapolis: University of Minnesota Press, 2003.

Mullen, Harryette. *Recyclopedia*. Minneapolis, MN: Graywolf Press, 2006.

Muñoz, José E. *Cruising Utopia: The Then and There of Queer Futurity*. New York: New York University Press, 2009.

Neilson, Brett, and Ned Rossiter. "FCJ-022 From Precarity to Precariousness and Back Again: Labour, Life and Unstable Networks." *The Fibreculture Journal*, no. 5 (2015). five.fibreculturejournal.org/

fcj-022-from-precarity-to-precariousness-and-back-again-labour-life-and-unsta-ble-networks/. Accessed 5 June 2018.

Oppen, George. *Of Being Numerous* (1968) in George Oppen, *New Collected Poems*. New York: New Directions, 2008.

Philip, M. NourbeSe. *Zong!* Middletown: Wesleyan University Press, 2008.

Robinson, Randall. *The Debt: What America Owes to Blacks*. New York: Penguin, 2000.

Rousseau, Jean-Jacques. *On the Social Contract*. Mineola: Dover Thrift, 2003 [1762].

Rowe, Will. *Collected Poems*. London and Barcelona: Crater, 2016.

Sennett, Richard. *The Craftsman*. New Haven and London: Yale University Press, 2008.

Shaftesbury, Earl of. *Characteristics of Men, Manners, Opinions, Times*. Vol. 1. Indianapolis: Liberty Fund, 2001 [1737].

Shakespeare, William. *The Complete Works of William Shakespeare*, edited by W. J. Craig. London: Oxford University Press, 1943.

Shelley, Percy Bysshe. "Mont Blanc: Lines Written in the Vales of Chamouni." 1817.

Sidney, Algernon. *Discourses Concerning Government*. Edited by Thomas G. West. Indianapolis: Liberty Fund, 1996 [1698].

Simins, Elizabeth. The Womansplainer. hellogiggles.com/lifestyle/womans-plainer. Accessed 15 April 2018.

Spragg, Andrew. "Response: Andrew Spragg on J. T. Welsch's 'The Promise of Professionalism,'" 2018. poetrysociety.org.uk/response-andrew-spragg-on-j-t-welschs-the-promise-of-professionalism. Accessed 5 January 2019.

Srnicek, Nick, and Alex Williams. *Inventing the Future: Postcapitalism and a World without Work*. London: Verso, 2015.

Stewart, Susan. *Poetry and the Fate of the Senses*. Chicago and London: University of Chicago Press, 2002.

Warner, Michael. "Publics and Counterpublics." *Public Culture*, vol. 14, no. 1 (2002).

Weber, Max. *The Sociology of Religion*. Translated 1963 by Ephraim Fischoff. London: Methuen, 1971 [1920].

Weeks, Kathi. *The Problem with Work: Feminism, Marxism, Antiwork Politics, and Postwork Imaginaries*. Durham and London: Duke University Press, 2011.

Welsch, J. T. "Audit: The Promise of Professionalism." 2018. poetrysociety.org.uk/audit-the-promise-of-professionalism-by-j-t-welsch. Accessed 5 January 2019.

Wilensky, Harold. "Labor and Leisure: Intellectual Traditions Industrial Relations." *A Journal of Economy and Society*, vol. 1, no. 2 (February 1962): 1–12.

Winch, Alison. "Brand Intimacy, Female Friendship and Digital Surveillance Networks." *New Formations: A Journal of Culture/Theory/Politics*, vol. 84 (2015): 233. muse.jhu.edu/article/597741.

PART I

Essays

CHAPTER 2

Show Your Workings:
Other Forms of Labour in Recent Poetry

Peter Middleton

Each art has its own genres of rumours and anecdotes; contemporary poetry has a rich vein of subterranean gossip about the wealth of poets, trust funds, and capital that enable a poet not to have to take a job. A poet with plenty of free time to write must surely have plenty of money too, or be one of what Kit Robinson calls "the pure poets" who "pay the price of poverty to uphold the honor of the poet's art. More power to them!"[1] Charles Olson admonished writers with the terse advice, "Poet, get a job!": both warning aspirant writers how unlikely poetry was to be a paying profession for them, and also tacitly advising them that, for their poetry to be pertinent to their own culture, it would need to be grounded in first-hand experience of meeting the demands on mind and body made by their society's economic structures, whether or not they intended to treat modern labour as an explicit theme.

---

[1] Kit Robinson, "Get a Job," Poetic Labor Project (Labor Day, 2010), labday2010.blog-spot.co.uk/2011/07/kit-robinson.html, accessed 15 April 2018.

P. Middleton (✉)
University of Southampton, Southampton, UK

© The Author(s) 2019
J. L. Walton and E. Luker (eds.), *Poetry and Work,*
Modern and Contemporary Poetry and Poetics,
https://doi.org/10.1007/978-3-030-26125-2_2

Almost all poets take paid employment at jobs other than writing, and most have demanding jobs that require some ingenuity if they are to accommodate the requirements of their poetry.[2] William Carlos Williams writes on a prescription pad between patients; Wallace Stevens walks to his insurance office composing stanzas for later transcription; Karen Brodine's poems emerge from her printshop work, typesetting, union organising, daydreaming, contemplating, and observing; Allen Fisher dictates onto a tape recorder as he drives his company car from construction site to construction site; Ron Silliman rises early to write poems and a widely-read blog before going to work as a market analyst; and Vanessa Place fits her conceptual projects around challenging legal work. Many poets today teach in universities where reasonably flexible schedules may give them some space to write between marking essays and preparing lectures. The holdouts against the university's invitation to teach—factory worker and businessman George Oppen, language teacher and Buddhist monk Philip Whalen, editorial associate and biographer Barbara Guest, or train guard and post-office worker Lee Harwood—are the exceptions.[3] Teachers of mathematics tell their students not only just to present an answer to test questions, but they should also "show their workings," show the work of reasoning that led them to their results. Are modern poets showing their workings, finding ways to represent the worlds of work that they know well? Or are they hiding those worlds?

Although perhaps fewer poets die in poverty than in previous centuries, life for the more radical and most resistant to conformity of employment—poets such as Mina Loy or Bill Griffiths—remains hard. "Future Models May Have Infra-Red Sensors" (1973), a witty poem by one poet for whom the life of a poet was insufficiently remunerative, Tom Raworth, cuts between various topoi of unemployment and the monetary nexus.[4] The poem starts as if the poet were on an extended vacation

[2] The Poetic Labor Project contains an extensive online discussion by poets about the significance and impact of their paid labour: labday2010.blogspot.co.uk. One contribution to this project, by Amber DiPietra, is included in this collection.

[3] This list is not intended to be anything more than indicative, though I suspect readers will find if they try to add more names that most of them turn out to have done occasional semesters or years as temporary university teachers. From my knowledge of these writers, all of them struggled financially at times.

[4] Tom Raworth, "Future Models May Have Infra-Red Sensors," in *Collected Poems* (Manchester: Carcanet Press, 2003), 111–112.

from his job, lasting long enough to think: "take a taxi and go fishing / how do you like that?", though it soon becomes evident that he is out of work, when a voice interrupts with what could be the impatience of a partner or superego: "why don't you ever go / to work and earn money?" The syncopated line-break hints at serious discord. From there the poem cuts quickly between images of armoured bank vehicles, the luck of striking "wildcat oil," and the old joke—"money talks. I just don't understand"—contributing to an overall zany mood, and culminating in the voice of what might be a bank robber, wealthy investor, or chronically apologetic Englishman: "pardon me gentlemen / is there a bank / in the neighbourhood? you drove up from hillcrest?" One reason why poets have gravitated to jobs in higher education is that of all the arts, the work of poetic composition is not only the least financially rewarding, it is also often the least respected as genuine labour. Basil Bunting, who was compelled to work as a somewhat unwilling newspaper editor, memorably recounts Tom Pickard's encounter with a local company chairman who questions why Pickard should expect to receive government benefits:

> Poetry? It's a hobby.
> I run model trains.
> Mr Shaw there breeds pigeons.
>
> It's not work. You don't sweat.
> Nobody pays for it.
> You could advertise soap.
>
> Art, that's opera; or repertory—[5]

The chairman categorises poetry as the leisure activity it once was for the upper classes of earlier centuries. Poets may insist that poetry is *poiesis*, a word whose etymology should demonstrate that poetic composition is a productive, reputable mode of labour.[6] Cultural norms demur.

---

[5] Basil Bunting, "What the Chairman Told Tom," in *Collected Poems* (London: Fulcrum Press, 1970), 130.

[6] Hannah Arendt asserts that poetry "is less a thing than any other work of art," but concedes that poems are ultimately categorisable as objects resulting from the labour of cognition, a process required by all labour processes: "like fabrication itself, it is a process with a beginning and end, whose usefulness can be tested, and which, if it produces no

Despite their authors' near universal experience of paid employment, both manual and intellectual, contemporary poems appear to have an awkward relation to labour. There is a remarkable lack in modern and contemporary modernist poetry of explicit poetic treatments of contemporary labour conditions (Keith Thomas thinks this is nothing new— "for all its centrality to human existence, work has never been a popular literary theme"—I think, as I say below, that its popularity has been particularly low in the past century).[7] Where are the poems about alienated labour and its vicissitudes, low pay, unhealthy conditions, strikes, and unions? Where are the shop floors and the laboratories, the forms of agricultural, menial, production line, clerical and managerial and professional work? We don't have a rich poetry of banking (Eliot), insurance (Stevens), the furniture business (Oppen), editorial practice (Guest), factory production line work (many young poets when they are starting out), the computer industry (Ron Silliman and a considerable number of other American poets), or even of the world where a great number of poets work, a poetry of university teaching and management. Where is the poetry of the call centre?[8] I once commented a little unfairly in an

results, has failed, like a carpenter's workmanship has failed when he fabricates a two-legged table." Her analysis of work encompasses several issues that would be worth exploring in relation to poetry, including its distinction from labour, the "durability" of its products, and its relation to the spheres of action and history. Her distinction between labour and work relies on assumptions about the difference between embodied activity and conscious effort that have been widely questioned. Hannah Arendt, *The Human Condition* (Chicago, IL: University of Chicago Press, 1958), 167–174.

[7] Keith Thomas, ed., *The Oxford Book of Work* (Oxford: Oxford University Press, 1999), v. This is one of the best places to start considering literary treatments of work. A recent historiography of work in Europe by Andrea Komlosy also provides an excellent overview of this history. Komlosy is particularly good on the interplay of paid and unpaid labour, factory work and home laundry for instance, and the need for analysis therefore to consider households rather than individual (traditionally male) workers: "The extended household's capacity for social absorption, its limits and durability can be accounted for through the combination of incomes, subsistence farming, interregional expansion through labour migration and access to public support in the form of social and poverty policies." Andrea Komlosy, *Work: The Last 1000 Years*, translated by Jacob K. Watson with Loren Balhorn (London: Verso, 2018), 188.

[8] On a broad definition, the "poetry of the call centre" might include "Human Capital Solutions," a digital artwork by Bea Gibson, Sejal Chad, and Adrian Ward, which mimics a training tool for call centre workers. See Bea Gibson, "The Conference Game," *Mute*, 4 July 2003. www.metamute.org/editorial/articles/1-conference-game, accessed 15 April.

essay on Robert Creeley that reading his poetry, you would hardly know that he spent most of his life as an administratively active university teacher, because scenes of pedagogy and its management never appear.

A very brief glance backwards in time is enough to remind us that such apparent uninterest in labour is perhaps more noticeable today than it was in earlier poetic tradition. After all, the pre-modern poetic tradition frequently encompassed two different forms of significant work: fighting and farming. Military service is almost always portrayed in terms of epic struggles for cultural honour and survival, rather than as the necessary employment it mostly was for those in the ranks, and would require more analysis than is possible here, so I shall turn at once to agriculture. The labours of farming have been a recurrent theme in poetry from the earliest Greek poets until the nineteenth century, sometimes subsumed into the fantasies of pastoral, and sometimes more openly attentive to the burdens of outdoor work that strives to produce food despite the vagaries of weather, soil, and pests. English poetry includes many significant works by poets attentive to at least some of the realities of country life: William Langland, John Dyer, James Thomson, William Cowper, William Wordsworth, and Thomas Hardy, are all major figures. No one poem can wholly represent this history, but in short span, Wordsworth's poem "The Solitary Reaper" comes close, because it encircles many of the difficulties facing poets who tried to understand the impact of pre-industrial rural labour on the social being of the worker and their relation to those who benefit from their productiveness.

> Behold her, single in the field,
> Yon solitary Highland Lass!
> Reaping and singing by herself;
> Stop here, or gently pass!
> Alone she cuts and binds the grain,
> And sings a melancholy strain;
> O listen! for the Vale profound
> Is overflowing with the sound.
>
> ......
>
> Will no one tell me what she sings?—
> Perhaps the plaintive numbers flow
> For old, unhappy, far-off things,
> And battles long ago:
> Or is it some more humble lay,

Familiar matter of to-day?
Some natural sorrow, loss, or pain,
That has been, and may be again?

Whate'er the theme, the Maiden sang
As if her song could have no ending;
I saw her singing at her work,
And o'er the sickle bending;—
I listened, motionless and still;
And, as I mounted up the hill,
The music in my heart I bore,
Long after it was heard no more.

Few poets have managed to convey so effectively the emotional power of such a scene of labour and song, alongside the simultaneous estrangement of the listener, whose class, whose freedom of movement, and whose freedom from manual labour all hinder his understanding of the import of her music. She, it might appear, is the true poet.

J. H. Prynne's masterfully detailed analysis of this poem brings out sharply the ethical unease that courses through this poem, raising difficult moral questions that expose why such spectatorial poetry of labour became increasingly difficult to justify. To start with, there is the question of just what her art, her singing, can represent given the kind of labour she is performing:

> When he writes of her singing at her work, the use of *her* contrives to suggest that this work belongs to her, is part of what she is and does; but just as likely at this time is that she is owned and used by this work, that her family are captive tenants who must pay rent to others who take from the harvest 'in kind' which they neither sowed nor reaped. [...] There are songs of captivity that long for freedom, and songs of freedom that become meaningless anthems to those who get paid to sing them, 'just as' Wordsworth hopes to enhance his income by sales of the poem he writes about her song for which she got paid nothing.[9]

The tradition which Wordsworth knows so well, and wants to reconfigure, comfortably finds nobility in such a scene of close bodily affinity with the managed natural landscape. Wordsworth, by contrast, intimates

[9] J. H. Prynne, *Field Notes: "The Solitary Reaper" and Others* (Cambridge: J. H. Prynne, 2007), 59.

doubts about whether such work can embody the virtues and values that even the sophisticated observer of rural poverty once expected to find. Prynne's lengthy analytic tribute to Wordsworth's poem deftly unravels the tangled skeins of complicity in her fate, with determination to honour her autonomy and aesthetic sense.

Poems in which labour is an inspiriting spectacle raise tacit questions about the conditions that lie hidden in the scene, questions of ownership, employment, assumed interiority, and the degree of autonomy that the worker has. The poet could choose to ignore them; Wordsworth's poem cleverly allows the reader sufficient space of ambiguity to start in such ignorance before arriving at a more disenchanted appraisal. "If the poet-traveller chooses to set these questions aside, can claims to reality and dignity, the summoning of such values like the humble and the sublime, retain any coherent moral force?"[10] These are questions I think the reader must pursue in reading not just this poem but any poem about the labour of others, if they are to avoid what Prynne calls dismissively "home-made nostalgic ethnography."[11]

Wordsworth's poem is as much about the distance between himself and the reaper, as it is about her labourer's song, a distance between poet and worker that has increased with the sequestration of industrial labour within the requisite legally enforced enclosures of the mills and factories of modernity, inaccessible to the passer-by. The professional poet can see the agricultural worker from the road or path; seeing the worker at the loom or foundry or warehouse or printshop requires an authorised visit. These workers have mostly not been in any sort of position to learn the craft of poetry sufficiently to enter the ranks of the modernists, though there is a rich tradition of poems aiming to raise the spirits of campaigning workers by poets who themselves are manual workers, a tradition documented by Anne Janowitz, Cary Nelson, and others. Leading poets since the nineteenth century have engaged far less with the conditions of working-class labour than novelists, film-makers, and dramatists, who have managed to continue to ask the sort of questions that Prynne raises. It is not easy to think of twentieth and twentieth-century poems that avail themselves of the full range of modern poetic strategies that are primarily centred on the condition of labour, on factory life,

[10] Prynne, *Field Notes*, 98.
[11] Prynne, *Field Notes*, 98.

the tenant farmer's straitened circumstances, or the many forms of zero-hours unskilled labour that prevail today. The few major achievements with coherent moral force that come to mind—for instance, Muriel Rukeyser's *US 1*, Barry MacSweeney's *Black Torch*, or Mark Nowak's *Shut Up Shut Down*—though powerful accounts of industrial exploitation from the standpoint of an investigator, remain somewhat to the edge of the canon of modern poetry. Rukeyser's sequence of poems, "The Book of the Dead" (1938), was the result of extensive journalistic research, and includes prose based on court records and interviews that document the exploitation of miners during the reckless drilling of a long tunnel in West Virginia through a rock so rich in silica that it quickly induced silicosis in most of the workmen. A Black worker explains how little protection they had: "As dark as I am, when I came out at morning after the tunnel at night / with a white man, nobody could have told which man was white. / The dust had covered us both, and the dust was white."[12] White and toxic: Rukeyser lets the poem gather several tacit themes around alienated labour, poverty, health, and the chromatics of racism. MacSweeney's poem about the 1844 miner's strike also collages documents from histories of the period, while sometimes framing them with references contemporary to the 1970s when the poem was written: "if you get the intellectual notion / of coal / there will be a filthy / armchair theorist / hewing carboniferous seams / Beamish and Mickley."[13] In his study of MacSweeney, Luke Roberts cites a comment that underlines MacSweeney's interest in making connections between different workforces: "PC [Poet's Conference set up by Bob Cobbing] is the nearest poets have ever gotten to a representative trade union, and is an organisation concerned with all matters relating to the welfare of poets and poetry."[14] Roberts claims further that "MacSweeney saw his poetic work as contiguous with his professional involvement in the NUJ."[15] The final poem in *Black Torch*, "Black Torch Sunrise," makes explicit that MacSweeney directly connected his trade as a

[12] Muriel Rukeyser, "George Robinson: Blues," in *The Collected Poems of Muriel Rukeyser*, ed. Janet E. Kaufman and Anne F. Herzog, with Jan Heller Levi (Pittsburgh: University of Pittsburgh Press, 2005), 88.

[13] Barry MacSweeney, *Black Torch* (London: New London Pride, 1978), 50.

[14] Luke Roberts, *Barry MacSweeney and the Politics of Post-War British Poetry: Seditious Things* (London: Palgrave Macmillan, 2017), 65.

[15] Roberts, *Barry MacSweeney*, 65.

journalist with poetry: "I must protect my sources / to weld Press trivia / in low-key suburban rags."[16] Careful research is foregrounded even more in Nowak's account of the consequences of various strikes and closures of American industry in the Reagan era and since. One of the poems in the sequence was first launched at "the UAW Local 879 union hall in St. Paul, Minnesota" as part of a radical history conference. What makes all three poem sequences distinctive is their attempts to recontextualise poetry as a contributor to union struggles, labour history, and readerships drawn from outside the modernist poetic community. Each of these poets made a conscious effort to locate themselves where they could manage a feat that most poets are not able to achieve, because it requires an exceptional convergence of events and research access to labour struggles, as well as of course a strong political commitment that is everywhere made visible. The voices of the suffering workforce in these poems direct the reader to share this political commitment.

Keith Thomas begins his excellent survey of the literature of labour by reminding us with the extra emphasis of a scare quote that "'Work' is harder to define than one might think."[17] In the remainder of this chapter, I want to argue that there are scenes of labour in many more poems than we ordinarily notice. To consider what underlies the perception that labour is no longer a central theme for poetry, we might begin with two very familiar modernist poems, one early and one on the edge of late modernism, W. B. Yeats's "Sailing to Byzantium" and Frank O'Hara's "The Day Lady Died," and ask ourselves why we do not usually categorise these as poems that acknowledge the character and centrality of modern labour. From there, I want to go further and argue that although late modernist poetry, written by poets with varying degrees of personal political commitments to support anti-capitalist struggles and new social movements, may often appear to be looking elsewhere than labour when it is actually concerned with questions about the character and politics of forms of work that require intersubjective labour, especially if the poem does not foreground questions about political struggle. Prynne's insistence on the reader's need to ask ethical questions also raises the possibility that as readers we may easily overlook

---

[16] MacSweeney, *Black Torch*, 74.

[17] Thomas, *Work*, xiii. For a bibliography of the social science literature on work, as well as a sociological overview, see Randy Hodson and Teresa A. Sullivan, *The Social Organization of Work* (Belmont, CA: Wadsworth Cengage, 2011).

representations of labour in poems that ascribe to it values of humility or sublimity, or in contemporary terms, values of creativity, vitality, or political energy.

Yeats's poem "Sailing to Byzantium" is not ordinarily thought of as a poem about work, though it valorises artisanal craft quite openly. Poets often make analogies between their own supposedly undervalued art and the expertise needed for making jewellery or musical instruments or other highly skilled traditional crafts. Listen closely to this poem and you notice that the entire poem is organised around a shifting series of contrasting modes of labour.

> That is no country for old men. The young
> In one another's arms, birds in the trees,
> —Those dying generations—at their song,
> The salmon-falls, the mackerel-crowded seas,
> Fish, flesh, or fowl, commend all summer long
> Whatever is begotten, born, and dies.
>
> ......
>
> O sages standing in God's holy fire
> As in the gold mosaic of a wall,
> Come from the holy fire, perne in a gyre,
> And be the singing masters of my soul.
>
> ......
>
> Once out of nature I shall never take
> My bodily form from any natural thing,
> But such a form as Grecian goldsmiths make
> Of hammered gold and gold enamelling

One reason that this is no country for old men is that they are retired from the sorts of labour this country requires for its survival, fishing, farming, and even some of the public arts. The mention of the "mackerel-crowded seas" in the first stanza is there not just to be an image of bounty and vitality; it also alludes to the importance of the mackerel catch to Irish fisheries.[18] The singing school with its masters is usually

---

[18] Mackerel still matters to Ireland. Writing in 2004, historian John Molloy reports that "the mackerel fishery is perhaps the single most important entity of the Irish fishing industry." From a Marine Institute press release, www.marine.ie/Home/site-area/news-events/

read allegorically as a reference to spiritual training, but it also reminds us of the importance of choir teachers in the task of acculturation performed by both religious and secular systems, the churches and schools. The lovely word "perne," a bobbin used in traditional spinning of wool, that Yeats treats partly as a symbol of his metaphysics of history also glances at a disappearing craft, still to be found in corners of the countryside, though practised more as a pastime than an economic necessity. Nor is the spinning wheel just Yeatsian nostalgia; at the time he was writing, it had become a political icon for Indian independence in the hands of that skilled spinner Mohandas Karamchand Gandhi, while in Britain, reformers influenced by his example treated the spinning wheel as a practical token of a new type of social work.[19] Although the poem concludes with an allegedly historical figure of the consummate craftsman, the "Grecian goldsmith" working for the emperor, this is also a figure of the type of craftsman that made Fabergé and Tiffany possible, with many unsung counterparts today in the world of consumer goods for the very rich. These images of labour demonstrate that the poem, which appears to take place almost entirely on an immaterial plane of spiritual transformation imagined as transcendental time travel for souls, also relies on tacit recognition of the labour required for these souls to traverse youth into age accompanied by the products and crafts necessary even for the highest spiritual conditions. Critics have often commented on the poem's ambivalence towards transcendence; song represents the flesh so loudly that the call of the spirit is almost drowned out. The poem's array of forms of labour constitutes a survey of how we live: the fishermen provide food, the spinners help clothe us, the singing teachers enable us to express ourselves, and the art of the goldsmith, which sounds more like the art of the electronic engineer than the art of hammering metal,

---

press-releases/major-fishing-history-book-published, accessed 26 February 2018. See also John Molloy, *The Irish Mackerel Fishery and the Making of an Industry* (Rinville, Galway: Marine Institute, 2004).

[19] Gandhi's spinning wheel became iconic of the Indian independence movement because it represented the adoption of a technology that allegedly could free India of dependence on Britain, as well as giving poor workers a marketable skill. Roy Foster comments on Yeats's longstanding interest in Indian culture, and cites a letter Yeats wrote in 1932 revealing that he has been "watching with delighted amusement the controversies with Gandhi." R. F. Foster, *W. B. Yeats: A Life. II: The Arch-Poet* (Oxford: Oxford University Press, 2003), 536.

extends human agency across time and space just as the new telecommunications have done. If we don't think of this as a poem about work, it is partly because the poem does not directly confront ethical or political questions about the burdens of such labour, nor the sources of the privilege enjoyed by the poet, who may be a scarecrow (another metonym for the labour of the farmer whose worn-out clothes are likely to be dressing this figure), and insofar as we can glimpse any sort of political ideal, it is a regressive feudal one. But if we were to rethink (perhaps along the lines offered by Prynne) what we mean by ambivalence, and treat it as an aestheticised discomfort with complicity in such a society, we could work towards an understanding of the poem as indeed a poem about the conditions of modern labour.

Our second poem also avoids ethical questions about labour, at least until its concluding lines. Reading it we are brought forward in time just thirty years, though it might as well be a hundred given the differences in modernisation, to a city whose varieties of work are a world away from Ireland and Byzantium, and to the life of a poet who had little time for any sentimentalities about traditional craft. New York's midtown is the scene of Frank O'Hara's "The Day Lady Died," a tribute to Billie Holiday, a singing master for the soul of this American, though she leans along a nightclub piano rather than stepping out of holy fire.[20] The poem starts with a modern dilemma, the onerous prospect of a busy social life at the end of the working day, in what is often called misleadingly "free time," including a three-hour train journey to accompany close friends to a dinner party at the house of someone the poet has never met. Evening may ostensibly be free time, not governed by the constraints of employment, but it sounds like work of a kind, a social duty. This impending occasion sets in motion a narrative of the office worker's pause from salaried labour in order to prepare for this visit while meeting his immediate needs with food for body and thought, hamburgers and "new world writing." As the poet goes out in search of the means to satisfy these needs, he is the recipient of various services provided by workers

---

[20] Frank O'Hara, *The Collected Poems of Frank O'Hara*, ed. Donald Allen (New York, NY: Alfred A. Knopf, 1971), 325. Jasper Bernes proposes that we read O'Hara as a "poet of service work as much as poet of consumption," in his recent study of the "thematic convergence between artistic avant-gardes of the 1960s in the United States and the workplace struggles that emerge toward the end of the 1960s." Bernes makes a significant contribution to our understanding of the connections between poetry, service work, and the growth of routinised white-collar employment. Jasper Bernes, *The Work of Art in an Age of Deindustrialization* (Stanford, CA: Stanford University Press, 2017), 39, 10.

ranging from the very low-status shoeshine man to the slightly more elevated kiosk attendant, and on to the higher status bank teller who merits a name as she provides the cash necessary to pay for these services and the gifts social life requires. Almost all the workers—the cooks, the booksellers, the liquor store clerks—remain anonymous, as of course do the individual labourers who actually built the material infrastructure of the city environment, the sidewalk, the diner, the bank, and bookstore. In sharp contrast to the service of all these people he does not know, his memory of a Billie Holiday concert with Mal Waldron stands out, as it concludes the poem dramatically with a striking chiasmus, the moment when the singer casts such a spell on her audience that "everyone and I stopped breathing," a metaphorical suspension of life that is proleptic of the singer's own permanent loss of the breath of life. This ending turns what had been a minor *dérive* into a highly original reworking of a subset of the *carpe diem* tradition, the poem that smashes into a humdrum scene with death's unwelcome presence. Readers also know, as O'Hara knew very well indeed, that Holiday's most famous song, "Strange Fruit," depended on the awful ambiguity of the title's metaphor as a memorial to the thousands of young Black men lynched in America.

Here is an intense knot of ethical questions about the conditions under which these Black artists work. Since the aesthetic labour of Holiday and Waldron is metonymic of the arts as a whole, including poetry, of which this poem—made possible by a break in the use of body and mind in paid labour for his employer—is another token, the poem waits, like the strange fruit, for the reader to begin to ask questions that can potentially travel backwards through the poem and the poet's lunch break. To summarise: "The Day Lady Died" portrays the everyday in terms of urban labour, variously manual, white collar and aesthetic, labour that can be interrupted by the needs of the body for lunch, the needs of the mind for news and arts, and ultimately by the mortality of our human condition. Even the greatest of these workers, the famous singer, must come to the end of her labours. O'Hara's poem stops breathing at the moment that lyric art reaches what for him is its peak, Lady's performance, the moment when all the singer's labour is justified as art, yet as this happens, as the labour ends, so allegorically, does the art. Here is where the sequence of work modes glimpsed during the midday break culminates: the poem intimates that lyric poetry relies on a network of labour; without it the poetry stops.

The forms of labour in the background of these poems by Yeats and O'Hara are for the most part immediately recognisable though recessed

into the background of the narrator's self-preoccupation. Now consider
three poems that do not appear to be about labour at all. I want to show
that they too depend not only on the reader's tacit recognition that this
is a scene of labour, the labour poses thematic questions about what
we understand by work. The first of these poems, Douglas Oliver's *The
Diagram Poems*, a highly original meditation on the value of the affects
and reasoning elicited in overseas readers by news stories of violent political struggles for freedom, a questioning of what the poem calls "a sickening English insouciance / for anything beyond islanded sympathies."[21]
These melancholic poems are permeated with an unfulfilled longing to
bear witness to Western complicity in the killings in Latin America: "the
deaths of innocences we have known / and even caused a little in the
scarface heart."[22] Oliver's allusion to the film villain deliberately plays on
traditional poetic tropes of authentic affect in order to raise our awareness of the difficulty of making this point, a difficulty that is given visual
form in the drawings that make this text so original. Each poem alludes
to these drawings the way a textbook might allude to its explanatory diagrams, making us continually aware of the shifting remediations at work.
Each drawing intertwines the journalist's *aide-mémoire* diagram of the
insurgents' movements, with doodles arising from unconscious urges
that result in comic faces and troublingly ambiguous images.

> I let a Parisian journalist in me draw the pictures
> let him have his head
> it was an academic drew the arrows and the loss of hope
> letting him
> but now the picture transforms no longer; it is the picture.[23]

[21] *The Diagram Poems* exist in two forms: Douglas Oliver, *The Diagram Poems*
(Cambridge, UK: Ferry Press, 1979); Douglas Oliver, *Kind* (London, Lewes, and
Berkeley: Agneau 2, Allardyce, Barnett, 1987). The original Ferry Press edition is a large
format book that does full justice to the "diagrams" that look as if they were influenced by
British Pop art of the 1960s and early 1970s, particularly the work of Eduardo Paolozzi. A
cover photograph shows one of the diagrams drawn in black ink on a poster-sized sheet of
paper. This first edition has a brief prefatory note, and lacks the italicised head notes of the
version published by Allardyce Barnett a decade later in a standard-size book that unfor-
tunately renders the images much less effectively. This edition does however reframe the
enigmatic poems with a much fuller narrative of the Tupamaro incident. All my quotations
therefore come from this revised edition.

[22] Oliver, "The Diagonal Is Diagonal," in *Kind*, 126.

[23] Oliver, "The Diagonal Is Diagonal," in *Kind*, 126.

The drawings gesturally indicate a struggle between two different forms of labour, while the poem records a tangle of reactions that swirl around the complexities of communication across languages, the intensities of foreignness, and the helplessness of the journalist to influence events upstream, while acutely conscious of the potential to affect readers downstream.

For this poem about the work of its author, identified as a "Parisian journalist," originated during a night shift at the offices of Agence France-Presse in Paris where he was responsible for first-stage rewriting, in accessible form, of the terse often semi-legible reports coming over the teletype machines. Oliver's sequence of poems follows his attempts in words and pencil sketches to comprehend a fast-moving situation in Uruguay, a clumsy bank robbery by Tupamaro guerrillas that ends with their torture and slaughter by government security forces. "At HQ you were in the middle of news-making, but were not a pure element of transmission," writes Oliver in the preface to this unusually frank, immersive poetic account of journalism in action, and the difficulties the journalist has in maintaining psychological borders between laconic often context-less factual inputs, acts of interpretation, sub-conscious intrusions such as painful auditory hallucinations of his dead child's voice, other memories, personal political commitments, signs of murkier social forces that defy articulation.[24] It would be easy to miss a crucial moment when Oliver tries to push back the ghost voice with the thought: "I'd better put that down to feeling and feeling's / part of my work."[25] Here, he makes us realise that the work of the journalist is not only the task of transmitting news in readable form, it is not just the provision of information, it is also affective labour-at-a-distance on the downstream readers.

Such emotional labour is far more visible in Simone White's prose poem, "Lotion" from her recent book *Of Being Dispersed* (the title a deft allusion to George Oppen's *Of Being Numerous*, which though also not primarily concerned with the conditions of modern labour, has more allusions to work than most poems). "Lotion" deliberately risks telling readers what they do not want to hear, because as the poem says, "it is considered unseemly to speak of a woman's facial hair outside of a controlled and rigorously policed set of rules," and the poem subtly uses this

---

[24] Oliver, "Night Shift," in *Kind*, 102.
[25] Oliver, "Central," in *Kind*, 113.

taboo in order to intimate how other taboos on speaking out about racist behaviour also operate. Outwardly this is a poem about hair, hairdressing, and the body, as well as moments of racist microaggression elicited by the markers of difference associated with hair, such as when a white woman in a rest room responds negatively to the rationale of using an iron to shape one's hair. Only well into the poem is work itself explicitly mentioned, and then as a necessity that is at odds with haircare: "I am an intellectual and a woman who must go to work and tend to her own survival. I accept, in my fortieth year, that the work of caring for my natural hair can, at last, be foregone."[26] If we want to think further about what is being said about hair, we might look at a magnificent painting by Kerry James Marshall that dominated his 2016 exhibition at the Met Breuer in New York, "School of Beauty, School of Culture" (2012), depicting a hair salon where a whole range of African American women, children, and men are working, having their hair done, or playing.[27] This is a celebratory picture that might be read as a visual comment on Harryette Mullen's opening to *Muse & Drudge*, which also starts with the intersection of hair and poetry: "Sapphire's lyre styles / plucked eyebrows / bow lips and legs," beautifications which are later accessorised by "Honey jars of hair / skin and nail conjuration."[28] Marshall's painting not only offers a subtle allegory of the work of the artist as hairdresser, as a shaper of cultural bonds and textures, in its crowded space it also stages the labour, paid and unpaid, required to shape social identities. White's prose poem is insistent that she is the engineer of her own outward appearance—she herself does her nails, her hair, and waxing (reluctantly). Once having established poetically this intimate autonomy in some detail, the poem then concedes that attentiveness to her body is curated by others too, those who are paid to care for the social presentation of the body: the women who do her twice monthly pedicure, and above all, "the aestheticians who remove my hair from my face [who]

---

[26] Simone White, *Of Being Dispersed* (New York, NY: Futurepoem Books, 2016), 51.

[27] See www.artsy.net/artwork/kerry-james-marshall-school-of-beauty-school-of-culture. This website enables the viewer to enlarge the image. Note the dimensions of the work, and don't miss the anamorphic blonde head, an allusion to paintings such as Holbein's *The Ambassadors*.

[28] Harryette Mullen, *Muse & Drudge*, in *Recyclopedia* (Saint Paul, MN: Graywolf Press, 2006), 99, 119.

play a special role in my life."[29] Aestheticians? The poet wants us to grasp that art work and body care are both forms of creative work; hair is such a strong marker of the fine print of our identity that it requires poetic skill to present it well. Much more could be said about the poem's subtle eliciting of the labours behind the everyday, but one further significant point will have to suffice: its reminder of the historicity of such labour. The latter part of the poem develops a parallel between caring for one's body and for one's immediate home, after the poet's mother has criticised her daughter's housecleaning, which leads to an intensive purge of kitchen dirt that includes scrubbing hard to reach corners of the floor. Her mother then comments that her father once had to scrub floors as an imprisoned teenager and caught osteomyelitis which led to the partial loss of use of his right arm. Labour has a memory. White's poem demonstrates how paid labour is surrounded by a hinterland of unpaid care work necessary for the reproduction of the social body.

In these examples we see that poems do not have to be about specific modes of manual or white collar labour to thematise work in a wider sense. And the poems by Oliver and White remind us that there are forms of labour that can readily be treated as invisible either because they are primarily mental or intersubjective, or because they are gendered, or because the history and human agents of the labour required to provide an object or service have been carefully hidden by the organisation that provides them. Modern retail relies heavily on the illusion that the goods arrive in the world fully formed, so that we don't have to think of the sweat and low pay of their actual makers. In the remainder of this essay, I shall investigate whether these four poems I have discussed are exceptions to a broad poetic practice that ignores modern labour, or whether poetry does actually engage constantly with work. To see this, we should heed Thomas's reminder about the elusive complexity of work, and may need to find ways to be more attentive to how we conceptualise modern labour, asking questions about unremunerated labour, affective and reproductive labour, and about other less well recognised forms of labour such as the work done by the journalist or artist, forms of work that I shall suggest are profoundly intersubjective, and not easily captured by conceptual frameworks that centre on the transformation of a raw material by physical labour. Can it be that the impression that

[29] White, *Of Being Dispersed*, 53.

late modernist poetry is largely ignoring labour is mistaken? Might we be surrounded by a more abundant poetry of work and labour than we imagine, because it is partly hidden by our theories of work and literature, hidden even in poetic form?

Michael Golston argues that the shift of extended analogy or allegory from theme to form is characteristic of recent avant-garde poetry: "When the allegorical impulse is projected from the poem's narrative level, where it has traditionally been located, into its formal and linguistic features, then we have postmodern poetry."[30] Vanessa Place and Rob Fitterman concur, while claiming that this is a move required by a "repressive market economy" that disempowers aesthetic critique at every turn. Conceptual writing is therefore necessarily allegorical: it works by "drawing attention to the conflation of work (research) and play (composing), particularly as they tend to suggest the same received or hollowed modes of (non)production and (non)meaning."[31] They endorse Sianne Ngai's demonstration of the social structures underlying aesthetic categories, notably in her analysis of the aesthetic of the "zany" that dramatises the excessive activity of production line robotics.[32] Because the zany character is often portrayed in a domestic rather than industrial setting, Place and Fitterman infer that the zany figure is a critique of the alienation that arises when play and work become interchangeable. In their view, conceptual, or as they call it, allegorical, writing makes the effort of its production highly visible in the obviously worked *longueurs* of its usually extended proceduralist manoeuvres. This clever if perhaps questionable justification for conceptual writing, that it is our fate because it combines rule-governed physical and mental labour of late

[30] Michael Golston, *Poetic Machinations: Allegory, Surrealism, and Postmodern Poetic Form* (New York, NY: Columbia University Press, 2015), 6.

[31] Vanessa Place and Robert Fitterman, *Notes on Conceptualisms* (Brooklyn, NY: Ugly Duckling Presse, 2009), 31–32.

[32] My argument in this chapter is indebted to Ngai. She argues throughout her study of the aesthetic discourses of contemporary culture for a very close relationship between aesthetics and labour. For instance, she claims that "post-Fordist zaniness points to the increasing emotionalization of work in general, a phenomenon now well documented by an increasingly diverse group of sociologists, economists, and activists." She references Nancy Fraser, Luc Boltanski and Eve Chiapello, and Arlie Hochschild, among others. Sianne Ngai, *Our Aesthetic Categories: Zany, Cute, Interesting* (Cambridge, MA: Harvard University Press, 2012), 10.

capitalism with a play of the imagination that only thinks it is free, rests on an unexamined assumption that I want to question, a conviction that sites of social reproduction and intersubjective toil elude conceptualisation as labour.

Before I discuss how the history of attempts to theorise labour has influenced poetics, I want to consider the possibility that instead of searching for thematic treatments of labour, we might consider poetic form itself as sometimes actively homologous to current forms of labour other than Fordist production. Might it be possible to interpret certain abstract, procedural, formally structured texts as structural allegories of intersubjective labour, even if they do not explicitly thematise labour issues? My test case is Lyn Hejinian's *My Life*, which has been the subject of some excellent readings of its handling of closure, its implicit critique of narratives of identity, its feminism, and its relations to history.[33] Thanks to Ron Silliman's influential framing of the prose poems of the Bay Area as instances of what he dubbed "the new sentence" almost everyone follows his lead and treats Hejinian's text as a resistance of closure, and an exercise in syllogistic deconstruction that "keeps the reader's attention at or very close to the level of language, that is, most often at the sentence level or below."[34] In his study of allegories of poetic form, Golston paraphrases early Language writing poetics thus: the reader "of the disjunctive writing under hand, becomes a co-creator of the text in an activity construed as an analogy for a generalised politics of resistance."[35] This is not primarily what is happening in *My Life*. The disjunctive form sets in motion a form of reading that can be read as allegory of one of the main challenges for care work and intersubjective labour, the making and sustaining of the connections between selves in the face of the many modes in which the work of recognition can be intermitted.

---

[33] See, for example, Juliana Spahr's discussion of how the text keeps identity in play, a politically sophisticated analysis that relies extensively on the concept of the work identity requires. Juliana Spahr, *Everybody's Autonomy: Connective Reading and Collective Identity* (Tuscaloosa, AL: University of Alabama Press, 2001), and Craig Dworkin's discussion of the images of labour inherent in the text's "patchwork aesthetic." Craig Dworkin, "Penelope Reworking the Twill: Patchwork, Writing, and Lyn Hejinian's *My Life*," *Contemporary Literature*, vol. 36, no. 1 (Spring 1995), 58–81.

[34] Ron Silliman, *The New Sentence* (New York, NY: Roof, 1987), 91.

[35] Golston, *Poetic Machinations*, 128.

My chosen example is the section "Yet we insist that life is full of happy chance," the 29th in the sequence, which approximately represents within the constructivist logic of the poem the thoughts and memories of the author as she approaches the age of thirty around the year 1970: "It was the present time for a little while, and not so new as we thought then, the present always after war."[36] Several times in this section the poet alludes to her children. Sometimes directly: "I'm seldom in my dreams without my children." In other words, even my unconscious, let alone my consciousness, constantly interacts with my children. "The child looks out" is another direct sentence which follows one that may provide a context for this action: "At the beach, with a fresh flush." In addition to the idea of recognising the child's growing capacity to gaze outward and away from oneself as parent, is also the intimation that just as parenting involves a near constant care for the child's welfare, a continuous looking out for them, so the child gradually reciprocates by learning to look out for themselves and others. During "those troubled years" in the Bay Area when there were frequent political protests, the babysitter arrived "directly from the riots, and she said that she dreamed of the day when she would gun down everyone in the financial district." Whereas the poet dreams of her sustaining connection to the children, this babysitter harbours dangerous visions of violently destroying people she considers enemies, which would eliminate any vestige of connective interdependence on them. The poet also reflects on the distance she now feels from child that she herself once was (and only fifty pages earlier in the book), in the discourse of social otherness and estrangement: "I am a stranger to the little girl I once was, and more—more strange." In one subtle usage of vernacular idiom, she also positions herself as a child in relation to fate: "Once, for a time, anyone might have been luck's child."

---

[36] Lyn Hejinian, *My Life* (Providence, RI: Burning Deck, 1980), 71–73. My analysis works best with this first version, though because the expanded version of 45 sentences in 45 sections retains the original sentences of the 37 sentence, 37 sections version, readers can still see the outlines of the earlier preoccupations. My own view is that the combined effect of the added sentences in the later version is to shift attention away from a tight focus on the growth of the poet's mind as it passes through various stages of individual and interpersonal self-consciousness, to a more linguistic focus on a pragmatist investigation of language. Since the later version is now likely to be the only one readers can obtain, I will give the page references for the current edition. Lyn Hejinian, *My Life and My Life in the Nineties* (Middletown, CT: Wesleyan University Press, 2013), 62–63. References to this edition are in square brackets.

The section ends with a more conventional instance of strong intersubjectivity: "He looked at me and smiled and did not look away, and thus a friendship became erotic. Luck was rid of its clover." Good fortune no longer required an enabling device, and so from being luck's child, the speaker is now an adult more able to make her own good fortune.

Although scenes of labour can be glimpsed in this section, beginning with the arrival of the babysitter, labour other than parenting is well in the background. Instead the poem compels the reader, as many critics have noted, to reflect extensively on the cognitive labour required of the reader who is repeatedly faced with varying degrees of disconnection between the sentences that are sometimes apparently dovetailed ("At the beach with a fresh flush. The child looks out"), and sometimes abruptly severed. This is a regularity of disconnection that invites the reader to make connections as well as to realise that any such effort must remain unending (maybe the beach and the child have after all little or no relation, so we need to alter the pattern we have made). The text frequently encourages us to reflect on the work of reading: "Patterns promote an outward likeness, between little white silences." To read this text is to engage in the interpretive labour of working out what is happening in those white silent gaps between sentences and to figure out whether there is inward likeness or interaction there: "Arts, also, are links," as the section also assures us. Instead of primarily allegorising a break with the ideological work of language, as Silliman proposes, this poem's form prioritises a performative allegory of the work of intersubjective labour. Such labour is represented in several ways: most vividly as parental care; but also as falling in love, which forms another recurrent thread in this section. Love comes in more forms than parenthood or romance. It can be solipsistic obsession: "But can one imagine a madman in love"—if not, it will be because for love to be genuine there has to be reciprocity, a form of (unpaid of course) intersubjective work. Imagining and then instantiating the work of intersubjective labour: this is the task. And this is also why "desire is always embarrassing," because it always risks treating the other as a means to an end.

All of which brings us to the large question of what we actually mean by labour. I shall argue that in literary theory, we lack a strong theory of forms of labour that entail working constructively, transformatively *on* other people's minds and emotions. What is labour? This is a question to which most of us think we know the answer. The very name of the British political party embodies a reference to the history of class struggle for the representation of working people and the recognition of the rights their labour ought to confer. When we think of paid work we think of its physical, tiring labours. Lifting hot plastic bottles from the moulding machine into a box for a ten-hour shift, typing reports, moving cattle across fields, driving vans, repeatedly filling test tubes in the laboratory, sweeping factory floors, operating lathes, stocking shelves, spreadsheeting expenditures, and hammering nails—they are all familiar modes of waged work. What has been lacking in poetic theory is recognition of the relevance of the conceptual density of the labour of housework, caring, and other forms of hard work that so many sociologists, activists, and historians have identified as essential to capitalism. Also lacking is recognition of how many sorts of paid work, from teaching and training to nursing and aesthetic practice, are forms of intersubjective labour requiring hard work, expertise, and crucially responsive care.[37] These latter modes of intersubjective labour are widespread, and as the poems we have been discussing reveal, extend into areas seemingly as unlikely as journalism and hairdressing. This is quite ordinary work that relies on various extensions and co-ordinations of ordinary intimacy just as manufacturing is a systematic extension of simple productive acts of hand and eye. In addition, intersubjective labour, like reproductive and affective labour, would appear to require at least a minimal commitment to ethical virtues (possibly though not necessarily altruistic ones) in order to work at all, and this might make us wonder if more traditional forms of labour don't also require similar though mostly disregarded ethical input. When poems engage with ethical issues, they may sometimes be shadowing such labour even when that context is not explicit.

I am conscious that in other fields than poetry studies, there is an extensive literature on the changing character of modern labour, but since it remains at a considerable analytic distance from most of our lyric theory, I want to revisit a few cornerstones of modern thought to clarify what it is that we might be looking to alter in our understanding of labour in poetry. G. W. F. Hegel's abstract fable of the master and slave in *Phenomenology of Spirit*, has been the starting point for many twentieth-century thinkers, and was central to Karl Marx's project.

[37] For an interesting account of the complexity of intersubjective work and its extension beyond affective labour, see Davina Allen, *The Invisible Work of Nurses: Hospitals, Organisation and Healthcare* (London: Routledge, 2016).

Hegel's allocates work a central role in the achievement of self-consciousness. By working on an object, labouring on a substance, the "slave" gives such consciousness shape and permanence:

> The negative relation to the object becomes its *form* and something *permanent*, because it is precisely for the worker that the object has independence. This *negative* middle term or the formative *activity* is at the same time the individuality or pure being-for-self of consciousness which now, in the work outside of it, acquires an element of permanence. It is in this way, therefore, that consciousness, *qua* worker, comes to see in the independent being [translator: of the object] its own independence."[38]

Work is firmly located in this relation to the results of actions on the material world, and therefore distinguished from the struggle for recognition that is also taking place. Raymond Plant summarises Hegel's thinking in less gnarly language: "Labour, self-consciousness and freedom go together in Hegel's mind; at the same time, the transformation of natural objects by labour increases the range of objects of human desire. Through labour, a man develops beyond an indigent existence, tied as that is to the pressure for subsistence."[39] Plant sums up Hegel's understanding of labour with recourse to Hegel's *The Philosophy of Right*: "Hegel is concerned with three main features: labour, need, and the complex forms of social organization generated through the division of labour."[40] Here too we notice with hindsight that labour is separated from the social structures to which it gives rise. Although Marx would insist on translating Hegel's abstractions into a dialectic of actual historical economic conditions, the bifurcation of labour from recognition, of work from intersubjective effort, would largely remain, despite attempts in his earlier writings to raise difficulties that resist systematic conceptualisation within his primary model of capitalism.

In the first volume of *Capital*, Marx set out one of the most influential of all modern theories of labour, one that continues to influence our thinking more than a hundred years later. He is primarily analysing

---

[38] G. W. F. Hegel, *Phenomenology of Spirit*, translated by A. V. Miller (Oxford: Oxford University Press, 1977), § 195, 118.

[39] Raymond Plant, "Hegel and Political Economy—1," *New Left Review*, vol. 103 (May–June 1977), 79–92, 84.

[40] Plant, "Hegel and Political Economy—1," 92.

the economics of the new industrial labour so he defines labour as "a process between man and nature, a process by which man, through his own actions, mediates, regulates and controls the metabolism between himself and nature." Marx soon adds "raw material" to the provisions of nature on which mining, agriculture, and other extractive industries rely. Such human activity is a two-way exchange: man "acts upon external nature and changes it, and in this way he simultaneously changes his own nature." Although the gendering of the universal subject is the most salient feature of this argument for us today, we should also notice that by conceptualising labour in terms of a collective singular subject (indicated as much by the singular verbs as the nouns), Marx elides the interactivity of human labour, the way that labour frequently involves different subjects working with and through each other. In his analysis this is the aspect of control that will vary from one historical moment to another. His examples always tend towards actions by sole autonomous subjects whose work transforms non-human entities. Another consequence of Marx's assumption that labour is a transformation of raw material into something with use-value, is that he imagines that labour "uses up its material elements [...] consumes them, and is therefore a process of [productive] consumption."[41] If we now try to apply this model of labour to forms of work such as that of people in service, or care work, or even sex work, many of them would have been working not on raw material—their duties included more than scrubbing and cleaning and bodily attentions—and they would have been providing all sorts of emotional labour and intersubjective support for their masters. If we go slightly up the social scale and consider the labour of nurses and teachers, they too were doing more than working on raw material, and they could not be said to be "using up" the people whom they cared for and educated.

Intersubjective labour has enormously expanded in our own time, and continues to employ large numbers of people, including those on the lowest wages and from the poorest sections of society. Since Marx's theory of labour has been a conceptual foundation for socialism and later for the new social movements, a core idea for everything from campaigns for equal pay for women to anti-global campaigners targeting multi-national companies' exploitation of low-paid labour in developing countries,

[41] Karl Marx, *Capital*, Vol. 1, translated by Ben Fowkes (Harmondsworth: Penguin, 1976), 283, 287, 290.

this conceptual legacy has continued to obstruct the analysis of interactive labour. Argument long ago moved away from investigation of the explanatory power of the very concept of labour to issues of value, political representation, remuneration, and contribution to the social order, mostly leaving aside the role of recognition and intersubjective modes of labour, and thus creating a conceptual deficit that affects the cultural and literary theory on which lyric theory is based.

Much of the actual labour within our culture is as invisibly powerful a social force as the dark matter holding the universe together, making possible the maintenance of the capitalist order often without registering as visible on our instruments of analysis. As Nancy Fraser cogently argues, we need to reconfigure our conceptual frameworks of the labour processes that are so important to us, and develop better forensic terms of analysis, because the silence about intersubjective labour is no accident, it derives from a massive gender imbalance in the political domain, while late capitalism relies on exploiting indifference or unwillingness to perceive the value of many forms of unrecognised, and therefore unprotected or unrewarded labour. Fraser suggests that materialist models of work and its sites need revision if we are to continue to mount a viable oppositional politics: "While Marx looked behind the sphere of exchange, into the 'hidden abode' of production, in order to discover capitalism's secrets, I shall seek production's conditions of possibility behind that sphere, in realms that are more hidden still."[42] In other words, we need to ask new questions about the contemporary character of labour: "what must exist behind these core features [of the economic system] in order for them to be possible?"[43]

Fraser outlines four core features of Marx's analysis: private property, labour, expanding capital, and markets, and then goes on to argue that in order to do justice to our conditions today, his framework needs augmenting in several areas.

One is the epistemic shift from production to social reproduction—the forms of provisioning, caregiving and interaction that produce and maintain social bonds. Variously called "care," "affective labour" or

---

[42] Nancy Fraser, "Behind Marx's Hidden Abode: For an Expanded Conception of Capitalism," *New Left Review*, vol. 86 (March–April 2014), 55–72, 57.

[43] Fraser, "Behind Marx's Hidden Abode," 60.

"subjectivation," this activity forms capitalism's human subjects, sustaining them as embodied natural beings, while also constituting them as social beings, forming their habitus and the socio-ethical substance, or *Sittlichkeit*, in which they move. Central here is the work of socializing the young, building communities, producing and reproducing the shared meanings, affective dispositions and horizons of value that underpin social cooperation. In capitalist societies much, though not all, of this activity goes on outside the market, in households, neighbourhoods and a host of public institutions, including schools and childcare centres; and much of it, though not all, does not take the form of wage labour. Yet social-reproductive activity is absolutely necessary to the existence of waged work, the accumulation of surplus value and the functioning of capitalism as such.[44]

We should note in passing that Fraser's trenchant analysis depends on certain concepts with their own theoretical entailments—affect, *habitus*, and *Sittlichkeit*—each of which could be the subject of further analysis, not least for the manner in which they tend to underplay the importance of the work that takes place through intersubjective actions of recognition, moral adjustment, cognitive correction, and other performative alterations that are not readily encompassed by simple models of control, persuasion, or parentage. Affect theory has attempted, as Ruth Leys demonstrates, to decouple the emotional behaviours of embodiment from cognitive and especially conceptual activity with detrimental effects on the analysis of the relations between emotion and value, and on the contagion of moods and dispositions.[45] I think we need to be careful when we talk about affective labour that we don't lose sight of the degree to which much of this work entails intensive cognitive activity. *Habitus* is Pierre Bourdieu's useful concept for a dense net of memories, expectations, feelings, and traditions, that form localised life-worlds, putting the emphasis more on the inertial than the generative character of labour. *Sittlichkeit* has been widely used by contemporary moral philosophers trying to move away from individualised transactional morality to theories of normative moral communities, and here too the significance

---

[44] Fraser, "Behind Marx's Hidden Abode," 61.

[45] Ruth Leys, "The Turn to Affect: A Critique," *Critical Inquiry*, vol. 37, no. 3 (Spring 2011), 434–472. This essay provoked a series of responses in subsequent issues of the journal. See in particular her defence. Ruth Leys, "Facts and Moods: Reply to my Critics," *Critical Inquiry*, vol. 38, no. 4 (Summer 2012), 882–891.

of the active, creative labour on others can be eclipsed. All three concepts presuppose extensive intersubjective dependencies and negotiations that remain under-theorised in cultural theory. Fraser's attention is rightly on the vast amount of unrecognised and unpaid reproductive labour that is taken for granted by capitalism, and essential to its maintenance, so the conceptual darkening of the character of the labour itself does not matter so much.

The concept of intersubjective labour can be glimpsed around the edges of Foucault's idea of power, Habermas's theory of communicative action, and in Butler's later work on precarity. Intersubjective labour, paid and unpaid, acts in and through a relationship with another person in which one person works on the mind and feelings of another to help the development of the recipient in some way. The worker may or may not be of higher social or hierarchical status than the other, and the labour itself may normally come under the aegis of teaching, healing, politicking, journalism, or some other mode of work, for it is never purely intersubjective, it is always partly rooted in physical labour of some kind. There is intent, as well as a likely formal ethics, plus a two-way influence that is largely constrained so that most of the practical, ameliorative improvements are one-way.

At this point, I want to suggest that if we return to our consideration of contemporary poetry with Fraser's expanded concept of labour and my supplementary proposal that paid labour can be a form of intellectually active intersubjective work, we can now identify many more poems that reflect on the conditions of contemporary labour. Poems directly about reproductive labour come quickly into focus. Andrea Brady's *Mutability* is not only a series of poems and prose meditations on childbirth; its juxtaposition of prose with provisional poems written in the midst of child care provides a dialectical questioning of the transformations of lyric intersubjectivity. The poem "In League" and its accompanying note for 2 April 2009 explore the implications of the parents' "promise of mutuality" with their infant.[46] Images of self-assertion from the Pindaric tradition are playfully contrasted with the infant's loud self-assertion of its right to be in the world. A Pindaric ethos can lead its adherents to lose sight of their origins in the womb and the

---

[46] Andrea Brady, *Mutability* (London: Seagull Books, 2012), 47.

dependency of babyhood—the "career driver and company man / have forgotten their nine months." Brady subtly emphasises the trickier challenges of aspirations to mutuality by depicting the infant's self-affirmations in terms of another more modern poetic tradition that owes more to Pindar than it often acknowledges: "You shout, practising modulation and amplitude, and look at us as if we're understanding. Your intonation is Poundian, so is the sternness of your brow."[47] Ezra Pound is not the only Poundian; so too is the child who makes visible the diversity of the interactive labour of the adults around him. In other words, the *Cantos* presuppose other forms of labour than that of Malatesta and his ilk. In *Mutabilities*, Brady is attentive to the many-sidedness of the intersubjective labour of birthing and parenting in a manner that would not be adequately captured by categorising these poems solely as scenes of reproductive labour.

Fraser's proposal for a renewed theory of capitalism also encourages us to look for poems engaged in that "work of socializing the young, building communities, producing and reproducing the shared meanings, affective dispositions and horizons of value that underpin social cooperation." Such a definition would appear to include the arts, and if so then much contemporary poetry would now be open to consideration for its treatment of these forms of labour. A sample list of more radical poetry, in which we can find political critique and reflexive attention to types of intersubjective or affective labour, might include: Charles Bernstein's *Dark City* (1994), Theresa Cha's *Dictée* (1982), Allen Fisher's *Gravity* (2004), Susan Howe's *Europe of Trusts* (1987), Fred Moten's *The Feel Trio* (2014), Juliana Spahr's *Well Then There Now* (2011), or Keston Sutherland's *Odes to TL61P* (2013). Readers will be able to think of many more.

In conclusion, I shall show in more detail the value of a critical perspective that reads poetry through an expanded model of modern intersubjective labour, by discussing Marcella Durand's *Traffic and Weather* (2008). This poem has attracted attention as a powerful work of ecopoetics—a category that has been expanding to include a large range of poetry investigating the interconnectedness of life-processes across all kinds of site, not just poetry about non-human organic environments. One reason for the expansion of interest in ecopoetics is that it makes

---

[47] Brady, *Mutability*, 47.

visible not only the non-human, but it also makes visible aspects of the human that have been occluded. Durand's book-length poem is a good example; it looks into those hidden conditions of capitalist labour that Fraser invites us to investigate.

Traffic and Weather finds language acts in the mineral arts of the city: the constructing, housing, leaking, rusting, and rebuilding of a typical metropolis full of building sites, tower blocks, and plans for the future, "a conglomerate of mutual designs."[48] From one of the city's many high points, you can see new building projects jostle dereliction. Construction materials—sheetrock, ceramic tiles, steel and glass—insist on themselves amidst "ramps, trucks, grass, fences, workers, rivets, rain gear" (58). The inclusion of workers in this list reminds us of their reified labour; the inclusion of rivets and ramps reminds that the building blocks of the city do cultural and sometimes linguistic work: "The gravel as convincing. / Iron as supportive, vanadium as communicative" (15). Durand is also alert to the potential agency of matter. Though not explicitly advocating a new materialist standpoint, her vision of the city allows for the unknowns at work in materiality. As Diana Coole and Samantha Frost write in the introduction to a survey of this field: "materiality is always something more than 'mere' matter: an excess, force, vitality, relationality, or difference that renders matter active, self-creative, productive, unpredictable."[49] Materiality labours. A few lines earlier, the poet observes that a concrete wall is prone to "leakages and discoloration" because the architect thought concrete was concrete or "impervious." Concrete is not solid as its metaphorical intransigence implies; it can be permeable, and can undergo fairly rapid chemical change under the right conditions. Iron can obviously be thought of as structurally supportive; why might gravel be convincing? Is it because of its noisy physical presence underfoot? Or its stony visibility? Durand doesn't tell us more, but we can infer what she is doing with gravel, because in this and other passages, she is deliberately constellating several conceptual domains, the domain of analogy (comparing someone to iron is to think

[48] Marcella Durand, *Traffic & Weather* (New York: Futurepoem, 2008), 27. Subsequent page nos. in text.

[49] Diana Coole and Samantha Frost, eds., *New Materialisms: Ontology, Agency, and Politics* (Durham: Duke University Press, 2010), 9. Relevant to my themes in this chapter are also essays by Sara Ahmed on women's labour, and Pheng Cheah on alternatives to thinking of the labour relation to materiality in terms of negation.

of them as supportive and strong); the material qualities for which we use and value these materials; and the more implicit new materialist idea that these substances enable us to instantiate certain qualities because they carry with them the existential possibility of that quality (here my best example would be how glass, as it developed from the use in vessels into windows and optics, and plate glass, enabled people to think about mediation, distance and boundaries in new ways, and act accordingly).[50] Communicative vanadium is not just a conceit, based on its intimate bonding with ferrous ions, that is projected by the imagination onto the receptive walls of the city. The vanadium of high-tensile steels used in bicycles and construction can be a medium of communication.[51]

How does the poem model this urban material language? Durand's poem powerfully embeds us in the city, shows that to be in the city is to find that the city itself stages scenes of extended cognition and social interaction, where structures of feeling can be renewed and transformed.[52] At times, so the poem suggests, "each space is almost imaginable in your mind" (26). The city makes apparent certain aspects of the perspectival character of being: "Affected by someplace elsewhere and so distant as to be almost incomprehensible. If trying to imagine someplace else. Hard to be elsewhere when one is here, *viewing*" (60). Gazing is as much an action as walking and traversing the city in a text that is itself constantly rebuilt. A verse paragraph about the coded damage to surfaces that include bullet holes and charred edges proceeds by revision and reconsideration:

---

[50] For an extensive discussion of the materiality of glass, see Isobel Armstrong, *Victorian Glassworlds: Glass Culture and the Imagination 1830–1880* (Oxford: Oxford University Press, 2008).

[51] Durand sketches her methodology in an essay on ecopoetics: "Association, juxtaposition, metaphor are how the poet can go further than the scientist in addressing systems. The poet can legitimately juxtapose kelp beds with junkyards. Or to get really technical, reflect the water reservoir system for a large city in the linguistic structure of repetitive water-associated words in a poem. And poets right now are the only scientist-artists who can do these sorts of associations and get away with them." Marcella Durand, "The Ecology of Poetry," *Ecopoetics*, vol. 2 (Fall 2002), 58–62, 62. Archived online at ecopoetics.files.wordpress.com/2008/06/eco2.pdf.

[52] See in this connection Drew Milne's suggestion that we search for opportunities for the "rewilding" of structures of feeling. Drew Milne, "Rewilding Marxism: A Manifesto for Textual Praxis," *Textual Practice*, vol. 30, no. 7 (2016), 1153–1154; Drew Milne, "Poetry After Hiroshima: Notes on Nuclear Implicature," *Angelaki*, vol. 22, no. 3 (2017), 87–102.

the mechanics of light when splintered by construction
plastic is not crystalline, nor is metal intentional
some of it is planned, and mixed with the not-planned
a master-plan of substructures, detailing each lock-box, tube, dutch
    wall
or many plans, some forged and aged with vinegar and charring at
    the edges

......

our mirror peoples, one per person, or one per acre, or at least one
    per block
all of which need to be walked, and charted, and documented here
do we imbue more than necessary? very well, then we imbue
as cities are meant to be imbued and take on the patina of hordes
(52)

The labour of the painstaking process of construction is there in the shifting back and forth from the planned to the unplanned, from the confidence that there is a master plan, that there is someone wise and knowledgeable in control of everything, to the idea that a plan is nothing more than another material object, conceivably forged and artificially aged to give it a patina of authenticity, and that there will be competing, incompatible plans, somehow all co-existing. This is a poem that shows us how we might view the dark matter of capitalist resources.

Durand's city is a scene of extended cognition, cognition that crucially includes language.[53] Her city is as much a communicative medium as print or sky. The deliberate echo of Walt Whitman's defensive gesture—"Do I contradict myself, / Very well then I contradict myself, / (I am large, I contain multitudes.)"—makes us aware that her idiosyncratic use of an intransitive form of the verb "imbue" may have affinities with "contradiction," and that here in the twenty-first-century city, the multitude somehow contains us even as we imbue it with our walking, thinking, and language. The *OED* traces a history of suspicion in the etymology of the word "imbue." Matthew Arnold exclaims in *Essays in Criticism*: "How deeply the prejudices of the multitude imbued the educated class also." A century earlier, Bishop Berkeley thought that a human capacity to be imbued made such contagion possible: "To imbue the multitude with such notions as may control their appetites." In an essay in *Ecopoetics* journal Durand says that "close concentration upon systems as systems can lead to the animation of poetic processes."[54] Extending cognition builds language into the urban environment, so that, as *Traffic and Weather* says: "each space is almost imaginable in your mind" (26)—we should note that this "almost" implies that the urban spaces edge at least a little over into the unimaginable. City becomes what John Durham Peters in *The Marvellous Clouds* calls a "medium," whether mineral, animate, or imbued with some of the capacities we call language.[55] Media are also of course potential sites of labour; in Peters words, "they are fundamental constituents of organisation. They compose cities and beehives, archives and asterisms."[56]

Poetry as language art is capable of aesthetic investigations of the conditions of communication on which social-reproductive activity depends. As itself a mode of labour, it can provide allegories of work at the borders between the realms of what a capitalist society circumscribes as remunerative labour, and those other domains on which it free-rides, the work of maintaining mutual recognition, cultural and social care, the education of the young, empowering those with cognitive and physical differences, or curating the cultural memory. It is remarkable how much labour is happening around the edges of our poems and how often it is unrecognised as such. When Simone White says in "Preliminary Notes on Street Attacks" that "A nightmare is a dream in which you are in service to a rich woman of indeterminate ethnicity, forced to walk her thoroughbred Maine Coon about the City on a leash, for money," she is alluding at once to the ugliness of racism, labour, and inaesthetics, and also implicitly to the uncomfortable entanglement of poetry and labour. Or as the poem continues, "one possible metaphor for microaggression is aphorism." A possible metaphor for exploitation is what poetic device? It is questions like this that future research on poetry and labour is likely to address to poems that offer scenes of social interaction and the circulation of affects, as well as other themes that encompass education and care, the still often unacknowledged work of our societies, as well as formal strategies of many kinds.

[54] Durand, "The Ecology of Poetry," 59.

[55] John Durham Peters, *The Marvelous Clouds: Toward a Philosophy of Elemental Media* (Chicago: University of Chicago Press, 2015).

[56] Peters, *The Marvelous Clouds*, 19.

Works Cited

Allen, Davina. *The Invisible Work of Nurses: Hospitals, Organisation and Healthcare*. London: Routledge, 2016.

Arendt, Hannah. *The Human Condition*. Chicago: University of Chicago Press, 1958.

Armstrong, Isobel. *Victorian Glassworlds: Glass Culture and the Imagination 1830–1880*. Oxford: Oxford University Press, 2008.

Brady, Andrea. *Mutability*. London: Seagull Books, 2012.

Bunting, Basil. *Collected Poems*. London: Fulcrum Press, 1970.

Coole, Diana, and Samantha Frost, eds. *New Materialisms: Ontology, Agency, and Politics*. Durham: Duke University Press, 2010.

Durand, Marcella. "The Ecology of Poetry." *Ecopoetics*, vol. 2 (Fall 2002): 58–62.

———. *Traffic & Weather*. New York: Futurepoem Books, 2008.

Dworkin, Craig. "Penelope Reworking the Twill: Patchwork, Writing, and Lyn Hejinian's *My Life*." *Contemporary Literature*, vol. 36, no. 1 (Spring 1995): 58–81.

Foster, R. F. *W. B. Yeats: A Life. II: The Arch-Poet*. Oxford: Oxford University Press, 2003.

Fraser, Nancy. "Behind Marx's Hidden Abode: For an Expanded Conception of Capitalism." *New Left Review*, vol. 86 (March–April 2014): 55–72.

Gibson, Bea. "The Conference Game." *Mute*, 4 July 2003. www.metamute.org/editorial/articles/1-conference-game. Accessed 15 April 2018.

Golston, Michael. *Poetic Machinations: Allegory, Surrealism, and Postmodern Poetic Form*. New York: Columbia University Press, 2015.

Hegel, G. W. F. *Phenomenology of Spirit*. Translated by A. V. Miller. Oxford: Oxford University Press, 1977.

Hejinian, Lyn. *My Life*. Providence: Burning Deck, 1980.

———. *My Life and My Life in the Nineties*. Middletown: Wesleyan University Press, 2013.

Hodson, Randy, and Teresa A. Sullivan. *The Social Organization of Work*. Belmont: Wadsworth Cengage, 2011.

Komlosy, Andrea. *Work: The Last 1,000 Years*. Translated by Jacob K. Watson. London: Verso, 2018.

Leys, Ruth. "Facts and Moods: Reply to My Critics." *Critical Inquiry*, vol. 38, no. 4 (Summer 2012): 882–891.

———. "The Turn to Affect: A Critique." *Critical Inquiry*, vol. 37, no. 3 (Spring 2011): 434–472.

MacSweeney, Barry. *Black Torch*. London: New London Pride, 1978.

Marx, Karl. *Capital*, Vol. 1. Translated by Ben Fowkes. Harmondsworth: Penguin, 1976 [1867].

Menary, Richard, ed. *The Extended Mind*. Cambridge: MIT Press, 2012.

Milne, Drew. "Poetry After Hiroshima: Notes on Nuclear Implicature." *Angelaki*, vol. 22, no. 3 (2017): 87–102.

———. "Rewilding Marxism: A Manifesto for Textual Praxis." *Textual Practice*, vol. 30, no. 7 (2016): 1153–1154.

Molloy, John. *The Irish Mackerel Fishery and the Making of an Industry*. Rinville, Galway: Marine Institute, 2004.

Mullen, Harryette. *Recyclopedia*. Saint Paul: Graywolf Press, 2006.

Ngai, Sianne. *Our Aesthetic Categories: Zany, Cute, Interesting*. Cambridge: Harvard University Press, 2012.

O'Hara, Frank. *The Collected Poems of Frank O'Hara*. Edited by Donald Allen. New York: Alfred A. Knopf, 1971.

Oliver, Douglas. *Kind*. London, Lewes, and Berkeley: Agneau 2, Allardyce, Barnett, 1987.

———. *The Diagram Poems*. Cambridge: Ferry Press, 1979.

Peters, John Durham. *The Marvelous Clouds: Toward a Philosophy of Elemental Media*. Chicago: University of Chicago Press, 2015.

Place, Vanessa, and Robert Fitterman. *Notes on Conceptualisms*. Brooklyn: Ugly Duckling Presse, 2009.

Plant, Raymond. "Hegel and Political Economy—1." *New Left Review*, vol. 103 (May–June 1977): 79–92, 84.

Raworth, Tom. *Collected Poems*. Manchester: Carcanet Press, 2003.

Robinson, Kit. "Get a Job." Poetic Labor Project, 2010. labday2010.blogspot.co.uk/2011/07/kit-robinson.html. Accessed 15 April 2018.

Rukeyser, Muriel. *The Collected Poems of Muriel Rukeyser*. Edited by Janet E. Kaufman and Anne F. Herzog, with Jan Heller Levi. Pittsburgh: University of Pittsburgh Press, 2005.

Silliman, Ron. *The New Sentence*. New York: Roof, 1987.

Spahr, Juliana. *Everybody's Autonomy: Connective Reading and Collective Identity*. Tuscaloosa: University of Alabama Press, 2001.

Thomas, Keith. *The Oxford Book of Work*. Oxford: Oxford University Press, 1999.

White, Simone. *Of Being Dispersed*. New York: Futurepoem Books, 2016.

CHAPTER 3

Bird-Song by Everyone, for Everyone: Poetry, Work, and Play in J. H. Prynne's Prose

Lisa Jeschke

This is the opening of J. H. Prynne's "The Poet's Imaginary" (2013), a lecture in which Prynne develops a highly theatricalized figuration of the poet at work encountering language's "complex recalcitrance:"[1]

> Actions that culminate in some form of deliberate production, directed by purposeful agency as means to probable ends, are a familiar part of human behaviour. We do things and we make things, and the grammar of transitive

[1] J. H. Prynne, "The Poet's Imaginary," *Chicago Review*, vol. 58, no. 1 (2013), 94. Presented as a lecture at Sussex University, 12 February 2013.

This chapter builds on the paper I gave at the Work, Performance, Poetry Symposium at Northumbria University in 2015, as well as my PhD dissertation: *Theatricality and J.H. Prynne's Work* (PhD diss., University of Cambridge, 2015). I am grateful for the feedback, comments, and dialogue received in both contexts; the errors that persist are my own.

L. Jeschke (✉)
CAU Kiel, Kiel, Germany

© The Author(s) 2019
J. L. Walton and E. Luker (eds.), *Poetry and Work*,
Modern and Contemporary Poetry and Poetics,
https://doi.org/10.1007/978-3-030-26125-2_3

105

acts is well established in Western language systems. We light a fire, plant a tree, write a poem. In the first two cases the act converts the status of existing circumstance into another consequent form; but the third case is different because there may be no precedent phenomenal disposition from which a result can be considered to have come into being: "something out of nothing." We may call such special cases of transitive action "creative," to indicate the anomaly of effects without the usual prior array of causal origins.[2]

When Prynne speaks of actions that "culminate in some form of deliberate production," the phrasing corresponds closely to one of the *Oxford English Dictionary*'s central definitions of the noun "work": "[a]ction or activity involving physical or mental effort and undertaken in order to achieve a result." The *OED* definition adds: "esp. as a means of making one's living or earning money; labour; (one's) regular occupation or employment" (*OED*, "work," *n.*, I. 4.). This specification is not given in Prynne's lecture. Nor is the word "work" actually mentioned. Instead, we follow a whole sequence of words circumventing it: "deliberate production," "purposeful agency," "[w]e do things and we make things," "transitive acts," "'creative,'" "acts of creation," "process of gestation," "eventuated productions," "novel object-reality."[3]

The use of adjectives such as "purposeful," "deliberate" and "transitive" seems to further remove the setting from the socially really existing late-capitalist workplace, especially if the term "workplace" is understood in its wider sense—as I use the term in this chapter—as the site of one's occupation or lack thereof. Depending on one's subject position, in terms of ascriptions such as race, class, migration status, or gender, and depending on one's location in region or nation, such workplaces may encompass the office, the home in which unpaid domestic labour is performed, the cell in which a body is incarcerated, and so on; this is not to say that these are all the same, but that these are all different. Yet all conditions named stand in a relation to the institution of wage labour. As Chris Chen notes, even "those populations which have become redundant in relation to capital," often populations subjected to feminizing or "*racialising processes*,"[4] are nevertheless

---

[2] Prynne, "The Poet's Imaginary," 89.

[3] Prynne, "The Poet's Imaginary," 89.

[4] Chris Chen, "The Limit Points of Capitalist Equality," in *Endnotes* 3 (September 2013), 207.

trapped within the capital relation, because their existence is defined by a generalised commodity economy which does not recognise their capacity to labour. The management of such populations could be said to be "form-determined" by the capital relation without being subsumed by it.[5]

A serious engagement with work in its sociologically given manifestations would, then, have to involve attention not only to wage labour, but also to exclusion from wage labour. However, neither condition—being subsumed by or expelled from wage labour—is directly invoked in Prynne's passage. The passage's contrary emphasis on agential subjectivity is heightened by the prominence with which the first person plural subject form *we* is used: "[w]e do things and we make things," "[w]e light a fire, plant a tree, write a poem." Is a mock-unified "[w]e" that lights a fire, plants a tree, writes a poem not just an abstraction floating in the universe? What would have happened to Prynne's lecture had he instead noted, "We serve coffee at Pret, we are unemployed, we write poems"? That is, what does it do to the lecture to write exactly "[w]e light a fire, plant a tree, write a poem"?

If the overt use of words such as *work* or *wage labour* is evaded, and if the overt allusion to specific present-day conditions of work or related abjections is evaded, then such glaring evasion needs to be taken on its own terms, not as an accident. The lecture seems careful to establish a frame for the discussion of poetic production that precisely does not claim that poetry is identical with workplace-work. This can be taken as a distancing from professional approaches to poetry as much as an acknowledgement that most people's primary experience of work does have to do with money-earning while not involving poetry—to think otherwise would be an aggrandization of poetry. Few people are career poets: but everyone can write poetry.

In this sense, "[w]e light a fire, plant a tree, write a poem" reads not as a presumptive universalization, rather as a claim that poetry is open not only to a set of "I"s of outstanding genius, but can be thought of as (1) a fundamentally collective activity and as (2) a fundamentally quotidian activity, as basic to human life as lighting a fire or planting a tree. The three activities named are as quotidian as mythically emancipatory: in cultural history, the stealing of fire from the gods by Prometheus has

---

[5] Chen, "The Limit Points of Capitalist Equality," 212.

represented a foundational act of human making (*poiesis*). "[W]e plant a tree" further affirms an understanding of landscape, of nature, as man-made—and such a shaping of nature then also forms part, in accumulative force, of "we write a poem".[6] Poetry is conceptualized as an economic activity not in its relation to money-earning, but in its relation to processes of production; this constitutes a positioning away from a reception- or consumption-based aesthetics.

As poetry is chained to the sequence of productive activities described, it is given the status of a special case. For Prynne, whereas in lighting a fire and planting a tree, "the status of existing circumstance" is transformed "into another consequent form," what is at stake in poetry is the creation of something absolutely new, something with "no precedent phenomenal disposition." The extra quotation marks around "'something out of nothing'" and "'creative'" appear as marking the difficulty of speaking of the possibility of the appearance of the new. There would be an uncomfortable ring to an unqualified use of "creative" in the early twenty-first century, when the term has become so central to movements of urban gentrification.[7] The kind of creation at issue here is at a later point in the lecture denoted as "surprise": "each strong new poem is in some sense a turning point for the poet, as in a more distant future it may also be for the reader possessed by its intrinsic power of surprise."[8] To state that "surprise" could be intrinsic to an object is to remove the affect from personal psychological experience. Surprise

---

[6]Also see Prynne's following note: "*harmony* is not part of nature. It can have no meaning to say that one tree is in harmony with another, or that summer is in harmony with winter, unless the meaning is man-made" (J. H. Prynne, "A Brief Comment on 'Harmony' in Architecture" [Xi'An, P.R. China, 23 September 2006], www.cai.cam.ac.uk/sites/default/files/harmony.pdf, 1, accessed 23 March 2018).

[7]Especially the person-based nominalization of "creative" in phrases such as "spaces for creatives" seems to attribute an essence of creativity to the elect; see, for instance, "Best Coworking Spaces in London for Creatives and Makers," Hubble, hubblehq.com/blog/best-co-working-space-in-london-for-creatives-and-makers, last modified 18 January 2018. If anything, all workplaces should be spaces for creatives; this demand is currently being pseudo-realized in exclusive form at the higher levels of digital economy workplaces. At the time of revising this essay in March 2018, the Google careers page features a header in which the words "for everyone" remain stable in grey and are preceded, in alternation and with changing colours, by "Build," "Create," "Design," "Code." See "Google Careers," Google, careers.google.com, accessed 27 March 2018.

[8]Prynne, "The Poet's Imaginary," 97.

appears in objectivized form, as shining forth from within a poem. An intrinsically surprising poem would have to be surprising every time I reread it. What is posited is that any practical or theoretical knowledge or analytical categories we may think we have for poetry become useless.

Were poetry completely severed from any relation to work in its real existing manifestations, it would be difficult to conceive of it as anything but a luxury pastime. If, on the other hand, poetry were claimed to be contained fully by what we experience at our various workplaces, such a claim would, firstly, constitute a ridiculing of the suffering experienced when in or out of work, and secondly, set the present as necessarily eternal—both the present of the current historical period and, more concretely, the stretch of present experienced during a shift. Positing poetry as economic, and yet removed from the realities of (un)employment, does not suggest that we find in poetry an escape from the need to earn money, as if poetry could hover in a vacuum. Rather, it suggests that a different past (the Promethean labour of emancipation) and a different future ("surprise") still or already form part of the present. The present appears not as a sleek monolith, but as a layered, internally fractured structure.

Such a modelling of the present may become clearer if compared to the following geography of space presented in an article by Endnotes:

> Within sight, there's a garden on wasteland reclaimed by local residents. The route that leads north-south from here has connected not just capitalist conurbations, but also medieval towns and hamlets. The kinds of vessels whose shards litter deep layers of the earth are still currently in use, with the same affordances. The spaces between these words were invented by feudal scribes. To the north, the woodless hills that roll either side were cleared not by capital, but by neolithic people. If capital is the motive factor in shaping social forms which in turn leave their imprint on all the stuff of the world, we would of course be distinctly overestimating its spread and power if we really thought that there was nothing here that was not referable to – and explicable in terms of – capital. To theoretically project capital's totalisation beyond what capital can legitimately explain is to make a false – merely imaginary – totalisation.[9]

[9]Endnotes, "Error," in *Bad Feelings*, ed. Arts Against Cuts (London, 2016), n.p.

If this is a non-totalizing geography of landscape, the definition of the creative act of writing a poem presented at the beginning of "The Poet's Imaginary" could be considered as beginning to establish corresponding non-totalizing geographies of work and time.[10] These point, ultimately, to a non-totalizing geography of our (social) lives, whereby becoming and making yet remain possibilities. There is scope not only for plants, but also for human beings to grow downwards, build tunnels, build countering temporal systems into the past and future.[11] Prynne's prose, as much as his poetry, can be deeply optimistic.

In "Mental Ears and Poetic Work" (2009/2010), the strange position poetry inhabits in the midst of work, yet not, is further specified by Prynne's positing of "noise" as a mediating quality between poetry and work. More specifically, the "sub-lexical acoustic noise" of poetry, its phonology, is declared to be analogical to "the striking clatter of real work in the material world":

> The poet works with mental ears. Via this specialized audition the real-time sounds of speech and vocalized utterance are disintegrated into sub-lexical acoustic noise by analogy with the striking clatter of real work in the material world. Plus also bird-song, weather sounds, and the cognates.[12]

The following passage from Prynne's earlier double-lecture "Stars, Tigers and the Shape of Words" (1992/1993), which critically explores Ferdinand de Saussure's model of the arbitrariness of the linguistic sign, already provided a concrete example of the analogy between poetry ("sounds of speech and vocalized utterance") and "the striking clatter of real work in the material world":

---

[10] Leisure appears less totally enclosed within regimes of work in Prynne than in Adorno, who notes: "free time is shackled to its opposite" (Theodor W. Adorno, "Free Time," translated by Nicholas Walker, in *The Culture Industry: Selected Essays on Mass Culture*, ed. J. M. Bernstein [London and New York: Routledge], 187).

[11] On plant time as a form of time that can go both forward and backward in Prynne's "The *Plant Time Manifold* Transcripts" (1974), see Justin Katko, "Relativistic Phytosophy: Towards a Commentary on 'The *Plant Time Manifold* Transcripts'," in *Glossator 2: On the Poems of J.H. Prynne*, ed. Ryan Dobran (New York: Glossator, 2010).

[12] J. H. Prynne, "Mental Ears and Poetic Work," *Chicago Review*, vol. 55, no. 1 (2010), 128. Presented as a lecture at the University of Chicago, April 2009.

the themes of volcanic smelting and forging and hammering are recurrent in Blake's work, just as are the abrupt blow-upon-blow accent patterns of his verse, in which some readers have heard the echo of hand-held or even water-powered metal hammers.[13]

This passage is embedded in a discussion of William Blake's poem "The Tiger," with focus placed on Blake's activity as an engraver.[14] Prynne displays how assembling a poem occurs, in Blake's case, literally, letter by letter. "The Tiger" can be assembled from—and disassembled into—its "individual *letters*, such as a child would use in learning to spell and an engraver take care to inscribe."[15] In a further addition to the chain of analogies we gradually see emerging, child and engraver are shown to engage in parallel activities: the child's learning corresponds to the adult's work, and the adult's work is a form of child's play.

If poetic composition is considered as a form of manual labour[16] and a form of play at once, it appears to constitute a genre that explodes installed orders of wage labour specifically insofar as it explodes installed divisions between work and play. This point is made nowhere more poignantly than when in "Mental Ears and Poetic Work," after positing the analogy between "the real-time sounds of speech and vocalized utterance" and "the striking clatter of real work in the material world" noted above, Prynne casually adds: "[p]lus also bird-song, weather sounds, and the cognates."[17] A sharply humorous effect is achieved by the syntactically incomplete addition. Just where we thought we had encountered a serious statement concerning poetry and its relation to the world of work through shared sound, Prynne allows what could be read as an entirely irrelevant intrusion not only of leisure, but also perhaps of nature in the guise of "bird-song."

---

[13] J. H. Prynne, *Stars, Tigers and the Shape of Words* (London: Birkbeck, 1993), 27. Presented as *The William Matthews Lectures* at Birkbeck College, London, 1992.

[14] "The Tyger" was originally part of *Songs of Experience*; see William Blake, *Songs of Innocence and of Experience* [1794], ed. Robert N. Essick (San Marino, CA: Huntington, 2008), Plate 40. Prynne uses as foundation of his discussion the re-print from Benjamin Heath Malkin, *A Father's Memories of His Child* (London: Bensley, 1806), from which "Dorothy and William Wordsworth copied out the poem into their commonplace book" (Prynne, *Stars, Tigers and the Shape of Words*, 51).

[15] Prynne, *Stars, Tigers and the Shape of Words*, 27.

[16] The desk- and computer-based work that has replaced the work of the engraver is no less manual.

[17] Prynne, "Mental Ears and Poetic Work," 128.

This risks reproducing the naturalized worlds of leisured harmony Prynne critiqued so fiercely in his "Brief Comment on 'Harmony' in Architecture" (2006), worlds that live the "dream of a sweet balance with nature" while ensuring "that the supportive work required to produce lunch is done by others."[18] It is unlikely that those who serve lunch at Pret have the time to have either a mental or a physical ear out for bird-song. And even in their spare time, a worker living on a polluted noisy road in the middle of a polluted noisy city in today's urban conglomerates will be much less likely to be able to catch a note of bird-song than the steady hum of car traffic. The reference to bird-song might be far removed from either their experience or their desires.

This is not all there is to the image, however, as the reference to bird-song as part of a negotiation of poetry, work, and play finds a prominent precursor in trajectories of German idealism and materialism. If Friedrich Schiller's elaboration of the significance of play and the play drive in *On the Aesthetic Education of Man* (1801) would yet seem to confirm a flawed idealism in Prynne's prose,[19] the motif of a possible reconciliation of work and play finds an openly revolutionary context in Rosa Luxemburg's frequent references to both bird-song and poetry in her letters from prison. The following is an extract from a letter to Sophie Liebknecht written on 24 November 1917:

> Every day at about this hour, high in the sky, hundreds of crows pass diagonally across the prison yard [...]. They fly with their wings flapping leisuredly and exchange peculiar calls – quite different from the sharp *krah* with which they rapaciously chase their prey during the day. Now the call sounds soft and muted, a deep, throaty call that somehow gives me the impression of a little metallic globule. And when several of them take turns gargling this *kau-kau* one after the other, to me it is as if they were at play, tossing one another little metal balls that arc gently through the air. They're chatting calmly about what they've experienced, talking 'of the day, of the day enjoyed today...'. ['*vom Tage, vom heute genossenen Tag*'].[20]

---

[18]J. H. Prynne, "A Brief Comment on 'Harmony' in Architecture," 1–2.

[19]See the fifteenth letter in Friedrich Schiller, *Über die ästhetische Erziehung des Menschen* [1801] (Stuttgart: Reclam, 2013), 58–64.

[20]Rosa Luxemburg, *The Letters of Rosa Luxemburg*, ed. Georg Adler, Peter Hudis, and Annelies Laschitza, translated by George Shriver (London and New York: Verso, 2013), 450. I am grateful to Luke Roberts for pointing me to the recurring significance of bird-song in Luxemburg's letters and to this passage.

Of crows we might expect not the calm "chatting" evoked by Luxemburg, but agitation and "a series of loud caws"; you may also "hear crows making a 'subsong': a mixture of hoarse or grating coos, caws, rattles, and clicks."[21] To Luxemburg, however, they seem to have taken on the qualities of a calmly gurgling mountain spring. For their talking "of the day, of the day enjoyed today" takes up, in slight misquotation—it should read "[o]f the day that has been today" ("Vom heute gewesenen Tage," l. 8)—a line from Eduard Mörike's poem "At Midnight" ("Um Mitternacht" [1827]) in which "springs," or "streams," or "sources" ("Quellen," l. 5) sing to the "night" ("Nacht," l. 6) of the day that has passed.[22] The "night," grammatically feminized in German, is also described as the springs' mother ("Mutter," l. 6). In a reversal of conventionalized roles, the springs, like children rushing by, sing the "lullaby" ("Schlummerlied," l. 9) of the day that has been— to their mother. It is a lullaby not perceived by her as calming, but as "wearying" ("sie ist es müd," l. 10).

Mörike is not known as a wildly revolutionary poet—given his repu- tation as a restrained poet of nature and inwardness, Luxemburg may as well be quoting bird-song by quoting Mörike[23]—yet the poem implies a notion of irreverence in that the mother is described as either not pay- ing attention or not respecting the song: she "does not heed" it ("Sie achtets nicht," l. 10).[24] Not only that, but the night's/mother's lack of

---

[21] "American Crow: Sounds," Cornell Lab of Ornithology, www.allaboutbirds. org/guide/American_Crow/sounds, accessed 23 March 2018. *Sub Songs* is also the title of a poetry sequence by Prynne from 2010: see J. H. Prynne, *Poems* (Hexham, Northumberland: Bloodaxe, 2015), 607–626.

[22] The German and English quotations above and below are taken from the poem's translation in Eduard Mörike, *Mozart's Journey to Prague and a Selection of Poems*, trans- lated by David Luke (London: Penguin, 2003), Kindle. Where further alternatives are given, these are my own. I have given the line numbers from the German. The translation features slightly variant line numbers.

[23] There is a song-realization of the poem, namely Hugo Wolf's *Lied* of the same title forming part of his *Mörike-Lieder* from 1888. See Jack M. Stein, "Poem and Music in Hugo Wolf's Mörike Songs," *The Musical Quarterly*, vol. 53, no. 1 (January 1967), 22–27.

[24] Helmuth Nürnberger notes that while "Mörike's timeless art forms, as it were, an opposite pole to the demands made by the political poetry committed to the present that, from 1840, increasingly dominated the events of the day," it was nevertheless "a misun- derstanding" for Mörike to have long been seen merely "as the sentimental pastor now and then writing beautiful verse" (Helmuth Nürnberger, *Geschichte der deutschen Literatur* [Munich: Bayerischer Schulbuch Verlag, 2006], 229–230, my translation).

respect postulates a radical longing for activity, for not-death, for the day: to her the "deep blue sky" is "sweeter" ("Himmels Bläue süßer," l. 11). Rosa Luxemburg, in prison, does pay attention to the crows' song, perhaps as this is the closest she can get to the sweetness of the day sky's blue. Her projection of a line from Mörike's poem onto the crows establishes a morbid neo-gothic optimism: the crows are not merely symbolic harbingers of death but appear as a communication technology from the live outside world ("the day enjoyed") to the coffin of prison (life to death), as much as from the coffins of the workers killed in wage labour or revolutionary activity ("the day enjoyed") to a live and alert Rosa Luxemburg in prison (death to life). Bird-song, it becomes evident, is not necessarily an index of luxurious leisure but can function as a channel piercing bubbles of totalized constraint, can pierce even, microscopically, the direct exertion of state power in imprisonment.

Bird-song appears not as an index of luxurious leisure in Luxemburg's letters from prison firstly because bird-song is, here, not an end in itself (as it would be in the following statement: 'given that *I* have a garden, I think everything is good enough as it is') but a means (of communication). Secondly bird-song here does not affirm an eternal present (the state; nature) but speaks of separation and longing, of lives lived, of unreachable outsides that can, nevertheless, already be perceived in flashes in what there is, now, in the present. If these flashes of pleasure in the present remained entirely unrecognized, socialist activism would form not much more than a joyless hatred of those we love. Read against this foil, the evocation of bird-song in "Mental Ears and Poetic Work," like the reference to processes of production in "The Poet's Imaginary," again seems to affirm a non-totalizing approach to the present, as bird-song comes to express a fissure in that brutal present—a fissure pointing to a future, yet already part of the present.

The line between an aristocratic or liberal self-satisfaction with the "dream of a sweet balance with nature"[25] and the progressive modernist "dream of humanity" is a thin one.[26] With Luxemburg and Prynne, the latter might alternatively be articulated as: 'Bird-song by everyone, for everyone!'; poetry in its wider sense as *poiesis*, as agential "creative"

---

[25] Prynne, "A Brief Comment on 'Harmony' in Architecture," 1–2.

[26] T. J. Clark, *Farewell to an Idea: Episodes from a History of Modernism* (New Haven, CT and London: Yale University Press, 1999), 71.

expression, would be "bird-song by everyone!". Slogans contenting themselves with "for" allow for emancipation only on the site of the consumer,[27] slogans featuring only "by" allow for no relaxation, veering towards a state-socialist obligation to enjoy work, always.

Prynne's triangulation of work, poetry, and bird-song is not merely oblivious of wage labour and relational states, but rather can be seen as working towards loosening their grip. Nevertheless there remains the risk, always, of carving out a proto-revolutionary—yet ultimately non-revolutionary—niche for poetry ('my garden') as a form that can provide glimpses of a better life and so distract from the struggle to turn a better life for all into a reality. Such a niche would be what Jacob Taubes has termed "the bourgeois apotheosis of culture," culture posited as an "ersatz for human emancipation": "bourgeois society was unable to realize human emancipation, and its apotheosis of culture becomes a lie, given that the economic foundation, dominated by inhumanity, is left untouched."[28] Under the given economic conditions, Prynne's alignment of work and bird-song, and hence his gesture towards a reconciliation between work and play, work and leisure, can only evade the apotheosis Taubes cautions us against and become critically productive if it is not understood as the fixed claim that all poetry always already harmoniously unites work and play, but if it is taken as a critical gesture: in historical motion.

---

[27] This is the formulation used in Google's careers site quoted in footnote 7 above.

[28] Jacob Taubes, "Kultur und Ideologie," in *Spätkapitalismus oder Industriegesellschaft? Verhandlungen des 16. Deutschen Soziologentages*, ed. Theodor W. Adorno (Stuttgart: Ferdinand Enke, 1969), 121–122, my translation. How might this economic foundation be touched? Perhaps by appropriating the gardens of those that owe us. This hint, at least, is given by Rihanna's music video "Bitch Better Have My Money" (2015), which presents a self-conscious synthesis of bird-song's image as indicative of privileged leisure only so as to launch from this imagery an attack against white privilege. The beginning and the end of the video shows Rihanna lying on top of a trunk, covered in blood and money, smoking a cigar, the faux-innocent bird-song marking her killing of the accountant, the "bitch" (played by Mads Mikkelsen), who has not paid her. The lyrics express Rihanna's claim to payment that has been withheld from her as a worker. Motifs of political dissent merge with motifs of a pop-cultural revenge violence taken to an extreme. Not least, a policeman is repeatedly tricked in the video, which may be read as an expression of solidarity with the Black Lives Matter movement: even if this is highly monied capitalist art, the video's stakes exceed aesthetic representation. See Rihanna, "Bitch Better Have My Money (Explicit)," video, 07:01, www.youtube.com/watch?v=B3eAMGXFw1o, published 1 July 2015, accessed 12 January 2017.

We have seen that in Mörike, the song of the day that has been is a *Schlummerlied*, a lullaby sung to the night, denoted as mother, who irreverently does not (want to) pay attention. In Luxemburg, this lull- aby reappears as the bird-song of crows who speak of life lived. In con- tinued cross-reading from Prynne to Luxemburg to Prynne, a further twist emerges in Prynne's close-reading of the nursery rhyme "The Star" (1806; "Twinkle, twinkle, little star [...]") in "Stars, Tigers and the Shape of Words"; this reading precedes his close-reading of Blake's "The Tiger" already mentioned above. Having made extensive notes on the diminutive etymological forms governing "The Star," having noted that "each word reduces the scale to the friendly and protective charm of little things," and having remarked on the fact that "a specific early sense of 'spark', going back to the seventeenth century and beyond, was 'a small diamond'," Prynne presents the following sketch of a mother "tacitly present" in the poem.[29]

> The diamond [...] crowns the upward mobility of this first stanza by an imperial validation; [...] *Mama* is the brightest star in this nursery firma- ment, and her personal ornaments confirm the ambitious, even fairy-tale transfer of presumed income into displayed capital; just as the child invests totalising amounts of hope and trust and need in the treasure-form of the mother. She is tacitly present here as the adult maternal voice which stoops benevolently towards the child as from a lofty sky above. [...] Form (bright twinkling, twinned by its word-repetition) endorses, and is endorsed by, superlative value; the relation is protected from anxiety about diminishment or loss of validation by means similar to, and derived from, the entrainments of trade with the diamond-producing colonies ("the jewel in the crown") to the domestic consumption of an apex economy within the affluent English upper-middle classes.[30]

Historically we find ourselves c.1800, in terms of the diurnal cycle again at the breaking point between day and night. This satirically sketched theatrical scene is one of a mother singing a lullaby to her child to ward off their "loneliness at bed-time."[31] What is claimed is that it is

---

[29] Prynne, *Stars, Tigers and the Shape of Words*, 9–10.

[30] Prynne, *Stars, Tigers and the Shape of Words*, 10–11.

[31] Prynne, *Stars, Tigers and the Shape of Words*, 10.

of all things the management of littleness in this song which contributes to the management of no less than the British Empire: the child learns that it owns a graspable universe, including the very stars. The passage refuses to idealize the mother-child relation into something that could exceed capitalism. To consider the mother a "treasure-form" is to understand her as an economic mother and the child as an economic child in the very heart—the economic heart—of familial relations.

There is an element of misogyny in the conjuring up of a mother "from almost nowhere" in the poem, as a *"Mama"* whose "personal ornaments" safeguard capitalism—all this seems to base itself on a particular kind of caricature of feminized wealth.[32] If the image is read as a depiction of work, however, it opens itself as a critique of gendered labour relations. To take the economic constitution of the mother seriously implies not only that she is a "treasure-form," but also that she is a (care) worker. This is a reading in excess of Prynne's own reading, and, significantly, of the projected historical context, as neither the mother herself nor her time could have understood her song as worksong. Precisely that failure, however, is the point. The underside that seems implied in this sketch of a mother planting the idea of the expansion of the British universe in a little boy's mind would be this: could this mother, it seems possible to argue with Silvia Federici's *Wages Against Housework* (1975) manifesto,[33] have claimed her singing not (only) as the act of loving, but as work, could she have understood her home as a workplace, to return to the wider definition of the workplace indicated at the beginning of this essay, then the British Empire as such would have crumbled; "if the mothers are revolutionized, there is nothing left to revolutionize."[34]

Thinking poetry through work and play becomes effective not where poetry is assumed to configure a premature reconciliation between the two, but as a critical method towards attending to concrete historical situations, even where these may be constructed model situations such as the one just discussed. Neither "[w]e light a fire, plant a tree, write a

[32] Prynne, *Stars, Tigers and the Shape of Words*, 11.

[33] Silvia Federici, *Wages Against Housework* (Bristol: Power of Women Collective and Falling Wall Press, 1975).

[34] Walter Benjamin, *Understanding Brecht*, translated by Anna Bostock (London: NLB, 1973), 34.

poem" nor "the striking clatter of real work in the material world [...] also bird-song" constitute, then, stable claims as to the status of any and all poetic production as already embodying agential, productive, play-like work. Not only do they gesture towards that which has been and that which might be, but they can serve as critical starting points for tracing particular conditions of work and play experienced by particular subjects in particular forms of a historical present; "the day enjoyed today." The study of poetry, conceived of as the study of who (economically) gets to speak and sing, who gets income from it or does not, who is speaking from which subject position, and which mechanisms of exploitation or exclusion may be involved, becomes central to the study—and negation—of work relations in capitalism.

Works Cited

Adorno, Theodor W. "Free Time." Translated by Nicholas Walker. In *The Culture Industry: Selected Essays on Mass Culture*, edited by J. M. Bernstein, 187–197. London and New York: Routledge, 2001.

Benjamin, Walter. *Understanding Brecht*. Translated by Anna Bostock. London: NLB, 1973.

Blake, William. *Songs of Innocence and of Experience* [1794]. Edited by Robert N. Essick. San Marino, CA: Huntington, 2008.

Chen, Chris. "The Limit Points of Capitalist Equality." *Endnotes*, vol. 3 (September 2013): 202–223.

Clark, T. J. *Farewell to an Idea: Episodes from a History of Modernism*. New Haven, CT and London: Yale University Press, 1999.

Cornell Lab of Ornithology. "American Crow: Sounds." www.allaboutbirds.org/guide/American_Crow/sounds. Accessed 23 March 2018.

Endnotes. "Error." In *Bad Feelings*, edited by Arts Against Cuts, n.p. London, 2016.

Federici, Silvia. *Wages Against Housework*. Bristol: Power of Women Collective and Falling Wall Press, 1975.

Google. "Google Careers." careers.google.com. Accessed 27 March 2018.

Hubble. "Best Coworking Spaces in London for Creatives and Makers." hubblehq.com/blog/best-co-working-space-in-london-for-creatives-and-makers. Last modified 18 January 2018.

Jeschke, Lisa. *Theatricality and J.H. Prynne's Work*. PhD diss., University of Cambridge, 2015.

Katko, Justin. "Relativistic Phytosophy: Towards a Commentary on 'The *Plant Time Manifold* Transcripts'." In *Glossator 2: On the Poems of J.H. Prynne*, edited by Ryan Dobran, 245–293. New York: Glossator, 2010.

Luxemburg, Rosa. *The Letters of Rosa Luxemburg*. Edited by Georg Adler, Peter Hudis, and Annelies Laschitza. Translated by George Shriver. London and New York: Verso, 2013.

Mörike, Eduard. *Mozart's Journey to Prague and a Selection of Poems*. Translated by David Luke. London: Penguin, 2003. Kindle.

Nürnberger, Helmuth. *Geschichte der deutschen Literatur*. Munich: Bayerischer Schulbuch Verlag, 2006.

Oxford English Dictionary. www.oed.com.

Prynne, J. H. "A Brief Comment on 'Harmony' in Architecture" [Xi'An, P.R. China, 23 September 2006]. www.cai.cam.ac.uk/sites/default/files/harmony.pdf. Accessed 23 March 2018.

———. "Mental Ears and Poetic Work." *Chicago Review*, vol. 55, no. 1 (2010): 126–157.

———. *Poems*. Hexham, Northumberland: Bloodaxe, 2015.

———. "The Poet's Imaginary." *Chicago Review*, vol. 58, no. 1 (2013): 89–105.

———. *Stars, Tigers and the Shape of Words*. London: Birkbeck, 1993.

Rihanna. "Bitch Better Have My Money (Explicit)." Video, 07:01. www.youtube.com/watch?v=B3eAMGXFw1o. Published 1 July 2015, accessed 12 January 2017.

Schiller, Friedrich. *Über die ästhetische Erziehung des Menschen* [1801]. Stuttgart: Reclam, 2013.

Stein, Jack M. "Poem and Music in Hugo Wolf's Mörike Songs." *The Musical Quarterly*, vol. 53, no. 1 (January 1967): 22–38.

Taubes, Jacob. "Kultur und Ideologie." In *Spätkapitalismus oder Industriegesellschaft? Verhandlungen des 16. Deutschen Soziologentages*, edited by Theodor W. Adorno, 117–138. Stuttgart: Ferdinand Enke, 1969.

CHAPTER 4

"The Stitching of Her Wake": The Collaboration of Pamela Campion and Ian Hamilton Finlay

Lila Matsumoto

In handicrafts that are two-sided, such as embroidery or rug making, there is often a front for viewing and a back that shows evidence of touching and making. Whether we are thinking of paintings on canvas or the reliefs on sarcophagi, all visual forms, including the visual forms of poetry, have as well a tactile dimension that comes into play even if it is repressed.[1]

Susan Stewart evokes embroidery in her discussion of poetry to make the point that like needlework, poetry involves tactility in both its creation and consumption. Thinking about poetry's "front for viewing and a back that shows evidence" speaks not only to its potential appeal to the sense of touch, but to the cultural, social, and material conditions of its production and reception. As Stewart states, this dimension is often repressed, such as in the wilful obscuring of the working conditions of

[1] Susan Stewart, *Poetry and the Fate of the Senses* (Chicago and London: University of Chicago Press, 2002), 162.

L. Matsumoto (✉)
University of Nottingham, Nottingham, UK

© The Author(s) 2019
J. L. Walton and E. Luker (eds.), *Poetry and Work*,
Modern and Contemporary Poetry and Poetics,
https://doi.org/10.1007/978-3-030-26125-2_4

121

those who make our clothing in factories and sweatshops. Asking questions about the labour behind all visual forms brings to the fore hierarchical divisions, historical and extant, between activities considered art and those named craft. As Roszika Parker states, the "real differences between [art and craft] are in terms of *where* they are made and *who* makes them."[2] Another difference is for *whom* the work is made.[3]

This chapter examines the collaboration of poet Ian Hamilton Finlay and embroiderer Pamela Campion as a site of art/work. Campion and Finlay's "poem-embroideries" (as Finlay called them in his letters to Campion) animate continuities between the domestic sphere and public sphere, the emotional and the political, by counterpoising historical and cultural associations of embroidery's form with themes of warfare and radical politics. Exploring a selection of collaborative works alongside materials that surround them (letters, maquettes, and invoices), this chapter will consider how the historical and cultural idea of embroidery as domestic activity—as opposed to art—informed the dynamics of Campion's and Finlay's output and at the same time determined the social and economic terms of their working relationship.

Rozsika Parker's pioneering study *The Subversive Stitch: Embroidery and the Making of the Feminine* (1984) interrogates the prevailing status of embroidery in the West as domestic women's work, imbued with associations of sentimentality, tradition, homeliness, and femininity. Parker argues that the development of an ideology of femininity coincided historically with the emergence of a clearly defined separation of art and craft. This division emerged during the Renaissance, when embroidery became increasingly an activity of women amateurs who worked with the needle at home, outside the realm of paid labour. The Victorian period saw the codification of embroidery as a feminine craft, aligning needlework with nineteenth-century ideologies of female subservience and virtue. Popular conception of the creative work of these women amateurs was not that they exhibited a powerful artistic personality, as Parker explains, but a feminine presence.[4] Drawing on Parker's study,

---

[2] Rozsika Parker, *The Subversive Stitch: Embroidery and the Making of the Feminine* (London: The Women's Press, 1984), 5.

[3] For instance, practices by those who have little or no institutional art training are accepted within those institutions' gates when they are recalibrated as 'outsider art.'

[4] Parker, *The Subversive Stitch*, 5.

this chapter argues that embroidery's enduring status as woman's work informed Campion and Finlay's collaboration in multiple ways.

Beyond their collaborative works, Campion carried out embroidery work for Finlay's exhibitions where her role was markedly that of employee rather than co-artist. The duality of her position highlights the complex nature of collaboration, and how the term smooths over the variance of agency, power, and visibility of working relationships. For Finlay, the stitch was an alluring multivalent metaphor in his poetics, and also the medium which bound together objects in his exhibitions. Metaphors as cultural constructions arise out social realities. For Campion, the stitch was not only a mode of expression. It was also a mode of work and economic sustenance.

THE LITTLE SEAMSTRESS

Finlay and Campion never met. The two conducted their artistic partnership entirely through letters and occasionally phone calls, producing numerous pieces together over the course of a twenty five year period. Co-working was a vital element of Finlay's practice from early on in his career: issues of his little magazine *Poor. Old. Tired. Horse.* (1961–1967), co-edited with Jessie McGuffie (now Sheeler), were illustrated, typeset, and/or formatted by an artist, which gave the magazine a visual interest as much as a literary one.[5] Finlay produced works with established artists as well as craftspeople, drawing on his co-workers' expertise and familiarity with materials, forms, and techniques.[6] The range of Finlay's poetic forms, from sculptures to greeting cards, created compelling intersections between different cultural traditions and synergies between text and object. The aspect of correspondence was also integral to Finlay's poetic work; letters to his collaborators were platforms through which he could discuss, shape, and articulate his plans and processes, as well as exchange ideas and advice.

[5] Sheeler stated in an interview with author, 20 January 2012, that while Finlay was director of the magazine, she economically funded the first few issues of the magazine through holding down multiple jobs and doing much of the administrative aspects, including letter-writing, advertisement, and distribution.

[6] Arguably his most prominent collaborator—and at the same time most overlooked until recently—was his (then) wife Sue Finlay, who was responsible for much of the gardening of Little Sparta, Finlay's garden in Dunsyre, Scotland.

In his first letter to Campion, dated April 1972, Finlay wrote to ask whether she would be able to reproduce into embroideries several previously published poem-postcards he had created with collaborators. Finlay explained, "I like to interpret a basic idea in different mediums and in different ways."[7] One of these cards was "A Heart-Shape" (1971) made with Ron Costley, which depicts a red square "patched" onto an orange background. In another letter a month later, Finlay elaborated to Campion: "the Patch is the sign of care, affection, the wish to preserve." Finlay held associations of homeliness and nurturing to acts of the needle and thread even before he began working with Campion. It is interesting to speculate how these ideas of caring and affection are tied to needlework, especially when needlework has historically been associated with domestic women's work. Finlay's letters to Campion highlight both this association and its attendant complications for their collaboration. In September 1972 he wrote to Campion to ask whether she had completed the embroideries, writing: "I entirely understand that you are perhaps too busy with your children, to do the embroideries more quickly." A few weeks later he wrote:

> I do of course understand about the difficulties of time, in relation to doing the embroideries. On the other hand, it is much nicer for me to have one person who I collaborate with, rather than several, and I feel you are very sensitive in the matter of translating the works into your own medium. So I hope we may go on, with the idea of always having a work in progress, and of my eventually exhibiting them together, in an exhibition.

Because there are no (known) extant copies of Campion's responses to Finlay, we are not in a position to understand to what extent Campion made her working conditions known to Finlay.[8] What is pertinent to this exploration is to acknowledge that Finlay, as an artist working towards an exhibition deadline, and Campion, a working mother, held different

---

[7] All letters are from Finlay to Campion (with the exception of one from Sue Finlay), and are drawn from the Pamela Campion Papers, 1972–2000, GMA A04/5 Scottish National Gallery of Modern Art. All subsequent citations from letters are from this source.

[8] Though the correspondence is one-sided, being only from Finlay (and occasionally from his then-wife Sue Finlay), there are still glimpses into Campion's working methods as well as suggestions and responses to their collaborative projects which can be picked up in Finlay's letters and in the notes Campion made on the margins of their correspondence.

positions to embroidery in terms of its physical reality as work. What is also notable is Finlay's underestimation of embroidery as a time-consuming activity, frequently incompatible with the timescales and deadlines of art funding and exhibitions. Finlay's letter on March 1973 asks, "Could you give me some idea of whether you would be able to produce embroideries more quickly? [...] At our present speed it would take something like ten years to gather enough embroideries, and we have less than 6 months." Going against his earlier statement that he preferred to collaborate with one person at a time rather than several, he asked Campion whether she knew anyone else to take on some of the embroideries, or whether it would be possible for her to "increase the pace."

Despite these setbacks, Finlay was enthusiastic about working with Campion, writing that he would "very much like to go on with more embroidery works with you, and because one learns something from each." This learning included not only what new themes and iconographies could be conveyed, but what was physically and economically possible to realise through embroidery. Finlay held expectations for collaborative working methods, writing "I wonder if it would be better if you felt freer to interpret the designs, rather than just copy them?" and "I don't want to make you feel that you can't interpret the designs into embroidery's own terms." His attempts to redress what he saw as an imbalance of agency in their collaboration, however, did not extend to an acknowledgement of a more acute imbalance of their positions: an established male artist appropriating embroidery—historically linked to tropes of domesticity and femininity—working with a woman, not widely known as an artist in her own right and making at least part of her living through embroidery. The appropriation of tropes is what gives the poem-embroideries their unique charge. But what needs to be addressed more prominently is the gendered division of labour which enabled Campion's and Finlay's collaboration to "work," both in the sense of activating metaphors within the artworks and in the sense of characterising their co-labour.

Nowhere is the gendering of embroidery's labour in Finlay's work more sharply demonstrated than in "The Little Seamstress" (1970), made in collaboration with the artist Richard Demarco.[9] In May 1973 Finlay sent Campion the poem-postcard, which featured a line illustration of a

---

[9] Commenting on this work, Stephen Bann writes that the eponymous seamstress is "metaphorically represented as a boat picking her way across the water and leaving the stitching of her wake behind her" (15).

Fig. 4.1 Ian Hamilton-Finlay, with Richard Demarco, *The Little Seamstress* (1970) (©Tate, London 2018. By courtesy of the Estate of Ian Hamilton Finlay)

boat making its way through the water. Following the logic of the boat as a needleworker, the boat's mast can be seen as a needle "drawing" the horizon line. Finlay asked Campion in an accompanying letter to translate the postcard into the medium of embroidery. He wrote: "The idea is that the little boat stitching its wake across the water [and] is compared to a little seamstress, toiling away at her stitching. (I hope that my embroideries do not make *you* feel like a little seamstress.)" (Fig. 4.1).

Like boats, sewing has historically been linked to women and embedded in the ideology of femininity as protecting and virtuous. A boat with a female moniker was supposedly blessed with nurturance; sewing belongs to the same realm of womanly care and sanctity. Finlay/Demarco's "The Little Seamstress," in imagining the boat as needleworker, calls to attention the contrast between the feminine, domestic and interior sphere of home-making (the verbal signifier of the seamstress) and the masculine, public and out-of-doors space of exploration, commerce, and warfare (the visual signifier of the ship). The idea of the seamstress, appended with the affectionate "little," evokes the image of a charming lady sewing at home, the image of peace and wellbeing, at odds with the male maritime world.

The uncanniness of "The Little Seamstress" is the incursion of the feminine domestic craft into the public masculine sphere. Yet "seamstress" does not only denote a woman who sews, but can mean a woman who earns her living by sewing. Penelope is no longer at home, sewing and waiting for Odysseus, but on the seas, plying her skill and trade on the water.

AT HOME AND AT WAR

This section will discuss the idioms of embroidery which Finlay and Campion's pieces evoke by examining three works: *Terra/Mare* (1973), *Homage to Kadinsky* (1973), and the *French Revolution* samplers (1986–1987). The medium of embroidery is placed in relation to the pieces' iconographies; historical associations of embroidery as traditional, simple, wholesome, domestic, and charming are placed in a striking—and sometimes troubling or humorous—relation to the imagery and language of Roman conquest in *Terra/Mare*, twentieth-century warfare in *Homage to Kadinsky*, and radical politics in the *French Revolution* samplers (Fig. 4.2).

Terra/Mare (1973) is a textile panel. There is a twisted blue cotton type string stitched horizontally and a brown un-twisted wool stitched vertically. They intersect on a linen-covered mount encased within a

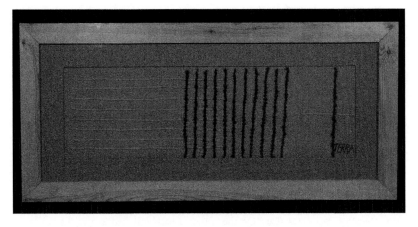

Fig. 4.2 Ian Hamilton-Finlay, with Pamela Campion, *Terra/Mare* (1973) (©Tate, London 2018. By courtesy of the Estate of Ian Hamilton Finlay)

pine wood frame.[10] "Terra/Mare" is Latin for Land/Sea, or Earth/Sea. A "key" is provided on the extreme right side of the piece, with "MARE" stitched next to a blue line and "TERRA" stitched next to a brown line. This panel could be understood as a semiotic poem. The thread is an interpretable language, the meeting and intersection of the land with water symbolised in the crossing of the threads. The piece alerts the viewer to the visual correspondence between land lines and sea lines: as tracks follow the wake of a plough, foamy lines follow a ship's passage. We can further interpret the lines as receipts of mechanical industry: the farming of the land through agriculture and the sea via fishing. We may also consider the historical lineage of passage lines through both sea and land as activated by "Mare": *Mare Nostrum,* Latin for "Our Sea," a byword of Roman conquest and antiquated imperialism (and later, in Mussolini's fascist propaganda campaign).

The use of modest materials in *Terra/Mare* and its geographic abstraction sit in strange contrast to the weighty and fraught history of human toil and conquest it seeks to represent. Finlay suggested to Campion in a letter that she should use string for its "simple" and "earthy" connotations. He explained further that, as this piece relates to "Greek philosophers […] we need to use materials which keep a simple homespun sort of feeling – avoiding silks," and preferably with an "open texture," a "hessian-y feel." It is interesting to consider how Finlay's (and indeed our own) association of wool as homespun, and evoking the domestic space in particular, is not an ancient trope but a relatively recent phenomenon. In its technique and use of wool, *Terra/Mare* could be classified as crewel work, where thin, loosely twisted yarn is embroidered on linen, often producing a "raised" effect. Parker writes that crewel work was an ideal method for decorating homeware, as the materials are relatively inexpensive and can withstand constant use.[11] Crewel work's link with the home was secured when house building increased in England in the late sixteenth century. Middle class families moved into bigger homes with subdivided rooms, so that tenants now had their own private bedrooms. As Parker explains, embroidery became a means of

---

[10] Sandra Deighton, "Technique and Condition," August 2005, www.tate.org.uk/art/artworks/finlay-terra-mare-collaboration-with-pamela-campion-t11739, accessed 26 May 2018. Deighton also notes that "On the reverse a backing board is overlaid with paper sealing tape."

[11] Parker, *The Subversive Stitch*, 106.

Fig. 4.3 Ian Hamilton Finlay, with Pamela Campion, *Homage to Kandinsky* (1973) Reproduced in the Scottish Art Council exhibition catalogue "Inscape", 1976 (By courtesy of the National Galleries of Scotland at the Scottish Gallery of Modern Art Archive and the Estate of Ian Hamilton Finlay)

expressing developing ideas of privacy and individuality, as the women of the household embroidered designs on cushions, curtains, clothing, coverlets, and wall hangings for the private bedrooms (Fig. 4.3).[12]

The link between homeliness and conquest is also made in *Homage to Kadinsky* (1973), exhibited at the "INSCAPE" exhibition at Fruitmarket Gallery in Edinburgh in 1976.[13] The visual plane of the embroidery is divided into seven compartments, with a warship stitched in the largest and central area and other instruments of modern warfare embroidered in the six surrounding compartments. The images are rendered in an almost cartoon-like or naïve style. Finlay wrote to Campion, "there is the fact that one thing can serve to underline the qualities of another thing; the waterships make one see Kadinsky in a strangely vivid, new way." A crude comparison of this piece to Wassily Kandinsky's practice alerts us to several

---

[12] Parker, *The Subversive Stitch*, 106–107.

[13] As he did with all exhibited flat-surfaced pieces he made with Campion, Finlay lay an emphasis on the colour and material of the mounts on which the works rested. The mounts formalise the pieces: it is what moves the piece from pastime to art (as when we mount a completed jigsaw puzzle into a frame).

contrasts at play: medium (painting versus embroidery); valuation (high art versus craft); approach (abstraction versus pictorial representation). Yves Abrioux writes that "[Finlay's] collaborations seek to bridge [...] modernity and traditional crafts [and] noble and trivial materials".[14] Following this idea, the viewer may well ask which is noble and which is trivial: the embroidery's childish rendering or the serious toys of modern warfare.

In 1984 Finlay and Campion began work on a series of samplers based on Finlay's speculative slogans for the French Revolution. These included "Justice is a Cottage Industry," "Teapots are the Navels of Happy Households," and "Let Us Invite Nature and All The Virtues To Our Festivals."[15] On each sampler the slogan is framed by a decorative motif of flowers and teapots, in keeping with the patterns used in traditional European samplers. As with *Terra/Mare* and *Homage to Kadinsky*, these poem-embroideries set in relation ideas of naiveté and domesticity with belligerence and worldliness. In his initial proposal of the project Finlay wrote to Campion:

> What I would like to try to do, is to use the sentimental idiom, in a way that restores something of its original association with a vision of political or ethical change – specifically, by using the 'sampler' form, by which I mean those kind of embroidered texts one used to see on the walls of bedroom in farmhouses: only, instead of having HOME SWEET HOME or whatever, I would use little sentences of my own, to evoke that medium, rather than being of it.

The medium which Finlay sought to evoke came to popularity in the early seventeenth century, taught as part of embroidery lessons considered an indispensable aspect of "feminine" education. Samplers, however, have been in circulation as early as the sixteenth century. The sampler was, in this historical context, a cloth containing a memorandum of patterns and stitches: literally a sheet of examples. John Palsgrave's Anglo-French dictionary *Les Clarcissement de la Langue Francoyse* (1530)

---

[14] Yves Abrioux, *Ian Hamilton Finlay: A Visual Primer* (London: Reaktion Books, 1985), 309.

[15] Other ideas included: "Don't Put All Your Heads In One Basket," "Spare the Blade and Spoil the Factions," "Don't Cast Your Revolutions Before Swine," "Happy States Are States With A Single Idea," "Revolutions Dethrone Kings and Enthrone Columns and Watering-Cans," and "Everything Under Heaven Has A Beginning."

defines the sampler as an "exemplar for a woman to work by."[16] Samplers were not traditionally considered works of art. Girls generally between the ages of five and fifteen modelled their work on their teachers' works, following particular patterns although they were allowed to choose their own arrangement of motifs, colours, and kinds of stitches used.[17] The historical idiom of the sampler is therefore deeply entrenched in the inculcation of women into codes of domestication. In the sense that many samplers contained edifying messages and exemplar stitches, the act of stitching can be understood as encoding diligence and obedience.

Finlay wrote to Campion in October 1984, stating, "there are two main strands or aspects, which one might call the Epic and the Domestic; in a certain sense, much we think of as being sentimental (I am not using the word to mean bad, but rather, to mean innocent and sweet) seems to derive from that time, or to make its first appearance at that time, largely (I think) through the writing of Rousseau." Tracing the logic of eighteenth century Enlightenment sentimental philosophy, which connects capacity for emotion to moral virtue, the French Revolution samplers recast its "innocent and sweet" mode into a form of speculative propaganda, a vehicle of radicalisation, and charming memorialisation. Finlay's textual intervention here is in line with his suite of French Revolution works, where the pursuit of revolution, motivated by ideals of democracy, liberty, brotherhood, is cast into an uneasy relation to the realities of death and destruction that followed. Drew Milne suggests that Finlay's French Revolution works constitute a proposal to "remember the French Revolution [...] as part of an approach to an art of civic remembrance."[18] The sampler's particular association with "feminine" education poses the question of *whose* civic remembrance when the clarion call of *fraternité* overtly excluded women. The "Sew for Victory" posters, part of the "Victory Begins at Home" campaign during World War II, indicate that the teaching of chauvinistic values through "feminine" education are not unique features of the nineteenth century.

[16] Donald King, *Samplers* (London: Victoria and Albert Museum, 1960), 2.

[17] King, *Samplers*, 1.

[18] Drew Milne, "'Adorno's Hut': Ian Hamilton Finlay's Neoclassical Rearmament Programme," *Jacket*, 15 (December 2001), http://jacketmagazine.com/15/finlay-milne. html, accessed 26 May 2018. Finlay's French Revolution works are discussed in detail in places like Yves Abrioux's *Ian Hamilton Finlay: A Visual Primer* (London: Reaktion Books, 1985) and Jessie Sheeler's *Little Sparta: The Garden of Ian Hamilton Finlay* (London: Frances Lincoln, 2003).

Arts-or-Crafts

The potency of the embroidery pieces we have examined lie in their apparent challenge of sewing's status as *mere* craft or manual labour, because the themes being represented are at odds with the medium of its execution, the modesty of its materials, and the small scale of their production. Finlay's use of actual teapots, jam jars, and a rocking horse in his French Revolution exhibitions point to their dual status as objects *and* art. However, this artful reclassification depends on the initial classification of embroidery, teapots, jam jars, and rocking horses as distinctly set apart from fine art. Far from challenging the status quo, the poem-embroideries reconfirm embroidery's historical and cultural distinction from poetry or sculpture. Their placement in the museum or gallery space further highlights the disjuncture of elevated versus quotidian forms. Finlay wrote to Campion, explaining how he imagined the samplers to be exhibited: "not presented in a frame, but rather, presented with part of it gathered around one of those round wooden things which are used when one is actually doing the stitching—and with the needle and thread left in it." The poem-embroideries capitalise on embroidery's non-art status to make claims about culture within an arts context.

Re-categorising embroidery as art obscures the disparate historical developments of the two, and in particular the co-option of embroidery into what Parker calls "an ideology of femininity as service and selflessness and the insistence that women work for others, not for themselves."[19] In her study, Parker locates the emergence of the artist in the Renaissance, where "the new emphasis was on the intellectual claims of the artist as opposed to manual skill. Artists wanted to be distinguished from those who were mere manual executors of other people's ideas and designs."[20] She points out that women have traditionally called embroidery "work," which seems to confirm its stereotype as craft rather than art. Indeed, historical and contemporary practices of embroidery as a creative and imaginative genre have largely been overlooked by surveys of art.

Finlay was an enthusiastic collaborator. In his letters he was profusely appreciative of Campion's output as well as input. He continually

---

[19] Parker, *The Subversive Stitch*, 6.

[20] Parker, *The Subversive Stitch*, 6.

encouraged her to interpret his designs, and often left the choice of colours, textures, and decisions about the mounts to her. Their collaboration also tempered Finlay's ambitions; the letters and mark-ups show that his ideas often required adjustment, and even at times abandonment. The maquettes, sketches, and facsimile diagrams give insight into how their work was made and, notably, how frequently Finlay came to realise that some projects were simply not feasible. Campion's invoices to Finlay demonstrate the difficulty of trying out experiments. The cost of the materials were more often than not paid in credit by Campion, and she had to first realise a work before Finlay could reject or accept it. This of course took time and money, neither of which Finlay nor Campion could readily afford.

In addition to their formally acknowledged collaborations, Campion sewed many elements of Finlay's works for his exhibitions, including velvet bags (for "Nox"); felt columns ("Corinthian Columns" exhibited at the gallery/temple at Little Sparta); flags sewn with "Arcadia," "Utopia," and "Little Sparta" (for an exhibition in Nevers in 1985), cushions (for "Pacific War Boardgame" (1975)), sails for a model boat, and swags, rosettes, and wall hangings for his French Revolution exhibitions. Finlay called these projects "pleasing 'extras,'" writing to Campion in April 1984 with excitement after receiving the flags "you have made of them real works of art. I am extremely appreciative […] I must try to have some ideas that meet your most delightful talents." Finlay also expressed enjoyment of the "Corinthian" columns Campion sewed and constructed out of felt and wooden batten in 1981; he called these "Embroidered Architecture" and claimed them as his favourite pieces in the gallery/temple at Little Sparta.

Considering these commissions alongside the poem-embroideries raises questions about what is or is not collaborative work, and what objects are deemed art whilst others remain seen as craft. These "pleasing extras" were not accredited to Campion. This was not due to neglect but because the sewn objects in themselves were not regarded as the central points of attention.[21] They were intended to contribute to and convey the general ambience or idiom of the exhibition. The conversation about the slippers that Campion sewed for the gallery/temple is a telling

---

[21] Finlay for the most part diligently gave due acknowledgement of others' work in the formal pieces.

example of this distinction-making. It was Sue Finlay who contacted Campion about the slippers in May 1981:

> The gallery floor is oiled quarry tiles: the slippers should help keep them polished + therefore be moderately soft materials, or at least non-scratchy. The tiles are quite cold so a warm material would be appreciated. However, I have to clean everything myself so a non-dust-producing materials would be <u>much</u> appreciated (i.e. not felt)!

Once the slippers had been received, Ian Hamilton Finlay wrote to Campion that "[They are] very practical in respect of the mud outside, and they also make a special feeling in the wearers, who probably pay more attention to things because of having them on. The also make them chatter less. So they are all I had hoped for them – and more." Whilst Ian Hamilton Finlay focuses on the aesthetics (or the enabling of an aesthetics or mood), Sue Finlay's emphasis, as the caretaker of the gallery, is on their practicality. The materials of the slippers must be chosen not only for their interpretative possibilities, but for their warmth and efficiency.

Women's Work

Finlay's status as a renowned male artist, exhibiting his poetry and artwork in galleries, and Campion's status as a woman and a relatively obscure artist, cannot be overlooked when considering their collaboration. This dimension is particularly important in light of embroidery's historical and cultural association as women's work, and its perceived inferior status in relation to more commercial forms of art. Faith Wilding discusses how avant-garde movements of the twentieth century such as Russian constructivism and Dada demanded the elimination of the division between arts and craft through their championing of traditional handicrafts such as embroidery. However this did not occasion a space for women to be acknowledged as artists. Wilding critiques successful contemporary male artists such as Mike Kelley, who she sees as working within the legacy of avant-garde traditions in the seventies by using embroidery in his work:

> The appropriation of a traditionally female and domestic tropes by a famous white male in a retrospective museum effectively rehabilitates them

for high art use (at least by men), but the connection to the feminist project which engendered this work is erased.[22]

On occasion, Finlay conflated the homeliness that he associates with embroidery to Campion herself. He wrote, "I like the world much better when I feel you are safely there, in the middle of England, with your sane and cosy life," and "I expect this is JUST the wrong time to write you, as you will be up to the waist in plum-pudding mixture. Still, perhaps you can tuck the letter in your apron pocket and read it when you are waiting for something to boil." It may be inequitable to hold Finlay accountable for statements made in private correspondence, and we are not privy to Campion's responses. However, it is telling that Finlay's conceptualisation of embroidery as a "delightful old-fashioned idiom" went hand-in-hand with his invocation of the embroiderer as a domestic housewife. Finlay's delight of embroidery, enmeshed in associations of the feminine, did not fully take into account its labour- and time-intensive production process.

That their collaboration was realised entirely through letter correspondence is an important aspect of Finlay's and Campion's working relationship. These letters are a record of the articulation, working out, abandoning, and picking up of ideas. They also chart the passing of days through cycles of personal crises, weather systems, and Christmases. They show that the making of art is shaped profoundly by welfare conditions both economic and physical.[23] Investigating their collaboration as a site of work, this chapter contends, is integral to an engagement of their art. This view is in contrast with Stephen Bann's statement from 1972, where he describes Finlay's collaborations as "the recognition and assumption of the 'Other.'" He considers

Whether Finlay can in the same way represent 'otherness' for his collaborators is an interesting question, but one which is obviously subsidiary to the problem of assessing his work.[24]

---

[22] Faith Wilding, "Monstrous Domesticity," in *M/E/A/N/I/N/G: An Anthology of Artists' Writing, Theory, and Criticism*, ed. Susan Bee and Mira Schor, 87–104 (Durham and London: Duke University Press, 2000).

[23] Illnesses on both sides often halted work for months and even years.

[24] Stephen Bann, *Ian Hamilton Finlay: An Illustrated Essay* (London: Shenval Press, 1972), 17.

It is clear that Finlay does not go far enough to engage with or address the gendered inequalities which conditioned the power of his poetic idioms. The enduring association of embroidery to domesticity and femininity has, as Johanna Drucker discusses, led to a generation of women artists moving away from handmade and tactile modes of production. She writes, "It seems that the farther the work is from any trace of or imprint of the woman's body, the more likely it is to achieve a measure of critical success".[25] Yet the view to extricate embroidery from women's creativity and expression is not shared by everyone; as Mary Mellor writes, images of weaving and spinning energised radical feminist writing of the eighties and nineties. This can be seen in scholarship such as Hazel Henderson's article "The Warp and the Weft: The Coming Synthesis of Eco-Philosophy and Eco-Feminism" (1983), and *Reweaving the World* (1990) edited by Irene Diamond and Gloria Feman Orenstein.[26]

The repressed dimension of Finlay and Campion's poem-embroideries is the burden of gendered labour. The taut threads conveying poetic metaphors trace every stitch Campion created, as well as act as metaphors themselves for the tension between Campion and Finlay in their different relation to embroidery. The nature of collaborations is that both co-workers are made visible, in spite of the social and economic inequalities that may distinguish them from each other. When collaborators work in different mediums and different contexts of production and reception, audiences must be alert to the ways in which each collaborator's practice and medium gains or loses charge from the new relation. Finlay and Campion's poem-embroideries are primarily perceived as Finlay's works, situated within his extensive oeuvre as a successful poet and artist. To engage with the poem-embroideries' "back that shows evidence of touching and making" as Susan Stewart suggests, is to encounter them as the collaborative and material works that they are. Only then can we begin to respond to Campion's co-work as not only labour but as art.

[25] Johanna Drucker, "Visual Pleasure: A Feminist Perspective," in *M/E/A/N/I/N/G: An Anthology of Artists' Writing, Theory, and Criticism*, ed. Susan Bee and Mira Schor, 167 (Durham and London: Duke University Press, 2000).

[26] Mary Mellor, *Feminism and Ecology*, 8 (Cambridge: Polity Press, 1997).

WORKS CITED

Abrioux, Yves. *Ian Hamilton Finlay: A Visual Primer*. London: Reaktion Books, 1985.

Bann, Stephen. *Ian Hamilton Finlay: An Illustrated Essay*. London: Shenval Press, 1972.

Beauty and the Revolution: The Poetry and Art of Ian Hamilton Finlay. Exhibition Catalogue, 6 December 2014–1 March 2015, Kettle's Yard University of Cambridge, Cambridge.

Deighton, Sandra. "Technique and Condition." *Tate Website*, August 2005. www.tate.org.uk/art/artworks/finlay-terra-mare-collaboration-with-pamela-campion-t11739. Accessed 26 May 2018.

Drucker, Johanna. "Visual Pleasure: A Feminist Perspective." In *M/E/A/N/I/N/G: An Anthology of Artists' Writing, Theory, and Criticism*, edited by Susan Bee and Mira Schor, 163–174. Durham and London: Duke University Press, 2000.

Finlay, Ian Hamilton. Ian Hamilton Finlay to Pamela Campion, various dates. Letters Series GMA A04/5. Scottish National Gallery of Modern Art. Pamela Campion Papers, 1972–2000.

King, Donald. *Samplers*. London: Victoria and Albert Museum, 1960.

Mellor, Mary. *Feminism and Ecology*. Cambridge: Polity Press, 1997.

Milne, Drew. "'Adorno's Hut': Ian Hamilton Finlay's Neoclassical Rearmament Programme." *Jacket*, 15 (December 2001). http://jacketmagazine.com/15/finlay-milne.html. Accessed 26 May 2018.

Parker, Rozsika. *The Subversive Stitch: Embroidery and the Making of the Feminine*. London: The Women's Press, 1984.

Sheeler, Jessie. *Little Sparta the Garden of Ian Hamilton Finlay*. London: Frances Lincoln, 2003.

Stewart, Susan. *Poetry and the Fate of the Senses*. Chicago and London: University of Chicago Press, 2002.

Wilding, Faith. "Monstrous Domesticity." In *M/E/A/N/I/N/G: An Anthology of Artists' Writing, Theory, and Criticism*, edited by Susan Bee and Mira Schor, 87–104. Durham and London: Duke University Press, 2000.

CHAPTER 5

Basil Bunting and the Work of Poetry

Annabel Haynes

Basil Bunting, who was born in the North East of England in 1900, was apprenticed in the 1930s to Ezra Pound, and wrote poetry until he died in 1985, was an important progenitor for a number of late modernist poets. He is a major link between poets writing in the modernist tradition today and the high modernism of the 1920s and 1930s. In "What the Chairman Told Tom," poetry is framed "a hobby":

> Poetry? It's a hobby.
> […]
> It's not work. You don't sweat.
> Nobody pays for it.
>
> Basil Bunting, "What the Chairman Told Tom"

As the Chairman then explains to Tom, a young poet: "You *could* advertise soap." By contrast, in a lecture celebrating Yeats's work, published in 1974, Bunting describes poetry as "a craft hard to learn and only acquired by long apprenticeship."[1] Moreover, throughout

---

[1] Basil Bunting, "Yeats Recollected," *Agenda*, vol. 12 (1974), 45.

A. Haynes (✉)
University of Sussex, Brighton, UK

© The Author(s) 2019
J. L. Walton and E. Luker (eds.), *Poetry and Work*,
Modern and Contemporary Poetry and Poetics,
https://doi.org/10.1007/978-3-030-26125-2_5

Bunting's precise, condensed oeuvre, work emerges as a major concern—if not *the* primary concern. Bunting pays attention variously to Horatian odes, Francois Villon, Persian poets Saadi, Hafez and Ferdowsi (among others), the wartime teashops of Britain and the spring soundscape of the Northumbrian Fells, but this theme of work—and the notion of poetry-making as a vital form of work, despite its social relegation to the status of "hobby"—remains present throughout.

Key to Bunting's presentation of work is his advocacy of craft as an antidote to the alienated and enervated work culture of modernity. In this chapter I read his influential mid-century modernist poem, *Briggflatts*, and collate, for the first time, the numerous instances of work that appear in the poem. By applying the lens of work to *Briggflatts* I also consider what the work of poetry meant to Bunting, and the effort he made to promote poetry as a kind of work, rather than an activity that takes place after, or around work. This essay therefore provides a background to the tradition of post-war experimental writing infused with ideas about work and labour.

The association that craft has with a particular kind of manual, physical labour is important here. So, too, is the process of learning a craft, though Bunting regrets that in the twentieth century, the poet must be their own apprentice.[2] Additionally, the notion of the craft practitioner as one who engages in a type of unalienated work that is disavowed, maybe even eradicated, by industrialisation and the capitalist mode of production, is also evoked. Craft, in late capitalism, risks losing its radical potential as it becomes associated with leisure activity, or the pastime of an amateur conducted outside the boundaries of the working day, rather than a tradition and history of vernacular artistic practice and work, a tradition that Bunting upholds by aligning poetry with craft.

Richard Sennett's *The Craftsman*, a detailed inquiry into historical and contemporary meanings of craft, provides a flexible definition that furnishes even a twenty-first century civilisation with the possibility of engaging in craft practice, or perceiving the craft models in everyday life. "Craftsmanship," writes Sennett,

---

[2] Bunting, "Yeats Recollected," 45.

names an enduring, basic human impulse, the desire to do a job well for its own sake. Craftsmanship cuts a far wider swath than skilled manual labor; it serves the computer programmer, the doctor, and the artist; parenting improves when it is practiced as a skilled craft, as does citizenship. In all these domains, craftsmanship focuses on objective standards, on the thing in itself. Social and economic conditions, however, often stand in the way of the craftsman's discipline and commitment: schools may fail to provide the tools to do good work, and workplaces may not truly value the aspiration for quality.[3]

Sennett is particularly interested in the union between hand and head that craft facilitates. His definition suggests, with its reference to the "thing in itself," that the product of craft is ultimately concrete. How might poetry-making fit with this understanding of craft? Language is the poet's material and a poem is something that is made, and that exists as an object: something outside and beyond the maker. A poem, once made, can be picked up by someone with no knowledge of the maker and can be admired, used, copied, like a pot, suggests Bunting, in a letter to Zukofsky of 1953:

Haven't we all, poets, been riding much too high a horse for a long time? A bit of the Yeatsian Grecian gold-smith or just plain potter (not for tea-cups though) or the guy who paints the Sicilian cars and British canal boats... Poets still act as though they thought they had some special claim. A skill worth preserving, with possibly some rather tenuous uses from the economic-social point of view: but if nobody buys my pots I don't accuse the customers of anything worse than poor taste, if nobody buys my poems what's the difference?[4]

Comparing a poem to a woodcut, Bunting also stated, in an interview in 1973: "I have never supposed a poem to be organic at all. I don't think the thing grows, it's built and put together by a craftsman."[5] Sennett similarly explains, according to his definition of craft, that "all skills,

---

[3] Richard Sennett, *The Craftsman* (New Haven and London: Yale University Press, 2008), 10.

[4] Dale Reagan, "Basil Bunting Obiter Dicta," in *Basil Bunting: Man and Poet*, ed. Carroll F. Terrell (Orono: National Poetry Foundation, 1981), 232.

[5] Dale Reagan, "An Interview with Basil Bunting," *Montemora*, vol. 3 (Spring 1977), 78.

even the most abstract, begin as bodily practices."[6] Craft is a dedication to "good work for its own sake."[7] Informed by Arendt's distinction between work and labour, Sennett believes that craft is work that is not "a means to another end." Instead, "[t]he craftsman represents the special human condition of being engaged."[8] So, is it possible to be a craftsperson at one moment, and a different kind of worker another, or can craft constitute a more enduring identity? Does craft merely describe the action of making, or a set of beliefs? To maintain the political potential of craft as an alternative to the capitalist mode of production, it is important to bear in mind the social structures necessary to the cultivation and practice of craft, as well as the rich socialist tradition and history behind craft work, and craft societies. Bunting would agree with Sennett's view that craft work is about practised expertise: "All craftsmanship is founded on skill developed to a high degree."[9] In terms of poetry, concision is the definitive skill that Bunting believes the poet-craftsperson must hone. In *ABC of Reading*, Pound, who was similarly opposed to superfluity and verbosity, attributed the phrase "dichten = condensare" (poetry = condensation) to Bunting.[10] Bunting wrote, in a letter to Denis Goacher, 26 May 1965, that even Allen Ginsberg still needed to master "the respectably ancient art of the pumice." His work was "far too diffuse," in Bunting's view (Letter held in Basil Bunting Poetry Archive, Durham University Library, UK).

Bunting's own mastery of concision is apparent throughout his poems, and his presentation of stonemasonry as akin to the precision of good poetry-making is repeated throughout his work. The following example, taken from his 1930 poem, "Nothing," is brief in both content and syntax as the poem rises in its middle to the climactic imperative:

> Celebrate man's craft
> and the word spoken in shapeless night, the
> sharp tool paring away
> waste and the forms
> cut out of mystery!
> (111)

---

[6] Sennett, *The Craftsman*, 10.

[7] Sennett, *The Craftsman*, 20.

[8] Sennett, *The Craftsman*, 20.

[9] Sennett, *The Craftsman*, 20.

[10] Ezra Pound, *ABC of Reading* (London: Faber and Faber, 1991 [1934]), 36.

Only two adjectives, "shapeless" and "sharp," make it into this stanza. Carefully placed and close in sound, the two words contrast each other to highlight the skill of the mason in chipping away all that is unnecessary or that clouds or confuses the final product, resulting in the revelation of clarity: out of the unknown or unintelligible comes solid meaning in object form.

Bunting first performed *Briggflatts*, at the Morden Tower in 1965 and it was published by Fulcrum in 1966. The long poem, "an autobiography," is exemplary of the methods, themes, and concerns that run throughout his oeuvre. The poem itself is an intricate work of craft: its structure based, partly, on the plaited patterns in the illuminated Lindisfarne Codex. In the twenty-first century it continues to represent a significant conceptual, temporal, and transnational link between the high modernist experiments of Williams, Eliot and Pound (who was a close friend and poetic mentor to Bunting) and the avant-garde and some of the regional scenes of British poetry in the post-war period for whom Bunting was a sort of poetic pater familias. Bunting represents a vital, and vitalising, transition between these stages and schools. He was also a socialist with connections to the Fabians and to William Morris's politicised craft philosophy and practice, and his poetry constantly attended to the universalising idea of work. Bunting's poetry shows that work—from the unalienated chip of the stonemason's chisel (*Briggflatts*) to the tearing of coal from the earth by the miner ("They Say Etna"), to the scrutiny of the government bureaucrat ("The Passport Officer"); from the "knack" and unpredictability of fishing to the serving work of "teashop girls" ("Mesh cast for mackerel"); from the counsel and support of the poetic muse ("The Well of Lycopolis") to the poet racking their brains and enduring poverty to keep up the art (Part II, *Briggflatts*)—is something everyone does.

Bunting's own work is manifestly masculine, even masculinist, and this is something that warrants more criticism than it has heretofore received. Indeed, the traditional craft model that Bunting draws on is stereotypically masculine. Elsewhere, I have written about Bunting's exploitation of female characters, and their work, sometimes included to provide a soft, idle, or trivial contrast to the physicality, hardship, or importance of men's labour, but this chapter will focus on the more progressive aspect of Bunting's presentation and philosophy of work.

Bunting's poetry raises important questions about work: what constitutes work? Why do we do it? How are we judged by what we do? How is twentieth-century society and beyond set up to favour and support certain kinds of work, and to devalue others? Bunting is both for and against work—perhaps this has something to do with being caught between two stages of modernist writing that represent earlier and later periods of capitalism. Bunting is pro-work when depicting specific forms of handicraft, always carried out by male characters, which tend to be portrayed as unalienated (surplus value is not appropriated by an owner of industry). The sort of making-work, including the making of poetry, portrayed by Bunting, is vitalising, redemptive, and contrasts with the hardship of mining work, the tedium of service work, or the emptiness of white-collar and office work. Bunting's positive work ethic leads him to repeatedly justify in poems and letters the validity of poetry as a form of work, and this project boils to outraged ridicule in "What the Chairman Told Tom" (quoted at the beginning of this chapter), which satirises the young poet Tom Pickard's encounter with the Chairman of Newcastle Council in the 1960s, and indicates the general antipathy that local and even arts councils had towards poets in the post-war period. Pickard was friend, supporter and apprentice to Bunting in this time and his poetry, which grows out of Bunting's, is even more explicitly outraged by the hardships which poets are expected to bear in order to produce their work.

So, on the one hand using the term "work" to describe poetry-making lends the activity credibility and a sense that it is a serious and worthwhile pursuit. On the other hand "work" gets in the way of writing poetry. Bunting's oeuvre is relatively compact as a result of his commitment to concision. However, his correspondence and his biography reveal a poet constantly distracted from writing by the need to earn a living. He is anti-work in the sense that he appears to have hated many of the jobs he was forced to do in order to survive: work that got in the way of writing poetry; another reason for his modestly sized collected works. He refuses to attribute value to all forms of work, and while he fights for poetry to be recognised as a form of labour, he scorns other kinds of work. The apparent work ethic that Bunting's idea of craft as something that redeems base human existence is at odds with his apparent desire to be free from work. We might ask why the word "work," associated in the post-war period as it is with alienated, alienating, piecemeal, unrewarding, even useless, toil is of any use or interest at all to a poet describing their art and practice.

I have suggested that craft is increasingly understood as an alternative to work, rather than a component or an example of it. Reinforcing the original sense of craft as a type of specialised, skilled work is therefore important, conceptually, as a matter of maintaining the dignity and value of work that entails making. More practically, it is important to a crafts-person, or an artist, that their making activity is recognised as a form of work as opposed to a form of leisure, so that they may claim time and a wage for that work. Even in the early twentieth century, Bunting scorned what he perceived as a privileged dilettantism of the British elite that jeopardised the job of the poet, and this was epitomised in his view by what he saw as the closed-system of the Bloomsbury Group. His poem, "The Well of Lycopolis," attacks the group, via an extended homophobic and sexist conceit about emasculation and idleness: floppy writing. By the mid-1960s, however, Bunting was living even further on the out-skirts of mainstream literary society. After a protracted hiatus, he was res-urrected by the Newcastle poet, Tom Pickard, and began to write again. The result of this friendship (and Pickard's apprenticeship to Bunting) was *Briggflatts*.

Nothing sounded like *Briggflatts* when Bunting first read the poem at Tom and Connie Pickard's Morden Tower Book Room, Newcastle, in 1965. Popular British poetry chugged along to Betjeman's train track beat, or bounced ironically through the well-worn forms that Larkin had reached back into the pre-war era to reclaim for his disillu-sioned lyrics. Established verse forms were back to stay, and it seemed that for many British poets, the high-modernist experiment had ended. But for Bunting, the work that the poet should be *engaged* in—I refer to Sennett's conditions of craft—is work which produces verse prior-itising its sound over its verbal comprehensibility. Bunting represents the continued experimentalism and honing of the craft of poetry of late modernist poetics, that imagines formal experiment as a progres-sion. Contributing to a collection of essays on writers and craft, Mark Rudman considers the "free verse" of *Briggflatts*, as "a good example of how free verse can be seen as an advance over the strictly metrical." He describes the poem as having "rhythm drawing its sound from the world's body."[11] For Rudman, an American poet, free verse marks a progression in English language poetics, thus "it is retrograde to write

[11] Nicholas Delbanco and Laurence Goldstein, *Writers and Their Craft: Short Stories & Essays on the Narrative* (Detroit: Wayne State University Press, 1991), 154–155.

primarily in fixed forms."[12] Rudman notes the difference between external form and the ethics of a poem (which might constitute form in another way). Rudman also cites Pound's project, expressed in Canto 81 (a poem in which Bunting features): "to break the pentameter, that was the first heave."[13] The physical, combative words Pound uses to describe the change imply that this was a violent revolution.

Briggflatts does not give up the hard-won ground of a post-pentameter poetics, and even without a prescribed verse form, it is structured around sound. Rudman writes that the occasional instances of rhyme that feature in the poem's free verse "have been dictated by the materials, the 'solemn mallet' repetitions" and so his reading links the work of poetry to the work of the poem's stonemason.[14] In this way, the poem is built from primary material gathered in the outside world—often from the natural world—in the same way that a mason makes an object from natural resources.

Nature often features in Bunting's poetry, often alongside human work, and there are many examples of this coalescence in *Briggflatts*, which develops earlier concerns into a long poem. The following analysis of the poem's presentation of work is broken into numbered parts and a "coda" corresponding to the six parts of *Briggflatts*.

I

The long poem's scene is set by the sounds of nature coming together, like the start of a symphony. We hear the descant brag of the bull; the splashing of Rawthey providing the main refrain; pebbles bouncing in the river's water. The second stanza introduces the mason whose work provides the recurring conceit for poetic labour, impermanence, memory, and life's close relationship with death:

> A mason times his mallet
> to a lark's twitter,
> listening while the marble rests,
> lays his rule

---

[12] Delbanco and Goldstein, *Writers and Their Craft*, 153.

[13] Ezra Pound, "Canto 81," in *The Cantos of Ezra Pound* (New Directions, 1993 [1948]), 538.

[14] Delbanco and Goldstein, *Writers and Their Craft*, 155.

at a letter's edge,
fingertips checking,
till the stone spells a name
naming none,
a man abolished.
(61)

The mason's work takes place within the sounds and the rhythms of the natural symphony that surrounds him, and his labour provides an example of non-alienated work. The next stanza maintains the interplay between nature, work, life, and death: "Decay thrusts the blade," suggesting that death compels work, and gives life on earth rhythm and purpose (61).

Two children, representing Bunting and his first love, Peggy, take a journey on the mason's cart, from the hamlet of Brigflatts, through the fells and dales of Cumbria (Bunting would say Northumbria) to the quarry at Stainmore. Then, the quarry-workers' labour joins the soundscape: a macrocosmic version of the mason's mallet. "Their becks ring on limestone, / whisper to peat." Such is the synchrony with nature, that the fruits of the quarry workers' labour are abundant and so in this real-life idyll, even the horse's work is done for it: "The clogged cart pushes the horse downhill." The air is "soft": the atmosphere of this scene of making within nature is gentle, and within this landscape, the poet makes his first foray (as far as the poem shows us) into verse: "laying the tune frankly on the air" (62). The ease and honesty involved in making song presented here contrasts with the "bogus," still-birthed lines in the next section (65). "Knotty wood, hard to rive" is not struggled with here, as it is later on, but it "smoulders to ash" (76, 63). The interplay of nature and human life and work is responsible for the "insufferable happiness" the protagonist experiences (64).

II

The work portrayed in the opening part of the poem is idyllic, but the references are to tough work: "[f]ingers / ache on the rubbing stone"; "[p]ainful lark, labouring to rise!"; and show that the work is not Arcadian (61). This is poetry that retains the Romantic tradition of a belief in the deep relationship between humankind and nature, but dismisses the ideas of poetic superiority, special purpose, or spirit. Part II abandons the idyll altogether as the poet-protagonist moves to London. Within the city's confines, his creativity is stifled by an unnatural urban world and capitalist industry:

> Poet appointed dare not decline
> to walk among the bogus, nothing to authenticate
> the mission imposed, despised
> by toadies, confidence men, kept boys.
> (65)

These "bogus" prefigure the journalists in Part III, who steal, exploit, and scavenge for a career. London is presented an unreal world full of horror; an artificial landscape in which true craft (making poetry) is impossible. Bunting presents the poet's work:

> Secret, solitary, a spy, he gauges
> lines of a Flemish horse
> hauling beer, the angle, obtuse,
> a slut's blouse draws on her chest,
> counts beat against beat, bus conductor
> against engine against wheels against
> the pedal, Tottenham Court Road, decodes
> thunder, scans
> porridge bubbling, pipes clanking, feels
> Buddha's basalt cheek
> but cannot name the ratio of its curves
> to the half-pint
> left breast of a girl who bared it in Kleinfeldt's.
> (65)

The unhappy, uninspired poet is an outsider, a misogynist and a misanthrope in this melodrama: his job has been degraded; he spies on women, and the bile-filled insult, "slut," is demonstratively aggressive. A list of quotidian sounds pause at the suspended word, "feels," bathetically aligning strong emotion with "porridge" and "pipes." His work is even sacrilegious: Buddha's basalt cheek (such a statue is held in the British Museum, just off Tottenham Court Road) is compared to a Bloomsbury bar-goer's breast. All the poet's observation and scansion produces nothing: "mating / beauty with squalor to beget lines still-born" (65).

Escaping from London, the poem develops one of its most sonically rich sections as it turns to the sea, depicting a group of rowers instructed by a pilot, who faces the rowers, and steers the boat.

> Thole-pins shred where the oar leans,
> grommets renewed, tallowed;
> halliards frapped to the shrouds.
> Crew grunt and gasp. Nothing he sees
> they see, but hate and serve. Unscarred ocean,
> day's swerve, swell's poise, pursuit,
> he blends, balances, drawing leagues under the keel
> to raise cold cliffs where tides
> knot fringes of weed.
> (66)

Bunting's use of specialised nautical terminology diverts most listeners' attention from the meaning of the words, forcing focus on the sound of the words. The excerpt again portrays labour as a physical interaction between humans and nature, and again this links to Bunting's poetics and politics. Worried about the perceived split between manual and intellectual labour and consequent association of poetry with elite leisure activity, Bunting warned that if poetry and music

> lose touch altogether with the simplicity of the dance, with the motions of the human body and the sounds natural to a man exerting himself, people will no longer feel them as music and poetry. They will respond to the meaning no doubt, but not with the exhilaration that dancing brings. They will not think of them as human concerns. They will find them tedious.[15]

The whole work system of the boat is displayed, and it's not ideal. The rowers "hate and serve"; they don't share the perspective of the pilot: "Nothing he sees/they see" so this seems to be an example of divided and hierarchical labour. However, the poetry, sounding grunts and gasps, the "sounds natural to a man exerting himself," maintains that invigorating contact with the physicality and movement of the

---

[15]Basil Bunting, "The Art of Poetry" (lecture, 1970), quoted in Dale Reagan, "Basil Bunting Obiter Dicta," in *Basil Bunting: Man and Poet*, ed. Carroll F. Terrell (Orono: National Poetry Foundation, 1981), 232.

human body at work. Bunting is surely comparing this sort of making work with sexual energy and exhilaration, too.

The scene changes again and, as a counterpoint to Part I's Northumbrian stonemasonry, the poem portrays the Carrara marble-quarrying industry:

> White marble stained like a urinal
> cleft in Apuan Alps,
> always trickling, apt to the saw. Ice and wedge
> split it or well-measured cordite shots,
> while paraffin pistons rap, saws rip
> and clamour is clad in stillness:
> clouds echo marble middens, sugar-white,
> that cumber the road stones travel
> to list the names of the dead.
> (67)

William Wootten's study of the meaning of stone in *Briggflatts*, describes this part of the poem as a denunciation of Pound's fatal faith in monumentalism. In a Duchamp-esque move, Bunting renders the marmoreal medium, that Pound celebrates throughout *The Cantos*, urine-stained. According to Wootten, Bunting "amends the Poundian description of marble [...] [It] is described in terms that link it inextricably with human, industrial and economic process, and, especially, with excretion and death."[16]

The noisy and destructive machinery, coupled with sweaty industrial toil in this section of the poem clearly contrasts with the earlier (in both senses) stonemason's work, and even the quarrying of Part I. The visual landscape presented here "stained like a urinal" and surrounding the local environment with clouds of dust is starkly different from the "stone white as cheese" which "jeers at the dale" in the earlier landscape (63). The contrast in sound, too, suggests that the stonemason's work has an affinity with nature: in Part II we hear rapping and ripping: a centre of "clamour" in an otherwise still landscape; whereas the stonemason's landscape "in such soft air" is so quiet that he hears not only larks, but the stone "resting" (62, 61).

---

[16]William Wootten, "Basil Bunting: 'Uneasy Mason'," *English*, vol. 51, no. 201 (2002), 237.

A sudden staccato of four quatrains of emphatic trochaic dimeter follow the Carrara scene, depicting metal mining that might be ancient or modern, and the stonemason reappears "reproached" and "uneasy" (68). "Shaping evasive ornament," like the poet struggling to find and, through articulation, regain what he has lost, the mason now "litters his yard / with flawed fragments" (68). A few paragraphs later, the connection is made between uneasy mason and poet who has lost his landscape, love and labour, as the poet's work is directly portrayed, and questioned:

> But who will entune a bogged orchard,
> its blossom gone,
> fruit unformed, where hunger and
> damp hush the hive?
> A disappointed July full of codling
> moth and ragged lettuces?
> (69)

III

Part III is based on Ferdowsi's *Shahnameh* story of Alexander the Great encountering the Angel and harbinger of apocalypse, Israfel. The section descends, "[d]own into dust and reeds" into a Dantean Hell holding journalists, fat cats, and politicians. A surreal scene is created mingling city life with the natural world, in which "scavengers" "scoop droppings / to mould cakes for hungry towns."

> [...] One
> plucked fruit warm from the arse
> of his companion, who
> making to beat him, he screamed:
> Hastor! Hastor! but Hastor
> raised dung thickened lashes to stare
> disdaining those who cry:
> Sweet shit! Buy!
> for he swears in the market:
> By God with whom I lunched!
> there is no trash in the wheat
> my loaf is kneaded from.
> (71)

Richard Burton suggests Hastor is a caricature of Bunting's former boss, the *Times*-owner Lord Astor, and calls this section "grim portrait of the journalist's trade."[17] The "scavengers" who scream out to the protagonist, their shit-scooping, and their theft from each other, which is work carried out for a "hungry" audience, indicate Bunting's feelings about the relationship journalism has with language. Journalism is presented as a commodified, sold-out, form of writing, headed by a grotesque capitalist aristocrat who is so powerful that he has the Divine as a dining partner. Hastor swears that "there is no trash in the wheat / my loaf is kneaded from," but this protest reveals either his mendacity or the unnaturalness of his product, as it contrasts with the positive organic quality of the trembling wheat at the beginning of the poem. Rhythmically synchronous with the river, Rawthey, and the mason's mallet knocking in non-alienated labour, in Part I: "wheat stands in excrement/ trembling. Rawthey trembles" (61).

The vista of hell then expands to include alongside journalists, entrepreneurs, financiers, tricksters, or even world leaders: all the "[g]uides at the top" who "claim fees / though the way is random" (72). Chaos and horror ensue until Alexander's epiphany occurs, thanks to Angel Israfel, and a prophetic slowworm, to remind the reader of mortality and the swift march of time, of natural "measure" reminiscent of the mason's mallet:

> Sycamore seed twirling,
> O, writhe to its measure!
> Dust swirling trims pleasure.
> Thorns prance in a gale.
> In air snow flickers,
> twigs tap,
> elms drip.
> (74)

[17] Richard Burton, *A Strong Song Tows Us: The Life of Basil Bunting* (Oxford: Infinite Ideas, 2013), 355.

IV

Part IV imagines poetry's relationship to nature. Images of hunting represent the hierarchies in the natural life that are turned into tiers of death in the food chain:

> Aneurin and Taliesin, cruel owls
> for whom it is never altogether dark, crying
> before the rules made poetry a pedant's game.
> (75)

Aneurin and Taliesin, ancient Welsh bards, represent the freedom of the oral poetic tradition and the affordances for unalienated labour within wholesome and unalienated craft work. Bunting links this earlier freedom with the freedom granted by progressive, modernist "free verse," against the excessive prosodic pedantry that constrains poetry to trivialities.

Bunting also relates the history of the natural world to the human world through poetry (and poetry's history). The poem at this point develops its nonlinear chronology through the proliferation of transcultural and transhistorical references, and the random sounding of various voices. The section, at the same time, makes repeated reference to the poem's structure through the recurring "weaving" conceit. With its references to the bardic tradition there is a nod to storytelling and chronicle, and this links the poem again to the Lindisfarne Codex. Thus voices and historical figures, and events, are woven together into an alternative British history. In notes to the poem Bunting writes: "Northumbrians should know Eric Bloodaxe but seldom do, because all the school histories are written by or for Southrons" (226).

Bunting is explicit about the need to record, or retrieve, a northern history; but *Briggflatts* is also a history of work. A vista of the work that makes the world is compared to weaving, as the scenery moves from "text carved by waves / on the skerry" to an address to the reader:

> Can you trace shuttles thrown
> like drops from a fountain, spray, mist of spiderlines
> bearing the rainbow, quoits round the draped moon;
> shuttles like random dust desert whirlwinds hoy at their
> tormenting sun?
> (75)

This bustling scene of natural creative activity has an unpleasant side: the lice that feed on the result of the collaborate work of the rest. Bunting wards off scholarly exegesis, but perhaps also hints at his wider life view which finds pattern and sense in the big picture of nature, and not through individual acts of human intellection or reasoning:

> Follow the clue patiently and you will understand nothing.
> Lice in its seams despise the jacket shrunk to the world's core,
> crawl with toil to glimpse
> from its shoulder walls of flame which could they reach
> they'd crackle like popcorn in a skillet.
> (75–76)

The music of the poem continues to build. A reference to piping, which Bunting's earlier poem about creative hermitism, "Chomei at Toyama" suggests, is a reference to the redemptive and individual work of making music with one's breath, lifts the poem's mood. The poem now presents work taking place in harmony with nature:

> As the player's breath warms the fipple the tone clears.
> It is time to consider how Domenico Scarlatti
> condensed so much music into so few bars
> with never a crabbed turn or a congested cadence,
> never a boast or a see-here; and stars and lakes
> echo him and the copse drums out his measure,
> snow peaks are lifted up in moonlight and twilight
> and the sun rises on an acknowledged land.
> (76)

Sara R. Greaves' eco-poetic reading of *Briggflatts* considers Bunting as a late Romanticist. She looks in particular at how Wordsworth and Bunting connect the work of poetry to the natural world. She recognises in *Briggflatts*, the preponderance of "men whose livelihood relies on their intimacy with the natural world," naming among these "local men and Wordsworthian simple folk."[18] According to Greaves, Bunting's

---

[18] Sara R. Greaves, "A Poetics of Dwelling: In Basil Bunting's *Briggflatts,*" *Cercles*, vol. 12 (2005), 75.

references to weaving and webs aim to "heal" (with craft) what the modern world severs: the relationship between person and place.[19]

V

As the poem approaches its end—"[s]olstice past, / years end crescendo" (78)—nature comes to the fore and provides a way of understanding mortality. The message that the cyclical natural world delivers is that death is a part of life, not other or separate. Part V aligns the seasons with stages of human life as it conjures the dead of winter. Natural imagery abounds and seems to redeem the futility of life and here we see nature at work, making, and weaving, continuing the conceit introduced in Part IV:

> Even a bangle of birds
> to bind sleeve to wrist
> as west wind waves to east
> a just perceptible greeting –
> sinews ripple the weave,
> threads flex, slew, hues meeting,
> parting in whey-blue haze.
>
> Mist sets lace of frost
> on rock for the tide to mangle.
> Day is wreathed in what summer lost.
> (78)

Even maggots, "gentles," are creative and generative, rather than destructive: feeding on dead flesh they "compose decay" rather than decompose, borrowing from the ongoing musical theme. The increasing patterning and interweaving of images, themes, sounds, and phrases at this point not only portray memories re-remembered, but also Bunting's bigger vision: the overarching pattern of life; the "soft / web" woven "not for bodily welfare nor pauper theorems / but splendour to splendour, excepting nothing that is" (75). The song laid "frankly on the air" by the children in Part I is recalled in the instruction to "[s]ing / strewing the notes on the air / as ripples skip in a shallow" (78). Poetry is compared to other kinds of natural noise. A voice repeats Part II's

---

[19] Greaves, "A Poetics of Dwelling," 71.

instruction to "Go/bare," encouraging the precision, concision and sim-
plicity in making verse that Bunting repeatedly recommends:

> [...] the shore is adorned
> with pungent weed loudly
> filtering sand and sea.
> (78)

The implication is that the natural world balances usefulness and dec-
oration: the useless excess that predominates in modern human culture
does not exist in the natural world. Even rotting seaweed is doing something: death and decay are not purposeless.

In this web of memories and images, the mason is summoned once
more: this time his craft is aligned with the sea's marks made on stone (a
recurrent image itself, appearing in parts IV and V):

> Silver blades of surf
> fall crisp on rustling grit,
> shaping the shore as a mason
> fondles and shapes his stone.
> (79)

The next verse moves inland, and shows "[s]hepherds," who are
able to "follow the links," contrasting the nature attuned work of the
shepherd to the pedantic poetry-reader's futile effort to "follow the
clue patiently" (79, 75). "Links," also a term for bumpy grass terrain,
plays with the former lines to suggest that local, natural knowledge sur-
passes institutionalised learning. The poem praises the shepherds' "silent,
accurate lips": precision, skill, and the oral tradition are celebrated once
again.

Stars, light and musical analogies take the poem towards another sea-
scape some lines later until suddenly bookbinding is portrayed in the last
few verse paragraphs of the fifth part, the book's necessarily fixed (and
thus chronological) order contrasting with the poem's advocacy of layered chronology and looping patterns:

> The sheets are gathered and bound,
> the volume indexed and shelved,
> dust on its marbled leaves.
> (80)

The diminishing stanzas, containing fewer and fewer lines, mime the dying light of the year's end. In these last few lines of the Part V, Bunting draws attention to the poem's construction, defying his authorial supremacy by highlighting the poem's fabrication and subjectivity. It attempts to effect what he repeatedly called for: that all that should remain are his poems.

CODA

In the last part of *Briggflatts* the rhythms of work and song unite to compel the speaker, and the listener, towards the final lines. Time has moved on, and the change of pace and of mood is reflected by the decreased line length. In contrast to the long verse paragraphs of Part IV that reflected a final burst of communicative energy, the coda's terse, rhymed lines communicate the closing down of the poem and the poet's life, too:

> A strong song tows
> us long earsick.
> Blind, we follow
> rain slant, spray flick
> to fields we do not know.
>
> Night, float us.
> Offshore wind, shout,
> ask the sea
> what's lost, what's left,
> what horn sunk,
> what crown adrift.
>
> Where we are who knows
> of kings who sup
> while day fails? Who,
> swinging his axe
> to fell kings, guesses
> where we go?
> (81)

As the poet's work reaches completion, blindness, uncertainty, and darkness arrive. It is "[n]ight" and only sounds, memories, and visions remain.

Bunting was adamant that his poems should stand by themselves; that scholarly resort to letters and manuscripts was futile, so his occasional statements about poetry are particularly meaningful. In a lecture on "The Codex," given at Newcastle University as part of a series (1968–1974), he claimed:

> A poet must write by ear (nearly all poets compose *aloud*); if he starts counting syllables and heeding the rules prosodists invent, writing verse becomes a pedantic game on a par with crossword puzzles.[20]

In *Briggflatts*, Bunting is not only inventing his own forms, but opposes contemporary poetry that writes to a prescribed metrical form; to "heeding the rules" like a pedant. His natural rhythms are rooted in the environment and in human work that takes place in that environment, and they distinguish his works from those of his more popular contemporaries. Though his experimental poetics link him with other modernists, his rural, local, and natural sounds distinguish his work *even* from that of his predecessors. So, not only is his poetry highly crafted—the product of a long labour—but it is also about work. Bunting believed his sound-centred poetics made his work more accessible to a wider audience, as well as granting more freedom to the poet. He worried in 1932 that, due to the dominance of upper-class writers, the gulf between literature and "the British subject" was "unpassable."[21]

Rather than turning to established forms, Bunting's sounds and rhythms are derived from nature, and from humans' interaction with nature, in the way we see in the opening verses of *Briggflatts*. Work is essential, Bunting's poem suggests, to this process and transformation. Later, the poem comments wryly on the job of the poet in modern society, and asks: "But who will entune a bogged orchard"? (69). The music of the poem comes from "entuning" the natural scenes and the historical events of the poem, writing them into verse. Bunting believed that

---

[20] Basil Bunting, *Basil Bunting on Poetry*, ed. Peter Makin (Baltimore: Johns Hopkins University Press, 1999), 36.

[21] Basil Bunting, "English Poetry Today," *Poetry*, vol. 39, no. 5 (1932), 265.

sound was of primary importance to the poem, sometimes even asserting that it was the only "meaning" worth looking for in a poem.[22]

It is significant that Bunting continues to write about poetry and work in the 1960s. In this era of cultural optimism, and a shakeup of regional arts councils, the public were enjoying a burgeoning poetry scene, featuring the proliferation of small press publications, new bookshops dedicated to supplying poetry magazines and pamphlets from across the UK and from further afield. People—particularly young people—were attending small, underground readings. There is an inherent craftiness in this small-scale production that bypasses the alienating production process of mass culture. But the trouble lies in supporting these activities in a big—and growing—capitalist society, and this is where the Chairman of Newcastle Arts Society, quoted at the top speaking to Tom Pickard in Bunting's satirical poem, comes in. Even in this era of optimism, and apparent institutional beneficence towards the arts, poets had to fight for their reputation as artists, and as workers. Tom Pickard's journals—recounted in *Work Conchy* (2009); *More Pricks Than Prizes* (2010); and "Kronika: A Warsaw Journal" (*Chicago Review*, Summer/Autumn 2015)—reveal a constant struggle with the establishment to keep his poetic projects going. Bunting, who had reached retirement age by the 1960s, endured financial hardship in his later years. Asides from a stint working for British Intelligence in Tehran, which he enjoyed, finding paid work seems to have been the scourge of Bunting's poetry-writing.

Bunting's preface to *Collected Poems* in 1968 gives a rare insight into his poetry-making process:

> With sleights learned from others and an ear open to melodic analogies I have set down words as a musician pricks his score, not to be read in silence but to trace in the air a pattern of sound that may sometimes, I hope, be pleasing.[23]

Although he is typically wry in implying his work is a kind of trickery, the craftiness implied by a sleight of hand also signals his more sincere beliefs about training and working as a poet. "Sleights" refers to specifically manual practice, and the propensity to wield a tool, and so

---

[22] Jonathan Williams and Basil Bunting, *Descant on Rawthey's Madrigal: Conversations with Basil Bunting* (Lexington: Gnomon Press, 1968), 32.

[23] Basil Bunting, "Preface," in *Collected Poems* (London: Fulcrum Press, 1968), 9.

its use here connects poetic skill to other, more physical, kinds of craft. Bunting writes, of poetry, "[i]f I ever learned the trick of it, it was mostly from poets long dead."[24] This modest, even dismissive, preface, a sleight of hand in itself, is easy to overlook, but his employment of the word, "sleights" at the outset of his *Collected Poems* is a key to understanding his work as a whole. In bringing to mind hands and handiwork, dexterity, and skilled manual work, Bunting's definitive "sleights" indicate the uniting concern of Bunting's life works: the link between the hand and the head forged by wholesome work, or craft.

Pre-empting the mason of *Briggflatts*, the 1941 poem, "These tracings from a world that's dead," aligns poetic work with the handicraft of the stonemason, who writes in stone. The mason's work is described as "sharp study and long toil" (129). In *Briggflatts* delivers an epiphany in Part I:

> Words!
> Pens are too light.
> Take a chisel to write.
> (63)

Bunting's representation of poetry-making as a form of skilled work bridges the divide between manual and intellectual labour. The interaction between human and nature envisaged in *Briggflatts* is an example of the means by which humans form an intellectual and physical relationship with the objective world, as Marx explains in *Capital*:

> Labour is, first of all, a process between man and nature, a process by which man, through his own actions, mediates, regulates and controls the metabolism between himself and nature. He sets in motion the natural forces which belong to his own body, his arms, legs, head and hands, in order to appropriate the materials of nature in a form adapted to his own needs. Through this movement he acts upon external nature and changes it, and in this way he simultaneously changes his own nature. He develops the potentialities slumbering within nature, and subjects the play of its forces to his own sovereign power.[25]

---

[24] Bunting, "Preface," in *Collected Poems*, 9.

[25] Karl Marx, *Capital: A Critique of Political Economy*, translated by Ben Fowkes and edited by Ben Fowkes and David Fernbach, Vol. 1 (London and New York: Penguin Books in association with New Left Review, 1981), 283.

Marx stresses the processual, as opposed to the merely productive, nature of work: time, energy, and human life go into the making of a commodity. In this extract, he outlines how primary the relationship between human beings and nature is: it gives humans a "sovereign power" and thus the freedom that comes with autonomy: the freedom of self-expression in work and the freedom to make and exchange the products of one's own labour. Marx describes labour as essential to the development of this relationship: it defines the human's spatial and physical boundaries; thus a sense of self, being, space, and purpose are created by work.

The work in *Briggflatts* that is attuned to the rhythms of nature represents the relationship a non-alienated worker has with their world. In aligning the work of the poet with the work of the stonemason, Bunting shows that even in 1965 an alternative model for work is possible, and it may be through writing poetry that a worker can find this potential for sovereignty, or freedom in work.

Morris's craft-oriented take on Marxist socialist thought has even more in common with Bunting's particular brand of non-conformist Quaker socialism, than Marx does. Morris, talking about craft, the so-called "Lesser Arts," or decorative arts, explains how craft practice contributes to a worker's well-being by forging a relationship between human and natural work:

> it is one of the chief uses of decoration, the chief part of its alliance with nature, that it has to sharpen our dulled senses in this matter: for this end are those wonders of intricate patterns interwoven, those strange forms invented, which men have so long delighted in[.][26]

His description of intricate patterns and strange forms, and an "alliance with nature" could be applied to *Briggflatts*, and thus the poem might reasonably count as a craft, according to Morris's definition. Morris's lecture, given in 1877 to the Trades Guild of Learning, represents one of his early forays into socialist thought, as he started to politicise his ideas about craft.

Bunting, like Morris, and Marx, was concerned about the well-being, or happiness, of the worker, including both the producer and consumer

[26]William Morris, "The Lesser Arts," in *Stories in Prose, Stories in Verse, Shorter Poems, Lectures and Essays*, ed. G. D. H. Cole (London: Nonesuch Press, 1934), 496.

of poetic works: he wrote in 1953 to Zukofsky that he wished "more people would have written in a way to give them pleasure."[27]

I will end by drawing upon a thinker with a different background to Bunting's, but whose thoughts on the political and liberatory potential of poetic practice contributes an uncharacteristically optimistic—but welcome—message to poets writing in the modernist tradition, who wish to reinstate the work of the poet as a type of work: one that is vital to society. Bunting spoke about the poet's role in society in his last interview in 1984. The excerpt, that mentions craft, politics, legislation, society, funding, and the work of poetry, weaves together the main threads of this chapter.

> [Interviewer]: Can you say how you define a poet's place in a society like this one? Are you an unacknowledged legislator of the race? an ordinary bloke with a job of work like any other? a vestigial craftsman? an oligarch? a democrat? It often seems to me that it requires more confidence than one can afford to find a *place* nowadays, so maybe you don't even think about these things?
>
> [Bunting]: There is no provision made for poets in this society. I try, under very difficult conditions, to maintain the art.[28]

In his essay "On Lyric Poetry and Society," Adorno refers to a system in which the practice of poetry-making, as a whole, is only permitted to the privileged members of society:

> poetic subjectivity is itself indebted to privilege: the pressures of struggle for survival allow only a few human beings to grasp the universal through immersion in the self or to develop as autonomous subjects capable of freely expressing themselves.[29]

However, Adorno suggests that a worker's articulation can nonetheless prevail, despite the prohibition of wholeness under the system of divided labour. He writes that of the need to express the consciousnesses of "those who stand alienated"—the workforce—who have the

---

[27] Reagan, "Basil Bunting," 232.

[28] Andrew McAllister and Sean Figgis, "Basil Bunting: The Last Interview [1984]," *Bete noire*, vol. 2, no. 3 (1987), 127.

[29] Theodor Adorno, "On Lyric Poetry and Society," in *Notes to Literature Volume One*, ed. Rolf Tiedemann (New York: Columbia University Press, 1991), 45.

greatest right "to grope for the sounds in which sufferings and dreams are welded." "This inalienable right has asserted itself again and again, in forms however impure, mutilated, fragmentary, and intermittent."[30] *Briggflatts*, with its proliferation of sources, sounds and voices, and its rejection of prescribed metrics, is surely an example of such a fragmentary form, and of late modernist work, that thus aligns itself with experimental poetics, progressive politics, and the promise of better work for the world.

WORKS CITED

Adorno, Theodor. "On Lyric Poetry and Society." In *Notes to Literature Volume One*, ed. Rolf Tiedemann, Vol. 1, 37–54. New York: Columbia University Press, 1991.

Bunting, Basil. *Basil Bunting on Poetry*. Edited by Peter Makin. Baltimore: Johns Hopkins University Press, 1999.

———. *Collected Poems*. London: Fulcrum Press, 1968.

———. *Complete Poems*. Edited by Richard Caddel. Newcastle upon Tyne: Bloodaxe, 2000.

———. "English Poetry Today." *Poetry*, vol. 39, no. 5 (1932): 264–271.

———. "Yeats Recollected." *Agenda*, vol. 12 (1974): 36–47.

Burton, Richard. *A Strong Song Tows Us: The Life of Basil Bunting*. Oxford: Infinite Ideas, 2013.

Delbanco, Nicholas, and Laurence Goldstein. *Writers and Their Craft: Short Stories & Essays on the Narrative*. Detroit: Wayne State University Press, 1991.

Greaves, Sara R. "A Poetics of Dwelling: In Basil Bunting's *Briggflatts*." *Cercles*, vol. 12 (2005): 64–78.

Marx, Karl. *Capital: A Critique of Political Economy*. Translated by Ben Fowkes and edited by Ben Fowkes and David Fernbach, Vol. 1: Penguin Classics. London and New York: Penguin Books in association with New Left Review, 1981.

McAllister, Andrew, and Sean Figgis. "Basil Bunting: The Last Interview [1984]." *Bete noire*, vol. 2, no. 3 (1987): 22–50.

Morris, William. "The Lesser Arts." In *Stories in Prose, Stories in Verse, Shorter Poems, Lectures and Essays* (Centenary edition), edited by G. D. H. Cole, 494–516. London: Nonesuch Press, 1934.

Pound, Ezra. *ABC of Reading*. London: Faber and Faber, 1991 [1934].

———. *The Cantos* (New Collected edition). London: Faber and Faber, 1968 [1964].

---

[30] Adorno, "On Lyric Poetry and Society," 45.

———. *The Cantos of Ezra Pound.* New York: New Directions, 1993 [1948].

Reagan, Dale. "Basil Bunting Obiter Dicta." In *Basil Bunting: Man and Poet,* edited by Carroll F. Terrell, 229–274. Orono: National Poetry Foundation, 1981.

———. "An Interview with Basil Bunting." *Montemora,* vol. 3 (1977): 66–80.

Sennett, Richard. *The Craftsman.* New Haven and London: Yale University Press, 2008.

Williams, Jonathan, and Basil Bunting. *Descant on Rawthey's Madrigal: Conversations with Basil Bunting.* Lexington: Gnomon Press, 1968.

Wootten, William. "Basil Bunting: 'Uneasy Mason'." *English,* vol. 51, no. 201 (2002): 235–259.

CHAPTER 6

Art Takes All My Time: Work in the Poetry and Prison Writing of Anna Mendelssohn

Eleanor Careless

"Art made me thin," writes Anna Mendelssohn, "art takes all my time."[1] The all-consuming work of Mendelssohn's poetry is indelibly marked by her own experience of imprisonment and gendered discrimination. Mendelssohn (1948–2009) was an undergraduate at the University of Essex in 1968, and by 1970 she was deeply involved in activism around issues from industrial relations to internment in Ireland to the women's liberation movement (WLM).[2] In 1971 she was arrested as an alleged member of the urban guerrillas known as the Angry Brigade, and in 1972, she was

[1] Anna Mendelssohn, *Implacable Art* (Applecross, WA and Great Wilbraham, UK: Folio and Equipage, 2000), 42. My thanks to the Anna Mendelssohn Estate for their generous permission to quote and reproduce poems, artwork, and archival material at length; to Sara Crangle, for her suggestions and revisions; and to Hannah Proctor and the Under the Moon reading group for productive discussions around some of these texts.

[2] Christopher Walker, "Influences That Shaped the Philosophy of the Angry Brigade: People for Whom Protest Became a Profession," *The Times*, 7 December 1972, 18.

E. Careless (✉)
University of Sussex, Brighton, UK

© The Author(s) 2019
J. L. Walton and E. Luker (eds.), *Poetry and Work*,
Modern and Contemporary Poetry and Poetics,
https://doi.org/10.1007/978-3-030-26125-2_6

convicted of conspiracy to cause explosions and sentenced to ten years in Holloway Women's Prison. For women in Britain, inside and outside the prison, the 1970s were a crucial and transformative decade, bracketed by the first national conference of the WLM in 1970 and the election of Margaret Thatcher in 1979. In 1971, Holloway Prison, the largest women's prison in Europe, was transformed from a Victorian panopticon into a secure mental hospital. In the same decade, the Equal Pay Act (EPA) of 1970 and the Sex Discrimination Act (SDA) of 1975 were passed by Harold Wilson's Labour government. While these legislative watersheds for gender equality in the workplace marked an important political shift, they are as notable for their limitations and failures as for their successes. A small number of writers and artists have addressed the effects and limits of these events in their work. One of these is the poet, artist, and activist Anna Mendelssohn, for whom work is inextricable from its gendered dimensions. Her poetry is highly aware of its status not only as work, but as women's work, and participates in the "gender-marked lyric genre" of experimental British poetry that Linda Kinnahan associates with Denise Riley, Wendy Mulford, and Geraldine Monk.[3] In Mendelssohn's materialist poetics "woman uses syntax like a broom" and "i am found reading negative dialectics in laundry rooms," domesticity cross-wired with the production of poetry.[4]

The work of this work is to resist forms of silencing and oppression through frenetic and abjected productivity. Although only a small portion of her writing was published during her lifetime, Mendelssohn was a prolific writer and artist. Her archive stands testament to the extent and urgency of this process of production: the thousands of poems and drawings held in her archive are scribbled on the dust jackets of books and in the margins of letters, seemingly on the first thing that came to hand. Mendelssohn's was a punishing productivity: in a letter from 1987, she writes "I feel as though most of my life has been spent in voluntary (hard) labour."[5] A poem from *Implacable Art* confesses to being "[a]ddicted to dealing in out of work hours / Will not leave when

---

[3] Linda A. Kinnahan, *Lyric Interventions: Feminism, Experimental Poetry, and Contemporary Discourse* (Iowa: University of Iowa, 2004), 182.

[4] Mendelssohn, *Implacable Art*, 3; Grace Lake, *Tondo Aquatique* (Cambridge: Equipage, 1997) [unpaginated].

[5] Letter to Herbie Butterfield, 2 March 1987, SxMs109/3/A/1/3. All references beginning "SxMs" refer to the files of Mendelssohn's correspondence housed in the Anna Mendelssohn Archive, University of Sussex Special Collections, The Keep, Brighton, UK.

asked to, works on."[6] Without being "productive" in a capitalist sense, Mendelssohn can write with complete sincerity, "I always Overwork."[7] Traces of incarceration, political and gendered oppression, and economic hardship accrue across this body of work, which stands almost entirely outside any direct relation to capital. This is marginal work, work made in the margins of the establishment and of salaried labour, but also work of felt necessity, not profit. As Mendelssohn says, "[p]oetry was never a by-product for me."[8] Her only full-length published collection, *Implacable Art,* everywhere inscribes and confronts questions of gender and incarceration, and returns several times to the concept of "a Law to ensure her Equality" and the tensions and contradictions that surround the implementation of "Equal Opportunities for Women."[9] Drawing on archival as well as literary sources, this chapter will situate Mendelssohn's poetic responses to legislation for gender equality in the workplace alongside—because inseparable from—her prison and post-prison work. My argument builds on Judith Scheffler's insight that "women's prisons are paradigmatic of woman's place in society."[10]

The Limits of the Law

In poetry and correspondence, Mendelssohn satirises the limits of gender equality legislation and its abuses, and brings the temporal constitution of the political subject into sharp focus. A poem that contests legal jurisdiction and its capacity to effect social change reproduces what may be read as the accepted view that

> Before the Equal Opportunities Act became Law
> (over twenty years ago) women were at a decided disadvantage. There
> is no question about that. It is absolutely and incontrovertibly true.[11]

---

[6] Mendelssohn, *Implacable Art,* 84.

[7] Letter to Rod Mengham, undated, SxMs109/3/A/1/34.

[8] Letter to Noella Smith, undated, SxMs109/3/A/1/58.

[9] Mendelssohn, *Implacable Art,* 131.

[10] Judith A. Scheffler, ed., *Wall Tappings: An International Anthology of Women's Prison Writings 200 to the Present,* 1st ed. (New York: Feminist Press at the City University of New York, 2002 [1986]), xxiii.

[11] Mendelssohn, *Implacable Art,* 78.

The clipped understatement of "decided disadvantage" undercuts the sincerity of these lines, which take aim at the assumption that gendered inequality in the workplace is readily resolved through legislature. The "Equal Opportunities Act" appears to stand in as a conflation of both the EPA and the SDA, in keeping with the poem's suspension of formal reality. Through the repeated insistence upon an illusory clear-cut distinction between a regressive "before" and enlightened "after," the poem suggests that "in order to understand the background to the legislation one must understand the conditions of discrimination prior to 1976," that is, "Before the Equal Opportunities Act became Law."[12] A letter to Mendelssohn's friend and publisher Peter Riley dating from around 1993 also satirises the illusion of legal efficacy secured by the clean-cut notion of the "before" of the "Equal Opportunities Act, when a girl poet could not be included in the realms of poetry without being solicited for sex."[13] Here, Mendelssohn satirically imagines the prohibition against the solicitation of female poets as a clause in the statutes, as well as including "poetry" within the jurisdiction of the act, that is, as work.

What had been "before" was the entrenchment of the denial of the rights of women in the very foundation of British democracy. Albie Sachs and Joan Hoff Wilson make this argument in 1978: "The English common law which had so often been extolled as being the embodiment of human freedom, had in fact proved the main intellectual justification for the avowed and formal subordination of women."[14] In this conception, there is no "before," as the same legal apparatus used to guarantee gender equality is enmeshed in patriarchal, heteronormative logics. Feminist analysis of the efficacy of gender equality law reveals the extent of this enmeshment. For example, the "feminist disillusionment with the inability [...] of the EPA to achieve parity between male and female wages" is well documented.[15] The impetus for the EPA came from women's industrial action at the Ford car-manufacturing factory in Dagenham

[12] K. O'Donovan and E. Szyszczak, eds., *Equality and Sex Discrimination Law* (Oxford: Blackwell, 1988), 21.

[13] Letter to Peter Riley, undated, SxMs109/3/A/1/52/1.

[14] A. Sachs and J. H. Wilson, *Sexism and the Law: A Study of Male Beliefs and Judicial Bias* (Oxford: Martin Robertson, 1978), 40–41.

[15] O'Donovan and Szyszczak, *Equality and Sex Discrimination Law*, 121; see also Anne E. Morris and Susan M. Nott, *Working Women and the Law: Equality and Discrimination in Theory and Practice* (London and New York: Routledge, 1991); Anne Morris and

in 1968, but the act did not address the key issue raised by the women strikers. Although the EPA enshrined the right to equal pay for equal work, women's work continued to be valued, and therefore paid, less than men's. The SDA, which outlawed sex discrimination, should have reinforced the terms of the EPA, but its enforcement machinery rapidly transpired to be inadequate.[16] Both acts were widely considered to be "largely unsuccessful" and became illustrative of the limits of law and legal method to combat gendered oppression.[17]

Evidence of Mendelssohn's own commitment to women's unions in the 1970s can be found in the 1971 issue of the underground newspaper *Strike!*, to which Mendelssohn contributed a couple of small articles on unionising nightcleaners and the threat of deportation—still current today—faced by striking migrant workers. Her first piece is highly critical of the reluctance of the Transport and General Workers' Union (T&G) to support women workers: "Most women do not belong to Unions and where they do the Unions dont [sic] give a fuck about their fights for higher wages, against sackings, and for better working conditions."[18] In her second piece, she focuses on the striking "Punjab Sikhs and black workers" who face the threat of deportation, and the T&G's failure to take action to protect migrant workers.[19] In her opening speech

---

Therese O'Donnell, *Feminist Perspectives on Employment Law* (London: Cavendish, 1999); Nicola Lacey, "From Individual to Group?" in *Discrimination: The Limits of Law*, ed. Bob Hopple and Erika M. Szyszczak (London and New York: Mansell, 1992), 99–124; Susan Atkins, "The Sex Discrimination Act 1975: The End of a Decade," *Feminist Review*, vol. 24 (Autumn 1986), 57–70; and Nicola Lacey, "Legislation Against Sex Discrimination Questions from a Feminist Perspective," *Journal of Law and Society*, vol. 14 (1987), 411–421.

[16] The SDA's largest section, Part II, dealt with discrimination in the workplace; it also aimed to promote equality of opportunity between the sexes. Cf. *Sex Discrimination Act 1975*, accessed 17 November 2016, www.legislation.gov.uk/ukpga/1975/65; Anna Coote and Tess Gill, *Women's Rights: A Practical Guide*, 3rd ed. (Harmondsworth: Penguin, 1981), 23, 41.

[17] Carol Smart, *Feminism and the Power of Law* (New York: Routledge, 1989), 138; Stephanie Palmer, "Critical Perspectives on Women's Rights: The European Convention on Human Rights and Fundamental Freedoms," in *Feminist Perspectives on the Foundational Subjects of Law*, ed. Anne Bottomley (London: Cavendish, 1996), 225.

[18] Anon, "T&G Plays Hard to Get," *Strike!* no. 0 (1971) [unpaginated]. Mendelssohn asserts her authorship in trial transcripts.

[19] Anon [Mendelssohn], "T&G Plays Hard to Get."

in her defence, given in court in 1972, Mendelssohn explains that she wrote these articles after hearing May Hobbes (a nightcleaner who set up the Cleaners Action group) speak at a meeting.[20] The trial transcripts demonstrate the extent to which recent activism around women's work and other industrial disputes was closely imbricated with Mendelssohn's criminal conviction and subsequent imprisonment. The prosecution used evidence of non-violent activist work as corroborating, and even implicating, evidence for acts of political violence.

Mendelssohn's later poetry, which frequently disavows any association with political violence or the Angry Brigade, is concerned not with industrial work but with "creative work which is not even recognized as work."[21] Throughout the "Equal Opportunities Act" poem, which is titled "My Chekhov's Twilight World," a characteristically ludic defiance continues to undercut politically heteronormative categories and "the Law":

> pan & tilt. weft & warp. the earth does tilt. to define me as straight
> ignores the fact that my mother's family were Russian. Polish Russian
> relations have had a painful history. I was in the pain of that history.
> And I knew it to the last fibre of my body and soul. So whom you saw
> Standing there without the faintest conviction apart from the Drag &
>
> and pull of miscarriage was a Pole from Seville. Methought I had a Beard
> coming on twas so fulsome
>
> ......
>
>   I can't be Everywhere
> ensuring that no harm is done. My poetry is not the harmful type. It stems
> from the affections not their antithesis. Where I came from one requested a license
>
> to write. one did not suddenly Snatch momentum. At each stage there are
> moral considerations. Before the Equal Opportunities Act became Law
> (over twenty years ago) women were at a decided disadvantage. There
> is no question about that. It is absolutely and incontrovertibly true.
> I Live my life. I don't have two lives or five or nine. I have One Life

---

[20] Mendelssohn's opening speech in her defence (11 October 1972), SxMs109/2/D/5.

[21] Letter to Lynne Harries, undated, SxMs109/3/A/1/18. In her memoirs, Mendelssohn writes: "Give me money for poetry-readings and for publishing material. I work for what I am never paid for. I don't want charity." SxMs109/1/B/1/41.

My Own. And what I decide to do with my life is a matter between myself, my mind and the Law.

......

I doubted that the Law was pure.[22]

This tense, fractured lyric brings questions of history, identity, and ongoing harm into argumentative contact. A refusal of "straightness" in any form is evident in the "tilt," "warp," and "Drag" of these lines, which move across horizontal and vertical planes: "pan & tilt." The broken form and syntax troubles fixed categories of identity, as when "Drag" segues into "pull of miscarriage," or in the allusion to Shakespearean gender-bending: "Methought I had a Beard / coming on." A "Pole from Seville" likewise disrupts a straightforward alignment between race and identity. The poetic subject, moreover, is "in" the "painful history" of "Polish Russian relations," that is, as a descendant of victims of the Holocaust.[23] Through the half-submerged trauma of these historical intersections, which are as preoccupied with race as they are with gender, the poem approaches the "Equal Opportunities Act"—itself directly derived from the US Race Relations Act. The repetition of the "Law" refers back to but also away from these specific pieces of legislation and towards a more abstract notion of "the Law." To challenge the constitutive powers of the law at large, the poetic subject makes its own repeated claims to self-possession—"my life," 'My Own," "my mind." The repetition of "life," sometimes capitalised, sometimes not, alongside the "Law," suggests "life" in its criminal justice contexts: a life sentence. The flagrant repossession of "my life" "My Own" in these lines is shadowed by the threat of excessive (two, five, nine!) life sentences, and the perpetual negotiation between the unruly subject and the law which attempts to constitute her. A juridical speech-act, vested with considerable powers, takes place over a space of time that is not easily delimited; neither is

[22] Mendelssohn, *Implacable Art*, 78.

[23] Mendelssohn is highly cognisant of her own Russian-Jewish identity and the legacy of Nazism. Her poetry supplies an ongoing account of the complex intersections between Nazism and its enabling legal mechanisms.

its transformative effect upon its subject.[24] From a judge's sentence to the prescriptions of legislature, such as the Equal Opportunities Act which itself negotiates the non-legislative sentences of everyday interpellation, Mendelssohn's subject wryly locates herself and her volition in between all of these: "a matter between / myself, my mind and the Law." A resistance towards the law is palpable in the poetry of Mendelssohn's contemporaries such as Riley ("I won't place it or / describe it It *is* and refuses the law") and Mulford ("What in practice does it mean for [the woman writer] to talk about the revolutionary violation of the Law?").[25] The work of Mendelssohn's granular inscriptions of the "law" is to articulate and resist attempts to "define me as straight" in terms not only of gender, but of the political constitution of the subject, whether through categories of race, criminality, or labour legislation.

"My Chekhov's Twilight World" ends by troubling a term frequently deployed to police female sexuality: pure. To doubt that "the Law was pure" is to doubt its disinterest, or lack of bias. There are a number of instances spanning Mendelssohn's published and unpublished writing that trouble assertions of purity. In a poem from *viola tricolor* (1993), the poetic subject is conversely "accused of purity."[26] Processes of purification are closely associated with accusation and incarceration. In a letter, Mendelssohn writes of "having served a prison sentence in order to purify myself."[27] To her friend Kate Wheale, Mendelssohn writes that "purification has a social, ethnic historical echo which is very real still to me."[28] Purity, as theorised by Julia Kristeva (whose writings formed a notable part of Mendelssohn's library), "will be that which conforms to an established taxonomy."[29] Impurity "unsettles [purity], establishes

[24] Judith Butler, *Excitable Speech: A Politics of the Performative* (New York and London: Routledge, 1997), 3.

[25] Denise Riley, *Dry Air* (London: Virago), 19; Wendy Mulford, "Notes on Writing: A Marxist/Feminist Viewpoint," in *On Gender and Writing*, ed. Michelene Wandor (London: Pandora 1983), 31–41.

[26] Grace Lake, *viola tricolor* (Cambridge: Equipage, 1993) [unpaginated].

[27] Letter to Lynne Harries, June 1991, SxMs109/3/A/1/18.

[28] Letter to Kate Wheale, undated, SxMs109/3/A/1/64.

[29] Julia Kristeva, *Powers of Horror: An Essay on Abjection,* translated by Leon S. Goudiez (New York: Columbia University Press 1972), 98.

intermixture and disorder [...] the impure will be those that do not confine themselves to one element but point to admixture and confusion."[30] Mendelssohn's construal of legal impurity disturbs conventional alignments of taxonomy and order with systems of law more broadly, and in particular the putative neutrality of gender equality law. By placing an expression of scepticism regarding the purity of the law at the very end of "My Chekhov's Twilight World," the "Law" is coloured by the accumulative energies of the poem, its warping of taxonomical category, its inscriptions of legal inefficacy, and its temporal and prosodic drag.

In feminist accounts, the inefficacy of sex discrimination laws has been attributed in large part to an impoverished concept of "women's rights." Queer theorist Jasbir Puar and co-author Isabelle Barker understand this impoverishment in rights language as related to norms, and find that "feminist resistance to women's claims for universal rights stems from a concern that universality necessarily bears the markers of a parochial Western, patriarchal norm, masquerading as neutral."[31] The deep structures and norms that produce sex-based discrimination went mostly untouched by British equality laws, which reinforced the dichotomy between private and public; reified the categories of "women" and "men" through the establishment of men as the normative model; and made assimilationist demands that women act, and work, as men.[32] From its inauguration, the SDA was unabashedly justified through appeals to the productivity of the labour force. Home Secretary Roy Jenkins introduced the SDA by condemning gender inequality as "individual injustice and [a] waste [of] the potential talents of half our population at a time

---

[30] Kristeva, *Powers of Horror*, 98.

[31] Jasbir Puar and Isabelle Barker, "Feminist Problematization of Rights Language and Universal Conceptualizations of Human Rights," *Concilium International Journal for Theology*, vol. 5 (2002), 64–76 (?); also see Joan Scott, "Some More Reflections on Gender and Politics," in *Gender and the Politics of History* (New York: Columbia University Press, 1999), 215; and Lacey, "From Individual to Group?", 103–105.

[32] O'Donovan and Szyszczak, *Equality and Sex Discrimination Law*, 36, 43, 47.

when more than ever before we need to mobilise the skills and abilities of all our citizens."[33] Women were assimilated in the name of enhanced productivity, and deep, binary structures therefore remained in place.[34]

Another artistic response to the sex discrimination laws of the early 1970s—of which there are few—is *Women and Work: A Document on the Division of Labour in Industry*, a detailed sociological study of women's work in a metal box factory in Bermondsey. Conducted by artists Margaret Harrison, Kay Hunt, and Mary Kelly between 1973 and 1975, *Women and Work* was timed to coincide with the implementation of the EPA. The project draws together the stories of over 150 working women and supplies an account not only of their relationship to the workplace, but records the changes in this relationship brought about by the EPA. The piece is minimalist, compiled of charts, photocopied documents, type-written texts, punch-cards, wage slips, black and white photographs, and film footage. *Women and Work* displays not only records of women's work, but also of men's within the same factory, in order to show how the low-skilled, repetitive tasks were allocated predominantly to the female part of the workforce, and the more physical, supervisory work to the male. Interviews undertaken as part of the project found that while men talked readily about their factory work, women workers talked instead about the work they did at home, *after* work. Although the site of the project was the factory, that site was shifted "back to the domestic space" by the women workers: to the work after work.[35] "After work," in Leopoldina Fortunati's theory of gendered exploitation, is where that "'other' necessary labor time [...] supplied by the female houseworker" takes place in order "to transform exchange-values into directly consumable use-values."[36]

The history of *Women and Work* testifies to the general intermingling of art, activism, unionising, and politics in Britain in the early 1970s. Harrison, Hunt, and Kelly were involved in a group formed

---

[33] O'Donovan and Szyszczak, *Equality and Sex Discrimination Law*, 32.

[34] O'Donovan and Szyszczak, *Equality and Sex Discrimination Law*, 47.

[35] In an interview, Kelly recalls how "at first I looked it very sociologically but it became more and more obvious that you couldn't get rid of the irrationality of this event." Margaret Iversen, Douglas Crimp, and Homi K. Bhabha, *Mary Kelly* (London: Phaidon, 1997), 15.

[36] Leopoldina Fortunati, *The Arcane of Reproduction: Housework, Prostitution, Labour and Capital*, translated by Hilary Creek (New York: Autonomedia, 1995), 92. Fortunati's English translator, Hilary Creek, was one of Mendelssohn's co-defendants during the Stoke Newington Eight trial in 1972.

in 1972, the Women's Workshop of the Artist's Union, which aimed to advance women's causes within the union and end racial and sexual discrimination in the arts.[37] One of the actions proposed by the Women's Workshop was "to demand that art colleges hire female staff in proportion to the number of female students (could be enforced through the anti-discrimination bill)."[38] A project by the Hackney Flashers' feminist collective also called *Women and Work* (1975) combined documentary photography and statistics to make the conditions of women's work more visible. One caption from the project read: "All workers are exploited, some are more exploited than others."[39] This piece toured across Britain and abroad, including the 1977 Socialist Feminist International Conference in Paris.[40]

Produced apart from such collective projects, Mendelssohn's outsider poetry—doubly marginal, as non-mainstream writing *and* women's writing—satirises not only the judiciary, but organised activism and its hierarchies. "My Chekhov's Twilight World" states that "[i]t is / no disgrace for a practising artist to attend a formally chaired meeting / on Equal Opportunities for Women," and explains that "One of the reasons / Why meetings are Chaired is to contain and separate the personal emotions / of each member of the meeting."[41] The droll emphasis on the "chaired" nature of these meetings as a method of containment is linked in the poem to "the frameworks of democratic procedure." One possible reading is that the very political structures that enable liberal feminist organising are complicit in the perpetuation of gendered discrimination; but, contradictorily, an absence of "democratic procedure" leads to harm:

> I have attended many, many meetings
> which have all been chaired. Before my own reputation was damaged
> by people who refused to recognize the structural reasons for democratic
> procedure.

[37] For a brief history of the Women's Workshop of the Artist's Union see Hilary Robinson, ed., *Feminism Art Theory: An Anthology 1968–2000* (Oxford: 2001), 87.

[38] Robinson, *Feminism Art Theory*, 87–88.

[39] *Hackney Flashers*, accessed 17 November 2016, hackneyflashers.com/women-and-work-1975/.

[40] Paul Hill, *Three Perspectives on Photography* (London: Arts Council of Great Britain, 1979), 80–83.

[41] Mendelssohn, *Implacable Art*, 77.

There is a tension between the co-option of activism by traditional power structures and an anarchistic non-hierarchical model, baffling attempts at a single authoritative reading. Here is another "before" which alludes specifically to Mendelssohn's pre-1971, pre-prison life: "Before my own reputation was damaged." The series of bombings claimed by the British urban guerrillas known as the Angry Brigade between 1970 and 1972 prompted an unprecedented police crackdown on the counter-culture, and led to the longest criminal trial in Britain in the twentieth century. Arrested for alleged involvement with the violent activities of this nebulous organisation in 1971, Mendelssohn never recovered from the persecution and the imprisonment that followed.[42] Eight defendants, all in their early twenties, all social activists, stood accused of involvement in the bombings, and of these eight, four were acquitted of all charges. Although she maintained her innocence and defended herself in court, Mendelssohn was convicted along with three others of conspiracy to cause explosions and given a ten-year sentence.

VOLUNTARY (HARD) LABOUR

In 1971, when Mendelssohn was first incarcerated, the treatment of women prisoners in Britain was on the verge of significant change, and Holloway Women's Prison was at the heart of this transformation in penal policy and practice.[43] In 1968 the Prison Department took the decision to demolish Holloway Women's Prison, an imposing castle-like structure modelled on the Eastern Penitentiary in Philadelphia, and to rebuild a modern prison-hospital in its place. James Callaghan, the Home Secretary behind this extraordinary project of prison reform, voiced the therapeutic optimism which amounted to an official reclassification of female criminality: "[m]ost women in custody," in Callaghan's words, "require some form of [...] psychiatric treatment."[44] The aim was to install a rehabilitative penal regime based upon therapeutic principles that would treat its inmates not as prisoners, but as patients. The original Victorian

---

[42] Mendelssohn's memoirs record how she lived in relative poverty for the rest of her life: "I heard three operas. Two at Convent Garden and one at the Coliseum. I starved myself for the tickets." "One of the Forever Damned?" piece so titled, SxMs109/1/B/1/41.

[43] For a fuller account of Holloway's transformation, see Paul Rock, *Reconstructing a Women's Prison: The Holloway Redevelopment Project 1968–1988* (Oxford: Clarendon Press, 1996).

[44] Quoted by Rock, *Reconstructing A Women's Prison*, 106.

panopticon-like structure, with its tiered galleries of cells in wings radiating from a central point, would be replaced by a building that approximated a modern university campus—but with rather higher perimeter walls.[45] The rebuilt Holloway would act as the "hub of the female prison system."[46] Feminist criminologist Carol Smart finds the project symptomatic of a tendency to perceive female criminality as "irrational, irresponsible and largely unintentional behaviour, as an individual maladjustment to a well-ordered and consensual society."[47] This unprecedented psychiatric intervention in women's offending compounded the already compromised agency of the female criminal subject.[48] Due to considerable delays, the first buildings of the new prison were only opened in 1977. Mendelssohn would have spent the term of her incarceration in the old prison, even as building works and demolition went on in situ. In this period of transition, the operating prison was nominally treated as a "therapeutic community in waiting," but, under the pressures of an increased population and decreased capacity, it ended up being "torn between the imperatives of treatment and punishment."[49]

Even before the rebuild began, penal policy at Holloway aimed at resocialising incarcerated women into their normative social roles. A paper given at the 1970 WLM conference in Oxford recorded that

> large number[s] of women at Holloway are in on charges of defrauding Social Security [or for] child neglect... women are being punished for failing to live up to society's image of them as good mothers, when the society itself will not give them adequate means and facilities to do so.[50]

[45] Ben Weinreb, Christopher Hibbert, Julia Keay, and John Keay, eds., *The London Encyclopedia* (London: Macmillan, 2008), 409; Rock, *Reconstructing a Women's Prison*, 9, 13.

[46] Tony Madan, *Women, Prisons and Psychiatry* (Oxford: Heinemann, 1996), 7.

[47] Carol Smart, *Women Crime and Criminology: A Feminist Critique* (London: Routledge, 1977), 145.

[48] For psychiatrist Tony Maden, the New Holloway represented "the peak of psychiatric intervention in women's offending," 11, 8; as the prison abolitionist pressure group Radical Alternatives to Prison expressed it: "the 'bad' label is being replaced with a 'sick' label that is an even more insidious and degrading attack on the identity of an individual than before." Radical Alternatives to Prison (Holloway Campaign Group), *Alternatives to Holloway* (Christian Action Publications Ltd., 1972), 32.

[49] Rock, *Reconstructing a Women's Prison*, 211, 220.

[50] Raya Levin and Judith Brandt, "Women, Prison and Economic Independence," in *The Body Politic: Writings from the Women's Liberation Movement in Britain 1969–1972*, compiled by Michelene Wandor (London: Stage 1, 1972), 177–178.

Instead, in what is termed "the most pernicious irony of the prison process," "women in Holloway are often put through a course in management and child care, consisting of training in budgeting and diet"; and "the wing for child neglect offenders [in Holloway] is sprinkled with plastic doilies and ruffled curtains."[51] Angela Weir, one of Mendelssohn's co-defendants, wrote in *Spare Rib* in 1973 of how

> Work in Holloway is women's work. Packing pencils or machining clothes. Work training programmes are not even given lip service in Holloway as at least they are in men's prisons. Pay in Holloway is women's pay. Male prisoners earn up to 60p a week, women prisoners earn 25p a week.[52]

Questions of equal pay entered the walls of the prison, too: there are several mentions in Mendelssohn's prison notebooks of the imprisoned women organising for a basic rate of pay for their prison-work.[53] Weir also notes the difficulty of acquiring writing materials, "presumably because the prison doesn't expect women to write."[54] Enforced domesticity has long been a feature of female incarceration. Elaine Showalter records how old manacles in nineteenth-century Bethlem were, in a reformist spirit, converted into irons, in an "efficient transformation of restraint into domestic work."[55] As Weir puts it, "the society of women in prison becomes [...] a gross caricature of the position of women outside."[56]

The coercive mesh between the domestic and the carceral is a recurring motif in Mendelssohn's poetry. A poem that asserts that "I do not run the prison system" and demands that the interlocutor "Serve your own sentences" also recounts the speaker's domestic obligations: "cooking cooking cooking / corking corking clucking."[57] This warped repetition sounds like the frustrated boredom brought on by repetitive

---

[51] Levin and Brandt, "Women, Prison and Economic Independence," 175–178.

[52] Angela Weir, "When the Key Turns," *Spare Rib* (May 1973), 36–37.

[53] Exercise book, 24 February–2 May 1973, SxMs109/2/A/1.

[54] Weir, "When the Key Turns," 37.

[55] Elaine Showalter, *The Female Malady: Women, Madness and English Culture 1830–1980* (London: Virgo, 1985), 83.

[56] Weir, "When the Key Turns," 37; similar sentiments were expressed elsewhere in the underground press, i.e. "Everything in prison is a parody, a caricatured essence, of what happens in the outside world" ("women imprisoned," *Frendz* 3.30 [4 June 1971], 14).

[57] Mendelssohn, *Implacable Art*, 54.

domestic labour. The coalition between gendered domesticity and incarceration surfaces again in the long poem "1:3ng," where the speaker declares that "I am not going to stand there & tell him how my coloured pencils were taken & I was given a sewing machine," powerfully recalling the domesticated discipline much practised upon incarcerated women.[58] In a sonnet from Mendelssohn's pamphlet *Tondo Aquatique* (1997), published like all her work in the nineties under the name Grace Lake, the humdrum space of domestic labour—in this case, a laundry room—is re-imagined as a space of vitality and creativity:

> I am found reading negative dialectics in laundry rooms
> talking to sheets that take on a life of their own
> through the inspirational properties of starch & the light freight of
>   chartered flight
> we sing ooooooooooooo this world is unrecognizable.[59]

Academic and theoretical work is resituated within a domestic space which is also a creative space: "starch" and "sheets" carry the creative force of the poem. The farcical incursion of the philosophy of Theodor Adorno into the laundry room precipitates a movement "through" starch and sheets into flight and song, and a refusal to recognise the world as it is. In a less utopian vein, "talking to sheets" is identified a few lines before as the haunting effect of mental disorder and a conviction for conspiracy: "She was always a bit touched / She Talks to Inanimate Objects in the hope that they won't be mistaken / for conspirators." When Mendelssohn's poems make "allusion[s] to washing dishes," "ironing without irony," and "laundry rooms," these allusions are almost always in proximity to forms of criminality or punishment.[60] The washer of dishes is a **malfaisant,** a wrongdoer; those who do not undertake non-ironic ironing are "punished for poverty"; and the laundry is done by a "She" who is "suspected" of "something." The enmeshment of intellectual, creative, and domestic work figured here might be read as a version of what Fortunati describes as the female "work time

<hr>

[58] Grace Lake, "1:3ng," in *Gare du Nord: A Magazine of Poetry and Opinion from Paris,* ed. Douglas Oliver and Alice Notley, vol. 1, 1997.

[59] *Tondo Aquatique* [unpaginated].

[60] Mendelssohn, *Implacable Art,* 110; *Tondo Aquatique* [unpaginated]; "Cultural," *viola tricolor* [unpaginated].

Fig. 6.1 Anna Mendelssohn, *Implacable Art*, p. 7 (Courtesy of the Anna Mendelssohn Estate)

that is not easily separable from the time" of reproductive (domestic) work—framed and compounded by the legacy of persecution and imprisonment.[61]

The poem which begins "Art made me thin" similarly imagines "other worlds" and a work time that cannot be bracketed or clocked out from:

> Art made me thin, took me away, into other worlds,
> I was very quiet, art took all my time, i could
> do things, be a human being

"Art," in this conception, is a site of dialectical tension: consuming and sustaining, an enclosure and an escape. Many of the poems from *Implacable Art* are faced by intricate crypto-figurative line drawings whose heavy mass and sharp thin lines are held within a cell-like space (Fig. 6.1).

---

[61] Fortunati, 93.

Drawing, as well as writing, took "all" of Mendelssohn's post-prison time. Prison-work, for Mendelssohn, was not poetic work—that came after. Prison work began with the work of legal defence. Denied bail by the magistrate, Mendelssohn and most of her co-defendants were detained for over a year before being sentenced.[62] In court, Mendelssohn described prison conditions of "isolation and repression," prolonged confinement in a small cell, and, most crucially, no access to an adequate library or her co-defendants.[63] A sympathetic *Guardian* article reported that:

> [...] because it was unusual for women to defend themselves from prison the authorities at Holloway were not used to coping with the situation. At first it had been impossible to get the paper Anna Mendelson [and her co-defendant] Hilary Creek needed to prepare their defence.[64]

It is important to note that Mendelssohn and her fellow defendants, unlike the majority of prisoners in Holloway, were elite prisoners, politicised, aware of their rights, their voices amplified by the extensive media coverage of the trial. Mendelssohn's *Guardian* obituary recalls her extraordinarily "impassioned and eloquent self-defence at the Old Bailey" that took a day and a half of court time.[65] The WLM considered self-defence to be "an expression of the politics of women's liberation," a refusal to let paternalistic authority do all the talking.[66] Legal work, in this understanding, was emancipatory. However, the work of the women defendants was made harder than that of their male counterparts held in Brixton prison due not only to the gendered bureaucracy of the criminal justice system, but to the misogyny of the national media. Media coverage of the trial focused disproportionately on the female defendants, and featured sensational headlines such as "Bomb case Anna," "The Bomb

---

[62] "Woman on Plot Charge is Refused Bail," *The Times,* 18 May 1972, 4.

[63] Jill Tweedie, "The Trials and Tribulations of Preparing a Vital Defence: One Over the Eight," *The Guardian,* 6 November 1972, 13.

[64] Jackie Leishman, "Defendant Tells Jury: 'I Oppose Bombing on Political Grounds,'" *The Guardian,* 17 November 1972, 20.

[65] Peter Riley, "Anna Mendelssohn Obituary," *The Guardian,* 15 December 2009, www.theguardian.com/theguardian/2009/dec/15/anna-mendelssohn-obituary; Gordon Carr, *The Angry Brigade* (Oakland, CA: PM Press, 2010), 193–195.

[66] Levin and Brandt, "Women, Prison and Economic Independence," 253.

Girls," "Terror Girl Anna," and "Sex Orgies in the Cottage of Blood."[67] Mendelssohn's plea for the trial to be deferred in the face of huge amounts of negative publicity was rejected by the magistrate.[68] Mendelssohn herself sums up, in her statement to the magistrate, how her pre-trial detainment inhibited her defence: "although the law book states that we are innocent until proven guilty, we are in effect serving a sentence right now." The conditions in which the defendants undertook their defence work is reprised in a poem from *Implacable Art* as "Guilty before proven innocent."[69] Parodying the legal principle of innocence, this lyrical inversion critiques the supposedly impartial state of being "before the law."

There is scarce material documenting Mendelssohn's time inside Holloway Prison. The Anna Mendelssohn archive holds twenty exercise and drawing books which Mendelssohn used during her incarceration, but many of the pages are blank, and any writing tends to be brief and unsystematic. These slim, barely-used regulation-issue notebooks rebuff the myth of the prolific and productive writer behind bars, epitomised by male authors from Oscar Wilde to Ezra Pound, Antonio Gramsci to George Jackson. In 1991, Mendelssohn wrote that "Prison debilitated my writing—"; and in another letter, she asks

> do you think I learnt to write poetry in prison? I know that there are poets in prison [...] I don't like to be rounded-up and genre'd as a prison poet. I did not start writing in prison.[70]

To refuse the genre of "prison poet" is to trouble, again, questions of origins, of a "before" and "after." Most of Mendelssohn's poetry was published in or after 1985, some years after her release, but Mendelssohn alludes to her "early" pre-prison poetry more than once.[71] A short poem

---

[67] "Bomb Case Anna," *The Daily Mail*, 26 March 1973, 6; "The Bomb Girls," *The Daily Mirror*, 7 December 1972; "Terror Girl Anna," *The Daily Mirror*, 25 February 1977, 5; quoted in Steve Chibnall, *Law-and-Order News: An Analysis of Crime Reporting in the British Press* (Routledge: London, 2001), 114–115.

[68] Chibnall, *Law-and-Order News*, 114–115.

[69] Mendelssohn, *Implacable Art*, 116.

[70] Letter to Lynne Harries, June 1991, SxMs109/3/A/1/18; letter to Ian Patterson, undated, SxMs109/3/A/1/47.

[71] Letter to Lynne Harries, June 1991, SxMs109/3/A/1/18; a letter to Noella Smith, undated, records the "confiscation" of Mendelssohn's early poetry by the police, SxMs109/3/A/1/58; in a letter to Denise Riley, Mendelssohn claims that "I began writing poetry in earnest in 1966" (undated, SxMs109/3/A/1/51).

by "Anna" published by the magazine *Frendz* in 1972 alongside a double page spread on "Holloway: From the Inside Out" seems very likely to be a Mendelssohn prison poem, but the authorship is not certain.[72] There are drafts of poems as well as journalistic entries scattered through the prison notebooks, but these fragments are often whimsical and rarely developed at length. The lines "prison wall: pigeon perch / Prison wall bigger than us" begin to play with scale and deflationary tactics.[73] "The orders look like bars to me / They fix into the Wall / and once locked, stay locked" intimates an equivalence between speech acts and prison bars.[74] There is a fleeting assertion that "la poesie est la liberte" but the notes that follow trouble the possibility of emancipation: "LA PEUR C'EST UNE PRISON PLUS MAUVAIS QUE LA PRISON" ("fear is a prison that is worse than prison itself").[75] The implication is that the prison reaches further than the cell walls. Another journalistic entry offers no further detail than "Tied. Tired. Sick."[76] A quasi-poetic entry from 1975 records the suffocating monotony of prison life that "debilitated" Mendelssohn's ability to write:

> can't do anything. can't sleep can't read
> can't concentrate [?] battling for attention
> body screaming to move intellect impotent
> advice useless. Suffocated. Miserable.
> Makes me sad to unbearable. Want friends
> love, no more fear, care of [?]. Want sleep.
> What's happened? mind a prey [?] blank.
> lack of stimulus. lack of everything.[77]

Prison life evidently debilitates not only Mendelssohn's writing, but her capacity to sleep, read, focus, indeed to think at all. Other accounts of Holloway describe it as a "deadening environment."[78] The frequently

[72] *Frendz*, 26 May 1972, 8.

[73] Exercise book, 1974, SxMs109/2/A/3.

[74] Exercise book, 1974, SxMs109/2/A/3.

[75] Exercise book, April 1974, SxMs109/2/A/9.

[76] Exercise book, September 1974, SxMs109/2/A/5.

[77] Exercise book, from December 1974 to December 1975, 6 January 1975, SxMs109/2/A/6.

[78] *Time and Time Again: Women in Prison.* Nina Ward with Women & The Law Collective (1986).

illegible handwriting of this entry stands in contrast to the highly stylised hand evident throughout the post-prison notebooks. Similar accounts of the utter paralysis of prison life in the early 1970s are recorded by women writers such as prison abolitionist Angela Davis, who during her 1971–1972 detention in New York City Women's Detention Center found that

> [...] jails and prisons are deadly places. There was the mesmerizing inanity of television; a few boring high school texts, some mysteries and a lot of unbelievably bad fiction. The women could write if they wished, but the small notepaper, which was seldom available, discouraged serious writing in favour of casual notes which would be censored anyway before they were mailed. Even getting hold of a pencil could be an extensive and complex undertaking.[79]

Davis foregrounds the difficulty of obtaining writing materials, rather than the difficulty of writing itself (Davis herself wrote an essay, "Reflections on the Black Woman's Role in the Community of Slaves," while in prison). She also notes that the "overwhelmingly sexist" presence of a "washing machine, clothes dryer and ironing paraphernalia" that were always readily available.[80]

> [...] the 'reasoning' behind this was presumably that women [...] lack an essential part of their existence if they are separated from their domestic chores. The men's linens and jail clothes were sent elsewhere for laundering; the women were expected to tend to their own.[81]

For the left-wing journalist Ulrike Meinhof, imprisoned in Stammheim prison in 1972 for her involvement with the revolutionary Red Army Faction, prison "was grim—i COULD not write— EVERYTHING was just rubbish, mincemeat, not in my head but on paper."[82] Leith Passmore has written of how "it was in prison that writing failed Ulrike

---

[79] Angela Y. Davis, *Angela Davis: An Autobiography* (New York: International Publishers, 1974), 308–309.

[80] Davis, *An Autobiography*, 309.

[81] Davis, *An Autobiography*, 308–309.

[82] German Federal Archive, Holding 362, File 339:XI/20.

Meinhof."[83] A poem written by Meinhof during her incarceration, presented under the heading "letter from a prisoner in the death wing," replicates some of the incoherence and fragmentation of Mendelssohn's diary entry[84]:

> The feeling that your head is exploding (the feeling the top of your skull should really tear apart,   burst wide open)-
> [...]
> The feeling you are growing mute -
>
> Sentence structure, grammar, syntax - are out of control. When you write, just two lines, you can   hardly remember the beginning of the first line when you finish the second-
>
> The feeling of burning out inside -
> [...]
> Raging aggression, for which there is no outlet. That the worst.[85]

Meinhof here records her rapidly dwindling ability to articulate her experience and her anger. Unlike Mendelssohn, Meinhof had already had a long and high-profile journalistic career before being imprisoned, and was held in solitary confinement for long periods of several months at a time, in a soundproofed white cell lit 24/7 with bare fluorescent bulbs.[86] Mendelssohn did not experience this degree of prison torture, but does record "weekly interrogations" at Holloway, strip searches, her perpetual sense of injustice ("I didn't even agree with what I was in there for"), her increasing ill-health, and her resistance to prison psychiatry—refusing to take drugs, undergo treatment, or accept the label of "psychopath."[87]

---

[83]Leith Passmore, *Ulrike Meinhof and the Red Army Faction: Performing Terrorism* (New York: Palgrave, 2011), 13.

[84]Passmore, *Ulrike Meinhof*, 75.

[85]Ulrike Meinhof, "Letter from a Prisoner in the Isolation Wing, June 16, 1972 to February 9, 1973" cited in Karin Bauer, ed., *Everybody Talks About the Weather... We Don't* (New York: Seven Stories Press, 2008), 77–79.

[86]Amanda Third, "Imprisonment and Excessive Femininity: Reading Ulrike Meinhof's Brain," *Parallax*, vol. 16, no. 4 (2010), 83–100.

[87]"[...] neither did I undergo any psychiatric treatment, neither did I take the prison's drugs [...] according to the Home Office Psychiatrist whom I neither met nor was treated by, I [...] was defined in a Radio Broadcast as a forensic psychopath, on

In one example of how psychiatric surveillance acted as a form of literary censorship, Mendelssohn recalls how "I was reported to the Psychiatric Unit for reading Ken Kesey's book *One Flew Over the Cuckoo's Nest* [...] aloud."[88] Her later poetry repeatedly reminds its reader that it does not offer an intellectual account of carceral structures from the "outside," but is itself an ex-carceral subject, always-already subjected to interrogatory, invasive, gendered procedures and surveillance. One poem is titled "the arrested poem"; in another, "poetry can be stripped"; and in *viola tricolor* (1993), female-authored writing is "in the grip of a literary psychoanalytical gynaecology," a sinister coalition of literary, psychic, and medical forms of "surveillance."[89]

The prison notebooks indicate that Mendelssohn's prison work took the form not of writing but of teaching and directing theatrical productions involving her fellow inmates. In 1997, Mendelssohn describes in a letter how "I worked very hard in prison with the Labour Governments [sic] permission and taught seven days a week for five years without a break."[90] There are several mentions in Mendelssohn's letters, as well as in media coverage of her release, of teaching literature in prison between 1973 and 1976.[91] The Labour MP for Stockport (where her parents lived) advocated for Mendelssohn's release in the same breath as describing her prisoner-students as "prostitutes, dope smugglers and pickpockets."[92] A *Guardian* article notes that Mendelssohn won an award from the Tate Gallery for her art work in 1975, and reinforces the connection between her industriousness and the signing of her parole papers in 1977.[93] There was considerable controversy in the press

---

the evening of December 6th 1972." From a letter to Denise Riley, 10 October 1989, SxMs109/3/A/1/51. In a letter to Marion Stenner Evans, Mendelssohn describes herself as "exhausted and frail just like any political prisoner who has been interrogated more times than she can bear," June 1991, SxMs109/3/A/1/59.

[88] Letter to Rod Mengham, 8 February 2000, SxMs109/3/A/1/34.

[89] Mendelssohn, *Implacable Art*, 131, 31, 132, 77; Grace Lake, "Half," *viola tricolor* (Cambridge: Equipage, 1993) [unpaginated].

[90] Letter to Marion Stenner Evans, 13–14 February 1997, SxMs109/3/A/1/59.

[91] Letter to Rod Mengham, undated, SxMs109/3/A/1/34.

[92] "Concern at Impact on Police and Public of Granting Parole to Angry Brigade Terrorist," *The Times*, 14 February 1977, 5.

[93] Conor O'Clery, "Angry Brigade Release 'No Cause' for IRA Hope," *The Irish Times*, 15 February 1977.

regarding Mendelssohn's early release, and in response to the uproar, Mendelssohn herself put out a statement on the irresponsibility of the press.[94] In addition, her father gave an interview describing Mendelssohn as "a model prisoner," "teaching illiterates [...] and putting on shows at Christmas."[95] Her father also touches on the question of work and gender in the prison environment, describing women's prisons as "awful: in men's prisons there is a greater chance to become involved in work. There is no outlet for women." Various accounts, some sympathetic, some not, characterise Mendelssohn at the time of her release as "a broken and changed person," "suffering from acute depression," and with "all the stuffing knocked out of her."[96] In Mendelssohn's own words, a decade later:

> I don't even have a book out yet, and I feel as though most of my life has been spent in voluntary (hard) labour [...] I am very shaky at the moment [...] I started to have mild shaking fits in my last year in jail, whenever I was strip-searched and my cell searched without forewarning.[97]

"[V]oluntary (hard) labour" is a dialectical term that inscribes Mendelssohn's post-prison work as an outfolding from the condition of incarceration and its psychosomatic effects. Nominally released from carceral constraints, the poet finds herself marked and interpellated by the unwaged prison work she undertook as a means of bartering for her freedom. A feminist documentary on Holloway Prison in the seventies records the long-lasting trauma of incarceration as a form of debilitation: in the words of one of the women, following her release: "prison disables you."[98]

While Mendelssohn refuses to be "genr'd as a prison poet," and claimed to "have never discussed what I know to be the most vulnerable part of me, which is that I have served a prison sentence," traces of

---

[94] Malcolm Pithers, "Anna: Leave Me Alone," *The Guardian,* 17 February 1977, 24.

[95] Alan Dunn, "The Home Girl Who Became a Revolutionary," *The Guardian,* 15 February 1977, 15.

[96] Clive Borrell, "Mr. Rees Defends Angry Brigade Woman's Release," *The Times,* 15 February 1977, 2; "Breaking of Anna the Bomber," *The Daily Mirror,* 15 February 1977, 8.

[97] Letter to Herbie Butterfield, 2 March 1987, SxMs109/3/A/1/3.

[98] *Time and Time Again: Women in Prison.*

the carceral are everywhere in the poetry she wrote after her release.[99] A careful reader will readily encounter a series of references to being locked in/up/away, shut up, caged, interred, imprisoned, constrained, in quod; to busting up/out; to the prison system, sentences, persecutors, arrest, defence, mug shots, and hard labour. And despite utopic invocations of a romanticised "Twilight World," "inspirational starch," or "other worlds," Mendelssohn's carceral poetics contest the emancipatory capacities often ascribed to poetry. The understanding, emergent in the prison notebooks, of the imbrication of the lyric subject and language in real conditions and structures of oppression and constraint is fully realised in Mendelssohn's mature poetry. As a poem published in 1998 puts it: "words won't break these walls."[100]

Although the focus of Mendelssohn's carceral poetics is almost always upon the category of "woman," her poems of the late nineties understand, too, that the continuum between women's prisons and women's place in society is replicated at the level of race and class. One of her exemplary 'prison poems' opens with an inscription and translation of an Irish poem "Is e ar" from an anthology titled *Poems of the Dispossessed* (1981), a collection of writings on the theme of Irish dispossession and colonial oppression. The poem is illustrative of the ways in which conditions of gendered constraint are inexorably productive of Mendelssohn's poetic work:

> a woman cries in the night between her innocent shoulders
> mistress of her writing hand her arms her preferred feature
> erasing the parts of her body that have long caused offence
> but her mind was met by texts that held her
> in space she could find nowhere else to control
> [...]
> & she sings way out of human hearing in time to the time
> [...]
> that the sky hold her in simple hard labour
> that the text has been divided into single weights
> that the burdens she is detailed to lift are the words of her former pages
> that her body is all conjunction verb and boring

---

[99] Letter to John Kerrigan, 12 July 1990, SxMs109/3/A/1/26.

[100] Grace Lake, *Sneak's Noise: Poems for R.F. Langley* (Cambridge: Infernal Histories, 1998).

[...]
one by one she forces herself to remember adjectives
can lift to a certain height her wrist gives way
she drops, she bends, she cannot bear this kind of poetry.[101]

The distressed woman in the poem is morphed with her writing-work, a cyborg creature consigned to "lift [...] the words of her former pages." Her "preferred feature," her arms, are the instruments of her writing and the remainder of her offending body is absent or erased or grammatically tedious. Neither are those same arms or "innocent shoulders" implicated in that "offence." She is "held" or imprisoned by texts and the sky; the texts, too, are the weights she must lift—both prison walls and prison work. Under the strain of lifting word-weights, the woman figure collapses, physically as well as mentally unable to "bear this kind of poetry." Simultaneous to being figured as a jailer ("texts that held her"), writing emerges as a space of "control," of which the woman in the poem is "mistress." The text as a space of control, and the effort to "remember adjectives" recalls Meinhof's frustrations with out-of-control syntax. Here, too, the lines warp out of linear sequence and syntactical sense. The woman's control over what remains to her—a small part of her body, "her writing hand"—seems premised on a temporal condition. "In time" but "out of hearing," this poem inscribes a state of incarceration that exceeds prison walls and extends as far as the sky, a state in which writing work, which here is women's work, concomitantly exists as prison work, produced from within the inescapable condition of incarceration that exceeds itself in past and future directions.

Situating Mendelssohn's poetic responses to gender equality legislation alongside the work that she undertook in prison and post-prison revises an understanding of women's work that would divorce that work from its carceral contexts. "My Chekhov's Twilight World" is Mendelssohn's most sustained confrontation of the inefficacies and anachronisms of sexual discrimination legislation, and of the legal constitution of the subject *outside* (but always-already inside) the prison. *Tondo Aquatique,* where the speaker locates "laundry rooms" as a site of creative and intellectual activity, articulates the continuum between prison, domesticity, women's work, and writing. The utopian moments and vaunted agency ("what I decide to do with my life") articulated in these

---

[101] *Tondo Aquatique* [unpaginated].

poems are tempered by an anti-lyrical strain that refuses any easy transcendence ("art made me thin"). Mendelssohn's carceral poetics might be described as Foucauldian, in their understanding of how the "proliferation of the authorities of modern judicial decision-making" produces the modern subject.[102] As Mendelssohn wrote, in a prison notebook: "I understand the trap of systems."[103] Yet her concentration on and problematising of the categories of "woman" and a clear-cut "before" and "after" moves away from a strictly Foucauldian analysis. The granular and often parodic articulation of how the woman writer is constrained by carceral structures foregrounds this poetry's material conditions of composition and production, both before and after work.

Works Cited

Anon [Anna Mendelssohn]. "T&G Plays Hard to Get." *Strike!* no. 0, 1971. Unpaginated.

Atkins, Susan. "The Sex Discrimination Act 1975: The End of a Decade." *Feminist Review*, vol. 24 (Autumn 1986): 57–70.

Bauer, Karin, ed. *Everybody Talks About the Weather... We Don't*. New York: Seven Stories Press, 2008.

Borrell, Clive. "Mr. Rees Defends Angry Brigade Woman's Release." *The Times*. 15 February 1977.

Butler, Judith. *Excitable Speech: A Politics of the Performative*. New York and London: Routledge, 1997.

Chibnall, Steve. *Law-and-Order News: An Analysis of Crime Reporting in the British Press*. Routledge: London, 2001.

Coote, Anna, and Tess Gill. *Women's Rights: A Practical Guide* (3rd ed.). Harmondsworth: Penguin, 1981.

Davis, Angela Y. *Angela Davis: An Autobiography*. New York: International Publishers, 1974.

Dunn, Alan. "The Home Girl Who Became a Revolutionary." *The Guardian*. 15 February 1977.

Fortunati, Leopoldina. *The Arcane of Reproduction: Housework, Prostitution, Labour and Capital*. Translated by Hilary Creek. New York: Autonomedia, 1995.

Foucault, Michel. *Discipline and Punish*. New York: Random House, 1975.

---

[102] Michel Foucault, *Discipline and Punish* (New York: Random House, 1975), 21.

[103] Exercise book, December 1974–December 1975, SxMs109/2/A/6.

Hill, Paul. *Three Perspectives on Photography*. London: Arts Council of Great Britain, 1979.

Iversen, Margaret, Douglas Crimp, and Homi K. Bhabha. *Mary Kelly*. London: Phaidon, 1997.

Kinnahan, Linda A. *Lyric Interventions: Feminism, Experimental Poetry, and Contemporary Discourse*. Iowa: University of Iowa Press, 2004.

Kristeva, Julia. *Powers of Horror: An Essay on Abjection*. Translated by Leon S. Goudiez. New York: Columbia University Press, 1972.

Lacey, Nicola. "From Individual to Group?" In *Discrimination: The Limits of Law*, edited by Bob Hopple and Erika M. Szyszczak, 99–124. London and New York: Mansell, 1992.

———. "Legislation Against Sex Discrimination Questions from a Feminist Perspective." *Journal of Law and Society*, vol. 14 (1987): 411–421.

Lake, Grace. *Sneak's Noise: Poems for R.F. Langley*. Cambridge: Infernal Histories, 1998.

———. *Tondo Aquatique*. Cambridge: Equipage, 1997.

———. *viola tricolor*. Cambridge: Equipage, 1993.

———. "1:3ng." *Gare du Nord: A Magazine of Poetry and Opinion from Paris*, edited by Douglas Oliver and Alice Notley, Vol. 1, 1997.

Leishman, Jackie. "Defendant Tells Jury: 'I Oppose Bombing on Political Grounds.'" *The Guardian*, 17 November 1972.

Levin, Raya, and Judith Brandt. "Women, Prison and Economic Independence." In *The Body Politic: Writings from the Women's Liberation Movement in Britain 1969–1972*, compiled by Michelene Wandor. London: Stage 1, 1972.

Madan, Tony. *Women, Prisons and Psychiatry*. Oxford: Heinemann, 1996.

Meinhof, Ulrike. "Letter from a Prisoner in the Isolation Wing, June 16, 1972 to February 9, 1973" quoted in Karin Bauer, ed. *Everybody Talks About the Weather... We Don't*. New York: Seven Stories Press, 2008.

Mendelssohn, Anna. *Implacable Art*. Applecross, Western Australia and Great Wilbraham, UK: Folio and Equipage, 2000.

Morris, Anne, and Therese O'Donnell. *Feminist Perspectives on Employment Law*. London: Cavendish, 1999.

Morris, Anne E., and Susan M. Nott. *Working Women and the Law: Equality and Discrimination in Theory and Practice*. London and New York: Routledge, 1991.

Mulford, Wendy. *And Suddenly, Supposing: Selected Poems*. Buckfastleigh, Devon: Etruscan Books, 2002.

O'Clery, Conor. "Angry Brigade Release 'No Cause' for IRA Hope." *The Irish Times*. 15 February 1977.

O'Donovan, K., and E. Szyszczak, eds. *Equality and Sex Discrimination Law*. Oxford: Blackwell, 1988.

Palmer, Stephanie. "Critical Perspectives on Women's Rights: The European Convention on Human Rights and Fundamental Freedoms." In *Feminist*

Perspectives on the Foundational Subjects of Law, edited by Anne Bottomley. London: Cavendish, 1996.

Passmore, Leith. *Ulrike Meinhof and the Red Army Faction: Performing Terrorism*. New York: Palgrave, 2011.

Pithers, Malcolm. "Anna: Leave Me Alone." *The Guardian*. 17 February 1977.

Puar, Jasbir, and Isabelle Barker. "Feminist Problematization of Rights Language and Universal Conceptualizations of Human Right." *Concilium International Journal for Theology*, vol. 5 (2002): 64–76.

Radical Alternatives to Prison (Holloway Campaign Group). *Alternatives to Holloway*. Christian Action Publications Ltd., 1972.

Riley, Denise. *Dry Air*. London: Virago, 1985.

Riley, Peter. "Anna Mendelssohn Obituary." *The Guardian*, 15 December 2009.

Robinson, Hilary, ed. *Feminism Art Theory: An Anthology 1968–2000*. Oxford: 2001.

Rock, Paul. *Reconstructing a Women's Prison: The Holloway Redevelopment Project 1968–1988*. Oxford: Clarendon Press, 1996.

Sachs, A., and J. H. Wilson. *Sexism and the Law: A Study of Male Beliefs and Judicial Bias*. Oxford: Martin Robertson, 1978.

Scheffler, Judith A., ed. *Wall Tappings: An International Anthology of Women's Prison Writings 200 to the Present*. New York: Feminist Press at the City University of New York, 2002 [1986].

Scott, Joan. "Some More Reflections on Gender and Politics." In *Gender and the Politics of History*. New York: Columbia University Press, 1999.

Showalter, Elaine. *The Female Malady: Women, Madness and English Culture 1830–1980*. London: Virgo, 1985.

Smart, Carol. *Feminism and the Power of Law*. New York: Routledge, 1989.

———. *Women Crime and Criminology: A Feminist Critique*. London: Routledge, 1977.

The Daily Mail. "Bomb Case Anna." 26 March 1973.

The Daily Mirror. "Breaking of Anna the Bomber." 15 February 1977.

———. "Terror Girl Anna." 25 February 1977.

———. "The Bomb Girls." 7 December 1972.

The Times. "Concern at Impact on Police and Public of Granting Parole to Angry Brigade Terrorist." 14 February 1977.

———. "Woman on Plot Charge is Refused Bail." 18 May 1972.

Third, Amanda. "Imprisonment and Excessive Femininity: Reading Ulrike Meinhof's Brain." *Parallax*, vol. 16, no. 4 (2010): 83–100.

Time and Time Again: Women in Prison. Nina Ward with Women & The Law Collective. 1986.

Tweedie, Jill. "The Trials and Tribulations of Preparing a Vital Defence: One Over the Eight." *The Guardian*, 6 November 1972.

Valier, Claire. "Women's Oppression, Crime and Society." In *Theories of Crime and Punishment*. Harlow: Longman, 2002.

Walker, Christopher. "Influences That Shaped the Philosophy of the Angry Brigade: People for Whom Protest Became a Profession." *The Times*, 7 December 1972.

Weinreb, Ben, Christopher Hibbert, Julia Keay, and John Keay, eds. *The London Encyclopedia*. London: Macmillan, 2008.

Weir, Angela. "When the Key Turns." *Spare Rib*, May 1973.

CHAPTER 7

Queer Labour in Boston: The Work of John Wieners, Gay Liberation and *Fag Rag*

Nat Raha

BEFORE THE STRAIGHT CAPITOL: SITUATING JOHN WIENERS IN GAY LIBERATION

A column recounting Boston's Gay Pride Week 1972 published in Gay Liberation newspaper *Fag Rag*,[1] comparing the event with the tensions and police surveillance of the previous year, reads

---

[1] All references from *Fag Rag* Issues 1–3 (44) are from copies in the William J. Canfield Papers. Archives and Special Collections, Snell Library, Northeastern University, Boston, Massachusetts. All references from *Fag Rag* Issues 4–18 are from copies in the Alternative Press Collection (Thomas J. Dodd Research Center, University of Connecticut, Storrs, Connecticut).

This chapter would not have been possible without the insights and support of Jim Dunn, Maria Damon, Sam Solomon, Kevin Killian, and Melissa Batt (at the Thomas J. Dodd Research Center, University of Connecticut).

N. Raha (✉)
University of Sussex, Brighton, UK

© The Author(s) 2019
J. L. Walton and E. Luker (eds.), *Poetry and Work*,
Modern and Contemporary Poetry and Poetics,
https://doi.org/10.1007/978-3-030-26125-2_7

Our march was more a joy and a celebration. The speeches in front of the State House (renamed the 'Straight House') were short and interspersed with chants and poetry. John Wieners read a gay Boston poem; the Good Gay Poets presented an exorcism against the straight man demon. And in the end ... we just sat around on the Common with a little wine and lots of good feelings.[2]

In the early 1970s, the working-class, gay/bisexual, and psychiatric-survivor poet John Wieners became involved in the Gay and Lesbian Liberation Movement in Boston and beyond, alongside Boston's Mental Patients' Liberation Movement. Wieners' involvement in Gay Liberation included reading poems at movement events, such as that detailed above; attending national events as a Gay Liberation representative, including the National Democratic Convention in Miami, July 1972[3]; publishing

---

[2] *Fag Rag* Issue 4 (January 1973), 15. The article refers to Aaron Shurin, *Exorcism of the Straight/Man/Demon* (Boston: Good Gay Poets, 1972). Shurin's broadside was the first publication by the Good Gay Poets, who had been meeting since 1970–1971 as a group. Christopher Hennessy, *Our Deep Gossip: Conversations with Gay Writers on Poetry and Desire* (Madison, WI: University of Wisconsin Press, 2013), 128.

[3] Describing this trip and the politics of the group in Charley Shively's Obituary, Michael Bronski writes:

"In 1972 a few members of Boston Gay Men's Liberation, and part of the *Fag Rag* collective, drove to Miami in Charley's blue VW bug to deliver to delegates at the Democratic National Convention a list of ten demands that the group had drafted. The demands were visionary, earnest, and wonderfully theatrical—we knew they were never going to be met, but we wanted them to be heard. They included: the disbanding of all 'secret police (FBI, CIA, IRS, Narcotics squads, etc.) and uni-formed police';

'the return of *all* United States troops to within the United States border' to hasten the end of U.S. imperialism;

'an end to any discrimination based on biology,' including the state's collection of racial and gender data;

'rearing children' as a 'common responsibility of the whole community';

the legal emancipation of children from their parents;

free twenty-four-hour day care centers "where faggots and lesbians can share in the responsibility of child rearing";

and the legalization of all forms of sex between consenting individuals." (Bronski 2017).

Wieners' diary poem *Playboy*, written primarily while travelling to the convention, was published as a pamphlet by Good Gay Poets in 1972. It is reprinted in Wieners' *Cultural affairs in Boston: poetry & prose, 1956–1985*, ed. Raymond Foye (Santa Rosa: Black Sparrow Press, 1988), 114–128. According to the poem, the convention was attended by other poets including Amiri Baraka and Ed Dorn.

his work extensively in radical Gay Liberation newspapers such as *Fag Rag* and *Gay Sunshine*[4]; and attending "mental patient liberation meetings," likely those of Boston's Mental Patients' Liberation Front.[5] From 1972 to 1976 Wieners was part of the publishing collective for *Fag Rag*, an anarchist gay male newspaper published in Boston until 1987.[6] Wieners was also a member of the Homophile Union of Boston (HUB), and part of the Good Gay Poets collective, who would produce and publish his 1975 book *Behind the State Capitol, or Cincinnati Pike*.[7]

Wieners understood that his poetry could be used to support the transformations of everyday life engendered by the Gay Liberation movement. Responding to a questionnaire about involvement in Boston's Gay Community Center's (GCC) Coffee House, Wieners lists his talents and activities as including "entertainer," "patron," and "public relations," and writes that, "As a member of HUB, I lend support to GCC, by public performance, via poetry and political action."[8] This chapter contextualises the work of John Wieners in relation to his involvement as a poet in the Gay and Lesbian Liberation movement, which is inextricable from his writing from the 1970s and the context of his work's circulation in the decade. Drawing upon Wieners' own

---

[4] All copies of the *Gay Sunshine* newspaper referenced come from the Alternative Press Collection, Thomas J. Dodd Research Center, University of Connecticut, Storrs, Connecticut.

[5] Quote from Wieners' *Gay Sunshine* interview. Winston Leyland, *Gay Sunshine Interviews: Volume 2* (San Francisco: Gay Sunshine Press, 1982), 261.

[6] Wieners last appears on the contributor list for issue 18 (Fall/Winter 1976).

[7] It seems that incarceration in state asylums obstructed Wieners involvement in the collective. Describing forming the group in Winter 1971 with Aaron Shurin, Shively names the group as "David Eberly, Ron Schrieber, Charles River, John LaPorta, myself and on occasion John Wieners (sometime incarcerated in Taunton State Hospital)" ("Poetry Cocksucking and Revolution," *Fag Rag*, 10 [Fall 1974], 3–5, quote on 3). A poem by Wieners, "Here for the Night," appears in *Fag Rag*, 3 (Summer 1972, 19), attributed as the work of the collective's members, rather than to Wieners. While Shively's list names no lesbian poets, the Good Gay Poets published Stephanie Byrd's *25 Years of Malcontent* (1976) and Ruth Weiss' *Desert Journal* (1977).

[8] Series 1, 1:14, Gay Community Center—Questionnaire, William J. Canfield Papers. Archives and Special Collections, Snell Library, Northeastern University. The Center was based at the Charles Street Meeting House on Beacon Hill, and the coffee house was set up in Spring 1973. The coffee house was open daily, described as having "cheap, gay, fun food and entertainment," with poetry readings on Saturday nights (*Fag Rag*, 5 [Summer 1973], 22).

archives and those of Gay Liberation organisers and newspapers, this chapter situates Wieners' poetic praxis, the publication of his work, and its critical reception, within the work of the Gay Liberation movement.

Since the turn of the twenty-first century, Wieners' poetry has received growing critical attention, which continues to develop since the publication of *Supplication: Selected Poems of John Wieners* (2015) and *Stars Seen in Person: Selected Journals* (2015), and may be given further boosts by the potential publication of a collected poems, and the forthcoming publication of *For The Voices: The Letters of John Wieners*, under the editorships of Robert Dewhurst and Michael Seth Stewart, respectively.[9] Work by Maria Damon (2011) and Christopher Hennessy (2015) has made important contributions to understanding the socio-political context and sexual politics of Wieners' poetry.[10] Hennessy's work also importantly considers poetry published across numerous Gay Liberation papers and journals by a variety of less well-known writers. Further comments on the importance of sexuality in Wieners' poetry have been made by Michael Davidson (1998), Marjorie Perloff (1975), Andrea Brady (2006, 2007) and John Wilkinson (2007), addressing the socio-political context of Wieners' writing to varying, albeit limited, degrees.[11]

[9] See Dewhurst and Stewart's doctoral dissertations: Robert Stuart Dewhurst, *Ungrateful City: The Collected Poems of John Wieners* (State University of New York at Buffalo, 2015); Michael Seth Stewart, *"For the Voices": The Letters of John Wieners* (CUNY Academic Works, 2014). I discuss the importance of *Supplication* as a volume in my essay "A Queer Excess: The Supplication of John Wieners" (*The Critical Flame*, no. 38 (September/October 2015), http://criticalflame.org/a-queer-excess-the-supplication-of-john-wieners/).

[10] See Maria Damon, *Postliterary America: From Bagel Shop Jazz to Micropoetries* (Iowa City: University of Iowa Press, 2011), and Christopher Hennessy, *Homosexuality Is a Poem: How Gay Poets Remodeled the Lyric, Community and the Ideology of Sex to Theorise a Gay Poetics* (Doctoral Dissertation, University of Massachusetts, 2015). Damon reads Wieners' poetry as a form of auto-ethnographic lyric penned by a minoritised subject, situated and speaking of marginal worlds while retaining a (temporal) distance. Damon argues that—in poems such as "A Poem for Tea Heads" (aka "A Poem for Vipers")—the socially marginalised poet's "dissociated lyric I," observing itself, functions as a buffer for the trauma of double-consciousness (*Postliterary America*, 181). Hennessy's doctoral work specifically addresses sexuality and lyric in Wieners' work in relation to Cold War discourses of privacy and the closet, arguing that, by representing and "formally reflect[ing]" oppressions facing the homosexual lyric poet through a form of "queer failure," Wieners' "transform[s] [...] the lyric into a vehicle able to critique the closet, [and] the false protection of privacy ethics" (*Homosexuality is a Poem*, 216).

[11] In an essay critiquing homogeneous erotic poetry spurred by the Liberation movements, Perloff singles out Wieners alongside Adrienne Rich as the two poets of the era producing innovative erotic lyrics. Marjorie Perloff, "The Corn-Porn Lyric: Poetry 1972–73,"

However, this work does not meaningfully address the poet's sexuality and gender non-conformity (beyond Freudian familial models), and has a tendency to individualise the social, political, and emotional struggles felt by many gay, lesbian, bisexual, and trans people in the decades prior to Gay Liberation.[12] This includes the naturalisation of the violence of psychiatry and psychiatric incarceration.[13] Furthermore, with the exception

---

Contemporary Literature, vol. 16, no. 1 (1975), 84–125. Davidson's work argues that Wieners inaugurates a "community of difference" by addressing marginal subjects, deploying "terms of deviance" to challenge the hierarchical logic of (white) heteronormative society and its scrutiny of deviant subjects (as witnessed in McCarthy's Congressional investigation committees. Michael Davidson. "From Margin to Mainstream: Postwar Poetry and the Politics of Containment," *American Literary History*, vol. 10, no. 2 (Summer 1998), 275–276.

[12] For instance, Brady's work on Wieners' archive—during a lengthy consideration of parental figures in Wieners' work—identifies that "Wieners described himself as a hermaphrodite, possessing a woman's mind" (Andrea Brady, "Making Use of This Pain: The John Wieners Archives," *Paideuma*, vol. 36 [2007], 175). Brady makes no attempt to historicise this description, but instead emphasises the idealised and demonising representations of women in Wieners' archive, and his idealisation of maternal and feminine roles. Brady's Freudian reading of Oedipal familial relations (including Wieners' relation to Charles Olson) makes little address to the position of homosexuality within the Oedipus complex, instead pointing to the incest fantasy and placing Wieners within "an infantile position" desiring maternal love (175), which in turn reinstitutes the heterosexism of Freud's model of sexual development in his *Three Essays on the Theory of Sexuality* (1905). Furthermore, Brady repeatedly emphasises the 'shame' around Wieners' sexuality in relation to living with his family (Brady, "Making Use of this Pain," 174–175). While shame in this reading can be redeemed through feminine expression (174), Wieners' personal expressions of femininity remain unaddressed beyond these passing references. Brady comments briefly on Wieners' "feminized persona" in another essay, but only as a means "to express his relative powerlessness as a lover or as a 'mentally ill person'" ("The Other Poet: John Wieners, Frank O'Hara, Charles Olson," in *Don't Ever Get Famous: Essays on New York Writing after the New York School*, ed. Daniel Kane [Campaign and London: Dalkey Archive Press, 2006], 333). The agency of Wieners' feminine gender expressions (even when they cannot be realised) or empowerment as a psychiatric survivor are evacuated from this reading. Furthermore, Brady's treatment of 'shame' in her reading of "Making Use of this Pain" appears somewhat divorced from a wider understanding of the complex role of negative affect within queer cultural production. Christopher Hennessy's work notably fails to address Wieners' gender deviance in his reading of 'Memories of You' and figures of drag queens in the work of Frank O'Hara, simply bracketing them as "other gay men" (Hennessy, *Homosexuality is a Poem*, 220–226, 2–3).

[13] Nat Raha, "The Survival of John Wieners: Psychiatric Incarceration, Poetics and Liberation," in *Queer Capital: Marxism in Queer Theory and Post-1950 Poetics*. Doctoral dissertation (University of Sussex, 2018), 189–229.

Lisa Tatonetti's work *The Queerness of Native American Literature* (2014) and Christopher Hennessy's doctoral dissertation (2015), critical work on Gay Liberation and its media and literature has paid little attention to either *Fag Rag* or the poetry of Wieners.

Situating Wieners' writing in the context of the radical social critique and transformations of the Gay and Mental Patients' Liberation movements produces a series of questions regarding the poet's labour beyond the page, and the reception and position of poetic labour when its products circulate within different subcultural contexts. This is also a question of what is recognised as labour within the poets' life and archive, especially given the heteronormative readings of Wieners' work and archive and the heterosexism that gay poets faced from publishers. For instance, Wieners' suggested titles for what became *Selected Poems 1958–1984* (1986) included *Queen for a Day* and *She Can Turn on a Dime*, the latter as a "roman à clef,"[14] which his publisher John Martin at Black Sparrow Press outright refused:

> Very important: when looking for a title, PLEASE nothing "campy" or cute. Queen for a Day is wildly inappropriate. Ditto She Can Turn on a Dime. Look for something literary, dignified and strong. Granted John is a gay poet, but first and foremost he is a poet, period.[15]

By claiming that these camp titles "wildly inappropriate" and not "literary," requesting instead "something literary, dignified and strong," Martin instigates a dichotomy where camp, queer femininity, and sex work are positioned outside of the sphere of 'literary' production. By extension, much of Wieners' writing from the 1970s, such as the work first published in *Fag Rag* addressing gay sexuality and culture and expressing queer femininity, could be relegated outside of the 'literary' sphere. As I discuss below, such a dichotomy was precisely what *Fag Rag* was trying to dethrone; such divisions permit gay male poets into the literary establishment only insofar as they remain in their closets.[16]

---

[14] John Wieners to John Martin, "Tuesday, July 9, 1984" (Wieners/Stewart, Forthcoming, 245).

[15] John Martin to Raymond Foye, 9 July 1984, Series 2, 2:63, John Wieners Papers. Archives & Special Collections at the Thomas J. Dodd Research Center, University of Connecticut Libraries. The paragraph concludes: "The best art has no gender."

[16] Charley Shively, "Poetry Cocksucking and Revolution," *Fag Rag* 10 (Fall 1974), 3–5.

Work within queer Marxism has begun to consider the relationship between labour and queerness,[17] and the social reproduction of LGBTQ subjects.[18] Work by Allan Bérubé—a founder member of *Fag Rag*—and Matthew Tinkcom provides two different models of exploring how labour becomes queer as workers undertake jobs that transgress gender and racial stereotypes; and how queerness and camp can signify in coded representations through certain forms of labour. Opening this chapter by developing this work, I will formulate the poetic praxis and political labour of Wieners and the *Fag Rag* and Good Gay Poets collectives as a form of 'queer labour.' This took the forms of activism and production of the *Fag Rag* newspaper, and thus the circulation of radical political knowledge, consciousness and critique, and (often through) the publication of poetry. By historically situating such cultural production and political work, I will argue that the labour of Wieners and of the collectives was an important and necessary example of 'queer world-making' for the Gay Liberation era.[19] Such world-making enabled the political, cultural, and emotional transformation of life for gay, lesbian, bisexual, and trans people (to varying degrees).

In the case of Wieners, such transformations impacted on the reception, circulation and production of his poetry; furthermore, alongside the consciousness-raising and action of the Mental Patients' Liberation, Wieners' poetics of the 1970s pursued a radical aesthetics of liberation, exploring gay sexuality and community, queer femininity and transgressive gender expressions, avant-garde camp, and a politicised psychiatric

---

[17] Allan Bérubé, *My Desire for History: Essays in Gay, Community and Labor History*, ed. John D'Emilio and Estelle B. Freedman (Chapel Hill: University of North Carolina Press, 2011); Matthew Tinkcom, *Working Like a Homosexual: Camp, Capital, Cinema* (Durham and London: Duke University Press, 2002); J. D. Rhodes, "Fassbinder's Work: Style, Sirk, and Queer Labor," in *A Companion to Fassbinder*, ed. Brigitte Peucker (Malden and Oxford: Blackwell Publishing, 2012); José E. Muñoz, *Cruising Utopia: The Then and There of Queer Futurity* (New York: New York University Press, 2009); and Rosemary Hennessy, *Fires on the Border: The Passionate Politics of Labour Organising on the Mexican Frontera* (Minneapolis: University of Minnesota Press, 2013).

[18] Miranda Joseph, *Against the Romance of Community* (Minneapolis and London: University of Minnesota Press, 2002); Meg Wesling, "Queer Value," *GLQ: A Journal of Lesbian and Gay Studies*, vol. 18, no. 1 (2012); Robert McRuer, *Crip Theory: Cultural Signs of Queerness and Disability* (New York and London: New York University Press, 2006).

[19] Lauren Berlant and Michael Warner. "Sex in Public," *Critical Inquiry*, vol. 24, no. 2 (1998); Muñoz, *Cruising Utopia*.

survivor consciousness.[20] In the context of the political aesthetics of *Fag Rag*, I will argue that *Behind the State Capitol*, alongside contemporaneous work, emerges from this socio-political context as a poetic experiment to realise such expressions and consciousness in content and form.

First, a brief note on the language of the chapter: in the late 1960s and 1970s, 'Gay' was used by men, women, transvestites, and gender variant people. Unlike today, it was an explicitly politicised term, implying the right to be free from heteronormative persecution and shame, and at its most radical, to intone the negation of heteronormative society. This chapter primarily addresses the work of a 'gay male' newspaper collective and thus directs less attention to lesbian cultural production from the same period and location[21]; indeed *Fag Rag* itself was founded following the split of Boston's Gay Liberation Front (into Gay Male Liberation and Lesbian Liberation), and of the paper *Lavender Vision* (from a gay and lesbian paper in 1970, into a lesbian liberation paper in 1971 and *Fag Rag*).

The Fag Rag collective's use of the pejorative word 'faggot'—and particularly in the name *Fag Rag*—were both points of criticism addressed within the paper. A 1971 editorial in *Fag Rag* #2 highlights the decision to reclaim this degrading and othering term used by "the straight man," emphasising the pride and anger in not fitting "the ster[e]otyped definitions of manhood Amerikan style" that is "essentially anti-human."[22] The editorial also emphasises that, next to the increasing trivialisation of 'gay' by the straight man, 'faggot' both cannot be co-opted and retains a sense of humour that was thus reflected in the newspaper's title.

---

[20]For more on the development of Wieners' consciousness as a psychiatric survivor, see Raha, "The Survival of John Wieners."

[21]For critical work addressing lesbian cultural production from the Gay Liberation era, see for starters Karla Jay and Allen Young (eds.), *Lavender Culture* (New York and London: New York University Press, 1994); Cherríe Moraga and Gloria Anzaldúa (eds.), *This Bridge Called My Back: Writings by Radical Women of Color* (Watertown: Persephone Press, 1981); Elly Bulkin (ed.), *Lesbian Fiction: An Anthology* (Watertown: Persephone Press, 1981); and Elly Bulkin and Joan Larkin (eds.), *Lesbian Poetry, an Anthology* (Watertown: Persephone Press, 1981); for an account of lesbian life and newspaper production in 1970s Boston, see Amy Hoffman, *An Army of Ex-Lovers: My Life at the Gay Community News* (Amherst: University of Massachusetts Press, 2007); and for accounts of (Black) lesbian activism in 1970s Boston, see the work of the Combahee River Collective.

[22]"About *Fag Rag*," *Fag Rag*, no. 2 (Fall 1971), 2.

Further, it is important to understand that the work produced by, and the gender expressions of, the collective's members exceed that typical of cisgender gay men, and that the newspapers include some content by, for, and about trans-feminine people who self-identified as transvestites (and to a less extent transsexuals or 'half-sisters'). Defining these identifications in 1971, Sylvia Rivera writes that "[t]ransvestites are homosexual men and women who dress in clothes of the opposite sex. Male transvestites dress and live as women."[23] The marginal position and oppression faced by such trans subjects is well documented—furthermore, a group of transvestites writing in *Fag Rag* #3 state that despite the numerous gay organisations in Boston, "there are none that speak to us."[24] It is important to acknowledge that not only did Wieners have sexual relationships with men and women, he was also a drag queen, and his writing includes numerous assertions of trans subjectivity. This includes directly stating "I have a woman's / mind in a man's body"[25]; regularly inhabiting feminine voices and personae; undertaking public 'experiments' with drag and describing dragging up; featuring drag queens and gender deviant figures in poems—including "Times Square" and "Ballade," the latter of which details the life and trials of, and the speaker's experiences working with, a drag queen named Alice O'Brian.[26] Furthermore, between 1974 and

[23] Rivera continues: "Half sisters like myself are women with the minds of women trapped in male bodies. Female transvestites dress and *live* as men. My half brothers are men with male minds trapped in female bodies." See "Transvestites: Your half sisters and half brothers of the revolution" (reprinted in Untorelli Press, *Street Transvestite Action Revolutionaries* [Untorelli Press, 2013], 19–20, quote on 19, emphasis added; originally published in *Come Out*). Some difference in usage is likely, and heterosexual transvestites exists, I here intend to emphasise the decision and needs of transvestites to inhabit lives and roles other to those they were assigned at birth. A detailed study of the identities half sister and half brother to that of transsexual identities and the Harry Benjamin transsexual narrative is yet to be written.

[24] "Transvestites," *Fag Rag*, no. 3 (Summer 1972, 4). For a historical account of the oppression of trans subjects in the 1960s and 1970s, see Susan Stryker, *Transgender History* (Berkeley: Seal Press, 2008), 59–120. For contemporaneous accounts, see Marsha P. Johnson, and Allen Young, "Rapping with a Street Transvestite Revolutionary: An Interview with Marcia Johnson" (Jay and Young 1992: 112–120) and Untorelli Press, *Street Transvestite Action Revolutionaries* (Untorelli Press, 2013).

[25] "Memories of You," in John Wieners, *Supplication: Selected Poems of John Wieners*, ed. Joshua Beckman, Robert Dewhurst, and CAConrad (Seattle: Wave Books, 2015), 74.

[26] "Times Square" in John Wieners, *Selected Poems 1956–1984*, 1986: 117. "Times Square" is published contemporaneously to the Stonewall Riot and the activities of members of Street Transvestite Action Revolutionaries, who included Sylvia Rivera and

1976 Wieners signed various pieces of work in *Fag Rag* with the name Jacqueline Wieners, including the paper's "Second Five Year Plan" and an otherwise-unpublished play "Harlem Bodyguard," with the signature reproduced in print in these cases.[27] In a letter to Neeli Cherkovski, Wieners' editor Raymond Foye recounts a lecture that Wieners gave on Olson and Black Mountain College at Harvard University (in a class taught by Bill Corbett), dressed in an outfit that sounds like an early '70s gay femme take on Marlene Dietrich's infamous outfit from the film *Morocco*:

> On the day of the lecture, he arrived wearing red high heels, pink hot-pants, a ladies 1940s tuxedo jacket w. rhinestone buttons, white Brooks Brothers shirt & bow tie, & a Nehru cap. And red lipstick. He lectured in a wonderfully erudite manner for about an hour, and then answered questions from the students. When one student asked why he was dressed this way, he simply replied, 'It's an experiment,' & moved on to the next question.[28]

Thus, all reference to Wieners as a 'gay male' poet must also recognise the permeability of this description with the fact that Wieners ought to be considered as, in Trace Peterson's words, a "proto-trans poet."[29]

Marsha P. Johnson. "Ballade" (published in *Angels of the Lyre*, 216–217) details the life of a drag queen Alice O'Brian—including the physical abuse Alice faced, the speaker's experiences of working with Alice and their engagement with gay bar culture, and Alice's suicide in Charles Street Jail in Boston (*Angels of the Lyre*, 216–217). The poem is dated November 1955.

[27] "Harlem Bodyguard," *Fag Rag*, 13 (Summer 1975), 6–7; "Second Five Year Plan," *Fag Rag*, 16/17 (June/July 1976), inside cover. *Fag Rag*, 10 (Fall 1974) features "Upon Mata Hari Paul Mall," reproduced as handwritten, signed Jacqueline Wieners (5), alongside "A comparative study of *Studies for an actress and other poems*; Women's Newspapers; Homophile Bulletins; and The Underground," printed with the names John Wieners and Jean Carrigue (22–23). The signature to the work is usually accompanied by the name John Wieners elsewhere in the paper.

[28] Raymond Foye to Neeli [Cherkovski], 16 July 1984, Series 2, 1:44, John Wieners Papers. Archives & Special Collections at the Thomas J. Dodd Research Center, University of Connecticut Libraries. Also cited in Brady (2006: 382, fn. 10).

[29] Peterson, T. Trace, "Being Unreadable and Being Read: An Introduction," in Tolbert and Peterson (2013: 15–22, quote on 21).

QUEER LABOUR

In his uncompleted work on the history of the Marine Cooks and Stewards Union in 1930s California, Allan Bérubé began to analyse what he called 'queer work,' "work which is performed by, or has the reputation of being performed by, homosexual men and women."[30] Following the lead of labour historians working on the gendering and racialisation of certain lines of employment, Bérubé traces references of queer work to the nineteenth century, to salesmen who sold fabric to women known derogatorily as 'counter-jumpers.' In the twentieth century, he notes African American men who undertook service work for white families and took part in drag balls; the classifications of certain 'choice' occupations of homosexual men according to a psychiatrist; and the masculine jobs undertaken by many lesbian women serving the US military in World War II.[31] Bérubé uses 'queer' intentionally to denote the stigma that was attached to such work. Queer work often involved some form of gender transgression when it came to the jobs undertaken, though of course it should also be noted that not everyone undertaking such work was gay. Considering contemporaneous stereotypically queer work for women and men, Bérubé writes

> Many but not all of these jobs are filled by people who are crossing gender roles: jobs where men do women's work and women do men's work, or where effeminate men and masculine women can make a living. Queer work also includes jobs in same-sex environments, especially where women live with women and men live with men, like colleges, jails, and the military. Queer work for men also includes personal service jobs – like waiters – and work that focuses on the decorative, designing and self-expressive arts. Queer jobs range from working class to middle class, but they're usually marginal to the primary labor force.[32]

Bérubé astutely notes that such roles were often racialised—either due to segregated workplaces and/or stereotypes around jobs.[33] In the

[30] Allan Bérubé, *My Desire for History: Essays in Gay, Community and Labor History*, ed. John D'Emilio and Estelle B. Freedman (Chapel Hill: University of North Carolina Press, 2011), 261.

[31] Bérubé, *My Desire for History*, 261–263.

[32] Bérubé, *My Desire for History*, 263.

[33] Bérubé, *My Desire for History*, 263.

case of the queer work undertaken onboard the Matson liner cruise ships around San Francisco bay in the '30s, Bérubé highlights how work undertaken by white gay men at sea—who were referred to and referred to each other at work using she/her pronouns—was typically the service work undertaken by African American women on land. Other forms of work aboard the liners were explicitly racialised, for instance, as one participant in Bérubé's oral history remembers, laundry workers were usually Chinese men. Thus queer work on the liners likely developed part of its derogatory character through the fact it involved socially degraded working class white men undertaking work typically considered to be Black women's work, transgressing what was expected of the racialised formation of their class.

However, Bérubé also emphasises that working environments where gay men and women were in the majority also enabled the development of queer cultures and sociality on and off the job, along with specific forms of resistance. Lesbian women and gay men could follow twentieth-century cultural references—including insults—"as signposts to identify what work was queer," which would attract gay and lesbian workers while deterring people who wouldn't want to work among them.[34] Arguing that such queer work was "a stigmatized ghetto, a trap that confines lesbian and gay workers to a few acceptable jobs," Bérubé writes that such work could also be a "refuge," where workers needn't hide their (sexual and/or gender) deviance and where lesbian and gay people were materialising "our own place in the economy."[35] Furthermore, in the case of the Marine Cooks and Stewards Union in the San Francisco Bay area during the period, as the union began to integrate Asian and Black workers, the union's reputation as queer developed, becoming known as the "Marine Cooks and Fruits," described as "a third red, a third black, and a third queer"—while Bérubé points out that some workers were all three.[36] This constitution became an important point of solidarity, as queens and Black workers fiercely defended each other against hostility on the ships. The union thus developed the slogan,

---

[34] Bérubé, *My Desire for History*, 266. Here Bérubé also points to the example of lesbian women driving vehicles and working as mechanics in the Army and Marine Corps during World War II, where the example of such working as being undertaken by lesbian women in *The Well of Loneliness* signposted this work as queer.

[35] Bérubé, *My Desire for History*, 266–267.

[36] Bérubé, *My Desire for History*, 267.

"If you let them red-bait, they'll race bait, and if you them race-bait, they'll queen bait."[37] (Emphasis in the original).

Matthew Tinkcom's work provides another model of thinking about the queerness of certain forms of labour. In *Working like a Homosexual,* Tinkcom "pervert[s]" Marx, and his *1844 Economic and Philosophic Manuscripts* (1959) in particular, to posit what he calls "camp labour"— the sensuous work of producing objects and actions encoded as camp, and the self-consciousness that may be gleaned through such labour.[38] Addressing the films of the '50s and '60s by Vincente Minnelli, Andy Warhol, and Kenneth Anger, Tinkcom historicises the labour of gay male subjects working in Hollywood in the era of McCarthyism as moving within a dialectic of concealment and coded expression. Tinkcom understands that in Marx's labour theory of value, capital reduces the qualitative character of human labour to homogenous quantities of value; and furthermore, that capital demands proletarians "make themselves adequate for their abstraction and insertion into the labour process"— both these points seem to prevent the recognition of queerness in value production.[39] By defining camp "heuristically," "as an alibi" for queer men working within and amid the historical contradictions of capitalist production, Tinkcom suggests that the abstraction of labour and societal homophobia function together to "suppress camp style *and* specific kinds of work [such as cinematic production and performances] that are enabled by the camp emphasis on stylistic commodity differentiation."[40]

Tinkcom is interested in the consciousness subjects have of their own conditions of labour, and highlights the importance of "the political dimensions of camp in the popular form as *a knowledge of, and delight in,* the apparent uselessness that travels with the commodity in its trajectory towards the moment after its seeming consumption."[41] His reading moves in a "contrary direction" to the homogenising abstraction of value production, to ask if the movement of the commodity through the spheres of circulation and consumption might reveal "the fact of its having been shaped by some anomalous labor and laborer."[42]

---

[37] Bérubé, *My Desire for History*, 268.

[38] Tinkcom, *Working Like a Homosexual*, 4, 23.

[39] Tinkcom, *Working Like a Homosexual*, 8.

[40] Tinkcom, *Working Like a Homosexual*, 4, 10, original emphasis.

[41] Tinkcom, *Working Like a Homosexual*, 23, 9, emphasis added.

[42] Tinkcom, *Working Like a Homosexual*, 8.

Given the critical engagement of camp with seemingly valueless objects that have passed beyond the moment of consumption, he suggests that commodities might "betray the knowledge that they were destined to become 'useless.'"[43] Thus, through the embodiment of labour and value in material things and commodities, Tinkcom argues that the camp labourer is able to work under the alibi of value's homogenising abstraction, whereby the commodity *appears* to its recipient as the product of labour in general; but by conceptualising camp as the product of the labour of queers, camp opens the *possibility* that the commodity may be "marked" by such labour in an unforeseen manner, revealing its specific, qualitative production at a certain points in its cycle, or through a *knowing* mode of engagement.[44] While Tinkcom doesn't undertake an analysis of the value-form of the commodity, we might say that the labour of camp describes an undercover means of anonymised expression for queer men—to externalise a form of camp expression through the physical body, or natural form, of the commodity—that *may* be picked up by knowing queers at some point during or beyond the cycle of the commodity's circulation. While the abstraction of the value form of the commodity would seem to prevent any recognition of its producer—removing physical traces of its conditions of production as quantified value—Tinkcom's argument provides camp consumers with a sense of belonging, activated through the knowledge that someone strapping worked on the object of their gaze. Such a perspective challenges the fetish character of the commodity, by speculatively reading the imprint of an anonymous queer labourer back onto the commodity. The domain of cultural production, for Tinkcom, seems to provide a potential site of exception to value's homogenising abstraction.

Returning to the labourer, Tinkcom argues that the work of camp is often disguised under the sign of playfulness, as signified by a "lack of seriousness."[45] He argues that the *pleasurable* work of camp provides its active subject the possibility of a glimpse beyond themselves *through* their activity, that is the possibility of the camp labourer exteriorising a camp self-consciousness. Putting a queer spin on the young Marx's

---

[43]Tinkcom, *Working Like a Homosexual*, 9.

[44]Tinkcom, *Working Like a Homosexual*, 23–24, 10.

[45]Tinkcom, *Working Like a Homosexual*, 13.

consideration of the sensuous, corporeal character of self-consciousness to consider the erotics of labour under capital, he argues that

> Marx's recognition of human self-consciousness as 'other' to itself is fundamental to his account, and it is not, as he suggests, an otherness steeped only in negation; otherness from the physical world as a thinking creature and from the social subjects who surround us has its own rewards of knowledge.[46]

Compared the self-consciousness of negativity when performing estranged labour, camp labour may provide a queer subject the knowledge of his qualitative difference in light of the demands of heteronormative capitalist society—within which labour must be subordinated to the homogeneous reproduction of value and profit for capital through the wage relation. Camp labour enables the queer subject to mark his otherness through labour and pleasurable work, his difference from heteronormative cultures that require social conformity in order to be reproduced, while his difference simultaneously remains under the radar of these heteronormative cultures, recognised only through a particular mode of engagement.[47] To elucidate this possibility, Tinkcom considers the "inappropriate emotions" of queerness, "which themselves have strong homologies with the status given to homosexuality within normative imaginations."[48] The *labour* of these emotions in cinema, for instance, is a mode of camp expression; this labour also denotes a consciousness of how to survive the negative reactions and violence of homophobia in the world. Hence, such "labor on the commodity, stage[s] in deflected fashion such forms of affect again in the world."[49] The affective, qualitative character of camp labour in such cultural production thus becomes a mode of exterior expression and production for queer men, to both realise themselves as the subjects of camp, and as a strategy of resistance to homophobia that also creates a coded product of queerness, which can be received by knowing audiences.

---

[46] Tinkcom, *Working Like a Homosexual*, 25.

[47] Tinkcom develops a distinction between labour and work-as-play in relation to camp labour though Hannah Arendt's critique of Marx in *The Human Condition* (Tinkcom, 2002: 11–13).

[48] Tinkcom, *Working Like a Homosexual*, 26.

[49] Tinkcom, *Working Like a Homosexual*, 26.

Between the two models of queer work and camp labour developed by Bérubé and Tinkcom, respectively, we have a historicised conception of queer work amid the racialised and gendered division of labour within pre-World War II, white America, where certain labour practices emanate queerness through the transgression of this division of labour. Through such practices, Bérubé's research bears witness to the (re)production of queer cultures on and off the job, which enables the creation of particular forms of resistance and resilience. Furthermore, we have a mode of camp labour amid the contradictions of the capitalist production of value, one that enables the exteriorisation of queerness and queer self-conscious through forms of pleasurable work, deflecting the recognition of camp to only knowing audiences. Bérubé's model importantly understands the historicised, public forms that queer work takes in relation to white heteronormative society, while at a later historical moment Tinkcom's camp labourer works under the radar, under the alibi of camp hidden through the value-form, read as queer only through particular forms of engagement. Both models give importance to the affective, qualitative character of this labour, which can provide queer subjects an important outlet for sexual and emotional exteriorisation. While capital demands conformity and homogeneity—varying at different historical moments—from the bearers of its labour-power, which collides with societal homophobia, transphobia, and racism, queer subjects find ways to remain engaged in the labour process. The concealment and expression of our sexual and gender deviances may be confronted, or disappeared, by capital and the commodity fetish—at times violently, as witnessed with the *Fag Rag/Gay Community News* fire discussed below.

Building upon the models formulated by Bérubé and Tinkcom, we can propose the concept of queer labour to describe historically situated forms of work labour, within racialised and gendered divisions of labour under capitalism, whereby gender and sexual transgressions may materialise within production, either in the cultural context of the labour itself or through the reception of its products. Under the working conditions of queer labour, certain expressions of queerness may be immediately expressible to one's colleagues and employers, or may become intelligible through particular forms of consumption. Amid the heteronormative cultures of the workplace, queer labour (or queer work) elaborates a space, both positively and negatively, for gender and sexual deviants to work: as Bérubé describes, it can be both "a trap that confines lesbian and gay

workers to a few acceptable jobs" and a "refuge."⁵⁰ Such a space can also
be a world, in a sense similar to that theorised by Berlant and Warner:

> 'world', like 'public', differs from community or group because it neces-
> sarily includes more people than can be identified, more spaces than can
> be mapped beyond a few reference points, modes of feeling that can be
> learned rather than experienced from birthright.⁵¹

Reading the labour of queer performers of colour through the
workerist theory of C. L. R. James, Muñoz suggests that such performers can be conceived of as workers and "world-historical entities",
undertaking "queer world-making as a mode of labor."⁵² For Muñoz,
performing queerness as a form of labour is "a doing for and toward
the future," amid capitalist societies where the "here and now is a
prison house."⁵³ Queer labour may describe the work that posits such
worlds—that forges knowledges, cultural products, sites and new needs
through which the qualitative difference of queerness is reflected back
to its producers, creating networks and enabling affectivities, where
its alterity is acknowledged, received, and consumed by other queers.
Queer labour may create worlds of possibilities that influence, impact,
and transform the lives and work of others. While queer labour is not
production *after* the end of alienated labour under capitalism,⁵⁴ it is

---

⁵⁰Bérubé, *My Desire for History*, 266–267.

⁵¹Warner and Berlant, "Sex in Public", 558.

⁵²Muñoz, *Cruising Utopia*, 56, see 49–64. Muñoz reads James' momentary examples
of supposed, "actually existing socialist realit[ies] in the present"–such as a factory where
the division of labour has been restructured by the workers to enable a worker, who was
no longer able to carry out his work, to retain his position (55). He relatedly "gestures"
to "sites of embodied and performed queer politics" through this reading, to "describe
them as outposts of actually existing queer worlds" (49). In his definition, "minoritarian"
describes "citizen-subjects, who, due to antagonisms within the social such as race, class
and sex, are debased within the majoritarian public sphere" (56).

⁵³Muñoz, *Cruising Utopia*, 1.

⁵⁴In the closing of his 1844 *Comment on James Mill*, Marx considers what labour
would look like if we "carried out production as human beings," once the conditions of
alienated labour were superseded, i.e. under communism. He writes that "Our products
would be so many mirrors in which we saw reflected our essential nature," in that one
would objectify their individuality through labouring; and that "In your enjoyment or
use of my product I would have the direct enjoyment both of being conscious of having
satisfied a human need by my work, that is, of having objectified man's essential nature,

work that challenges the alienation of labour under capitalism, in part by enabling the collective possibilities of LGBTQ life and communalism by directly producing queer and trans cultures. In the sense that queer labour may enable intimacies that are or have been subject to duress and criminalisation within white heteronormative and ableist capitalist society, such work would necessarily overlap with forms of queer and trans social reproduction.[55] Furthermore, the potentiality of queer labour—in terms of what work and worlds become possible—remain mediated by the demands of capital.

Bérubé's work provides a significant example of how such worlds can be posited within the capitalist workplace, and the politics of Gay Liberation might be read as forging the demand to radically transform the conditions under which we work and what may be actualised through one's labour. The challenge to the closet of Gay Liberation is not limited to the social sphere, and its demand for the self and communal actualisation of gays, lesbians, and other queer and trans people include challenges to overcoming alienated labour and capitalism. As Wieners pens in *Behind the State Capitol,*

and of having thus created an object corresponding to the need of another man's essential nature." Such work would be "a free manifestation of life, hence an enjoyment of life." The freedom and the possibilities of self-expression and validation expressed by Marx in this text are somewhat different from my and Tinkcom's descriptions of queer labour and camp labour, in that these labours remain bound to the conditions of labour and production under capitalism. The self, or collective, expression that may be enacted through queer labour may enable queer and trans life and may be enjoyable; however it is work that is undertaken when one inhabits an abject position within or adjacent to wage labour—abjection inflected by societal prejudice and a gendered and racialised division of labour. Camp labour explicitly engages with the conditions of homophobia of forms of labour in America in the 1950s. Note that Marx's early definition of alienation, or estranged labour in the *1844 Economic and Philosophic Manuscripts,* is considerably different to its definition in *Capital.*

[55] Indeed, Muñoz's definition of queerness as an affective "ideality" that "lets us feel that *this* world is not enough" comes with the call to both "dream and *enact* new and better pleasures, other ways of being in the world, and ultimately new worlds" (2009: 1, emphasis added). This can be read as tying affective understanding to a Marxist call for social transformation.

responding to an essay by Charley Shively, with a highly complex syntax that echoes an idiom of Marx:

> A factor of consciousness developing in the gay world, conducive to those or whomever one's audience or prey is straightly reminding one, our people that despite sordid, past histories and oft-inherited bigotry from countless, other civilizations over the face of the earth, expressed to self-indulgence of the most blatant matter, gaining some satisfaction in self-effort, that they are real and different persons with the largest potential of the whole, human race for the realization of their own, since they have been blasphemed for so long, morally good selves.[56]

Demanding the fullest possible realisation of gay life, Wieners here articulates the Liberation-era consciousness of the potential of gays and lesbians. As we have seen and as I discuss further below, such a consciousness claims a public and (inter)national stage, and materialises into forms of cultural production and political intervention—such as newspapers, poetry, and/or protest—that challenge the alienations of hetero- and cis-normative capitalist society. Compared to the labour that reproduces white heterosexist capitalist society and its subjects, queer labour in the Liberation era works to inaugurate alternative publics and worlds.

The Labour of Queer World-Making, in Wieners' San Francisco, 1958

To this effect, we can consider queer labour as taking the historically situated forms of work in relation to racialised and gendered divisions of labour under capitalism, including forms of socially reproductive labour of queer lives. To undertake queer labour is to undertake a "world-making project" in the sense formulated by Berlant and Warner and dovetailed by José Esteban Muñoz. Berlant and Warner argue that "every cultural form, be it a novel or an after-hours club or an academic lecture, indexes a virtual social world." In their formulation

> 'world', like 'public', differs from community or group because it necessarily includes more people than can be identified, more spaces than can

---

[56]Wieners, *Behind the State Capitol*, 88.

be mapped beyond a few reference points, modes of feeling that can be learned rather than experienced from birthright.[57]

Furthermore, Muñoz suggests that minoritarian performers can be conceived as workers and "world-historical entities," undertaking "queer world-making as a mode of labor."[58] Hence, queer labour might be oriented towards the forms of physical and emotional labour that enable such worlds to be posited, to potentially cohere, or to enable intimacies which are or have been subject to duress and criminalisation within white heteronormative and ableist capitalist society. Indeed, Muñoz's definition of queerness as an affective "ideality" that "lets us feel that *this* world is not enough" comes with the call to both "dream and *enact* new and better pleasures, other ways of being in the world, and ultimately new worlds" (emphasis added).[59] Performing queerness as a form of labour is "a doing for and toward the future."[60] Bérubé's work provides a significant example of how such worlds can be posited within the capitalist workplace; the labour of Gay Liberation provides us with an example of how such labour claims a public and (inter)national stage, to enact a world necessary for the survival and potentially the fullest realisation of gay and lesbian life. Compared to the labour that reproduces white heterosexist capitalist society and its subjects, we have the work that reflects its deviations to the worker who undertakes it, to those who have learned to read the queerness of such work, in the cause of inaugurating an alternative queer world.

Wieners' "A poem for cock suckers" captures the beauty and politics of San Francisco's bar scene of the late 1950s, a queer world enabling

---

[57] Berlant and Warner, "Sex in Public," 558.

[58] José E. Muñoz, *Cruising Utopia: The Then and There of Queer Futurity* (New York: New York University Press, 2009), 56. Also see Muñoz, *Cruising Utopia*, 49–64. Muñoz reads James' momentary examples of supposed, "actually existing socialist realit[ies] in the present"—such as a factory where the division of labour has been restructured by the workers to enable a worker, who was no longer able to carry out his work, to retain his position (55). He relatedly "gestures" to "sites of embodied and performed queer politics" through this reading, to "describe them as outposts of actually existing queer worlds" (49). In his definition, "minoritarian" describes "citizen-subjects, who, due to antagonisms within the social such as race, class and sex, are debased within the majoritarian public sphere" (56).

[59] Muñoz, *Cruising Utopia*, 1.

[60] Muñoz, *Cruising Utopia*, 1.

sexual and gender transgressions while stabilising its legal right to exist.[61] "Well we can go / in the queer bars," suggest, simply, the first lines, in a plurality of honest fatalism, "after all / what have we got left." Wieners' use of the possessive plural pronoun "our"—"*our* long hair," "*our* songs / of love like the black mama on the juke box"—demonstrates a sense of belonging through the image and pleasures possible here and the social identification of queer persons with other marginal voices such as Black female singers (who may also be queer). "On *our right* the fairies / giggle in their lacquered / voices & blow / smoke in your eyes let them" (emphasis added)—the golden coating of queer beauty and the flirtations of the fairies enable the desiring of the queer bar's patrons and aid them to "retain strength" in "a nigger's [sic] world"; although while not uncommon in the logic of white gay people (contemporaneously and in the present day), as Somerville discusses in *Queering the Color Line*, analogies which "assume that being a person of color is 'like' being gay" often "obscure those who inhabit both identifications," positing whiteness as a dominant norm and erasing the historical specificity of both positions.[62] The bars, as Wieners sees them, provide a condition of collective solidity ("The gifts do not desert us, / fountains do not dry") and possibly ("there are mountains / swelling for spring to cascade"). These are utopian situations, as Andrea Brady suggests, "defined through the poem's own remastery of abusive language"; however, contra Brady's suggestion that the poet also "neuters" these words by "placing such words in a frame of camp or ornate language," evacuating and explicitly de-sexualising the political possibilities of camp in the poem, these are also concrete sites of queer struggle.[63] In her important book on the queer history of San Francisco, Nan Alamilla Boyd argues that the

[61]Wieners, *Supplication*, 18–19. Wieners discusses his relationship to San Francisco's North Beach and Tenderloin LGBTQ scenes from the 1950s in his second *Gay Sunshine* interview (Leyland, *Gay Sunshine Interviews: Volume 2*, 274).

[62]Siobhan B. Somerville, *Queering the Color Line: Race and the Invention of Homosexuality in American Culture* (Durham and London: Duke University Press, 2000), 7–8. Davidson's reading of 'A poem for cocksuckers' argues that the poet's comparison of "forms of social marginalization," such as of blackness and sexual deviance, "reinforces" his linguistic challenges to the logic of white heteronormative society (1998: 276). This citation of Somerville is also used by Tatonetti in her discussion of *Fag Rag* 18 and Maurice Kenny's disruption of white space and what she describes as "'Indigenous' filler art" (2014: 55–61, citation on 58, quote from 55).

[63]Andrea Brady, "Making Use of This Pain," 337.

San Francisco queer bar and tavern scenes of this era had "the greatest amount of community interaction and mounted the heaviest challenge to mainstream law and order." The bars provided a world for queers and gender non-conforming groups that "expressed multiple and overlapping social identities based on class, race and gender," who "fought to secure public space for themselves," and furthermore "worked to protect that space from hostile outsiders."[64] Such labour of both the creation and maintenance of queer space and the sexual and gender expressions flourishing within them was thus a direct challenge to the law and order stabilising late '50s California. While the threat of law and order cannot be expunged entirely from the reality shrouding the queer world of the bars ("Take not / away from me the small fires / I burn in the memory of love."), Wieners' poem evidences these conditions, which maintain the space and possibility of desire and queer memory:

> It is all here between
> the powdered legs &
> painted eyes of the fair
> Friends who do not fail us
> Mary in our hour of
>   despair.

The body of the fairy, the space between her dressed limbs and decorated, lustrous eyes—the space of her gender deviance and the work this requires to maintain—holds a queer world ideologically positioned against the reality of the law. Furthermore this is an alternative world to that of the Catholic morality that Wieners struggled with throughout the 1950s–1970s. The fairy, in her pleasure and beauty, posits the antithesis of the Virgin Mary. Wieners writes in "The Address of the Watchman to the Night" that "the form of the poem, with its order, expressions and release" provides the possibility of "Communion"—with both "the ordinary things of life" and furthermore, the subject of the Wieners' text, "those dark eternals of the nightworld: the prostitute, the dope addict, thief and pervert."[65] For the mutuality of such marginalised figures and

---

[64] Nan Alamilla Boyd, *Wide Open Town: A History of Queer San Francisco to 1965* (Berkeley, Los Angeles and London: University of California Press, 2005), 14.

[65] John Wieners, "The Address of the Watchman to the Night," in Allen and Tallman (1973: 351–352). Wieners' text is dated "Saturday April 27th 1963."

their "interior beliefs [to] mingle with a cohesion of world"—that is, to achieve communion in a world thus reflected in a poem like "Cock suckers"—Wieners suggests that the poet must plumb the depths of their lives by "becom[ing] every one of them." Through this, the poet may "let live the divine reign" through the word, such that "The world [is] revealed in a word." As witnessed across *The Hotel Wentley Poems*, here the divine is found in the places that straight white America wishes to destroy on moral grounds—which in "Cock suckers" is embodied in the figure of the fairy, who provides pleasure, beauty, and support to the queer bar's patrons when they are low, blasphemously negates in rhyme the Holy Virgin, in the world of queer communion.[66]

Boyd discusses the development of politicised community and support through the bar and tavern scene: following increased surveillance of queer bars and taverns in California across the 1940s,

> in 1951, Sol Stouman, the owner of the Black Cat bar, won a state supreme court case against the State Board of Equalization that affirmed the right to serve alcohols to homosexuals. Explicit in this decision was the right to public association, a conclusion that overturned the most effective tool of local policing agencies: the presumed illegality of gay bars and taverns.[67]

Following the case, there was a proliferation of queer bars and nightlife in the city, which was challenged again in 1955 by the state's newly created Alcoholic Beverage Control Board; however, the owners and patrons of bars challenged the state with a number of legal cases

---

[66]The word "Mary" is deleted in both Wieners' *Selected Poems* (1972) and *Selected Poems: 1958–1984* (1986). Arguably, given Wieners' challenges to God and religion across *The Hotel Wentley Poems*, the deletion of the word in the republishing of the poem with the retention of the space the word occupied, still carries the echo of the deleted rhyming word:

It is all here between
the powdered legs &
painted eyes of the fairy
friends who do not fail us
in our hour of
   despair (Wieners 1986: 36).

[67]Boyd, *Wide Open Town*, 16.

asserting their right to public association and emphasising their "understand[ing of] the power to collective action" as a group in "defend[ing] their territory from police intrusion."[68] Furthermore, the working class life and transgender expressions of the bars were part of a subculture that the contemporaneous homophile movement—who had been active in San Francisco from 1950—were trying to distance themselves from, as their largely white middle-class constituents pursued assimilation into American society.[69] With the existence of the bars amid the threat of the law, Boyd argues that a "siege mentality" developed, within which lay the conditions of the "swelling" of queer consciousness, borne out of the labour to protect the public life of these queer worlds and their patrons.[70] The labour of political challenges to the law was necessary for the basic existence of these public queer communities and spaces, and a means to an income for those who ran the bars. Through such work, queer worlds within such public spaces were made possible, including the gender and sexual expressions that emerge and occupy them, alongside the expressions of desire and possibility that are borne in cultural products like Wieners' poem. Both the collective work protecting the bars, and the socially reproductive labour taking place within them, provide the conditions whereby the figure of the fairy may hold the communion captured by the queer poet, enabling his utterances ("On our right").

MAKING GAY LIBERATION

We can extend the thesis of queer labour to address the historical moment of Gay Liberation—whereby gay activist labour and that of social reproduction is socially necessary for the survival and coming into being of lesbian and gay life, defined by breaking taboos around self and collective proclamation and affirmation, alongside the establishment of a visible gay media and culture. At its most radical, this work intended the transformation of society to enable the life of sexual and gender deviants to their utmost—the production and creation of a sexually and politically

---

[68] Boyd, *Wide Open Town*, 17.

[69] Boyd, *Wide Open Town*, 14. For one account of homophile organising in the 1950s among many, see John D'Emilio, *Sexual Politics, Sexual Communities: The Making of a Homosexual Minority in the United States* 1940–1970 (Chicago and London: University of Chicago Press, 1983), 57–125.

[70] Boyd, *Wide Open Town*, 17.

revolutionary society. The political consciousness that developed across the '50s and '60s, as we have seen above in the case of gay and lesbian organising among the San Francisco bar and tavern scene, sometimes took the form of a specific struggle against law and order and led to numerous "militant" uprisings against police repression—including the incident at Cooper's Donuts, a coffeehouse in Los Angeles, May 1959; a less violent incident at Dewey's lunch counter in Philadelphia, April 1965; the riot at Compton's Cafeteria in the Tenderloin District, San Francisco, 1966[71]; and the Stonewall uprising in Greenwich Village, New York City, June 1969.[72] In each of these queer riots, police harassment centred on street queens, i.e. transvestites and transsexuals who had no material means of survival beyond sex work, who lived between hotels and the pavement; and poor and/or working class gay men and lesbians, who primarily or only had access to public queer spaces such as bars or coffeehouses. Many of those rioting were queer persons of colour, who would be distanced by racism from the political organising that followed. The radicalisation of gay and lesbian political organising in the United States formed a continuum emerging out of the more liberal struggles of the homophile movements, struggles for public space such as bars, taverns, and cafeterias, and the hugely significant political struggles of the sixties—the Black Civil Rights and Black Power movements, the Anti-War Movement against the US's imperialist war in Vietnam, the Women's Movement, the New Left, the student movements of 1968, and Native American struggles against US colonialism within North America. The Stonewall uprising was catalytic for national and international gay and lesbian activism, and in New York the weeks after Stonewall would see the founding of the Gay Liberation Front (GLF), naming itself in solidarity with the National Liberation Front of South

[71] Stryker, *Transgender History*, 59–75. For detail on the latter, see also Stryker, "Transgender History, Homonormativity, and Disciplinarity," as well as her documentary *Screaming Queens: The Riot at Compton's Cafeteria.*

[72] Accounts of the Stonewall riot are too numerous to detail. For starters, see Donn Teal, *The Gay Militants* (New York: Stein and Day, 1971); Martin Duberman, *Stonewall* (New York: Dutton; Plume, 1994); David Carter, *Stonewall: The Riot that Sparked the Gay Revolution* (New York: St Martin's Press, 2004); and Stryker, *Transgender History*, 82–86. While Duberman's book is sometimes criticised for mistakes on historical details, his work is important given the subjects of his oral history (Craig Rodwell, Yvonne Flowers, Karla Jay, Sylvia Rivera, Jim Fouratt and Foster Gunnison Jr.) and the differences of their experience that intersect with gender, race and class.

Vietnam. While many of those in the GLF and its cells had been involved in the important movements of the sixties and experienced homophobia within these movements, the GLF would importantly pledge and find solidarity with various parts of the 'movement of movements,' leading to the support of demonstrations by the Black Panther Party and the Young Lords, among others.[73]

Gay Liberation as an ideology was based on a critique of the repressive heteronormative social institutions of the state and capitalist society (the police, prisons, psychiatric institutions and psychiatry, homophobic schools and universities), the church, the media, workplaces, and the nuclear family. It would politicise the slogan 'Gay is Good,' arguing, in the words of Martha Shelley, that it is "too late" for a liberal attitude of tolerating homosexuality.[74] As Shelley among others argued, gay men and women existed as the negation of heteronormative society. Addressing "straights" in a second person address, she writes "we are

[73] In Duberman's *Stonewall* (1994), Karla Jay and Jim Fouratt recount their experiences of homophobia in the Women's Liberation movement and the anti-war and Yippie movements respectively. Jay describes her experience and that of lesbian women involved in Redstockings.

Homophobia in the Black Panther Party would become an important issue for the Gay Liberation movement, especially following the publication of Eldridge Cleaver's *Soul on Ice* (1968). While the rhetoric of the Panthers originally deployed words like 'faggot' to describe white capitalist oppressors, Huey P. Newton wrote an important letter in 1970, calling for members of the Party to "relate to the homosexual movement because it's a real thing." Emphasising the oppression of homosexuals in society, including that from the Panthers' own homophobic fear of homosexuality, he writes that homosexuals "might be the most oppressed people in society." Furthermore, he argues that "we must understand [homosexuality] in its purest form: That is, a person should have freedom to use his body in whatever way he wants to"; and, emphasising the potential allies in the Women's liberation and Gay Liberation movements, Newton calls for their "full participation" in "revolutionary conferences, rallies and demonstrations" ('Huey Newton on Gay Liberation,' in Leyland, *Gay Roots*, 207–208, also published in *Gay Sunshine* [No. 2, October 1970]). The movements involvement in the People's Revolutionary Conference in Philadelphia, September 1970, saw the Panthers supporting a statement made by the male caucus of Gay Liberation (reprinted in Jay and Young, *Out of the Closets*, 346–352), however women and black people in the movement struggled with sexism and issues of white dominance.

I discuss the intersection of Third World Liberation and Gay Liberation groups in New York in my essay, "'out of jail and into the streets': Street Action Transvestite Revolutionaries and the praxis of transfeminism of color" (Raha, forthcoming).

[74] Martha Shelley, "Gay Is Good," in *Out of the Closets: Voices of Gay Liberation*, ed. Karla Jay and Allen Young (New York: New York University Press, 1993).

alien. You have managed to drive your own homosexuality under the skin of your mind – and to drive us down and out into the gutter of self-contempt."[75] In a politicised response and understanding of selves as 'Gay,' gay men and women emerge as "the extrusions of your unconscious mind – your worst fears made flesh."[76] Positing Gay Liberation as a form of class struggle, Karla Jay writes in the 1972 introduction to *Out of the Closets*:

> We perceive our oppression as a class struggle and our oppressor as white, middle-class, male-dominated heterosexual society, which has relentlessly persecuted and murdered homosexuals and lesbians since the oppressor had power. We are the negation of heterosexuality and of the nuclear family structure, and as such we have been driven from our jobs, our families, our education, and sometimes from life itself.[77]

Such class struggle is articulated in Wieners' 1973 poem "Viva," which—in comparison to Jay's analysis of gay and lesbians having been driven out of White heteronormative 'mentalist'[78] capitalist America—figures the struggle of Liberation as a struggle *for* queer life that cannot leave even the familial dead of this society undisturbed:

> Drag them out of their places,
> for they block the progress of our lives, our times,
> drag them out of their graves,
> even if they were our parents,
> for they barricade the streets of our protest, our loves;
> contaminate afternoons with lanterns from poems
> by questions of industry and idleness,[79]

---

[75] Shelley, "Gay Is Good," 33.

[76] Shelley, "Gay Is Good," 31.

[77] Karla Jay, "Introduction" [1972], in *Out of the Closets: Voices of Gay Liberation*, ed. Karla Jay and Allen Young (New York: New York University Press, 1993), lxi.

[78] Judi Chamberlin describes mentalism as a belief in the inferiority of ex-patients (survivors of psychiatric incarceration), primarily discussing its internalisation by ex-patients, "which must be consciously rooted out," and which consciousness raising in the Mental Patients' Liberation movement worked to challenge (Chamberlin, *On Our Own*, 173).

[79] Wieners, *Supplication*, 115.

In the poem's present, the fabric of straight white America is literally blockading a liberated future for those it has exiled, as the poem posits the 'poisonous' morality of this "smug aristocracy" through a series of statements beginning with transitive verbs ("barricade," "contaminate," "encourage"). Against the illumination of literary, subcultural forms we hear the echo of straight white America's rhetoric of productivity and productive labour. Even the "graves" of straight white Americans form a half rhyme with "barricade," preventing the public demonstration of Gay Liberation and the desires that grow with it, these seemingly "weird needs" that have "rewards sweet." Indeed white America has "refused to consider" them, answering with the sentences of "poverty" and incarceration in prisons and hospitals. Thus white America's dead block the transformation of life; 'their' living "breed death and young graves," and "heartless despair" for oppressed peoples, that is the reproduction of straight life and heteronormativity breeds queer social death.[80] The poem closes with a denunciation of straight white American values, piling up alliterative consonants to illuminate the toxic plagues of this society: "Stealing beneath bosoms to fester automatically in leeches / As enormous tumours out from the poverty of their lusts."

Furthermore, Jay's formation of Gay Liberation's struggle as one of class does not preclude the heterogeneities within this class—the oppression of gay women by gay men, black gays by white gays, transvestites (and other gender non-conformists) by "straight-looking gays" also gave the need to "combat our own chauvinism, our own sexism, our own racism."[81] The failure to combat these latter challenges would create major friction within many aspects of the movement, ultimately creating splits and the part of the conditions of this radical political project's downfall. However, the emphasis on challenging both one's own consciousness, the consciousness of one's peers, and that of heteronormative white capitalist society, highlights the distinctiveness of the movement (and other movements of the late '60s and early '70s), when compared with the liberal political project that would emerge and overtake it, exemplified by the single-issue yet militant politics of the Gay Activist Alliance.

We can argue that the activist labour of the Gay Liberation movement—of demonstrations against repressive state organs and

---

[80]Wieners, *Supplication*, 116.
[81]Jay and Young, *Out of the Closets*, lxi–lxii.

organisations, attending movement meetings and developing activist groups, the work of consciousness-raising groups, writing letters to incarcerated gays and lesbians, creating centres for homeless queer and trans people, writing and publishing poetry, fiction and interviews with queer cultural producers, et cetera, and (importantly) the forms of social and sexual life that cohere within, between, and through such work—represent the necessary labour for the production of a *world* where Gay Liberation can blossom.[82] At the historical moment of Gay Liberation, queer activist labour directed towards the negation of white heterosexual capitalist society to enable life for sexual and gender deviants importantly involves challenging heteronormative "modes of feeling,"[83] that in Wieners' and Shelley's formulations breed social repression and death for gay women and men. Sexuality and gender expressions must necessarily and creatively be relearnt from the normative expressions assigned to certain genders, and the heteronormative lives expected of men and women—varying significantly in regard to class, race, dis/ability, and mental health—challenged and reconstructed.

Printing Liberation:
Fag Rag and Gay Liberation in Boston

Newspapers, providing reports on activism, resources, and events, addressing queer social issues, spreading critique, and publishing literature and art, were an important part of the movement, supporting consciousness-raising and cultural production. The number of gay and lesbian newspapers proliferated from a handful representing the homophile movement of the '60s (and earlier) into the hundreds during the '70s. John D'Emilio suggests that this explosion was partly due to the fact that in the '50s and '60s "[m]ainstream journalism had been one of the bastions of homophobia."[84] Furthermore, he writes that "[t]he community press was, really the only resource other than word of mouth for letting people know that *a new world, a new outlook, and a new*

---

[82] The pages of *Gay Sunshine* and *Fag Rag* regularly included letters from and addressing issues of gay men in prison.

[83] Berlant and Warner, "Sex in Public," 558.

[84] Quoted in Tracey Baim (ed.), *Gay Press, Gay Power: The Growth of LGBT Community Newspapers in America* (Chicago: Prairie Avenue Productions and Winder City Media Group, 2012), 9.

community were in formation" (emphasis added).[85] Indeed the methods of producing and typesetting were undergoing a revolution in the late '60s and early '70s, which enabled the thriving production of countercultural newspapers.[86] Thus newspapers were fundamental for the world-making of Gay Liberation, enabling the knowledge and the consciousness of Gay *being*. A 1973 *Fag Rag* editorial describes the "elementary level" of this gay world-making that enables subjects to index themselves as Gay: "you give her, him a face, a reality.... We open the pages and let the queers talk about themselves. We listen. And it starts with this fact: I see, I perceive, I think."[87] Through engaging with Liberation newspapers, gays and lesbians are able to posit an 'I' among a communally produced, gay consciousness; these 'I's and the subjects they belong to must explore and develop themselves through thought, critique and praxis, through the multiple forms of labour and sociality described as 'Gay.'

Through content and form, newspapers were fundamental in providing reflexive and political critique—where politics involves the diverse forms of queer work described above. As was the case *Fag Rag*, newspapers were a significant platform for the revolutionary programmes of Gay Liberation, alongside the quotidian, artistic, and creative productions of the movement. Through such labours we see the expansion and spread of gay political consciousness; we see the transformation and politicisation of gay consciousness reflected in the work printed in movement papers, undoubtedly aided by consciousness-raising groups, alongside the production and design of movement papers themselves. Furthermore, while oral history has been an important mode of documenting LGBTQ history and that of other liberation movements, newspapers provide significant documents of the work—practical, material and theoretical—of the movement.

Alongside a significant amount of poetry, *Fag Rag* published influential and controversial essays, literature, graphic illustrations, and photography addressing intersecting issues of gay sexuality, race, cultural production, gender-fucking, prisons and psychiatric incarceration,

---

[85] Quoted in Baim, *Gay Press, Gay Power*, 10.

[86] Charley Shively, "*Fag Rag*: The Most Loathesome Publication in the English Language," in *Insider Histories of the Vietnam Era Underground Press, Part 2*, ed. Ken Wachsberger (East Lansing, Michigan: Michigan State University Press, 2012).

[87] *Fag Rag*, no. 4 (January 1973), reverse cover (n.p.).

capitalism, the Left, and state legislation. It also published practical information of Boston/Cambridge Massachusetts area resources for lesbians and gay men. While the paper and its Californian sibling paper *Gay Sunshine* seem to be largely forgotten pieces of gay liberation history, further marginalised by their radical content, the papers have been the subject of recent academic attention, in particular in Lisa Tatonetti's *The Queerness of Native American Literature* (2014) and work by Robbie Dewhurst.[88] In *Beyond Shame*, a book addressing the lost history of "Radical Gay Sexuality," Patrick Moore briefly highlights the importance of *Fag Rag*'s synthesis of "Gay Fairie sensibility with left politics" and pornography:

> *Fag Rag* is of singular importance because it articulated a far more radical and isolationist view than the earnest coalition-building so common in gay politics. It also resisted a commercialized version of gay life where the 'correct' body, disco, gym, and vacation spots were carefully identified as markers of belonging. *Fag Rag* embraced gay male sexuality while insisting on critiquing it from a political perspective and denouncing a uniformity of male beauty.[89]

Moore further highlights the paper's significant commitment to a critique of the class constructions of gay sexual and gender expressions, in part reflected by its attention to "the more 'vulnerable' members of the gay community," including working-class people, minors, sex workers, and transvestites.[90] Moore's reading of the paper is brief, although he argues that its ideas were significant in developing the political consciousness of gay men across the tumultuous 1970s, as single-issue and socially reformist tendencies became the dominant direction of the gay and lesbian movements.[91]

---

[88] See Robbie Dewhurst, "*Gay Sunshine*, Pornopoetic Collage, and Queer Archive," in *Porn Archives*, ed. Tim Dean, David Squires, and Stephen Ruszczycky (Durham and London: Duke University Press, 2014)

[89] Patrick Moore, *Beyond Shame: Reclaiming the Abandoned History of Radical Gay Sexuality* (Boston: Beacon Press, 2004), 7.

[90] Moore, *Beyond Shame*, 8.

[91] Moore's reading of *Fag Rag* as 'isolationist' ought to be understood in the context of the shift of gay and lesbian politics towards single-issue organising (around 'gay issues' only, i.e. white middle class and often cisgender gay male issues, rather than coalitional issues with other liberation movements). *Fag Rag* repeatedly refused this form of politics and also refused separatism in regards to their own politics.

In her recovery of Native American poet Maurice Kenny's work published in *Fag Rag*—the first publication of out queer writing by a Native American writer in the USA[92]—Lisa Tatonetti provides a critical reading of *Fag Rag* and work performed by Kenny's "regular inclusion" in the paper, which as she argues "disrupts a sense of these early journals as largely white and at the same time enlarges the parameters and concerns of a coeval literary moment Kenneth Lincoln termed the 'Native American renaissance.'"[93]

Winston Leyland, editor of *Gay Sunshine*, has emphasised the important role of the two papers as leading outlets for both the literary and socio-political aspects of what he describes as the "Gay Cultural Renaissance"—the "rediscovery of the Gay Cultural heritage and its expression, especially since Stonewall, through art, music, literature, film and many other ways."[94] Poet Aaron Shurin describes the papers as "the primary theoretical agents for the emerging gay literary sensibility,"[95] and in the case of Charley Shively's work, the papers took liberation politics to controversial extremes. As Leyland suggests, publication in such papers also provided an important retroactive space for writers to 'come out' and for the reception of their experiences.[96] Describing the physical growth of *Fag Rag's* size and the amount of poetry included in the publication, Tatonetti writes:

> By the time Kenny was first published in *Fag Rag* – issue 10, fall 1974 – the size of the newspaper had doubled, with most issues averaging thirty pages. The number of poems included in each edition had increased exponentially as well, and, as opposed to the practice of the early issues, most subsequent poems were attributed, though not always titled, from *Fag*

[92] Kenny's work first appears in *Fag Rag*, 10 (Fall 1974)—the '69 Poets' issue. Tatonetti provides a detailed reading of the different forms of work Kenny published in *Fag Rag* and *Gay Sunshine*, situating this work as part of a queer literary heritage of the Brooklyn Bridge, emphasising its diversions and re-encoding two spirit history and Gay Native experience in the 70s and its representations of age and disability. See Lisa Tatonetti, *The Queerness of Native American Literature* (Minneapolis and London: University of Minnesota Press, 2014), 28–66.

[93] Lisa Tatonetti, *The Queerness of Native American Literature*, 31.

[94] Leyland, *Gay Roots*, 19.

[95] Hennessy, *Homosexuality is a Poem*, 128.

[96] Winston Leyland (ed.), *Angels of the Lyre: A Gay Poetry Anthology* (San Francisco: Panjandrum Press and Gay Sunshine Press, 1975), 12.

Rag issue 5 onwards. In addition, the newspaper often interspersed two-page sections of poetry with the essays, letters and art that made up each issue.[97]

In the pages of these papers, we see a rapport between queer expressions and the worlds of such experience as addressed throughout Wieners' work and the work of other Gay writers, and the experiences of the readership of these internationally circulated newspapers.

The papers saw the publication and critical reception of Wieners' writing in the early-to-mid 1970s alongside that of numerous gay male writers and activists, American and international, past and present, including Jean Genet, Gore Vidal, Tennessee Williams, Allen Ginsberg, Peter Orlovsky, Jonathan Williams, John Giorno, Arthur Rimbaud, Paul Verlaine, Abu Newas, Maurice Kenny, W. H. Auden, Taylor Mead, Stephen Jonas, Frank O'Hara, Joe Brainard, Robert Duncan, Tommi Avicolli Mecca, and Anne Waldman. In 1973, Wieners was interviewed as part of *Gay Sunshine*'s influential interviews series of gay writers; and was featured prominently in gay male poetry anthologies published in the '70s.[98] Leyland described Wieners' *The Hotel Wentley Poems* as "the pioneering book" by a gay poet in the '50s, and gave the poet significant space in his gay male poetry anthology *Angels of the Lyre*.[99] Shively was a key champion of Wieners' writing within this context, composing numerous essays on the poet. Shively describes Wieners as "virtually the poet laureate of gay liberation," praising the magical quality and honest expressions of desperation, despair, and camp that characterised pre-liberation gay life in Wieners' poetry, highlighting these aspects as

---

[97] Lisa Tatonetti, *The Queerness of Native American Literature*, 34.

[98] Wieners' *Gay Sunshine* interview features in No. 17 (March/April 1973). It was also anthologised in Leyland, *Gay Sunshine Interviews: Volume 2*, and reprinted in edited form in Wieners' *Selected Poems 1958–1984* (1986), editing out a discussion of police surveillance. Ian Young (ed.), *The Male Muse* (Trumansberg: Crossing Press, 1973)—the anthology prints "Love-life," "Feminine Soliloquy," and "Paul"; and Gay Sunshine Press' *Angels of the Lyre* (Leyland, *Angels of the Lyre*, 212–223), which gives 11 pages to Wieners' work, printing "Impasse," "Act 2," "A Poem for the Old Man," "Ballade," "The Old Man," "In Love," "Contemplation," "Gusta with Madame Simone de Beauvoir," "How to Cope with This?" and "Two Years Later."

[99] Leyland, *Angels of the Lyre*, 8.

"lanterns" "[l]ighting paths through and beyond straight life"[100] (as echoed in Wieners' "Viva" and "The Lanterns Along the Wall").[101] Wieners also responded to Shively's radical liberation politics in his poetry, such as Shively's essay "Indiscriminate Promiscuity as an Act of Revolution," in which he argues that capitalism has influenced gay desire and the sexual valuation of certain bodies over others.[102] Furthermore, Wieners and Shively appear kissing in a photograph on the cover of *Fag Rag*, 44 (1987).[103] Rudy Kikel also penned essays on Wieners' writing.[104] However, while many of the above writers have been canonised inside and outside the sphere of LGBTQ literature, Wieners has become marginal to this canon—in the words of Black Mountain classmate and fellow queer writer Michael Rumaker, he remains one of the "invisible old fags."[105]

The labour of queer cultural production, the circulation of newspapers, the spread of poetry like that of Wieners, enables the political, social, intellectual, creative, sexual, and affective realisation of a world that held the promise of Liberation.[106] This was work largely unwaged,

[100] Review of John Wieners, *Selected Poems* (1972), in *Gay Sunshine*, no. 16 (January/February 1973), 20.

[101] Wieners, *Supplication*, 181–185.

[102] Throughout the '70s, Shively authored a series of radical and controversial essays on gay sexuality and sexual revolution, such as "Cocksucking as an Act of Revolution," "Indiscriminate Promiscuity as an Act of Revolution," etc. In the latter Shively argues for a "socialism of love and sex" and emphasising the materiality of bodies, he proposes the need to love all bodies indiscriminately of race, age, beauty, sex, or national origin (Leyland, *Gay Roots: Twenty Years of Gay Sunshine* [San Francisco: Gay Sunshine Press, 1991], 257–263, 261; first published in *Fag Rag/Gay Sunshine: Stonewall 5th Anniversary Issue* [Summer 1974]). Wieners responds to this article in *Behind the State Capitol* with the poem 'A Popular Belief as Practiced: Indiscriminate Promiscuity' (1975: 88–89).

[103] Issue 44's cover features John Wieners in a floral shirt, waistcoat and a large badge featuring Jackie Kennedy on his collar, lightly kissing Charley Shively, who wears a denim jacket and a flower in his top buttonhole. They appear to be at a demonstration in 1978. The photo is credited to Demian.

[104] Rudy Kikel, "Mythic Meaning in the Late Poetry of John Wieners," *Boston Gay Review*, no. 2 (Spring 1977), 7–10.

[105] Michael Rumaker, "Boston Tea Party," *Oyster Boy Review*, no. 8 (1998), online at www.oysterboyreview.org/archived/08/rumaker2.html (accessed 9 October 2015).

[106] However, we mustn't ignore the fact that the worlds produced by the work of gay liberation reproduced hierarchies of sexism, racism, classism, transmisogyny, ableism and ageism.

performed outside the reproduction of capital within heterosexist society; but by no means entirely outside, as writing, typesetting, printing and distributing newspapers required money and physical labour. Situating *Fag Rag* as one of many GLF newspapers produced across North America—alongside *Come Out* (New York), *Gay Liberator* (Detroit), *Body Politic* (Toronto), *The Furies* (Washington, DC), *Amazon Quarterly* and *Gay Sunshine* (Oakland and San Francisco), Shively argues that publication itself "could be an act of liberation," as it decentred the power of media and publicity, giving space to viewpoints even marginal within the Gay Liberation movement.[107] In addition, Tatonetti suggest that Maurice Kenny's work appearing in *Fag Rag* and *Gay Sunshine* in the 1970s constitutes an "intervention into the dominant narrative of *Fag Rag*."[108] Reading *Fag Rag*'s use of decontextualised images and art referencing 'Indigeneity' as "'Indigenous' filler art"[109] she argues that the white settler colonial logic reproduced through the two newspapers is disrupted by Kenny, where works such as his two 'Papago' poems "quietly break through this white noise to challenge the politics of the gay literary renaissance."[110] Besides the space given to marginal voices including those of incarcerated gay men, Native American writers, and transvestites, we might consider Wieners' own writing as one such marginal voice, given its radical aesthetics and its authorship by a working class, femme/drag queen, psychiatric survivor. The labour producing these papers in which radical ideas and marginal voices could be published against the norms of white heterosexist capitalist culture provided a significant, democratising space—if still a white space to be disrupted—as a queer social world; it leaves an important archive of such worlds, through which we can trace the labour of their production and the struggle and duress facing such work.

The GLF in Boston, Massachusetts developed out the Student Homophile League, which met at Boston University and produced a newsletter.[111] Like numerous other GLF groups, Boston GLF

---

[107] Shively, *Fag Rag*, n.p.

[108] Tantonetti, *The Queerness of Native American Literature*, 64.

[109] Lisa Tatonetti, *The Queerness of Native American Literature*, 58.

[110] Lisa Tatonetti, *The Queerness of Native American Literature*, 61.

[111] The *Boston Student Homophile League Newsletter*. In a letter to Wieners dated 22 February 1970, Shively writes to Wieners' of an exchange with female faculty member at Boston State that will be published in the paper, in which he quotes a poem by Wieners. Shively invites Wieners to the next SHL meeting (March 1970) and writes that "[s]ome

had a flash in the pan existence, from April to September 1970.[112] Out of this climate came the production of newspaper *Lavender Vision*. The first issue was published in November 1970 and produced with half the paper devoted to lesbian content and half to gay male content. However, charges of male domination in GLF meetings and the resultant necessity for autonomous lesbian organising would lead to the dissolution of the Boston GLF and its "reconstitut[ion]" as Gay Male Liberation (GML) and Gay Women's Liberation.[113] This led to the production of the second (and final) issue of *Lavender Vision* in May 1971 by lesbian women, alongside which appeared *Fag Rag* in June 1971, and the formation of the gay male collective that oversaw the latter.[114]

The production of *Fag Rag* was an endeavour of collective and politically minded labour. The paper was edited, compiled and typeset collectively, operating on a not-always-realised ethos of skill sharing; however, as few people involved in the paper had experience in publishing (except for Allen Young, who had worked at the *Liberation News Service*) and some people had some training in typing and photography, producing the paper enabled the development of skills. The paper was circulated nationally, numbering 5000 copies at times; and was a deviant quarterly, only managing to publish four issues in 1974. Tatonetti writes that

of the people in the Homophile League would be interested in hearing you read" (Charley Shively to John Wieners, 22 February 1970, courtesy of Michael Seth Stewart).

[112] For an account of the GLF in Boston, the micropolitics around its existence, and details of movement events in Boston 1970–1971, see John Kyper "Coming Out and Into the GLF: Banned No More in Boston" in Tommi Avicolli Mecca (ed.), *Smash the Church, Smash the State! The Early Years of Gay Liberation* (San Francisco: City Lights Books, 2009) 31–39.

[113] Kyper, "Coming Out and Into The GLF" in Mecca, *Smash the Church, Smash the State!*, 35. *Lavender Vision* (Issue 1, No. 2, May 1971) details information regarding Boston Gay Women's Liberation meetings in May 1971 (2). William J. Canfield Papers, Archives and Special Collections, Snell Library, Northeastern University, Boston, Massachusetts.

[114] Shively also suggests that part of the shift of *Lavender Vision* to be a publication by gay women came after "most of the male staff members moved to San Francisco" (2012). The issue of *Fag Rag* as a Gay Male newspaper—and not a paper complied by gay men and lesbians—would be repeatedly addressed and responded to in the letters section of the paper (typically on the first pages of the paper). This demonstrates a need by its publishing collective to consistently refer back to the papers' origin in the lesbian/gay male split of *Lavender Vision*.

"[t]here was rarely a set publication schedule for the newspaper during its sixteen-year run, and in fact, the fall 1971 editorial commentary in the second issue addressed the difficulty the volunteer editorial staff had in producing *Fag Rag* issue 2 at all due to disagreements over the content and scope of the publication."[115] *Fag Rag* also produced *Street Sheet*, a weekly, mimeographed publication with announcements and news that was distributed for free. In the 1970s, the paper was produced on an IBM Composer, which had a changeable typeset ball and could justify text. Given its gay and political content, and its rejection of commercial advertising, the paper had trouble with homophobic printers and grant-funders. Printers were able to refuse and censor material, while other printers that were sympathetic to the paper and its politics were also targets of FBI repression. However, the paper did receive sporadic grants in the mid-1970s from the Coordinating Council of Literary Magazines (although these promptly ended with Ronald Reagan's 1981 election).[116] Furthermore, in 1970 few bookstores would carry the newspaper, and one bookstore in Cambridge, Massachusetts even threatened members of the paper collective. The paper did receive wide distribution through demonstrations and Gay Pride events, and through the few gay and lesbian bookstores—such as the Oscar Wilde Memorial Bookstore in New York—which were significant outposts for movement newspapers.[117]

Alongside the emergence of *Fag Rag* from Boston's GLF, was that of Good Gay Poets, who in the words of Carl Morse "issued an important series of poetry books by lesbians and gay men."[118] Good Gay Poets

[115] Lisa Tatonetti, *The Queerness of Native American Literature*, 32.

[116] Shively describes the lack of response *Fag Rag* received from the CCLM in 1972–1973. After offering to present their "gay rage case" in person, the paper received annual grants between 1974 and 1977, and further grant in 1980. The Newspaper's politics created contention among the CCLM, who variously threatened to cut off their grant. Shively also discusses how "Reagan simplified the NEA [National Endowment for the Arts] so that artists could clearly identify it and the government as their out-and-out enemy" (Shively, "*Fag Rag*," n.p.).

[117] Shively, "*Fag Rag*."

[118] Carl Morse and Joan Larkin (eds.) *Gay and Lesbian Poetry in Our Time* (New York: St Martin's Press, 1989), xviii. Good Gay Poets published work by Stephanie Byrd, David Eberly, Sal Farinella, Maurice Kenny, Charley Shively, and Ruth Weiss. For work addressing Maurice Kenny's 1979 *Only So Far as Brooklyn*, published by Good Gay Poets, see Tatonetti (2014), 29, 61–62.

organised a poetry reading series in Boston and published Wieners' 1975 collection *Behind the State Capitol: or Cincinnati Pike* and 1972 *Playboy / We were there! … a gay presence at the Democratic convention* pamphlet. Next to their involvement Boston's GML and Good Gay Poets, members of the *Fag Rag* collective were active in various projects including Boston's Gay Community Centre, gay commune-collectives, a prison-mental hospital group/Boston's Mental Patients' Liberation Front, a twenty-four-hour gay phone, and consciousness-raising groups, among others.[119] The group took part in public protest, including protesting the 1971 Miss America competition in Atlantic City alongside numerous other groups, the 1971 May Day demonstrations in Washington DC, and a zap of the Eastern Psychological Association and the Massachusetts Psychological Association in Spring 1972 (contemporaneous to Wieners' incarceration in Taunton State Hospital, Massachusetts).[120]

The homophobic repression—including from the state and its capital interest—threatening such radical work was demonstrated in the 1982 arson attack on *Fag Rag*, *Gay Community News* and gay bookshop Glad Day's shared offices at 22 Bromfield Street in Boston's Downtown Crossing.

In an essay reviewing Wieners' *Selected Poems 1958–1984*, Shively details the increasing harassment of the newspaper's offices, alongside the policing of gay public sex sites, in the late '70s/early '80s— "[m]ysterious break-ins, bullet holes, phone threats of death and fire so frequent, soon our back windows were totally gone, replaced by aluminium and then iron bars."[121] During a season of arson attacks in Boston, and rumoured to have been instigated by off-duty fireman and police officers after *Fag Rag* led a demonstration for "the abolition of the vice squad" during Gay Pride season, the fire destroyed means of production, archives, stock and merchandise of both newspapers and Good Gay

---

[119] Shively, "Fag Rag"; Charley Shively, 'Reviews' of *The Gay Liberation Book* (Richmond and Noguera (eds.) (1973) and Jay and Young, *Out of the Closets: Voices of Gay Liberation* (Jay and Young [1992]), in *Gay Sunshine*, 17 (March/April 1973), 8.

[120] Shively, "*Fag Rag*"; "GML ZAPS Witchdoctors," *Fag Rag*, 3 (Summer 1972), 5. I discuss the Eastern and Massachusetts Psychological Association zaps in "The Survival of John Wieners" (Raha, forthcoming).

[121] Charley Shively, "SEQUINS & SWITCHBLADES: In Extremis Exegesis: A reading of John Wieners' *Selected Poems: 1958–1984*," *Fag Rag*, 44 (1987), 28–33, quote from 30.

Poets.[122] Discussing the fire in her memoir, *Gay Community News* editor Amy Hoffman writes that "the situation was so scary—someone, somewhere, hating us enough to threaten not only our project but our lives"; Hoffman emphasises the emotional toll of the fire and the work that this led to, such that after the fire the papers set up "a round-the-clock vigil over what was left of the building."[123] The fire destroyed the Good Gay Poets' stock, including the negatives for and remaining 750 copies of *Behind the State Capitol,* putting the book out of print, although Shively describes the fire as "the definitive exegesis of *Behind the State Capitol,*" in that it "revealed the void, the ashes, the destruction, the devastation. John Wieners had lived it first in his mind, in his poems, in his body."[124]

POETRY, COCKSUCKING, AND REVOLUTION
BEHIND THE STATE CAPITOL

This chapter has conceptualised and argued that the work of John Wieners as part of the Gay Liberation movement and the work of the *Fag Rag* collective were a form of queer labour, work that materialised a Gay Liberation newspaper and poetry as a form of queer worldmaking. To conclude the chapter, I turn to Wieners' poetic production in the context of *Fag Rag's* political aesthetics and the queer labour of the Good Gay Poets collective. *Fag Rag* regularly published work by gay poets, including by the Good Gay Poets collective, often giving them pride of place. For instance, the *Fag Rag/Gay Sunshine* Stonewall Fifth Anniversary Issue, which included poems by Allen Ginsberg, Jonathan Williams, Anne Waldman, and graphics by Joe Brainard, prints Wieners' "Gusta With Madame Simone de Beauvoir"

---

[122]Video footage of the fire has been posted online—Fourduce1, "Bromfield St. Boston MA 6 alarm fire 7/7/1982 05:30 hrs," YouTube. Online at www.youtube.com/watch?v=oFq3PfosM5c (accessed 24 January 2018).

[123]Amy Hoffman, *An Army of Ex-Lovers: My Life at Gay Community News* (Amhurst: University of Massachusetts Press, 2007), 155.

[124]Shively, "SEQUINS & SWITCHBLADES," 32, 33; Raymond Foye to John Martin, 10 October 1984, Series 2, 1:44, John Wieners Papers. Archives & Special Collections at the Thomas J. Dodd Research Center, University of Connecticut Libraries. Wieners' poem "September Eleventh" discusses the fire, with the title suggesting it was written in 1982 (Wieners, *Supplication,* 178).

on page 2.[125] Naming Wieners "Chair of Speculative History,"[126] *Fag Rag* published various works by him: including gay/Boston poems such as "Gardenias," "Broken-hearted Memories," "Dormant Lamont" and "The Gay World has Changed" (alongside a sketch of Wieners sleeping by Robert LaVigne); a play "Harlem Bodyguard" and other experimental prose texts that shift between high society type columns, memoirs, book reviews, and reflections on the changes in gay life and politics in Boston.[127]

> Sort of Greek canapes color my memories.
> Am I dead or alive? A feeling of embalming
> fluid, unfair from this governmental restric-
> tive use of private human beings threatens
> my future, including grand larcening my
> mother's past.
> ...in Fairy Temple
> company, Mr. Rufus Stephen Jones shot
> James Schuyler, forgetting my prepositions
> from class as witchcraft, in the building!
> here on Joy Street; Louis Bromfield's Joy
> Street. Just think of it, behind the State
> House, Sargeant's privy, said at the Napo-
> lean, without the ball and chain, come over
> and call on me anytime, I brought my bed-
> room down, if you can make the bail.[128]

---

[125] *Fag Rag/Gay Sunshine* Stonewall 5th Anniversary Issue (Summer 1974)—the poem is here titled 'imaginary interview' (between Greta Garbo and de Beauvoir), with the subtitle "in the style of beckett malanga, an a.k.g.b......"

[126] This is somewhat comical. *Fag Rag* 11 (Winter 1974), 10.

[127] The poems listed appear in *Fag Rag*, 4 (January 1973), 11. 'Harlem Bodyguard' appears in *Fag Rag* 13 (Summer 1975). Prose texts include "1972-73"—which discusses contemporary gay life in Boston and appears framed by graphic illustrations of penises in *Fag Rag*, 5 (Summer 1973), 13; "Gay American's Day in Rose Kennedy's Estate," *Fag Rag*, 6 (Fall 1973), 10, 28–29; "A Comparative Study of *Studies for an Actress and Other Poems*," [Jean Garrigue (1973) Indiana: Macmillan]; "Quart," *Fag Rag*, 7&8 (Winter-Spring 1974), 10; "Women's Newspapers; Homophile Bulletins; and The Underground," *Fag Rag*, 10 (Fall 1974), 22–23; "Conjugal Contraries," *Fag Rag*, 11 (Winter 1974), 11. For some of this work, see John Wieners, *Quart, and Conjugal Contraries* (Madras: Hanuman Books, 1987).

[128] "Quart," *Fag Rag*, 7&8 (Winter-Spring 1974), 10. This text is cited as it appears on the page.

Printed alongside a portrait of Jacqueline Kennedy, "Quart" opens with the juxtaposition of food and memory felt through a body that is unsure of its status in life. Such feeling is "unfair," emanating from the Massachusetts Government's limits and placed on incarcerated and psychiatrised persons, juridical, social, and sexual—as the text continues, "This is a cheated poet. A *chastised citizen* of The United States, a person illegally imprisoned over two years in the state of Massachusetts by Federal inmates from Hospitals for the Criminally Insane throughout the commonwealth" (emphasis added). This unfairness is also felt as a threat on both the poet's future and the felonious theft (grand larceny) of his "mother's past"—denoted through the present tense, transmuted verb "larcening." The text quickly runs into a micro-drama murder scene in the "Fairy Temple" of Thomas Mann's *Venice*[129] among the company of gay poets, where Stephen Jonas shoots James Schuyler; followed by a clause in which "prepositions" slip Wieners' memory before the word is itself connected to their site or status from which one learns learning ("prepositions *from* class"), forgotten as if through a spell. The build-up of clauses shifts the scene to Joy Street, apparently that of Pulitzer Prize-winning novelist Louis Bromfield; however, it is distinctly the Joy Street inhabited by Wieners, ulterior to the 'Straight House' and discussed in Boston's gay bars, in this case, bars for older men such as The Napoleon Club.[130] The queer references may be more or less familiar to *Fag Rag*'s readership, but the suggestive camp closing the paragraph solicits its reader to join the poet, in the bedroom or bathroom, provided they've the means to liberate him. The poem goes on to address: art and psychology; various celebrities (including Cary Grant, Bugsy Siegal and Baroness Maria von Trapp); Wieners' memories of the assassinations of John F. Kennedy and Lee Harvey Oswald (referencing various people who may or may not have been involved in the JFK assassination, such as New Hampshire's then Republican Governor Meldrim Thompson, implicated through a play on words); it makes references to various

[129] *Death in Venice*, trans. H. T. Lowe-Porter (Harmondsworth: Penguin Books, 1955).

[130] In 1974, the year this poem was published, The Napoleon Club won *Boston* magazine's award for "Best Gay Bar, Older People." The magazine described the Bay Village bar as "both the best and the worst. Known as the Wrinkle Room, Nappy's or the Geriatrics Institute, the Napoleon Club goes back decades—it's rumored JFK frequented it when he was at Harvard." See www.bestofboston.com/winner/best-gay-bar-older-people/the-napoleon-club-1974/ (accessed 30 November 2015).

hospitals where Wieners was incarcerated to political unrest of the 1960s; to poets including Stan Persky, Herbert Huncke, Janine Pommy Vega; it recalls a romantic scene in the first person, possibly *as* Joan Crawford, with Charles Olson; and it invokes the car crash at Black Mountain college whose wreckage was witnessed in 1955 by Wieners, his boyfriend Dana, and Michael Rumaker, as addressed in Wieners' poem '"You Can't Kill These Machines."'[131] The poem draws near to a close with a murder scene in which poem's speaker (at this point) runs into the street in a blood-stained dress and wig, before suggesting she may be socialite Gregg Sherwood. There follows a brief reference to Wieners' vision of the Virgin Mary, and the poem ends by denouncing 'priggish' political and royal elites who pollute Americans with fraudulent morals. The text is signed "Joe DiMaggio's Last Wife," i.e. Marilyn Monroe.[132] Wieners' poetics here shifts across temporalities of memory, culture, politics, and sexuality, all key sites of struggle for the poet across the '60s and '70s, moving between personae, anger, trauma, honesty, and sexual desire, piling up through a multiplicity of feminine voices in the text's clauses—in a form of highly politicised, avant-garde camp that would speak hilarious volumes to *Fag Rag*'s readers.

As a key outlet for experimental and erotic poetry, *Fag Rag* also addressed the politics of poetry and position of poets in the liberation movement. In "Poetry, Cocksucking and Revolution"—the editorial to the '69 Poets' issue of *Fag Rag*—Shively writes that despite the number of "faggot poets" across history and nations, and the number involved in the movement, "poetry has been the poor country cousin in the gay liberation movement no less than in the movement to conquer space. Even among our own we live unwelcome."[133] Shively also points towards the importance of challenging the politics that emerge in gay male writing—for instance challenging male supremacy in writing, and furthermore

---

[131] A version of '"You Can't Kill These Machines"' appears in *The Floating Bear* (Issue 10, 1961); see also John Wieners, Seth Stewart (ed.), "Letters, Poems, to Michael Rumaker, 1955-58," *The Battersea Review*, online at thebatterseareview.com/critical-prose/218-letters-with-poems-to-michael-rumaker-1955-58 (accessed 24 January 2018).

[132] Amy Hoffman, "Boston in the 1970s: Is There a Lesbian Community? And if There is, Who is in it?" *Journal of Lesbian Studies*, 18, no. 2 (2014).

[133] Shively, Charley, "Poetry, Cocksucking and Revolution," *Fag Rag*, 10 (Fall 1974), 3–5, quote on 3. Shively continues "nonetheless," following this with a stanza from Wieners' "A poem for cocksuckers."

theorising the position of out "faggot poets" in relation to what Shively describes as the "imperialist industry" of the competitive poetry world and its institutions, where gay poetry is not considered 'serious' and queer poets only retain their position if their sexuality remains discreet. Indeed John Martin from Black Sparrow Press' dismissal of Wieners' titles for his *Selected Poems, 1958–1984*, ten years later, is exemplary of this. Claiming that society positions the poet as an individual and irrelevant, Shively argues that the grading systems of literary criticism must be done away with; that the faggot poet must tear down the literary establishment; and that "EVERYONE MUST SPEAK; EVERYONE SHOULD HAVE ACCESS TO THE MEANS OF COMMUNICATION."[134] While a single newspaper alone is unable to fully democratise poetic production and the circulation of work, the labour of creating space for marginalised writers (with varying degrees of public prominence) was a significant part of the work of *Fag Rag* and Good Gay Poets collectives. Between Spring 1973 and Spring 1975 the Good Gay Poets organised readings with Wieners, William Burroughs, John Giorno, Gerard Malanga, Paul Mariah, Jonathan Williams, Sylvia Sidney among other gay and lesbian poets, and a tribute reading to Boston homophile/gay activist Prescott Townsend.[135] As Amy Hoffman recalls of Boston's lesbian community at the time, "concerts and poetry readings could be organized by ad hoc, task-oriented committees, and the events themselves were usually fun, illuminating, and full of opportunities for flirtation."[136] While occupying a diminished place in the wider movement, for the *Fag Rag* collective poetry was important for configuring, challenging and expressing the joys and ambivalences of the world of Gay Liberation, and an inextricable part of the world produced in print and through gay cultural spaces, enabling the circulation of gay desire. Furthermore, producing, publishing, and publicly performing poetry were important forms of collectivised labour, through which could be waged an anti-establishment politics for social transformation (as we have seen in the case of Boston's 1972 Gay March).

From this context emerged *Behind the State Capitol,* published by the Good Gay Poets collective. This context has been unacknowledged

[134] Charley Shivley, 3–5, quote on 5.

[135] *Fag Rag*, no. 12 (Spring 1975), 14; Shively (2012).

[136] Hoffman, "Boston in the 1970s: Is There a Lesbian Community?", 139.

and fundamentally misunderstood by some of Wieners' critics. For instance, in the two and half pages dedicated to describing the appearance and materiality of the book, John Wilkinson writes that it gives "overall an impression of the most comprehensive disorder and complete lack of reverence for the text. Indeed the effect is reminiscent of the home publishing and websites of conspiracy theories for whom the urgency of communicating the threat Prince Philip poses to civilisation outweighs any aesthetic concerns." Wilkinson concludes that "[i]nconsistency appears to be a principle."[137] While the infamous string of offensive phrases Prince Philip has uttered towards people from a multiplicity of countries, minorities, and ethnic backgrounds might be reflective of the poetics aligned to the British establishment and aristocracy dating back to the Renaissance, more significantly, Wilkinson seems to miss how his own negative description of the book highlights the challenge to normative values offered by the radical Gay politics of *Fag Rag* and the Good Gay Poets collectives. Wilkinson describes the "reproductive quality" of the book as "of an indifferent photocopy," with the "[a]uthor's name and book title appear[ing] in a Broadway stencil typeface on the cover, in lipstick pink, and set with a notable lack of visual taste and technical competence."[138] However, Shively recollects that the book was typeset on a Compugraphic machine shared by various liberation groups, which was both "more expensive and more complicated" than the IBM Composer on which *Fag Rag* was produced, and furthermore "the entire text [of *Behind the State Capitol*] faded and had to be reset (because the developer had not been properly changed)."[139] Furthermore, the book was typeset collectively by members of the Good Gay Poets collective, including Shively, Dave Stryker, Rich Kinman, and John Mitzel.[140]

While the collectively used equipment led to additionally challenging work for the book's publishers, it was produced on equipment that directly facilitated the spreading of the politics and consciousness of various liberation movements, through an organic division of queer labour created by Gay Liberation. The author's name and book title in 'lipstick

[137] John Wilkinson, *The Lyric Touch* (Cambridge: Salt Publishing, 2007), 234–236.

[138] Wilkinson, *The Lyric Touch*, 234.

[139] Charley Shively, *Fag Rag*, n.p.

[140] Wieners, *Supplication*, 185.

pink' denotes from the outside a gay, high femme aesthetic referencing the queer labour behind the production of both the book as material object and its content. Given that Wilkinson can only recognise the Good Gay Poet's logo as "a curious splotch," it is unsurprising that his reading fails to recognise radical gay and Mad poetics and content of the book as a commodity—a political product of transformative, collectivised queer labour.[141] Indeed, *Fag Rag* even offered *Behind the State Capitol* to its readers for $1 with a ten issue subscription to the paper.[142]

> A factor of consciousness developing in the gay world, conducive to those or whomever one's audience or prey is straightly reminding one, our people that despite sordid, past histories and oft-inherited bigotry from countless, other civilizations over the face of the earth, expressed to self-indulgence of the most blatant matter, gaining some satisfaction in self-effort, that they are real and different persons with the largest potential of the whole, human race for the realization of their own, since they have been blasphemed for so long, morally good selves.[143]

Behind the State Capitol ought to be understood as Wieners attempt to aesthetically express and realise a liberated Gay and psychiatric survivor consciousness—including the political potential and historical ambivalence of such struggles and the suffering that necessitates them. This includes challenging the agents of repression that silence such voices—including auditory hallucinations that are labelled as psychotic—be they psychiatrists or the literary establishment. The book's title itself denotes the gay world of the north side of Boston's Beacon Hill, geographically situated 'behind' Massachusetts' State House—the legislative heart of straight politics and restraint.[144] It is a crucial volume of poetry and prose on class and social transformation ("After Dinner on Pinckney Street"), radical gay sexuality and the ambivalences of gay life ("A Popular Belief as Practiced: Indiscriminate Promiscuity," "By the Bars"), gender trans*gression ("The Rich and The Super Rich"), Wieners' life among poets and personal experiences with drugs ("Letters"), American

---

[141] Wilkinson, *The Lyric Touch*, 234–235.

[142] *Fag Rag*, 20 (Summer 1977).

[143] Wieners, *Behind the State Capitol*, 88.

[144] The scene of gay and lesbian politics on Beacon Hill, and in particular on Wieners' Joy Street, is captured by Dudley Clendinen and Adam Nagourney, describing an activist meeting on Joy Street in June 1972 (1999: 125–127).

politics, psychiatric survivor consciousness ("Children of the Working Class"), emotional nostalgia and avant-garde camp drama ("Vera Lynn")—often shifting between these aspects in one text or one paragraph. The book also contains "over forty collages," which as Jim Dunn writes, "isolate, layer and demonstrate Wieners obsession with his own memories and personal history commingled with movie stars, socialites, and random ephemera he includes in his creative process."[145] It stands as a key product of the collective labour and politics of Boston's Gay Liberation movement, remaining in discourse with Boston's liberation movements, all the while maintaining Wieners' religious commitment to his art.

WORKS CITED

Allen, Donald, and Warren Tallman. *The Poetics of the New American Poetry.* New York: Grove Press, 1973.

Baim, Tracey (ed.). *Gay Press, Gay Power: The Growth of LGBT Community Newspapers in America.* Chicago: Prairie Avenue Productions and Winder City Media Group, 2012.

Berlant, Lauren, and Michael Warner. "Sex in Public." *Critical Inquiry,* vol. 24, no. 2 (1998): 547–566.

Bérubé, Allan. *My Desire for History: Essays in Gay, Community and Labor History.* Edited by John D'Emilio and Estelle B. Freedman. Chapel Hill: University of North Carolina Press, 2011.

Boyd, Nan Alamilla. *Wide Open Town: A History of Queer San Francisco to 1965.* Berkeley, Los Angeles and London: University of California Press, 2005.

Brady, Andrea. "Making Use of This Pain: The John Wieners Archives." *Paideuma,* vol. 36 (2007): 131–180.

———. "The Other Poet: John Wieners, Frank O'Hara, Charles Olson." In *Don't Ever Get Famous: Essays on New York Writing After the New York School,* edited by Daniel Kane, 317–347. Campaign and London: Dalkey Archive Press, 2006.

Brathwaite, Edward Kamau. *X/Self.* London: Oxford University Press, 1987.

Bronski, Michael. "The Last Gay Liberationist." *Boston Review,* 20 December 2017. http://bostonreview.net/gender-sexuality/michael-bronski-last-gay-liberationist.

Carter, David. *Stonewall: The Riot that Sparked the Gay Revolution.* New York: St Martin's Press, 2004.

---

[145] James C. Dunn, "The Mesmerizing Apparition of the Oracle of Joy Street: A Critical Study of John Wieners' Life and Later Work in Boston," http://nrs.harvard.edu/urn-3:HUL.InstRepos:33826277 (Master's thesis, Harvard Extension School, 2017), 47.

Chamberlin, Judi. *On Our Own: Patient-Controlled Alternatives to the Mental Health System.* New York: Hawthorn Books, 1978.

Damon, Maria. *Postliterary America: From Bagel Shop Jazz to Micropoetries.* Iowa City: University of Iowa Press, 2011.

Davidson, Michael. "From Margin to Mainstream: Postwar Poetry and the Politics of Containment." *American Literary History,* vol. 10, no. 2 (Summer 1998): 266–290.

D'Emilio, John. *Sexual Politics, Sexual Communities: The Making of a Homosexual Minority in the United States, 1940–1970.* Chicago and London: University of Chicago Press, 1983.

Duberman, Martin. *Stonewall.* New York: Dutton, 1993; Plume (1994 edition).

Dunn, James C. *The Mesmerizing Apparition of the Oracle of Joy Street: A Critical Study of John Wieners' Life and Later Work in Boston.* Master's thesis, Harvard Extension School, 2017. http://nrs.harvard.edu/urn-3:HUL.InstRepos:33826277.

Freud, Sigmund. "Three Essays on the Theory of Sexuality (Trans. James Strachey)." In *The Standard Edition of the Complete Psychological Works* (Vol. 7), by Sigmund Freud, 125–148. London: Vintage Books, 2001 [1905].

Hennessy, Christopher. *Homosexuality is a Poem: How Gay Poets Remodeled the Lyric, Community and the Ideology of Sex to Theorise a Gay Poetics.* University of Massachusetts - Amhurst: Doctoral Dissertations 2014–Current. Paper 302, 2015.

———. *Our Deep Gossip: Conversations with Gay Writers on Poetry and Desire.* Madison, WI: University of Wisconsin Press, 2013.

Hennessy, Rosemary. *Fires on the Border: The Passionate Politics of Labour Organising on the Mexican Frontera.* Minneapolis: University of Minnesota Press, 2013.

Hoffman, Amy. *An Army of Ex-Lovers: My Life at Gay Community News.* Amhurst: University of Massachusetts Press, 2007.

———. "Boston in the 1970s: Is There a Lesbian Community? And if There is, Who is in it?" *Journal of Lesbian Studies,* vol. 18, no. 2 (2014): 133–141.

Jay, Karla, and Allen Young (eds.). *Out of the Closets: Voices of Gay Liberation.* London: GMP Publishers Ltd, 1992.

Joseph, Miranda. *Against the Romance of Community.* Minneapolis and London: University of Minnesota Press, 2002.

Lefrançois, Brenda A., Robert Menzies, and Geoffrey Reaume. *Mad Matters: A critical reader in Canadian Mad Studies.* Toronto: Canadian Scholars' Press, 2013.

Leyland, Winston (ed.). *Angels of the Lyre: A Gay Poetry Anthology.* San Francisco: Panjandrum Press and Gay Sunshine Press, 1975.

———.*Gay Roots: Twenty Years of Gay Sunshine.* San Francisco: Gay Sunshine Press, 1991.

————.*Gay Sunshine Interviews: Volume 2*. San Francisco: Gay Sunshine Press, 1982.

Marx, Karl. *Capital: A Critique of Political Economy*, vol. 1. London: Penguin Books, 1990.

McRuer, Robert. *Crip Theory: Cultural Signs of Queerness and Disability*. New York and London: New York University Press, 2006.

Mecca, Tommi Avicolli (ed.). *Smash the Church, Smash the State! The Early Years of Gay Liberation*. San Francisco: City Lights Books, 2009.

Moore, Patrick. *Beyond Shame: Reclaiming the Abandoned History of Radical Gay Sexuality*. Boston: Beacon Press, 2004.

Muñoz, José E. *Cruising Utopia: The Then and There of Queer Futurity*. New York: New York University Press, 2009.

Perloff, Marjorie G. "The Corn-Porn Lyric: Poetry 1972–73." *Contemporary Literature*, vol. 16, no. 1 (1975): 84–125. www.jstor.org/stable/1207786.

Raha, Nat. "A Queer Excess: The Supplication of John Wieners." *The Critical Flame*, no. 38 (September/October 2015). http://criticalflame. org/a-queer-excess-the-supplication-of-john-wieners/.

————. "'Out of Jail and on the Streets Again': Street Transvestite Action Revolutionaries and the Praxis of Transfeminism of Color." *Scholar & Feminist Online*, Forthcoming.

————. "Queering Marxist [Trans]feminism: Queer and Trans Social Reproduction." *Marxism in Culture Seminar.* London, 28 April 2017.

————. "The Survival of John Wieners: Psychiatric Incarceration, Poetics and Liberation." *Queer Capital: Marxism in Queer Theory and Post-1950 Poetics*. Doctoral dissertation. University of Sussex, 2018.

————. "The Survival of John Wieners: Psychiatric Incarceration, Gay and Mental Patients' Liberation and Poetics." In *Essays on John Wieners*, edited by Michael Kindellan. Montpeller: Presses Universitaires de la Méditerranée, Forthcoming.

Rhodes, J. D. "Fassbinder's Work: Style, Sirk, and Queer Labor." In *A Companion to Fassbinder*, edited by Brigitte Peucker, 181–203. Malden and Oxford: Blackwell, 2012.

Shelley, Martha. "Gay Is Good." In *Out of the Closets: Voices of Gay Liberation*, edited by Karla Jay and Allen Young, 31–34. New York: New York University Press, 1993.

Shively, Charley. "Fag Rag: The Most Loathesome Publication in the English Language." In *Insider Histories of the Vietnam Era Underground Press, Part 2*, edited by Ken Wachsberger. E-book (unpaginated). East Lansing: Michigan State University Press, 2012.

Somerville, Siobhan B. *Queering the Color Line: Race and the Invention of Homosexuality in American Culture*. Durham and London: Duke University Press, 2000.

Stryker, Susan. *Transgender History.* Berkeley: Seal Press, 2008.

———."Transgender History, Homonormativity, and Disciplinarity." *Radical History Review,* no. 100 (2008): 144–157.

Tatonetti, Lisa. *The Queerness of Native American Literature.* Minneapolis and London: University of Minnesota Press, 2014.

Teal, Donn. *The Gay Militants.* New York: Stein and Day, 1971.

Tinkcom, Matthew. *Working Like a Homosexual: Camp, Capital, Cinema.* Durham and London: Duke University Press, 2002.

Tolbert, T. C., and T. Trace Peterson (eds.). *Troubling the Line: Trans and Genderqueer Poetry and Poetics.* Callicoon: Nightboat Books, 2013.

Untorelli Press. *Street Transvestite Action Revolutionaries: Survival, Revolt and Queer Antagonist Struggle.* Untorelli Press, 2013.

Wesling, Meg. "Queer Value." *GLQ: A Journal of Lesbian and Gay Studies,* vol. 18, no. 1 (2012): 107–126.

Wieners, John. *Behind the State Capitol; or, Cincinnati Pike: Cinema Découpages, Verses, Abbreviated Prose Insights: A Collection of Poetry.* Boston: Good Gay Poets, 1975.

———. *Cultural Affairs in Boston: Poetry & Prose, 1956–1985.* Edited by Raymond Foye. Santa Rosa: Black Sparrow Press, 1988.

———. *Selected Poems.* London: Jonathan Cape, 1972.

———. *Selected Poems, 1958–1984.* Santa Barbara: Black Sparrow Press, 1986.

———. *Supplication: Selected Poems of John Wieners.* Edited by Joshua Beckman, Robert Dewhurst, and CA Conrad. Seattle: Wave Books, 2015.

Wilkinson, John. *The Lyric Touch.* Cambridge: Salt Publishing, 2007.

CHAPTER 8

Without the Text at Hand: Postcolonial Writing and the Work of Memorisation

Aimée Lê

While attending a reading of Kei Miller's, I noticed the author looking away from his book and asked if the poems had been memorised. Miller responded that, although he knew many of his poems well enough to recite them from memory, he still deliberately read them from the book. This moment (which is not as uncommon as one might imagine) he had described in more detail some years before:

> Although I almost never need to look at a book or a printed page to recite any of my poems, I have begun to take blank sheets of paper up with me to podiums, to shuffle through and glance down occasionally at their emptiness, all to give the illusion that I am reading.[1]

Given the absence of a written text, the revelation that these were not precisely "readings," but rather "the illusion that I am reading,"

---

[1] Kei Miller, "Literature from Where I Stand, or Rather Sit; No, Make That Stand..." *Caribbean Review of Books*, no. 15 (2008), caribbeanreviewofbooks.com/crb-archive/15-february-2008/literature-from-where-i-stand/.

A. Lê (✉)
Poetics Research Centre, Royal Holloway, University of London, Egham, UK

© The Author(s) 2019
J. L. Walton and E. Luker (eds.), *Poetry and Work*,
Modern and Contemporary Poetry and Poetics,
https://doi.org/10.1007/978-3-030-26125-2_8

may produce an anxious sense that the poem has disappeared. Miller's memorised poems challenge us to locate authority, and an authoritative version: firstly by undermining the notion that the authoritative version of a work is by necessity a specific written text, and secondly, through problematising the social processes by which such authority comes to be established. It would also seem (contrary to the relation of production between the poet and his writing) that the physical text, distinct from what we could call "the poem," takes on a role in authenticating the body of the poet. In other words, "the illusion" demarcates our sense of the written word's primacy over the body; Miller's blank pages pose the question of whether this has become a kind of fetish.

It is particularly significant, given that nothing about Miller's work requires theatrical performance, that he uses the term "performing"[2] (as opposed to, for example, recitation) to describe his engagement with his own poems. Miller suggests in the same account, however, that to describe him as a "performer" would dangerously inflect his work with the values of entertainment as opposed to literature. The racial affect of what Sianne Ngai calls animatedness[3] appears to have an echo in Miller's discomfort at appearing too "interesting" (although one could argue that by reading from a blank page the poet has made himself far more interesting): "*Oh, child — I'm no performer. I am a poet. Get it right! And don't you ever call me interesting again!*"[4] In this, and in his choice to read from a blank page, Miller therefore mobilises not only performance, but *performativity*, as the text becomes additionally racialised, gendered, etc., through being physically reproduced by a specific body. For the purposes of this discussion I will assume that, as in Miller's case, the writer and the reader are the same and that the only person to reproduce a text through memorisation is its author; the introduction of actors would inevitably mean understanding this process theatrically, but losing the significance that the written word carries within poetry. A poetry reading can be distinct from stage performance in its more

---

[2] Miller, "Literature from Where I Stand." "I politely declined reading a poem on a slam stage in front of five hundred people, but relished in performing the next night to a more distinguished audience of thirty."

[3] Sianne Ngai, "Animatedness," in *Ugly Feelings* (Cambridge: Harvard University Press, 2005), 89–125.

[4] Miller, "Literature from Where I Stand."

informal character and through the verifying presence of the author, but also in its attempt to express what is generally understood as a text.

While the past three decades of debate around slam, performance poetry, and indeed, spoken word and hip-hop, have challenged the primacy of the silent, solitary reader and reintroduced poetry readings as a popular art form, it is precisely this popularity which has been in many cases obfuscating for scholars and for poets who identify with the avant-garde and with innovative writing. Due to the preponderance of American institutional and literary referents through which the "stage vs. page" debate has articulated itself internationally, these terms need to be historicised, as they cannot be thought through abstract aesthetic categories, but must be comprehended through their determinate contexts. American literature has always emphasised disjuncture with the written past through employing the more vital qualities of speech, as can be seen even in its early antecedents, such as Ralph Waldo Emerson's address "The American Scholar." This turn towards speech and performance is simultaneously figured as a break with (often European) tradition in favour of something particularly American.[5] However, to temporally locate the performing body as new and innovative, in contrast to the conservative properties of written text, obscures many of the most important issues at stake in Miller's engagements with both memorisation and reading, including the historic reality that memorisation of poetry has served as a technique of conservative pedagogy as well as an innovative tool of performance. The question of speech's innovativeness should be put in relation to both postcolonial and Commonwealth intertexts, current and past, if it is to be properly understood. Furthermore, the problems of memorisation are not merely problems of performance, they problematise writing itself as a kind of performance.

Memorisation of a text can introduce a greater range to what we think of as a poetic practice, in part by moving language beyond the presence of writing. Laurence A. Breiner notes a range of possibilities within

---

[5] My Ph.D. thesis explores this further, along with the racial implications of an American "national literature." For one example of how these "breaks" with tradition have been figured recently, we can look to the collection *The Breakbeat Poets*, which references the previous "breaks" of both Black Arts and the New Negro Renaissance. See Kevin Coval, Quraysh Ali Lansana, and Nate Marshall, eds., *The Breakbeat Poets: New American Poetry in the Age of Hip-Hop* (Chicago: Haymarket Press, 2015).

"the interplay of speech and writing as models for the production of poetry," ranging from

> improvisation, to oral composition, to 'orature', to poetry written as a script for performance, to poetry written (or improvised) for distribution through recordings, to poetry written for performance with or to music (as well as to songs *per se*), and even to a kind of shaped poetry whose visual effects function remarkably as a metaphor for orality.[6]

I have here limited my attention to the memorisation of a written work, rather than including improvisational methods which nevertheless employ memory, because of the questions that arise when a "record" of the poem vanishes into the body, a process which, as we have observed, can both produce and allay various forms of anxiety. To "perform" too much can be to succumb to a sense of compensating for something. But while the memorised poem may call our attention to a semblance of formal mastery, it may also introduce the uncertainty of its physical generation, resituating the poem irreverently among the other bodily and speech acts of the poet.

Perhaps furnishing the kind of criticism in response to which Miller has chosen to pretend that he is reading from a page, the poet Ron Silliman has argued that the attention poems require is undermined by the process of memorisation and recitation, to the extent that "the memorized text [...] is the antithesis of [...] the read text."[7] Silliman's approach derives from his critical emphasis on parataxis set out in *The New Sentence*. He suggests that memorisation itself is inherently hypotactic, since one must keep the entirety of a memorised poem in mind to recite it.[8] The written poetry that Silliman finds unrewarding thus has as

---

[6] Laurence A. Breiner, "How to Behave on Paper: The Savacou Debate," *Journal of West Indian Literature*, vol. 6, no. 1 (1993), 1–10.

[7] Ron Silliman, "Whenever I've Been Paired Up at a Reading..." *Silliman's Blog*, 4 May 2005, ronsilliman.blogspot.com/2005/05/whenever-ive-been-paired-up-at-reading.html.

[8] Other writers, such as Umberto Eco, have deliberately invoked the hypotactic possibilities of mnemonic structures, but perhaps in so doing have suggested that these mnemonics *themselves* contain, extend, or simply are, our consciousness. From Simonides' method of loci to contemporary neuro-scientific study, investigations into our memory's capacity repeatedly relate it to metaphorical space (such as maps, attics, or cupboards) but simultaneously suggest it is highly plastic. See, for example, Donald R. Forsyke, "Long-Term Memory: Scaling of Information to Brain Size," *Frontiers in Human Neuroscience*, vol. 8 (2014), 397, www.frontiersin.org/articles/10.3389/fnhum.2014.00397/full.

a kind of corollary a reading which will be controlled by its narrative arc instead of marking out a series of encounters with language. Yet we have to ask whether the *written* text, in its seeming authoritative totality, may simply substitute another form of hypotactic proxy.

At times the text's pre-existing status as a mnemonic device that extends beyond the body can also be undermined and delegitimised, as we see in M. NourbeSe Philip's *Zong!*. The book uses the technique of erasure on a legal report of the *Gregson v. Gilbert* decision, in which an insurance claim was made on a "cargo" of enslaved Africans who drowned in 1781. Philip describes her decision to use only the pre-existing words of the text as a kind of bondage, as she "decided to lock [herself] in the body (the very limited body, I might add) of the text," and also as a form of mutilation.[9] Some of the sequences initially seem impossible to sound, even from the opening arrangement of letters: "w w w   w,"[10] yet their relation to embodiment beyond and through the text pertains: while Philip's writing plays with the difficulty of words being performed or remembered, as she writes the poems they do not exist only as texts, but also as "voices" which Philip actually stages and performs, often plurally.[11] In this regard, the subtitle, "As told to the author by Setaey Adamu Boateng," suggests that Philip's text, for all of its difficulty in being spoken, is more of a transcript than a record.[12]

When we read from a page (or screen), the interaction we ask the audience to receive is that of ourselves with a separate object, which can be deeply unexamined as its own form of practice. The memorised and performed poem may bring the poet and the audience into contact with one another in the present, rather than through the ostensible, always fantasised, proxy of the text—and when we do not have to divert attention to reading out the text, we may also be able to more fully activate our ability to articulate to the audience something it is capable of

---

[9] Travis Macdonald et al., "The Weight of What's Left [Out]: Six Contemporary Erasurists on Their Craft," Interview by Andrew David King, *Kenyon Review*, 6 November 2012, www.kenyonreview.org/2012/11/erasure-collaborative-interview/.

[10] M. NourbeSe Philip, *Zong!* (Middletown: Wesleyan University Press, 2008), 3.

[11] Katherine Verhagen, "Sound or Text: How Do You Heal a 'Foreign Anguish'?" *English Studies in Canada*, vol. 33, no. 4 (2007), 83–90, journals.library.ualberta.ca/esc/index.php/ESC/article/view/9123/7289.

[12] George Elliott Clarke, "Review: *Zong!*" *Maple Tree Literary Supplement*, 4, www.mtls.ca/issue4/writings-review-clarke.php, accessed 1 May 2017.

receiving (which is not necessarily the same as communication). The experience of the audience's response may even change the reading itself. As the poet Gahl Liberzon remarked, "The poem is music. The poet is the orchestra. *The audience is the conductor.* When you don't acknowledge this, what you're doing is recitation, not performance."[13] In performance, Liberzon's poem "What It's Like to Be a White Guy with a Black Eye in Detroit (After Lauren Whitehead),"[14] which describes him being punched in the face, would emerge differently when heard by majority white or black audiences, who treated it as, respectively, tragic or comic.

In listening to a poem read aloud, we shift emphasis from the text's spatial array in favour of a temporal experience of words as they arrive. Alternatively, hearing the words aloud might serve to produce a fantasy in which we envision the spoken as inscribed. The written text represents a range of potential readings for the poem that no single performance of the poem will ever approach, but it is equally impossible for that range of readings to be performed between people. If we accept the desire, the necessity, to read our own poems, then we must reckon with particular iterations of poems and passages between particular people at particular moments, as well as the history of spoken and heard language invoked and troubled through this process—and whether memorised or read from a page, in this the spoken text will always be distinct from the read text.

Perhaps analogously to the procedure of erasure, memorisation for performance can also function as a kind of erasure of the original written text. One thing stripped away in memorisation is the affective scaffolding of the sequence as associated with the fantasy of its integrity, as well as the identification of the words as formally coherent; through practice they become "mere" words. Along with its integrity, we also lose an initial fantasy of how the poem might be performed, its separate "voice," which is not our voice. Repetition enables the words of the poem to shed their initial allure, even their meaning, and reappear as our own speech in the present tense, among our own gestures and sounds. If one were once the author, perhaps one is now, rather, the speaker of the text. The kinds of memory we rely upon in everyday circumstances, known to

---

[13] Gahl Liberzon, Personal Conversation, October 2016.

[14] Gahl Liberzon, "What It's Like to Be a White Guy with a Black Eye in Detroit (After Lauren Whitehead)," in *Bodies, Bodies, Bodies, Bodies, Bodies* (Ann Arbor: Red Beard Press, 2013), 24–27.

neuroscience as nondeclarative memory (for example: saying hello, going to the store, riding a bicycle) may be activated by this practice.[15] Thus, Silliman's description of "the physical feat" of memory is worth greater attention (particularly given that he does not likewise describe literacy as a physical feat).[16]

Memory, as invoked in Miller's writing, engages with this question of mastery. In one notable episode in *The Cartographer Tries to Map a Road to Zion*, the titular character confronts an I-formant's sequence of description while asking for directions, receiving a reply that leaves him (seemingly habitually) "frustrated." "Awrite, you know the big white house at the bottom of Clover Hill..." the I-formant begins, describing a specific house "with all the windows dem board up..." As the poem progresses, the description of the house becomes clearer and clearer, spatially and temporally, through extremely precise details of characters, flora and fauna. The I-formant adds that in front of the house, "you always see a ole woman, only three teeth in her mouth, and she out there selling pepper shrimp in a school chair with an umbrella tie to it. And beside her she always have two mongrel dog..." Finally, when the description is painstakingly clear, the rug is pulled out from under: "Yes, yes, the cartographer insists. I know it. / Good, says the I-formant. Cause you mustn' go there."[17] What, we might ask along with the cartographer, is the point of this description, this knowledge, then?

In one sense, this almost too closely re-enacts Silliman's concern, in which the memorised poem "is sending the mind to other places, to characters & tales, to arguments and positions."[18] Yet it also demonstrates memory's non-instrumental quality. To directly approach one place, the poem suggests, one works through other possibilities, other purposes, incidents, and knowledge that seem unprofitable. One of Miller's implicit objects of critique therefore in this poem might be that of conscious knowledge, figured as productive labour.

---

[15] Larry R. Squire and John T. Wixted, "The Cognitive Neuroscience of Human Memory Since H. M.," *Annual Review of Neuroscience*, vol. 34 (2011), 259–288, www.ncbi.nlm.nih.gov/pmc/articles/PMC3192650/.

[16] Silliman, "Whenever I've Been Paired Up at a Reading...".

[17] Kei Miller, *The Cartographer Tries to Map a Way to Zion* (Manchester: Carcanet Press, 2014).

[18] Ron Silliman, Untitled Blog Post, *Silliman's Blog*, 4 May 2005, ronsilliman.blogspot.co.uk/2005/05/whenever-ive-been-paired-up-at-reading.html, accessed 15 April 2018.

The indeterminacy of the poet in relation to production (and indeed the lack of symmetry between libidinal "economies" and the capitalist economy) is brought out in Sophie Mayer's poetic text "rest,"[19] which begins "Today (International Women's Day 2017) I am on strike." Mayer writes, "what if rest (from *ro*) — that which is restful — is or could be a form of resistance (remaining in place, holding one's ground)?" In relating rest and resistance, Mayer implicitly connects her own attempted "strike" to a larger cultural imperative towards productivity which even reincorporates rest as an ideological category: "So you can be productive. So you can be normal." This trap inevitably recalls Adorno's discussion of division of labour and independence in the very first sections of *Minima Moralia*.[20] When Mayer describes "recognition," she introduces a similar paradox: to be able to rest, Mayer continues, one would "need to be heard by the system that does not recognise your existence." This fantasy of inscription proposes being written into "the system" as the only means of achieving the possibility of relief. So, can poets go on strike (*as poets*, that is, rather than as, e.g. workers or women)? If poetry does produce value, it is on a continuum with the ideological "healthy, normal" rest that Meyer criticises; in other words, it is complicit. However, if poetry does not produce value, poets cannot go on strike as a "resistance" to capital. Indeed, beneath the otherwise comic monologue of the I-formant, with its profusion of trivialities, Miller darkly hints that local geography may be due to be written out of the map, emphasising the layered and violent processes of inscription (the map, and implicitly, the poem) which impose their limits on the unformed possibilities of lives: to be free is to be worthless, to produce is to be exploited, in all cases we are written by others, and in some cases we even fantasise about it.

Yet, outside of the literal political economy of poetic labour, can we connect the poet's work to the body's labour in another way? There is some sense, however vague, in the Romantic notion of the genius, that there is a thinking in the body that extends beyond the work; or that at minimum enables the work. Inasmuch as this subjective heritage has

---

[19]Sophie Mayer, "Rest," TinyLetter, 7 March 2017, tinyletter.com/sophiemayer/letters/rest.

[20]Theodor Adorno, *Minima Moralia: Reflections on a Damaged Life*, translated by E. F. N. Jephcott (London: Verso, 2005), 3–5.

been taken up and defended, it generally has neglected the literal body as the repository for genius, and the material consequences of this figuration. On the other hand, "the body" or embodiment has generally been taken up by those who wish to pointedly oppose a Cartesian idea of the subject. In this sense, "the body" and subjectivity are not connected, or are even adversarial in an uneven hierarchy; being made of physical stuff tends to overwhelm, or serve as a critique of, "the subject," in much the same way that the I-formant's monologue might appear extraneous to a process of finding directions.

Keston Sutherland, however, comes close to recuperating this question of subjectivity through materialism. In defence of the poetic "subjective" labour neglected and denigrated by conceptual writers, Sutherland writes, "The ignorance of technique implies a casual and contemptuous attitude toward the history of work."[21] Sutherland's remarks introduce the question of the relationship of the work of poetry with other kinds of work, especially relevant in that the English word for the artist's "work," which in other languages contains specific reference to an aesthetic object, is identical with the verb meaning "to labour." One of Sutherland's readings of Marx, referenced briefly here, revisits Marx's term *Gallerte*—describing a commercial gelatin product—which, he explicates, has greater significance than the English translations which describe "congealed" or "frozen" labour. The labour process, Marx suggests through this specific commodity, is a violent and irreversible one, which boils down "the living hands, brains, muscles and nerves of the wage laborer."[22]

---

[21] Full quote: "The ignorance of technique implies a casual and contemptuous attitude toward the history of work. The antisubjectivist dogma is an optic for ironic theorisation of *value* alone; its implications for a theory of *labour* are wholly reactionary. Marx's account of the inhumanity of wage labour was precisely that it extinguishes the individual subject and reduces her to a mere quantity of 'socially necessary labour power' and finally to *Gallerte*. Capital itself is the fundamental 'antisubjective' force in the world and the pattern of all the others. Marxist revolutionary theory is about restoring the subject to society and abolishing the coercion that actually and in material reality desubjectivises workers." Keston Sutherland, "THESES ON ANTISUBJECTIVIST DOGMA," *Tumblr*, vol. 1 May 2013, afieryflyingroule.tumblr.com/post/49378474736/keston-sutherland-theses-on-antisubjectivist.

[22] Keston Sutherland, "Marx in Jargon," *World Picture Journal*, vol. 1 (2008), www.worldpicturejournal.com/World%20Picture/WP_1.1/KSutherland.pdf.

Thus there is another sense of performance, beyond the theatrical, that is at stake here: the way in which one speaks of one's performance at doing a job, or playing a sport, or having sex. The fact is that these are procedures we complete without *appearing to* have a script in hand. The development of printed matter has freed writers from the need to employ mnemonic devices to structure our poems, although we may choose to use them. Concomitantly, the signifying practice of memorisation and recitation brings forward tensions: between the relationship of "life" (our pre-existing bodily life) to the written text; between the poet's work and its relation to a Marxist analysis of labour; and about the uneasiness of forms of dominance illuminated through poetry. To locate the recitation and the writing of poetry as something which is practised (repeated and honed) places it side-by-side with other activities which depend on "performance" and initiates evaluations of skill, virtuosity, and relation to a tradition. That these traditions have indeterminate claim to be a writer's "own" further intensifies their significance.

The immediate consequence of memorisation as a practice is that of removing the visible limit of the written poem as script. This can in some sense "defile" poetic language by placing it indistinguishably among other actions, and thus many poets who routinely recite their work have developed analogous compensatory modes of delimiting the poem from the nonpoem (such as, for example, the number of formal constraints in slam poetry, especially regarding time limits). Yet one could equally argue that the memorised poem is elevated through attention, turned into something like a quotation, and given proximity to other words known by heart. There are also pragmatic considerations that have led writers to memorisation through deprivation from physical texts to read, such as exile, imprisonment, and forced illiteracy. Regardless, through demonstrating how subject our speech already is to being shaped into patterns, the poem that is memorised presents us with a fundamental confrontation with our own derivativeness, one particularly fraught for those already placed into an "imputed lack of history," without "a character and purpose of their own."[23]

The history of colonialism is not incidental to the images of the made work as they appear in Derek Walcott's writing, for example. In the exclamation "O Christ, my craft, and the long time it is taking!"[24]

---

[23] Edward Baugh, *Derek Walcott* (Cambridge: Cambridge University Press, 2006), 171.

[24] Derek Walcott, *Midsummer* (London: Faber and Faber, 1984), 23.

we can sense "craft" as sailing vessel or ship, as well as artisanal production that predates industrialism. This has a great deal to do with the role that "having-had-to-memorise" or "having been written" also plays in Walcott's writing. Edmund Hardy points out "a recurring idea in *White Egrets* (and throughout Walcott's poetry) that the text is found in the world or is translated from it — the name exists before the thing does; the thing's reality is its name."[25] Yet, as Hardy goes on to show, this question—nearly compulsive in Walcott—of naming breaks open to reveal a temporal and ontological ambivalence about the primacy of language or being, "the canefields set in stanzas."[26] The presence of textual forms within the landscape demonstrates a mutual unnaturalness: "And when they named these bays / bays, / was it nostalgia or irony?"[27] The repetition of "bays" suggests not only the possible "derivativeness" or "second order phenomena" of all language (although it does this), but also marks the act of naming in relation to a colonial fantasy of an original upon which Walcott must speculate that his landscape has been based. Phenomenal perception of the landscape for the colonial, and even the postcolonial writer sometimes arrives after its depiction and is held to scrutiny through the expectations of literature. Additionally, the model of *naming* rather than *writing* suggests a more primary relation to the word—suggests, among other things, that one might be made to memorise it.

English studies, or studies of the vernacular in English, were colonial in inception,[28] and this didactic purpose can still be detected in the educational practices of formerly colonised countries, which often continue to emphasise memorisation and recitation of poetry (particularly Shakespeare and the Romantics), long after these educational techniques have ceased to be widely practised in England. The second section of

---

[25] Edmund Hardy, "Derek Walcott/The Philosophy of Names/2011," *Tumblr*, 19 March 2017, bitetheweeds-blog.tumblr.com/post/158584535617/derek-walcott-the-philosophy-of-names-2011.

[26] Walcott, *Midsummer*, 2.

[27] Derek Walcott, "Names," in *Collected Poems 1948–1984* (London: Faber and Faber, 1986), 306.

[28] Robert Eaglestone, "Where Did English Come From?" in *Doing English: A Guide for Literature Students* (London: Routledge, 2000), 7–19.

Lorna Goodison's poem, "Bam Chi Chi La La/London, 1969" depicts the seeming temporal and spatial disjuncture:

> In Jamaica she was a teacher. Here, she is charwoman at night in the West End. She eats a cold midnight meal carried from home and is careful to expunge her spice trail with Dettol. She sings 'Jerusalem'to herself and recites the Romantic poets as she mops hallways and scours toilets...[29]

This form of memorisation and recitation as a living practice serves as a potential counterpoint to a linear periodisation of aesthetic practices in English-language poetry, as well as a rejoinder to the reductive assumption that memorisation for non-white writers must be only in relation to oral tradition. Walcott, for instance, extended recitation as his own pedagogical technique, requiring his American students to memorise Milton's *Lycidas*.[30] To bring the works of Milton directly into the mouths of contemporary speakers may also serve to complicate the development of language in the metropole as the standard by which to assess a "progressive" literary history. One might examine Walcott's riposte that "Jacobean" English is still spoken: "If you hear a guy from Barbados, or Jamaica, speaking English, and you listen to that speech, you hear seventeenth-century constructions [...] my relationship to what's called Jacobean by critics is not nostalgia."[31] That postcolonial writers are thus already in reference to a tradition of English-language writing produced through imperial conquest is beyond a doubt. The persistence of memorisation as an educational technique has been read similarly in various ways: as a historical vestige nonsynchronous with "progress" in the imperial centres, through an emphasis on rhetoric rather than literacy, or as a deliberate form of practice.

One of the signal tropes of writing in response to colonial education is that the education precedes or supersedes knowledge of locality itself.

---

[29] Lorna Goodison, *Goldengrove* (Manchester: Carcanet Press, 2006), 120.

[30] Melissa Green, "Excerpt from *The Linen Way*," *Parnassus Poetry Review*, vol. 33 (2013), parnassusreview.com/archives/1651. We might also consider internationalism as a lens through which to understand Walcott's emphasis on declaimed poetry, given his affinity with Russian writers such as Joseph Brodsky and his sense of that tradition as more public and auditory.

[31] Derek Walcott, "An Interview with Nancy Schoenberger," in *Conversations with Derek Walcott*, ed. William Baer (Jackson: University Press of Mississippi, 1996), 90.

We see this, for example, in Merle Collins' poem "The Lesson," which depicts how, as J. Edward Chamberlin discusses, "names of local places and people were left out of the colonial curriculum and replaced by a litany of events and personalities."[32] The requirement to mimic colonial models puts the student in the place of the one who memorises and reproduces by rote, rather than "authentically" produces. The speaker of Collins's poem notes that her grandmother "Spoke/Parrot-like" of colonial history, but never of local history. We might connect the motif of the speaking bird to R. J. Owens's 1961 criticisms of Caribbean poetry, particularly Walcott's, as "jackdaw collections from other poets,"[33] and find a responsive image of literature through Walcott's birds: "Then all of the nations of birds lifted together / the huge net of the shadows of this earth / in multitudinous dialects [...]" where the use of "nations of birds" displaces a biological emphasis on species or breed, and the "dialects" of the birds and their collective agency suggests, at least implicitly, a relocation of the "repetitive" or "rote" properties of the birdsong.

"Rote reproduction" draws attention to multiple effects of estrangement that exist within language; firstly, through the replication of procedures out of their "natural" location (where the bareness of the procedure becomes more evident), and secondly through the uneasiness of reproducing the location of knowledge, as the words of authority arrive and are articulated by colonial subjects. We might view these unintended consequences through Homi Bhabha's concept of sly civility, in which the colonial apparatus undermines its own legitimacy by producing subjects fluent in the discourse of power.[34] Furthermore, for Bhabha, the discourse taken in by sly civility does not have to be linguistic; as other critics have addressed, a significant practice which is also repurposed in this way is sport.[35]

---

[32] J. Edward Chamberlain, *Come Back to Me My Language: Poetry and the West Indies* (Champaign: University of Illinois Press, 1993), 78.

[33] R. J. Owens, "West Indian Poetry," *Caribbean Quarterly*, vol. 7, no. 3 (1961), 120–127.

[34] Homi K. Bhabha, *The Location of Culture* (London: Routledge, 2012).

[35] Simon Eales, "'Get Ready for a Broken Fuck'n Arm': The Anti-instrumentalism of Postcolonial Cricket Poetry," *Don't Do It Mag*, 2, dontdoitmag.co.uk/issue-two/get-ready-for-a-broken-fuckn-arm-the-anti-instrumentalism-of-postcolonial-cricket-poetry/, accessed 25 October 2016.

The eighth section of Walcott's "The Schooner *Flight*" contains a moment of meta-reflection on the narrator, Shabine's, writing process:

> It had one bitch on board, like he had me mark—
> that was the cook, some Vincentian arse
> with a skin like a gommier tree, red peeling bark,
> and wash-out blue eyes; he wouldn't give me a ease,
> like he feel he was white. Had an exercise book,
> this same one here, that I was using to write
> my poetry, so one day this man snatch it
> from my hand, and start throwing it left and right
> to the rest of the crew, bawling out, "Catch it,"
>
> and start mincing me like I was some hen
> because of the poems. Some case is for fist,
> some case is for tholing pin, some is for knife—
> this one was for knife. Well, I beg him first,
> but he keep reading, "O my children, my wife,"
> and playing he crying, to make the crew laugh;
> it move like a flying fish, the silver knife
>
> that catch him right in the plump of his calf,
> and he faint so slowly, and he turn more white
> than he thought he was. I suppose among men
> you need that sort of thing. It ain't right
> but that's how it is. There wasn't much pain,
> just plenty blood, and Vincie and me best friend,
> but none of them go fuck with my poetry again.[36]

That Shabine writes his poems in an exercise book suggests Walcott's ironic invocation of students' presumed derivativeness. Furthermore, Shabine's willingness to demonstrate the book in question, "this same one here," suggests his gestural presence in front of us, speaking aloud. "The Schooner *Flight*" contains many of these doublings of writing and speaking: "in simple speech / my common language go be the wind, / my pages the sails of the schooner *Flight*. / But let me tell you [...]" The system of loose rhyme ("first/fist"; "men/pain/friend/again") stages the poem to be imagined aloud. Thus it is significant that Shabine's

---

[36] Derek Walcott, "The Schooner *Flight*," *Collected Poems 1948–1984*, www.poetryfoundation.org/poems/48316/the-schooner-flight.

"fight with the crew" is staked on a demonstration of physical, rather than written, mastery—mastery of a masculine script. While Vincie *reads* poetry out to mock Shabine, Shabine's dominance is re-established through the "flight" of a knife through the air and the consequent bloodletting, which he depicts as existing among a pre-existing set of options ("some case is for fist [...]"). As the section concludes, "none of them go fuck with my poetry again," the integrity of the poem, its voice, is preserved through a physical feat, in which a scripted bodily intervention is proxy for literary prowess.

When presenting the memorised poem, Silliman suggests, "One is perpetually other than present with the text at hand."[37] This is literally true, given that the text of a memorised poem does not need to be "at hand": "since most poems are memorised and recited without a script, the poet is able to move freely up and down."[38] But does this necessitate more of a distraction from the words of the poem than the form of reading in which the writer holds "the text at hand"? We must ask, then, if the seemingly forgettable pose of holding the text could be read as its own interference with interpretation. The recent explosion of the genre of the performance lecture suggests that far from being natural, the position from behind the lectern or microphone formally sustains an illusion of neutral distance in academic reading and presentation. Thus, once we have decided to read the poem aloud, questions of performativity become questions of providing a reading—and the concomitant issues of attention, difficulty, communicativeness, and, of course, power—which are unavoidable. "Text at hand" becomes a telling slip. If we accept, primarily, that such a form as the poetry reading ought to exist, instead of solitary readings where the audience encounters the poem in privacy, these are inescapable consequences. For those in the audience of a reading, of course, the text is precisely not in their hands, but in the hands of the poet. Is a reading of poetry, then, meant to be a form of witnessing the author's encounter with his own text? Or might it be an attempt to supply this text to the audience in a way that aids their own ability to encounter it—and how might this take place? The difference between

---

[37] Silliman, Untitled Blog Post.

[38] Christian Habekost, *Verbal Riddim: The Politics and Aesthetics of African-Caribbean Dub Poetry* (Amsterdam and Atlanta: Rodopi, 1993), 99.

the poet's and the audience's relation to the poem during a reading remains undertheorised.

In an interview, Walcott notes: "That minimal withdrawing, taciturn kind of composition begins to wither memory. In a sense, when one reads a poem out loud, one is, first of all, presenting a poem to an audience, and secondly, one is also asking them to memorise it."[39] While questions of literary "inheritance" in postcolonial settings are marked by relations of violence, past critics have perhaps overemphasised a seeming choice between colonial and nation language (often figured through the opposition of Walcott and Kamau Braithwaite). This opposition between the received and the innovative seems to avoid the otherness inherent to language, and therefore sociality, itself (an otherness that the subject is merely initiated into) in which language in every case penetrates the subject as "another's," and which serves as a medium for definitively marked expressive encounters.[40] This aspect of simultaneous, even constitutive, proximity and alienation through language may help to illustrate some of the ways in which abstract and occasionally even mundane procedures, such as a manner of reading from the page, might have an operant presence. Rather than being contradictory options, these mutual effects can also be perceived in the re-emergence of the memorised poem: the expressive extension of one's own body which simultaneously subjects it to the effect of a script.

Works Cited

Adorno, Theodor. *Minima Moralia: Reflections on a Damaged Life*. Translated by E. F. N. Jephcott. London: Verso, 2005.
Baugh, Edward. *Derek Walcott*. Cambridge: Cambridge University Press, 2006.
Bhabha, Homi K. *The Location of Culture*. London: Routledge, 2012.
Breiner, Laurence A. "How to Behave on Paper: The Savacou Debate." *Journal of West Indian Literature*, vol. 6, no. 1 (1993): 1–10.

[39] Walcott, "An Interview with Nancy Schoenberger," 94.

[40] This estrangement is extended even beyond Lacan's "symbolic order" by Laplanche, who addresses the unconscious "as an alien inside me, and one even put inside me by an alien. At his most prophetic, Freud does not hesitate over formulas which go back to the idea of *possession*." Jean Laplanche, "The Theory of Seduction and the Problem of the Other," *International Journal of Psychoanalysis*, vol. 78, no. 4 (August 1997), 653–666, www.ncbi.nlm.nih.gov/pubmed/9306181.

Chamberlain, J. Edward. *Come Back to Me My Language: Poetry and the West Indies.* Champaign: University of Illinois Press, 1993.

Clarke, George Elliott. "Review: *Zong!*" *Maple Tree Literary Supplement*, 4. www.mtls.ca/issue4/writings-review-clarke.php. Accessed 1 May 2017.

Coval, Kevin, Quraysh Ali Lansana, and Nate Marshall, eds. *The Breakbeat Poets: New American Poetry in the Age of Hip-Hop.* Chicago: Haymarket Press, 2015.

Eaglestone, Robert. *Doing English: A Guide for Literature Students.* London: Routledge, 2000.

Eales, Simon. "'Get Ready for a Broken Fuck'n Arm': The Anti-instrumentalism of Postcolonial Cricket Poetry." *Don't Do It Mag*, 2. dontdoitmag.co.uk/issue-two/get-ready-for-a-broken-fuckn-arm-the-anti-instrumentalism-of-postcolonial-cricket-poetry/. Accessed 25 October 2016.

Forsyke, Donald R. "Long-Term Memory: Scaling of Information to Brain Size." *Frontiers in Human Neuroscience*, vol. 8 (2014): 397. www.frontiersin.org/articles/10.3389/fnhum.2014.00397/full.

Goodison, Lorna. *Goldengrove.* Manchester: Carcanet Press, 2006.

Green, Melissa. "Excerpt from *The Linen Way.*" *Parnassus Poetry Review*, vol. 33 (2013). parnassusreview.com/archives/1651.

Habekost, Christian. *Verbal Riddim: The Politics and Aesthetics of African-Caribbean Dub Poetry.* Amsterdam and Atlanta: Rodopi, 1993.

Hardy, Edmund. "Derek Walcott/The Philosophy of Names/2011." *Tumblr.* 19 March 2017. bitetheweeds-blog.tumblr.com/post/158584535617/derek-walcott-the-philosophy-of-names-2011.

Laplanche, Jean. "The Theory of Seduction and the Problem of the Other." *International Journal of Psychoanalysis*, vol. 78, no. 4 (August 1997): 653–666. www.ncbi.nlm.nih.gov/pubmed/9306181.

Liberzon, Gahl. *Bodies, Bodies, Bodies, Bodies, Bodies.* Ann Arbor: Red Beard Press, 2013.

Macdonald, Travis, Janet Holmes, Srikanth Reddy, M. NourbeSe Philip, Matthea Harvey, and David Dodd Lee. "The Weight of What's Left [Out]: Six Contemporary Erasurists on Their Craft." Interview by Andrew David King. *Kenyon Review*, 6 November 2012. www.kenyonreview.org/2012/11/erasure-collaborative-interview/.

Mayer, Sophie. "Rest." TinyLetter, 7 March 2017. tinyletter.com/sophiemayer/letters/rest.

Miller, Kei. "Literature from Where I Stand, or Rather Sit; No, Make That Stand..." *Caribbean Review of Books*, no. 15 (2008). caribbeanreviewofbooks.com/crb-archive/15-february-2008/literature-from-where-i-stand/.

———. *The Cartographer Tries to Map a Way to Zion.* Manchester: Carcanet Press, 2014.

Ngai, Sianne. *Ugly Feelings.* Cambridge: Harvard University Press, 2005.

Owens, R. J. "West Indian Poetry." *Caribbean Quarterly*, vol. 7, no. 3 (1961): 120–127.

Philip, M. NourbeSe. *Zong!* Middletown: Wesleyan University Press, 2008.

Silliman, Ron. "Untitled Blog Post." *Silliman's Blog*, 4 May 2005. ronsilliman. blogspot.com/2005/05/whenever-ive-been-paired-up-at-reading.html.

Squire, Larry R., and John T. Wixted. "The Cognitive Neuroscience of Human Memory Since H. M." *Annual Review of Neuroscience*, vol. 34 (2011): 259–288. www.ncbi.nlm.nih.gov/pmc/articles/PMC3192650/.

Sutherland, Keston. "Marx in Jargon." *World Picture Journal*, vol. 1 (2008). www.worldpicturejournal.com/World%20Picture/WP_1.1/KSutherland.pdf.

———. "THESES ON ANTISUBJECTIVIST DOGMA." *Tumblr*, 1 May 2013. afieryflyingroule.tumblr.com/post/49378474736/keston-sutherland-theses-on-antisubjectivist.

Verhagen, Katherine. "Sound or Text: How Do You Heal a 'Foreign Anguish'?" *English Studies in Canada*, vol. 33, no. 4 (2007): 83–90. journals.library.ualberta.ca/esc/index.php/ESC/article/view/9123/7289.

Walcott, Derek. "An Interview with Nancy Schoenberger." In *Conversations with Derek Walcott*, edited by William Baer, 86–94. Jackson: University Press of Mississippi, 1996.

———. *Collected Poems 1948–1984*. London: Faber and Faber, 1986.

———. *Midsummer*. London: Faber and Faber, 1984.

CHAPTER 9

Body Burdens: The Materiality of Work in Rita Wong's *Forage*

Samantha Walton

water connects us to salmon & cedar, whales & workers ...
a gyre of karma recirculates, burgeoning body burden

Rita Wong's work is fundamentally concerned with exploring and exposing the entanglement of economic, subjective and ecological exploitation. Wong is an Asian Canadian writer who, as a critic, has addressed theories of work and labour, both in regard to Asian racialisation and labour in literature, and the 'work' of the writer within and against capitalism.[1] This chapter, however, focuses on Wong's poetry, specifically her 2007 collection *forage*. Much of the poetry collected in *forage* addresses the social and environmental injustices of global capitalism by following the disguised and mystified routes of supply chains to reveal the materiality of work. The forms and techniques of Wong's poetry—including ruptured lyric, found text, open field poetics and citation—reveal the movement of materials around the world, at the

---

[1] Rita Wong, "Provisional Mobilities: Rethinking Labour Through Asian Racialization in Literature," Unpublished Thesis (Simon Fraser University, 2002).

S. Walton (✉)
Bath Spa University, Bath, UK

© The Author(s) 2019
J. L. Walton and E. Luker (eds.), *Poetry and Work,*
Modern and Contemporary Poetry and Poetics,
https://doi.org/10.1007/978-3-030-26125-2_9

same time as they attend to the experiences of migrant and indentured workers exposed to noxious materials and degraded environments. Before the poetry is discussed, however, it is necessary to introduce the theories of trans-corporeality and slow violence central to this chapter's analysis. This theoretical framework will help reveal how Wong's poetry advances a new way of seeing work and exposing capitalist complicity in human suffering and environmental damage by making visible the materiality of labour exchange. Materiality emerges as a fundamental consideration in any theory of work, proposing a counter-narrative to theories of full automation, deterritorialisation and dematerialisation.

TOXICITY: THE CURRENT CRISIS AND THEORETICAL APPROACHES

In his 1989 essay, *The Three Ecologies*, Felix Guattari addresses the conditions of integrated world capitalism as socially, subjectively and ecologically devastating.[2] A few years later, the Nigerian poet and environmental activist Ken Saro-Wiwa defined oil extraction by Shell in the Niger Delta as an 'ecological war', simultaneously attacking the culture, health, social organisation, livelihood and land of the Ogoni peoples.[3] These insights from distinct theoretical and activist perspectives summarise the foundations of the environmental justice movement: the state of nature and the state of humanity are not in binary or tangential relation, but are fundamentally interwoven and interdependent.

More recent approaches have insisted upon the absolute integrity and interconnectedness of human (cultural, economic, social) and natural processes. Timothy Morton's 'ecological thought' exemplifies such thinking: everything is interconnected, and the constructions of 'cultural' and 'natural' must be rejected in order to reach a more holistic understanding of ecological interdependence. Morton states that '[t]he ecological crisis we face is so obvious that it becomes easy—for some, strangely or frighteningly easy—to join up the dots and see everything is

---

[2] Felix Guattari, *The Three Ecologies* (London: Bloomsbury, 2000).

[3] Ken Saro-Wiwa, *Genocide in Nigeria: The Ogoni Tragedy* (Port Harcourt: Saros, 1992), www.turntowardlife.org/essays/chapter5/chapter5.pdf, accessed 11 May 2018.

interconnected. This is *the ecological thought*. And the more we consider it, the more our world opens up'.[4] Morton establishes the 'mesh' as the most appropriate way of conceiving of these interconnections, adapted from the Hindu model of Indra's Net: 'The mesh of interconnected things is vast, perhaps immeasurably so. [...] Nothing exists by itself, so nothing is fully "itself"'.[5] Ecological thinking and 'the mesh' forces a re-examination of human exceptionalism and human–nature binaries. Instead of privileging either anthropocentric or ecocentric values, human health must be seen as an environmental concern, and environmental flourishing as fundamental to human health.[6] Most importantly, environmental justice emerges as one of the key stakes in the confrontation between capitalism and indigenous people, the poor and low-skilled workers, all of whom are disproportionately affected by environmental issues from climate change to resource conflict, toxic dumping to chemical industries.

The racial, ethnic, gendered and class dimension of environmental risk are written large across the globe. They have been addressed in scholarship concerned with exposing the interdependence of social, economic and environmental justice. In *Bodily Natures*, Stacy Alaimo notes how in North America, 'exposure to toxins correlates most directly with race, and then with class, as toxic waste sites, factories, and other sources are most often located near the neighbourhoods of African Americans or other people of colour'.[7] A small selection of high-profile and ongoing conflicts can be called on to demonstrate the ubiquity of what Alaimo refers to, including, but by no means limited to: the state of water emergency in Flint, Michigan, where lead-poisoned water is, at the time of writing, still being supplied to predominantly African American communities; in the Athabasca watershed of Alberta, Canada, where First Nation communities experience high levels of rare cancers and autoimmune diseases associated with tar sands extraction; and in the monumental struggle between indigenous activists and the corporate group, supported by the US government, behind the Dakota Access Pipeline.

---

[4] Timothy Morton, *The Ecological Thought* (Harvard: Harvard University Press, 2011), 1.

[5] Morton, *The Ecological Thought*, 15.

[6] Lawrence Buell, 'Toxic Discourse,' *Critical Inquiry*, vol. 24, no. 3 (1998), 639–665.

[7] Stacy Alaimo, *Bodily Natures: Science, Environment and the Material Self* (Bloomington and Indianapolis: Indiana University Press, 2010), 117.

On a global scale, flows and movements of resources, people, capital, water and toxins are inextricably intertwined. Raw materials are extracted in regions defined, problematically, as 'developing' or 'Third World'; they are then processed and manufactured cheaply in nations with lower degrees of industrial and economic autonomy and environmental regulation than the Global North; next they are imported as high-end goods to wealthy nations. At the end of the supply chain, toxic materials return to Global South/'Third World' countries from an array of industries, leaching into water and impacting on the health of workers, residents, animals and ecosystems. The Blacksmith Institute currently identifies 3241 toxic sites in low and middle income countries, affecting around 54 million people.[8]

In some cases, the catastrophic incidents which expose poor communities to toxins are devastatingly visible. Such is the case of the 1984 Bhopal gas tragedy, in which an accident at the Union Carbide Factory led to over 500,000 people living around the site being exposed to deadly methyl isocyanate. More difficult to make visible are the long-term human health and ecosystem implications of leaching toxic materials, from disasters like Bhopal, or from industrial practices globally. As Jennifer Beth Spiegel notes, ongoing protests by survivors in Bhopal are deeply concerned with the politics of visibility. Activities include marches to deliver collections of urine to government buildings, led by local mothers who attempt to '[alter] the power dynamics relating to the way biochemical flows become publicly visible'.[9]

Precarious migrant workforces also accompany flows of raw and processed materials around the world. As Vandana Shiva notes, neocolonial practices ensure that nature, matter and humanity are all treated as raw materials for the appropriation of capital: 'it is the Third World's biodiversity and human diversity that is being pirated by Northern corporations'.[10] These workers' lives and bodies are shaped and often poisoned by their labour, for example through chemical injury sustained in work that involves

---

[8] "Global Commission on Pollution and Health," Pure Earth Blacksmith Institute, www.pureearth.org/global-commission-pollution-health/, accessed 11 May 2018.

[9] Jennifer Beth Spiegel, "Subterranean Flows: Water Contamination and the Politics of Visibility after the Bhopal Gas Disaster," in *Thinking with Water*, eds. Cecelia Chen, Janice MacLeod, and Astrida Neimanis (Montreal: McGill-Queens University Press, 2013), 91.

[10] Vandana Shiva, "Bioethics: A Third World Issue," Native Web, www.nativeweb.org/pages/legal/shiva.html, accessed 11 May 2018.

exposure to noxious substances, or by living on land which bears the burden of resource extraction, dangerous manufacturing practices and toxic dumping. However, theorists writing from the Global North have been slow to address materiality in theories of economics and labour. Coole and Frost note how '[a]mong social theorists it has become fashionable to talk about deterritorialized, dematerialized capital flows', but immediate and long-term material affects accompany any interruption or crash in financial markets, while flows of capital are paralleled by flows of toxins in and raw materials out of areas subject to processes of Third Worldisation.[11]

Toxicity and environmental pollution demand reconceptualisations of agency, materiality and violence, as well as a renewed politics capable of addressing issues played out across deep temporal and planetary scales, and across different cultures, nations, language traditions, watersheds and land-masses.[12] Two key concepts will, however, be particularly useful in understanding the materiality of labour and examining representations of work in Wong's poetry. Firstly, 'slow violence' as defined by Rob Nixon will assist in considering distributed forms of responsibility and harm as they are played out over generations and across multiple scales and long distances. Slow violence is 'a violence that occurs gradually and out of sight, a violence of delayed destruction [...] incremental and accretive, its calamitous repercussions playing out across a range of temporal scales'.[13] Slow violence is a particularly appropriate lens to adopt in the analysis of Wong's representations of work. The forms of Third World labour that she addresses—manufacturing, mining, waste disposal, electronics recycling—often do cause immediate harm in devastating accidents. More difficult to perceive, however, are the forms of violence which are gradual and accretive, and whose moment of origin can be difficult to determine. Even in the UK and North America, where employees enjoy relatively expansive workplace rights and stringent health and safety protection, medico-legal insurance policies are geared against awarding damages to workers who suffer from diseases and disorders connected to long-term or life-long working conditions. Beyond the life-changing injury, there is a need to adjust perceptions of damage

---

[11] Diana Coole and Samantha Frost, *New Materialisms: Ontology, Agency, Politics* (Durham and New York: Duke University Press, 2010), 31.

[12] Gayatri Chakravorty Spivak, 'Planetarity,' *Paragraph*, vol. 38, no. 2 (2015), 290–292.

[13] Rob Nixon, *Slow Violence and the Environmentalism of the Poor* (Cambridge, MA: Harvard University Press, 2011), 2.

within occupational health and environmental management. Slow violence provides a means of pinpointing the brutality of the tumours, birth defects, sullied waterways—into which pesticides leach at 'a tenth of a mile in a day'[14]—and other 'body burdens' experienced by the world's poor, and addressed in poetry by Wong.[15] Slow violence helps reconnect human agency and responsibility with injuries seemingly distant in space and time.

The second key concept, trans-corporeality, describes the movement of materials between bodies, gesturing towards our own materiality and continuity with the rest of the physical world. Stacy Alaimo, who coined the term, states: 'trans-corporeality suggests that humans are not only interconnected with each other but with the material flows of substances and places'.[16] Carried by water, air, food and other means of influx: 'matter flows through bodies, substantially recomposing them in the process'.[17] Trans-corporeality is transgression because it challenges subject/object relations and binaries of self/other, human/environment and inside/outside on which modern individualistic classifications of personhood and 'the human' rest. Awareness that the human body is material and trans-corporeal demands reconsideration of environmental crisis as well as the body burden of labour; as Alaimo puts it: 'Humans are vulnerable because they are not in fact "human" in some transcendent, contained sense, but are flesh, substance, matter'.[18]

Ecopoetry and Wong's Poetics

Themes of slow violence and trans-corporeality can be seen across Wong's poetry, particularly so in her representations of work. The formal and linguistic innovation of Wong's writing exposes the movement of material around the globe, at the same time as it attends to the experiences of workers who are subjected to the damage of labour in sickening bodies and degraded environments. To this extent, she participates in a

---

[14] This quote is taken from Rachel Carson's *Silent Spring*. Wong, "reverb" *forage*, 60.

[15] Wong, "after 'Laundry Song' by Wen I'to," *forage*, 22.

[16] Stacy Alaimo, "The Naked Word: The Trans-Corporeal Ethics of the Protesting Body," *Women and Performance*, vol. 20, no. 1 (2010), 23–24.

[17] Spiegal, *Thinking with Water*, 86.

[18] Alaimo, "Naked World," 15.

modernist ecopoetic project to reject and innovate beyond pastoral and Romantic constructions of nature and to challenge a modernist, capitalist, extractivist understanding of *time* in terms of efficiency, *place* in terms of property relations, and *nature* in terms of multiply interlocking and destructive binaries: feminine, raw, passive, primitive, innocent, Other, and ripe for exploitation. Linguistic innovation and formal experimentation are particularly attractive techniques in ecopoetry because they help denaturalise the language of 'nature', reveal nature–culture interdependencies, and model ecological relations in new ways. According to Lynn Keller 'experimental poetics [...] might be helping shift our sense of human/nonhuman relations away from the anthropocentric and might enhance our sense of kinship and interdependence with other life forms'.[19]

Modernist poetics has proved to be influential on ecological theory as well. Morton describes ecology as 'more like a Mallarmé poem than a linear, syntactically organized, unified work. The words spread out on the page: we can't tell whether to read them from left to right, nor can we tell which words go with which'.[20] Stacy Alaimo developed trans-corporeality in part through analysis of Muriel Rukeyser's 1938 modernist long-poem, *The Book of the Dead*. In this work, Rukeyser exposes the interconnection between systemic racism and slow violence in the Hawk's Nest Tunnel industrial disaster, in which a workforce of predominantly African-American miners were exposed to fatal levels of silica while carving out a new hydroelectric dam. Modernist literary techniques were used and developed by Rukeyser to reveal the unseen hazards of mining: these include found text (from court transcripts), mixed registers (scientific language interspersed with lyrical testimony), and multiple, discordant framing devices and points of view, including X-Rays, technical photography and perspectives associated with landscape painting. As *The Book of the Dead* contends, workers at Hawk's Nest were exploited not just subjectively and economically, but materially, as they bear the toxic burden of their labour in the sickening body.[21]

[19] Lynn Keller, "A. Rawlings: Ecopoetic Intersubjectivity," *Jacket2* (2015), jacket2.org/article/arawlings-ecopoetic-intersubjectivity, accessed 2 December 2016.

[20] Morton, *The Ecological Thought*, 61.

[21] Muriel Rukeyser, *The Book of the Dead* (Columbia: University of Missouri Press, 2015).

Like Rukeyser's, Wong's poetry advances the project of making the materiality of labour visible. In a manifesto-poem from her 2015 water-themed collection *Undercurrent*, she states:

> water connects us to salmon & cedar, whales & workers
> its currents bearing the plastic from our fridges & closets
> a gyre of karma recirculates, burgeoning body burden.[22]

Intentionally advancing the theory of trans-corporeality, this excerpt emphasises human and non-human entanglement. It attempts to overcome limitations on perceiving relations across vast spatial and temporal scales through the endlessly cycling medium of water. It also addresses ecological enmeshment in the movement of matter through natural processes, in this case, the ocean gyre in which the Great Pacific Garbage patch has collected.

Bringing such relations of exploitation to light may be seen to constitute the 'work' of the poet. However, at the same time as she commits herself and her poetics to revealing the misuses and abuses of industrial capitalism, Wong is alert to the limitations of lyric and the ethical problems with evoking empathy as a political gesture. This paradox is at the heart of *forage*, which the rest of this chapter will now address. In the balancing act between situated lyric and writing that foregrounds material relations over individual experience, the figure of the Chinese migrant—both in nineteenth and twentieth-century North America, and the contemporary industrial worker in China—recurs as a motif and a rallying cry. These are the bodies who bear the burden of capitalism: culturally, spiritually and materially. How, Wong asks in *forage*, can the poet evoke this worker and demonstrate solidarity without participating in the same dematerialised fantasies which make real workers distant, other and theoretical?

FORM AND CONNECTIVITY

forage is comprised of many short poems of mostly a page or two; some are organised as tightly constructed blocks of text, some are organised across two pages in open form style, and others are composed of

---

[22]Rita Wong, "Declaration of Intent," *Undercurrent* (Gibsons: Nightwood Editions, 2015), 14.

fragmentary sentences with a full line space in-between. Many poems are also surrounded by handwritten text that coils around the poems' margins. In the printed, page-centred text, each formal choice contributes in distinct ways to the collection's overall themes. In the poem 'fester', the word 'trade' is placed in proximity to 'traitor', implying a relationship between the two, while the compression of words in the line 'sweatshoparoundyourthroat' emphasises the experience of entrapment in a class and labour position which is felt as a direct attack on the body.

Many other poems are arranged as collections of spaced-out sentences, including 'value chain', 'mess is lore' and 'forage, fumage'. This form is suggestive of a cut-up composition process. Fragments in different voices and registers are slotted next to one another, proving resistant to both enjambment and any run-on reading, for example:

> the internal frontier: my consumer patterns
> what is the context for "you people are hard workers?"
> electromagnetic fields of refrigerator, phone & computer hum
>   bewildered static[23]

Lines are not, however, to be read in isolation. They can be held in parallel associations: above, for example, Wong's speaker reflects on her own consumption, presumably including electronics (referred to two entries down), between which is an attempt to make sense of a restated racist stereotype of the hard-working Asian (perhaps both the wealthy tech-savvy descendent of migrants in North America, and the immiserated industrial worker in China). While no ultimate synthesis of meaning or context can be reached, accepting a disguised relation between the fragments urges the kinds of thinking necessary for the ecological thought, in which only traces and fragments of more complex interconnectivity can be seen.

Many of the 'run-on block of text' poems emphasise trans-corporeality and entanglement, at the same time as they demonstrate the difficulties of perceiving flows through disjunctive phrasing and harsh enjambment. In the poem 'fluorine', agencies designated as human, animal, natural and material pursue diverse intentions in work, consumption, life-patterns and in the global cycles of the hydrological system:

---

[23]Wong, "value chain," *forage*, 11.

> arsenic in calculators, mercury in felt
> hats, mad as a poisoned hatter
> pyrophoric undercurrent in mundane
> acts assume poison unless otherwise
> informed crowded alloys detect no

Chemical flows connect bodies and ecosystems through water. As the opening lines suggest, toxic mercury and arsenic are emitted routinely in the energy market, particular in China, and are used in the production of everyday objects, building up in aquatic systems and in the bodies of higher-level species, due to biomagnification.[24] Toxic release into aquatic systems produces immediate health and environmental disasters at the point of release—as in Minamata Disaster of 1956—and more long-term effects both locally and in distant bodies and places. The non-standard grammar and fit-start enjambment throughout alludes to processes without containment, while anacoluthon—change of syntax mid-flow—alludes to the moment that human control of industrial chemicals is lost as they enter geological and ecological systems.

Towards the second half of "fluorine," a lyric 'I' of sorts is asserted. Wong notes how no health damage is detected

> [...] until generations later i
> brush my teeth with nuclear intensity
> the cavities i avoid destined for others
> fall into hazardous-waste piles up as
> i sleep smells though i don't see it
> transported across oceans & into sad
> rural neglect [...] [25]

Whilst emphasising the collective nature of this daily chore and the paradoxical minuteness of brushing one's teeth, the emergence of a small 'I' places some responsibility on the speaker. Collapsing commonsense notions of scale and responsibility, the poem makes materiality visible. The tooth-cavity that the speaker avoids is transplanted elsewhere. Accretive toxic burden builds up in the water system, contributing, Wong implies, to cancerous manifestations and long-term chronic health problems in other burdened bodies.

---

[24] Michael S. Bank, ed., *Mercury in the Environment: Pattern and Process* (Oakland: University of California Press, 2012), 9–10.

[25] Wong, "flourine," *forage*, 14.

Body Burdens

The phrase 'body burden' appears in both *forage* and *Undercurrent*. In this phrase, Wong alludes to a fundamental problem with the labour contract model under toxic working conditions. The labour contract emerged historically in the social contract theory of Thomas Hobbes, John Locke and Jean-Jacques Rousseau. Labour contracts are based on the premise that individuals are free to contract their labour, and thus to enter into agreed conditions of servility and become, for the purposes of work, the property of another. In *The Sexual Contract*, Carole Pateman critiques the foundations of Locke's contract by revealing the ways in which the labour contract is premised upon forms of self-denigration which, within the theory of contract itself, it is beyond the worker to contract away. This is because no one can fully contract away their own rights to life and liberty, because to do so would destroy the 'free' terms of the contract itself. At the heart of Pateman's critique—which touches upon slavery, marriage and sex work—is a resistance to all forms of labour contracts for the reason that, due to differentiations of power between the buyer and the seller of labour, they always exceed their own terms.[26] Marxist and feminist theorists concerned with labour have further addressed the additional forms of affective and emotion labour demanded by employees and consumers, beyond traditional models of disembodied, genderless and machinic models of worker productivity.[27] Wong's poetry contributes to existing critiques of the labour contract by revealing bodies materially burdened by work. The bodies that 'inhale carcinogenic toner dust' and the 'disposable factory girls' of Wong's poetry are not liberated by their work [28]; they have been forced into the paradoxical position of contracting away their health and physical integrity as if they had entered into a 'normal' work contract. [29] The toxicity of modern labour, and the forms of slow violence enacted over decades and generations, adds an essential dimension to critiques of the labour contract.

[26] See Carole Pateman, *The Sexual Contract* (Stanford: Stanford University Press, 1988).

[27] For starting points, see Michael Hardt and Antonio Negri, *Empire* (Harvard: Harvard University Press, 2000) and Arlie Russell Hochschild, *The Managed Heart: Commercialization of Human Feeling* (Berkeley: University of California Press, 1983).

[28] Rita Wong, "sort by day, burn by night," *forage* (Gibsons: Nightwood Editions, 2007), 46.

[29] Wong, "chinese school dropout," *forage*, 51.

Wong's commitment to making obscured global networks of relations and responsibilities visible involves following links of material connections from privileged consumers to the burdened bodies of workers. In 'after "Laundry Song" by Wen I'to', Wong updates older Chinese literatures of work to address the body burden of modern labour. According to Renqui Yu, in 1888 there were around 10,000 Chinese people living in New York and around 2000 Chinese laundries.[30] The hand-laundries offered opportunities for occupation outside of factory work, at a time when Chinese workers were denied employment due to prejudice and the limitations on rights to work enshrined in the Chinese Exclusion Act (1882). In spite of the higher degree of autonomy these small-business owners achieved, hand-laundry work was often exhausting and poorly paid. Wen I'to's 'Laundry Song', after which Wong's poem is named, was written in 1926. Here is a short excerpt:

> I can wash handkerchiefs wet with sad tears;
> I can wash shirts soiled in sinful crimes.
> The grease of greed, the dirt of desire ...
> And all the filthy things at your house,
> Give them to me to wash, give them to me.[31]

As the poem suggests, hand-laundry work involved physical and affective labour, connecting the suffering body and mind of the worker with the act of cleaning clothes sullied by wealthy employers. In washing the clothes dirtied through desire and greed, the laundry worker becomes the unseen conduit for purification, occupying an ulterior world in which the sins written on the clothes are fully manifested and registered. It is these sinful traits—greed, desire, conspicuous consumption—that may be seen as fundamental to the strivings and financial successes of the white Americans who use the laundry's services.

Wong's adaptation of 'The Laundry Song' develops and expands upon the affective and symbolic labour of washing clothes to address the chemical body burden of late-capitalist laundry work. In Wong's poem,

---

[30] Renqui Yu, *To Save China, to Save Ourselves: The Chinese Hand Laundry Alliance of New York* (Philidelphia: Temple University Press, 1922), 9.

[31] Wen I'to, "The Laundry Song," in *Twentieth Century Chinese Poetry: An Anthology*, trans. and ed. Kai-Yu Hsu (Ithaca, NY: Cornell University Press, 1963), 51.

hands are 'soapworn', as of old, but coughs are now toxic: 'kidneys and livers mumble / to the brass of cash registers', and clothes are 'laundered in endochrine disrupters / the sudsy chemicals gurgle flames / sulk in your blood for a decade'.[32] As well as the more immediate physical and existential suffering of the original migrant Chinese laundry worker, modern chemicals leach material suffering into multiple bodies over extensive distances and temporal scales, enacting slow violence through trans-corporeality.

THE CHINESE LABOURER

Wen I'to's poem reflects specifically on the experience of the migrant worker, but the figure of the worker has a special place in non-diaspora Chinese literature and art. During the New Cultural Movement of the 1910s and 1920s, a new vernacular literature proliferated in China, taking the lives of working people as its theme.[33] After the Communist Revolution and during the years of Maoist rule, the peasant and worker were centred in cultural narratives of China, both through state-sanctioned Soviet-influenced Socialist Realist art, which celebrated healthy rural peasantry and bucolic fertile farmlands, and in new Chinese literary conventions promoted by Mao Zedong.[34]

Wong's writing fixates upon the historical figure of the Chinese migrant worker, both within China and across the USA and Canada. With this comes a deep self-consciousness that her work is contributing to tropes of the Asian labourer which make real workers more difficult to empathise with, because they become more stereotyped and more theoretical. In the first poem of the collection, she asks 'what is the context

---

[32] Wong, "after 'Laundry Song' by Wen I'to," *forage*, 22.

[33] For example, see Lu Xun, "The Real Story of Ah Q" in *The Real Story of Ah Q and Other Tales of China: The Complete Fiction of Lu Xun*, translated by Julia Lovell (London: Penguin Classics, 2009), 79.

[34] Dong Xiwen, *Thousand-year Old Earth Has Turned over*, date unknown. Watercolor, in Liu Ding and Carol Yinghua Lu, 'From the Issue of Art to the Issue of Position: The Echoes of Socialist Realism, Part I,' *e-flux Journal* 55 (May 2014), 4worker01.e-flux.com/pdf/article_8975853.pdf, accessed 14 May 2018; Mao Zedong, "Talks at the Yan'an Conference on Literature and Art. May 1942" *Marxists Internet Archive*, www.marxists.org/reference/archive/mao/selected-works/volume-3/mswv3_08.htm, accessed 14 May 2018.

for "you people are hard workers'"?[35] Throughout the collection, she deconstructs a range of literary and cultural representations, asking why it is that Chinese migrants workers have historically been figured as so little worthy of empathy and why they are forced to occupy the terrible roles they do in modern industry.

forage contains two photographs of Chinese workers. One is of Agnes Wong, a munitions worker at the Small Arms plant, Long Branch, Ontario.[36] The photo was taken in 1944 and shows Agnes assembling a Sten gun for use by Chinese soldiers in the Second Sino-Japanese War (1937–1945). Evocative of the 'We Can Do It!' Rosie the Riveter poster designed by J. Howard Miller in 1943, the image of the smiling and head-scarf adorned Agnes Wong reveals under-documented and ulterior histories of the cross-Pacific movement of arms, capital and workers. The second photograph is from c.1889 and shows the 'Interior of Victoria Rice Mills showing rice packaged in mats and Chinese worker'.[37] The image depicts a factory wall against which are stacked blocky packages of rice in neat rows. To the front right of the shot, a worker stands, hands on his waistband, his face almost entirely obscured in shadow. Next to it is the visual poem 'rise/riven/rice'. It is made of lone-standing words arranged in an inverted and shallow crescent, and includes the words *rise*, *riven* and *rice*, bookended above and below with the letters 'r / rr / rrr' and 'rrr /rr / r' respectively. The image itself is circular, and evokes the flag of the People's Republic of China, with the circular image standing in for the largest of the five red stars and the half moon replacing the semi-circle of four smaller stars arranged around it. Although the flag that the text and image represent was not adopted until 1949, the anachronistic placement of the image of the late nineteenth-century worker in the place of the largest star provides a commentary on the centrality of Chinese products and workers in the late 1880s in the making of global capitalism.

The neatly arranged packages of rice and the obliterated face of the Chinese worker show the personality and corporeality of labour flattened and the materiality of the product transformed into commodity. Marx,

---

[35] Wong, "value chain," *forage*, 11.

[36] 'Worker Agnes Wong of Whitecourt, Alberta, assembles a sten gun produced for China by the Small Arms Ltd. plant, Long Beach, ON, April 1944. Source: Library and Archives Canada. Reproduced in *forage*, 24.

[37] Wong, *forage*, 8.

of course, drew attention to how the 'sensuous characteristics' of things are 'extinguished' as they become commodities.[38] Recently, Anna Tsing has described the ways in which the social relations, lives and acts which create products are erased at the moment in which it is transformed into capitalist inventory.[39] Wong's poetic and visual arrangement addresses the alienation inherent in the production of the commodity, in this case, rice. In the crescent arrangement of broken words, 'riven' is at the centre, standing for the fragmentation of cultural practices in the globalised world, including but certainly not limited to: the loss of indigenous language traditions and attendant fracturing of identity; the disruption of pre-modern and non-Western rural economies; and the falsity and historicity of the nature/culture divide. The migrant worker is particularly vulnerable to fragmentation, identity displacement and loss of language and other cultural heritage. Appropriately, the face of the worker is erased in the photograph Wong selects for inclusion. In the process of turning a sensuous substance (rice) into alienated capitalist commodity, their identity and individual characteristics have also been erased.

Since the 1980s, many Chinese writers have responded to the deregulated conditions of work, marketisation, globalisation, cheap production, assembly line work and mining, in writing which is more emphatically critical of working conditions and state oppression. In *Iron Moon: An Anthology of Chinese Worker Poetry* (2017), worker-poets speak out against the immiserating conditions of mechanised labour. The collection includes poetry by Xu Lizhi, born in 1990, who worked in a Foxcomm factory making Apple products until his suicide in 2014, and Wu Xia, whose poem 'Sundress' demonstrates a tender care for the consumers to whose lifestyles her own life has been sacrificed: 'I want to press the straps flat / so they won't dig into your shoulders when you wear it'.[40]

Wong's poetry cannot, and does not try to, speak on behalf of these workers. However, her poetry is committed to revealing the conditions of a workforce exhausted and exploited in order to produce the materials

---

[38] Karl Marx, *Capital: A Critique of Political Economy*, trans. Ben Fowkes, Vol. 1 (Toronto: Penguin Books, 1990), 128.

[39] Anna Tsing, *The Mushroom at the End of the World* (Princeton: Princeton University Press, 2015), 127.

[40] Wu Xia, "Sundress," in *Iron Moon: An Anthology of Chinese Worker Poetry*, trans. and ed. Eleanor Goodman (White Pine Press: Buffalo, 2017), 165.

of a lifestyle that is in itself ecocidally destructive, and is disproportionately enjoyed by wealthy consumers in the Global North. In 'sort by day, burn by night', Wong describes how workers at China's electronic recycling plants '"liberate recyclable materials" / into canals & rivers'.[41] Using quotation marks to insinuate an ironic distance, followed by enjambment as a form of detournement, Wong reveals how the language of capitalism sanitises and censors the ecocidal realities of the e-waste industry. Another poem, 'perverse subsidies', begins with a command: 'will pay for you to take my garbage away so i never have / to look at it, never have to imagine the roaches & rats / crawling through cucumber rinds'. Romantic fantasies of unspoilt Nature are spared for the privileged, while the grotesquery and danger of waste disposal are deputised to underpaid workers. Low-skilled and domestic work is revealed to be none other than environmental censorship for the benefit of the rich. As the poem continues, Wong connects abject and suppressed material disposal, farmed out to anonymous workers, with acts of colonial violence and modern Western imperialism, centred on the oil industry: 'fill my car with the corpses of iraqi civilians, the ghost of ken saro-wiwa, the bones of displaced caribou'. The sanitised Western imaginary is strewn with ghosts that the speaker knows about—which are invoked—without experiencing guilt or revulsion. The final statement of the poem involves accepting responsibility for this suppressed and repressed knowledge and proclaiming a bodily solidarity with workers, animals and nature: 'disaffect, reinfect me', the speaker of 'perverse subsidies' finally demands.[42]

In spite of these invocations, Wong's poetry exhibits a profound self-awareness of the limits of poetry and any rhetorical act. While her speakers are often committed to making some form of change, individual acts of ethical consumerism are always a constrained way of contributing to environmental and social justice: *'somehow i will begin walking & bicycling for my life, for our lives'* goes the italicised coda to 'perverse subsidies'.[43] This desperate and guilt-stricken promise draws attention to the difference between the position of the 'i' and the experience of the worker. The resulting paradox produces an impasse: we can trace painful chains of harm between ourselves and others, at the same time as being

---

[41] Wong, "sort by day burn by night," *forage*, 46.

[42] Wong, "perverse subsidies," *forage*, 21.

[43] Wong, "perverse subsidies," *forage*, 21.

able to make limited change through ethical consumerism and individual behavioural change. The reader, who may be the direct target of these calls to arms—even the modest decision to use a bike—is left in the same position of powerlessness as Wong's speaker, cycling for her life, but not *really* cycling her life.

EMPATHY, ETHICS AND THE LYRIC

How is it possible to reverse these processes of erasure? Literature, in particular postcolonial writing, is frequently considered as able to effect change by provoking ethical engagement through empathy. Madhu Krishnan notes how, according to current trends, it is assumed that the (usually Euro-American) reader

> may enter into the mind, life, and experience of those who remain socially, politically, economically, and geographically remote, thereby both learning to better empathize with these far-flung others while simultaneously effecting social change through the empathic call to responsibility.[44]

As a window into another life, literature is assumed to be able to expand the 'Western' imagination and humanise readers whose own experiences are remote from troubled political circumstances, war, environmental degradation, and demeaning labour. In this way, literature ceases to be textual artifice or aesthetic object, and instead becomes

> an extension of life not only horizontally, bringing the reader into contact with events or locations or persons or problems he or she has not otherwise met, but also, so to speak, vertically, giving the reader experience that is deeper, sharper, and more precise than much of what takes place in life.[45]

However, the use of literature as a window into the life of another raises some problems. The ethical engagement it spurs may be heartfelt, but it may also be shallow and serve a primarily aesthetic or cathartic purpose: for example, in the 'slum tourism' and 'poverty porn' decried in

---

[44] Madhu Krishnan, "Affect, Empathy, and Engagement: Reading African Conflict in the Global Literary Marketplace," *The Journal of Commonwealth Literature*, vol. 52, no. 2 (2015), 215.

[45] Martha Nussbaum, quoted in Krishnan, 'Affect,' 216.

some media and development charity campaigns.[46] Furthermore, according to Krishnan, it may further entrench the relations of power which produce the conditions causing damage:

> By supposing ourselves to inhabit the struggles and experiences of those who remain socially, politically, economically, and geographically remote, we simultaneously run the risk of engaging in what Carolyn Pedwell has termed the "forms of projection and appropriation [...] which can reify existing social hierarchies."[47]

Krishnan's article addresses fictional representations of African nations and the idea of 'Africa' itself, but her and Pedwell's critique of the limitations of empathy may be extrapolated to an analysis of Wong's work through attention to the lyric form and its capacity to form empathetic connections between speaker and reader.

In recent years, there has been increased interest in the empathetic capacities of lyric within experimental poetics in the UK and North America. While Language Poetry's critique of the textual constructedness of the lyric 'I' has been extensively influential, more recent experimental reappraisals of the lyric within feminist, critical race theory, queer and postcolonial studies reassert the radicalism of new forms of lyric 'I' that attest to both the inconsistencies and constructedness of the subject, and the political significance of asserting a lyric voice as an outsider within a white, male and Western lyrical tradition.[48] In terms of evoking empathy as a means to ethical engagement, John Wilkinson has defended the lyric as productive of what he terms the 'lyric touch':

> it is poetry's contamination – the *touch* at the Latin route of contamination – that helps *me* to recognise *you* and to cease "ingrowing into ourselves" through an urgently needed distortion into the quickening of hope.[49]

---

[46] See Matt Collin, "What Is 'Poverty Porn' and Why Does It Matter for Development?" *Aid Thoughts* (July 1, 2009), aidthoughts.org/2009/07/01what-is-povertyPoverty-porn-and-why-does-it-matter-for-development/, accessed 11 May 2018.

[47] Krishnan, "Affect," 5.

[48] See Linda A. Kinnahan, *Lyric Interventions: Feminism, Experimental Poetry, and Contemporary Discourse* (Iowa: University of Iowa Press, 1998).

[49] John Wilkinson, *The Lyric Touch: Essays on the Poetry of Excess* (Cromer: Salt, 2007), 120–142. The phrase "ingrowing into ourselves" is taken from Andrea Brady.

Lyric, to Wilkinson, has the potential to produce moments of 'contamination'—the touch—in which the other becomes visible to the self and the loneliness of bourgeois individualism is replaced, momentarily, with generosity and hope. Lyric, seemingly offers a brief window if not into the emotions of another, then at least out of the private 'ingrowing' of the self.

Empathy and ethics are implicated, if not named, in this encounter, and yet the writing of identity intrinsic to writing of the self is tainted by one's complicity in social and environmental injustice. As Keston Sutherland states:

> Our identities are dependent for their making and sustenance on the catastrophic exploitation of the unfortunate inhabitants of other places. [...] How can lyric register the experience of ethical neutrality in acts of consumption which reap such harm elsewhere? How is suffering elsewhere figured by lyric poetry? And how can lyric document the rift in the identity of the consumer, that alienation from "my life" propagated by the commodities and advertisements of the society of the spectacle?[50]

These questions are all fundamental to Wong's poetics. In *forage*, she produces multiple forms of ruptured and ironic lyric which register an awareness of the material making of identity, revealing how the self is produced by ecological and trans–corporeal association with the 'I' of another. In the small 'i' of 'fluorine', washing poisons down her sink, and in the GMO-induced horrors of 'chaos feary', the capacities of lyric are stretched as the speaker comes to cognisance both of her dependence on the exploitation of workers, and her material and ecological entanglement in a world damaged by industry. 'chaos feary' provides a play on the autopoiesis of self-creating and regulating cellular life and biological systems, alongside connected notions of writing the self into existence and maintaining it through lyric self-production. The line 'me poetic auto me diverse' taken from 'chaos feary' acknowledges multiplicity and rifts in the self.[51] The poem's meditation on genetic modification further complicates the lyric, which must not only register the alienation from 'my life' propagated by commodities, to paraphrase Sutherland, but the contingency of the self on the technologically modified matter which constitutes it.

---

[50] Keston Sutherland, *Complicities: British Poetry 1945–2007* (Kindle Locations 4535–4540). Litteraria Pragensia. Kindle Edition.

[51] Wong, "chaos feary," *forage*, 37.

THE LIMITS OF EMPATHY

Wong's doubts about lyric's capacity to promote meaningful ethical engagement through empathy come through in her poem 'reverb'. She writes:

> i counted sweatshops in vancouver's eastside until i got dizzy
> and fainted
> assume spiritual plenitude—can you?[52]

The first line records a moment of collapse following an excursion around a deprived district. A seemingly earnest statement, it is however undercut by the second. Phrased as a directive and a challenge, the question to the assumed reader urges critique of the naturalised lyric voice of the first line. Who is the 'i', and why did they faint? Is it because of the horror of sweatshops, or are they simply exhausted by walking and counting? The first line seems to describe an act in which identification with those working in sweatshops overwhelms the speaker. This, in turn, is supposed to encourage empathy. The question, then, 'assume spiritual plenitude—can you'? poses a challenge to attribute the exact same degree of generosity and concern to the speaker. This chain of empathy highlights the difficulty of ensuring that ethical and empathetic equivalence is reproduced at each stage in the chain. In a collection concerned with intentionally obscured industrial supply chains, the passing on of empathy from one consumer to the next raises doubts about the value of empathy to the reader-consumer, and also the authentic reproducibility of affect through lyric production.

Instead, awareness of trans-corporeality produces a more material way of 'touching' others, with more discernible modes of lyric contamination. Although Wong's speakers do not live in the same degraded environments as the people she writes about, neither are they transcendent above the material world. Alaimo notes that with 'more consumption and exposure, [comes] more risk'.[53] In affinity with this sentiment, Wong states: 'you might carpenter a tree-house escape / but the assiduous rain will find your pores'.[54]

---

[52] Wong, "reverb," *forage*, 60.

[53] Alaimo, *Bodily Natures*, 117.

[54] Wong, "after 'Laundry Song' by Wen I'to," *forage*, 22.

SORT BY DAY, BURN BY NIGHT

The most direct statements concerning connection, responsibility and contamination in *forage* come in the poem 'sort by day, burn by night', which addresses the e-waste recycling industry sited, between 1996 and 2015, in Guiyu, China.[55] While the sites of production, labour, extraction and dumping mentioned within the collection are various and global, this poem forms the book's centrepiece. *forage*'s front cover features an image taken in Guiyu of a heap of burnt out motherboards, forming a simulated green hill nearly obscuring the natural hills rising almost picturesquely in the background.[56] On this site, e-waste workers are tasked with reclaiming precious metals from post-consumer computer and phone parts, including gold, silver and palladium. Lacking robust environmental legislation and worker's rights, workers handle lead and mercury with basic equipment and bare hands, while lead, chromium and tin run-off poisons the river and soil.

In his analysis of the poem, Matthew Zantingh uses Bruno Latour's Actor–Network Theory to address the ways in which workers and consumers are connected through networks of things: Wong's poetry 'asks us to consider how the material objects of everyday life emerge from networks that connect disparate places and peoples together'.[57] While the exchange of commodities flattens objects, ANT and the newer forms of philosophical materialism address the ways in which objects form a part of subjectivity and identity, at the same time as global commerce produces 'a crisis of urgent materiality' in e-waste and toxicity.[58] The situation in Guiyu and the e-waste crisis is of particular significance because digital technologies, new media and the internet are so frequently discussed in terms of the immateriality, instantaneity and lack of geographical location. What is found in Guiyu is the insistent materiality of the digital, while focus on consumer electronics urges an awareness that the text itself has been produced on the computers and devices which poison Guiyu's workers.

---

[55] Operations in Guiyu were shut down suddenly in December 2015. It is unclear where the production site has shifted to. For more information see Basel Action Network, www.ban.org/news.

[56] Wong credits these images to credited to LaiYun and Greenpeace.

[57] Matthew Zantingh, "When Things Act Up: Thing Theory, Actor-Network Theory, and Toxic Discourse in Rita Wong's Poetry," *Interdisciplinary Studies in Literature and Environment*, vol. 20, no. 3 (Summer 2013), 624.

[58] Zantingh, "When Things Act Up," 625.

'sort by day, burn by night' tests the capacity of the lyric to handle the confusing subject/object dilemma produced by awareness of the materiality of the self and material entanglement in global ecology. Wong quotes from Whitman's 'One's Self I Sing'—'Yet utter the word Democratic, the word En-Masse'—reframing Whitman's statement on the relationship between individual identity and the collective in an age of ecological entanglement. The poem also experiments with different forms of address, employing two forms of 'you' to implicate the reader in the situation in Guiyu. It asks, first

> if you live in guiyu village,
> one of the hundred thousand people who
> "liberate recyclable materials"
> into canals and rivers

and then follows this up with a series of interrogatory questions:

> where do your metals come from?
> where do they return
> what if you don't live in guiyu village?
> what if your pentium got dumped in guiyu village?
> your garbage, someone else's cancer?[59]

'You' is used as both a distancing technique, making things general and impersonal, and at the same time a tool to reveal entanglement, as a means of implicating the reader in the damage. Although Wong asks whether 'you' live in Guiyu village, the likelihood is that the reader will not be the e-waste worker, but the geographically distant consumer who benefits from digital technologies without considering the problem of sourcing metals or processing post-consumer electronics. Globalised capital relies on distance and the invisibility of social and environmental injustice to ensure consumer apathy and moral indifference. Wong's poetry asserts that these relations are not complex and overwhelming, but are *excessively easy to trace*. On the very devices which may one day end up in a heap of toxic metals in Guiyu, the concerned reader may access thousands of photographs of Guiyu's workers in seconds, as well as images of fields and waterways clogged with scrap electronics and metallic run-off.

[59] Wong, "sort by day burn by night," *forage*, 46–47.

Knowledge has never been so accessible. However, making these disguised connections more visible demands an ethical response beyond crass mitigating statements involving collective implication in capitalism and dialectical critiques of the limitations of consumer boycott: 'economy of scale / shrinks us all' she states at the poem's close.[60] While acts of slow violence are notoriously difficult to see and to fix blame for, in the lines quoted here Wong asserts that it is exactly the massiveness and comprehensiveness of capitalist industry which makes consumers particularly responsible. Increasing choice and access to products and technologies ironically bring us closer into connection with lives and places around the world.

Through poetry that collapses imaginative distances through an economy of language, Wong draws attention to a real, material 'touch', and produces a 'lyric contamination' between the 'me' and the 'you'. She does this while refusing, in the tradition of experimental and feminist lyric, to adopt a singular or finite subject position. As well as ironising the lyric form, Wong alludes to the classical tradition of the epic in 'sort by day, burn by night': 'o keyboard irony […] sing me the toxic ditty of silica'.[61] As the singular subject position—whether of worker or consumer—is insufficient to address the huge scale of interconnections, bodies, agencies and materials that Wong includes without synthesising in her poetry, so too is the epic form rejected as too preoccupied with closed, heroic and anthropocentric narratives. Her open form poetry of fragments and juxtapositions contributes to an eco-modernism which rejects grand human narratives at the same time that it acknowledges a deep ecological interconnectedness and trans-corporeality beyond the expressive scope of traditional literary conventions.

FORAGING, POETRY AND RESISTANCE

What, then, is the 'work' of the poet, if not to feel keenly, to produce or perform empathy? Rather than constructing an outraged lyric 'I', or sourcing and/or simulating worker testimonies, Wong uses documentation and citation as a form of activism. 'sort by day, burn by night' was, Wong notes, written upon watching the documentary *Exporting Harm:*

---

[60]Wong, "sort by day burn by night," *forage*, 47.

[61]Wong, "sort by day burn by night," *forage*, 46.

The High-Tech Trashing of Asia, which can be easily sourced online.[62] In the poem's footnotes, Wong includes the url for the Seattle-based Basel Action Network, an environmental health and justice not-for-profit committed to 'ending toxic trade; catalysing a toxics-free future; campaigning for everyone's right to a flourishing environment'.[63] The lists of References and Acknowledgements at the collection's close further enable readers to become amateur experts on the environmental issues the poetry addresses. Indeed, Wong includes information of various kinds in multiple poems; for example 'canola queasy' is 'Dedicated to Percy Schmeiser, the Saskatchewan farmer harassed and sued by Monsanto because genetically engineered canola blew into his fields'.[64] Facts, statistics and commentary feature in the body-text, while her handwritten marginalia features quotes, dedications, suppressed and underrepresented news stories about environmental disasters and corruption, including clarifications of terminology and advice on further reading: for example, a handwritten note which runs vertically up one top-right margin notes that 'chaos feary' was written 'upon reading <u>Biopiracy</u> by Vandana Shiva'.[65] This use of marginalia and citation gestures towards the marginalisation of postcolonial and environmental justice critiques within modernity's forms of cultural and industrial production. At the same time, it builds a tentative community for the exchange of knowledge, criticism and action. The margins become a fruitful and underregulated space for the emergence of ulterior knowledge and activism, within which the reader might 'forage'.

The book's title, obviously, alludes to the free collection of wildgrowing plants: a pre-modern, extra-capitalist and—ideally—sustainable way of collecting food for sustenance. In contrast, Guiyu's workers engage in an abject and inverted form of foraging: 'cooking' circuit boards to extract gold and picking heavy metals from computers by hand. Rather than sustenance accumulation, their work can be compared to 'salvage accumulation' as defined by Tsing. Salvage accumulation is the process, foundational to capitalism, 'through which lead firms amass capital without controlling the conditions under which commodities are produced'.

---

[62] "Exporting Harm: The High-Tech Trashing of Asia," Basel Action Network (May 2013), www.youtube.com/watch?v=yDSWGV3jGek, accessed 11 May 2018.

[63] Basel Action Network. Web, www.ban.org/what-we-do/, accessed 2 May 2017.

[64] Wong, "canola queasy," *forage*, 36.

[65] Wong, "canola queasy," *forage*, 37.

In this way, 'free' labour such as woodland foraging or peasant farming becomes capitalised when these *'pericapitalist activities are salvaged for accumulation'*.[66] Tsing's book about foraging, *The Mushroom at the End of the World*, focuses on the matsutake foragers of the North West US, but the same process applies when any foraged or peasant farmed goods are bought and enter global supply chains, becoming capitalist inventory. Foraged or salvaged goods are not irrelevant to capitalism: indeed, many of the products most valuable to capitalist industry are naturally produced outside of its control, for example coal, oil and metals created through geological processes. Salvage accumulation therefore describes the ways in which capitalism depends upon a store of raw materials that it cannot produce or control: from the flow of water to photosynthesis.

Salvage accumulation goes beyond raw materials such as plants and metals. As Tsing suggests, '[s]imilar processes happen with human labor as well. Even factory labor, that icon of capitalist production, cannot be *made* by capitalists, since capitalists can shape—but not manufacture—human beings'.[67] As well as the reproductive labour inherent in the creation of workers, a considerable stock of skills and physical attributes are 'salvaged' by capitalism in the creation of the most automated and alienated workforce. Capitalism, defined by Tsing, emerges from numerative generative life processes beyond itself in order to survive and thrive. This model of salvage accumulation presents new ways of reading *forage*. The work of e-waste recyclers in emphatically not the free, pericapitalist and life-sustaining act of foraging. Beyond the obvious sarcastic inversion, the use of 'forage' to describe labour in Guiyu alludes to additional processes of salvage accumulation in operation there. Workers are not just producing value by foraging materials from post-consumer detritus: value is being produced through the survival capacities of their bodies and the water and soil ecologies of Guiyu. As long as workers in these abusive industries continue to survive and arrive for work, and to use their own inventiveness, ingenuity and skill to extract metals from e-waste, they become victims and objects of capitalist salvage accumulation.

---

[66] Tsing, *Mushroom*, 63.

[67] Anna Tsing, "Salvage Accumulation, or the Structural Effects of Capitalist Generativity," *Cultural Anthropology* (30 March 2015), culanth.org/fieldsights/656-salvage-accumulation-or-the-structural-effects-of-capitalist-generativity, accessed 11 May 2018.

Like Wong, Tsing's writing addresses all that is exploitative and seemingly comprehensively entrapping about capitalist social and economic organisation. However, Tsing isolates some areas for resistance to capitalism, which in turn can be compared to the more hopeful sections of Wong's poetry. In the foraging activities of the matsutake pickers, Tsing observes forms of work that are experienced as 'freedom' by the pickers. While the fruits of their labour are finally salvaged—and consumed—by capital, the forms of life-making which take place prior to salvage suggest other possibilities to the labour contract. As she states, 'Only when we begin to notice the elaborate and heterogeneous making of capitalist worlds might we usefully discuss vulnerabilities, points of purchase, and alternatives'.[68]

Wong, likewise, is interested in different forms of exchange, economic models and ways of relating to human and non-human worlds. In the poem, 'for Lee Kyung Hae, Korean farmer martyred in Cancun (1947–2003)' she celebrates the anti-neoliberal protester who led a hunger strike at the WTO headquarters in Geneva in Spring 2003, and in September of the same year stabbed himself on top of a police barricade at the WTO conference in Mexico. Wong interprets this desperate and despairing act which as both sacrifice and gift, and in its tragic excess she foresees the possibilities of social organisation beyond capitalism. The notes of hope sounded in this poem are inspired by the generative capacities of both the earth and the human, and the potential for life to be otherwise:

> WTO
> smashes rice farmers into
> the enduring earth
>
> but your sacrifice
> invokes capitalism's fall
> so earth resurges
>
> gift economy
> socialism's red fist unclenched
> open palm stories[69]

---

[68] Tsing, "Salvage Accumulation".

[69] Wong, "for Lee Kyung Hae, Korean farmer martyred in Cancun (1947–2003)," *forage*, 62.

Poetry cannot produce alternative economic models or liberate the workers bearing the body burdens of capitalist industry; however, it can be used to accumulate and share knowledge, show solidarity, and offer counter narratives which reveal the interconnectedness of life and the vitality of earth and the human. Rita Wong's poetry insists on the interconnectedness of social, subjective and ecological damage. It proposes critical and collective means of intervening in social and environmental injustices through consciousness raising, activism, boycott and protest. Finally, it explores alternatives to the labour contract under capitalism, introducing the vital and significant notion of the body burden to bring an often-neglected awareness of materiality to theories of work.

WORKS CITED

Alaimo, Stacy. *Bodily Natures: Science, Environment and the Material Self.* Bloomington and Indianapolis: Indiana University Press, 2010.

Alaimo, Stacy. "The Naked Word: The Trans-Corporeal Ethics of the Protesting Body." *Women and Performance*, vol. 20, no. 1 (2010): 15–36.

Bank, Michael S, ed. *Mercury in the Environment: Pattern and Process.* Oakland: University of California Press, 2012.

Basel Action Network. www.ban.org/news. Accessed 11 May 2018.

Collin, Matt. "What Is 'Poverty Porn' and Why Does It Matter for Development?" *Aid Thoughts*, 1 July 2009. aidthoughts.org/2009/07/01/what-is-poverty-porn-and-why-does-it-matter-for-development. Accessed 11 May 2018.

Coole, Diana and Samantha Frost. *New Materialisms: Ontology, Agency, Politics.* Durham and New York: Duke University Press, 2010.

"Global Commission on Pollution and Health." Pure Earth Blacksmith Institute. www.pureearth.org/global-commission-pollution-health. Accessed 11 May 2018.

Guattari, Felix. *The Three Ecologies.* London: Bloomsbury, 2000.

Keller, Lynn. "A. Rawlings: Ecopoetic Intersubjectivity." *Jacket2*, 2015. jacket2.org/article/arawlings-ecopoetic-intersubjectivity. Accessed 2 December 2016.

Kinnahan, Linda A. *Lyric Interventions: Feminism, Experimental Poetry, and Contemporary Discourse.* Iowa: University of Iowa Press, 1998.

Krishnan, Madhu. "Affect, Empathy, and Engagement: Reading African Conflict in the Global Literary Marketplace." *The Journal of Commonwealth Literature*, vol. 52, no. 2 (2015): 212–230.

Lu Xun. *The Real Story of Ah Q and Other Tales of China: The Complete Fiction of Lu Xun.* Translated by Julia Lovell. London: Penguin Classics, 2009.

Marx, Karl. *Capital: A Critique of Political Economy*, Vol. 1. Translated by Ben Fowkes. Toronto: Penguin Books, 1990.

Morton, Timothy. *The Ecological Thought*. Harvard: Harvard University Press, 2011.

Nixon, Rob. *Slow Violence and the Environmentalism of the Poor*. Cambridge, MA: Harvard University Press, 2011.

Pateman, Carole. *The Sexual Contract*. Stanford: Stanford University Press, 1988.

Rukeyser, Muriel. *The Book of the Dead*. Columbia: University of Missouri Press, 2015.

Saro-Wiwa, Ken. *Genocide in Nigeria: The Ogoni Tragedy*. Port Harcourt: Saros, 1992. www.turntowardlife.org/essays/chapter5/chapter5.pdf. Accessed 3 July 2017.

Shiva, Vandana. "Bioethics: A Third World Issue." Native Web. www.nativeweb.org/pages/legal/shiva.html. Accessed 11 May 2018.

Spiegel, Jennifer Beth. "Subterranean Flows: Water Contamination and the Politics of Visibility After the Bhopal Gas Disaster." In *Thinking with Water*, edited by Cecelia Chen, Janice MacLeod, and Astrida Neimanis. Montreal: McGill-Queens University Press, 2013, 84–103.

Spivak, Gayatri Chakravorty. "Planetarity." *Paragraph*, vol. 38, no. 2 (2015): 290–292.

Sutherland, Keston. *Complicities: British Poetry 1945–2007*. Kindle Locations 4535–4540: Litteraria Pragensia. Kindle Edition.

Tsing, Anna. "Salvage Accumulation, or the Structural Effects of Capitalist Generativity." *Cultural Anthropology*, 30 March 2015. culanth.org/fieldsights/656-salvage-accumulation-or-the-structural-effects-of-capitalist-generativity. Accessed 11 May 2018.

Tsing, Anna. *The Mushroom at the End of the World*. Princeton: Princeton University Press, 2015.

Wen I-to. 'The Laundry Song.' In *Twentieth Century Chinese Poetry: An Anthology*, translated and edited by Kai-Yu Hsu. Ithaca, NY: Cornell University Press, 1963.

Wilkinson, John. *The Lyric Touch: Essays on the Poetry of Excess*. Cromer: Salt, 2007.

Wong, Rita. *forage*. Gibsons: Nightwood Editions, 2007.

Wong, Rita. "Provisional Mobilities: Rethinking Labour Through Asian Racialization in Literature." Unpublished Thesis. Simon Fraser University, 2002.

Wong, Rita. *Undercurrent*. Gibsons: Nightwood Editions, 2015.

Yu, Renqui. *To Save China, to Save Ourselves: The Chinese Hand Laundry Alliance of New York*. Philadelphia: Temple University Press, 1922.

Zantingh, Matthew. "When Things Act Up: Thing Theory, Actor-Network Theory, and Toxic Discourse in Rita Wong's Poetry." *Interdisciplinary Studies in Literature and Environment*, vol. 20, no. 3 (Summer 2013): 622–646.

CHAPTER 10

"Because We Love Wrong": Citizenship and Labour in Alena Hairston's *The Logan Topographies*

Lytton Smith

In her 1988 essay "Women and Theft," Canadian-Caribbean writer and activist M. NourbeSe Philip provocatively calls for "reparations for women, instead of affirmative action"[1] on the basis of the unjust and "traditionally unacknowledged" distinction between "labour and work" as it differently affects men and women.[2] Philip draws on an argument made by Hannah Arendt in *The Human Condition* (1958), who demonstrates that "labor and poverty (*ponos* and *penia*, *Arbeit* and *Armut*) belonged together in the sense that the activity corresponding to the

---

[1] M. NourbeSe Philip, "Women and Theft," in *Frontiers: Selected Essays and Writings on Racism and Culture, 1984–1992* (Toronto: Mercury Press, 1992), 76.

[2] M. NourbeSe Philip, "Women and Theft," 76.

Thanks to my creative writing and Black Studies students at SUNY Geneseo whose discussions of Hairston's book in our classes have led me in new directions. This essay also owes a debt to Lexi Rudnitsky.

L. Smith (✉)
SUNY Geneseo, Geneseo, NY, USA

© The Author(s) 2019
J. L. Walton and E. Luker (eds.), *Poetry and Work*,
Modern and Contemporary Poetry and Poetics,
https://doi.org/10.1007/978-3-030-26125-2_10

status of poverty was laboring."[3] For Arendt, and for Philip, labour connotes a twofold meaning: "the effort of [life's] sustenance and the pain of giving birth."[4] In either meaning, labour is a necessary precondition for "the freedom and potential productivity of masters and men; freedom to pursue whatever public activity they were engaged upon." Labour's connection to poverty is not just that it is undervalued in comparison to work but that, because it exists outside the sphere of work, on or beyond the margins of "public activity," it in itself produces the increased opportunity "masters and men" enjoy.[5]

This binary, in which female labour is "hidden" and viewed as effort without production while male work is "public" and equates to the production of material goods and tangible achievements, perhaps without concomitant effort, lies at the heart of Alena Hairston's debut collection of poetry, *The Logan Topographies* (2007), which explores African-American coal mining community and shifting attitudes to gender, sexuality, and civic membership therein during the twentieth century. The collection documents masculinist attempts to control women's behaviour: "because we love wrong we are no-one's daughter," explains the plural female voice, noting disinheritance as a consequence for deviating from an approved romantic script, defined especially in terms of sex, gender, and race.[6] This delimitation is countered through imaginative acts—"lonewalking" (57), speaking out (46), interracial childbearing— which threaten and provide alternatives to male-centred conceptions of labour. Drawing on a theoretical framework developed by Charles T. Lee, this chapter identifies what might seem quotidian actions outside of the realm of the political as activist ways in which women, particularly those whose labour is further devalued by dint of sexuality, race, or class, intervene in the script of citizenship, offering new models for communal participation.[7] Lee uses the phrase "ingenious citizenship" as a way to name

[3] Hannah Arendt, *The Human Condition* (Chicago: University of Chicago Press, 2013 [1958]), 110 fn56.

[4] Arendt, *The Human Condition*, 121.

[5] M. NourbeSe Philip, "Women and Theft," in *Frontiers: Selected Essays and Writings on Racism and Culture, 1984–1992* (Toronto: Mercury Press), 75.

[6] Alena Hairston, *The Logan Topographies* (New York City: Persea Books, 2007), 27.

[7] The notion of a citizenship script is used by numerous theorists of citizenship, including Lee; for example, in her monograph *Origin Stories in Political Thought*, Joanne Harriet Wright reads *Leviathan* as Thomas Hobbes' attempt to "provide a script of citizenship,

the political engagements of underprivileged citizens, means of being a citizen which often do not get valued as highly as familiar forms of citizenship like paying taxes or serving on a jury. Drawing on that phrase, I argue that *The Logan Topographies* is structured around a transformation in the terms of female agency within both domestic and mining spheres that re-identifies the kinds of behaviour that might produce citizenship. *The Logan Topographies* affirms labour, in both its senses, as a form of citizenship, despite patriarchal attempts to situate it outside work.

The Logan Topographies is set within Logan County, the history of which can be traced back to 1824, before West Virginia seceded from Virginia to join the Union in 1863.[8] The town of Logan existed first as Lawnsville, a village established in 1827, then later incorporated as Aracoma in 1852, and finally renamed Logan at the start of the twentieth century, three years after Harry. S. Gay opened Logan County's first coal mine in 1904. As Otis Rice and Stephen Brown note in *West Virginia: A History*, "mining profoundly changed the social and economic structure of most coal areas of West Virginia," bringing in a "managerial class" and introducing a "paternalism that had no counterpart in the yeoman farmer spirit that had prevailed."[9] *The Logan Topographies* exists within the framework of that "paternalism," which is both gendered and class-based in its nature.

The landscape of *The Logan Topographies* is precisely historical and geographic: one poem catalogs road closings, grocery prices, and local

encouraging citizens of England to behave as though they had entered into a social contract with one another" (55). Such scripts depend in part on governmental decree—the United States requires (new) citizens to swear an Oath of Allegiance, for instance—and in part on social and cultural patterns, which alter across time and geography, but which might include approved forms of work, expectations of volunteerism, and attitudes to health and education. Sherally Munshi's unpublished dissertation exploring early twentieth century Indian immigration to the U.S., for instance, explores how, faced with governmental attempts to "denaturalize citizens" of Indian origin after the Supreme Court, in United States v. Bhagat Singh Thind (1923), determined that Indians were 'racially ineligible' for citizenship," Indian immigrants such as Dinshah P. Ghadiali undertook projects that sought the "crafting of personhood or subjectivity through violent and mundane encounters with legal institutions, legal language, and legal form."

[8] Logan, WV History and Nostalgia: Preserving Logan County history, https://loganwv.us/ (accessed 29 April 2017).

[9] Otis Rice and Stephen Brown, *West Virginia: A History* (Lexington: University of Kentucky Press, 2010), 188.

news in the form "Shaheen's Grocery: Potatoes, 5lbs., $3; onions, 2lbs., $2; sport physical exam, $5; notary / Women's Club of Omar: Nancy Drew Book Club, every Wednesday, 6 pm" (28). The book's cover displays part of a 1926 topographical map of Logan County, while the book comprises four poetic sequences named for Logan County geographical landmarks: "22 Mountain," "Devil's Tea Table," "The Hill," "The Bottom." However, *The Logan Topographies* also often eschews names of people and place, allowing its geography to have figurative meaning; as Milton Welch has noted, "one reality of the United States is that in many regions the appellation *Bottom* identifies an historically African American community"—an area that is "historically segregated to the low end of social and economic opportunity."[10] That is, *The Logan Topographies* takes place somewhere between a particular historical experience of place and an experience of repetitions of the same in which minority experience in America can be mapped across locations.[11] The book operates less as a historical sourcebook and more as an exploration of language and subjectivity. This is signalled in the paratextual space of a full-page epigraph that weaves together eleven definitions for the noun "descent" from three dictionaries.[12] The first of these definitions

[10] Milton Welch, "A Review of *The Logan Topographies* by Alena Hairston," in *The Believer*, vol. 5, no. 8 (October 2007), 38. Existing discussion of *The Logan Topographies* amounts to a series of reviews, some largely academic journals such as *Appalachian Heritage* and *Journal of Appalachian Studies*, others in literary publications like *Rain Taxi*; these reviews largely emphasize the racial-ecological stakes of the poems. Warren Carson's laudatory review praises the book as "one of the finest sustained treatments of race, place, and culture since Jean Toomer's *Cane*" (2008, 104), while Chris Green suggests that alongside "the fragmentary style of postmodern lyricism" Hairston is able to "show [readers] the earth under their own feet" (2007, 256).

[11] The front matter includes the "author's note" that "While *The Logan Topographies* is based on existing places and is modeled on the lives of real people, certain events, places, and figures in the text are fictional."

[12] I use the term "paratext" specifically in the way Beth McCoy unpacks it within her article "Race and the (Para)Textual Condition": that is, as consisting of "marginal spaces and places [that] have functioned centrally as a zone transacting ever-changing modes of white domination and of resistance to that domination" (156). The paratext within African-American spaces was often a zone of white, male control, and the use of dictionary definitions in the prefatory material of *The Logan Topographies* both acknowledge the dispossession of women and black citizens involved in that space while reclaiming control of it, weaving together definitions to create a new script, one which highlights ironies of power.

gesture towards coal mining practice: "the act or an instance of descending"; "a way down"; "a downward incline or a slope" (xi). None of the
definitions, however, explicitly mentions mines or coal. Instead they
note the human implications of descent: "Hereditary derivation, lineage: *a person of African descent.*" The italicized example represents the
first emergence in the book of the racial stakes of topography and labour,
and the role of inheritance in both, an idea echoed in the sixth definition, "*Law.* Transference of property by inheritance." The possibility of
a united community of "African descent" is complicated in subsequent
definitions.

Cumulatively, the definitions suggest that *The Logan Topographies* is
concerned both with hidden assumptions about African-American identity and about the limitations placed on women within the United States.
The lone female pronoun in the definitions comes via the italicized
example accompanying definition 7: "a lowering or decline, as in status
or level," a definition exemplified as "*Her career went into a rapid descent
after the charges of misconduct.*" Female work emerges, barely, in this
example only in order to announce its reduction and even disappearance.
The unnamed woman's "lowering" might echo "the act or instance of
descending" in mining. However, as the eleventh and final definition
makes clear, "descent" is also "The passage of the presenting part of
the fetus into and through the birth canal." That this definition follows
the question of inheritance of property and the economic "lowering or
decline" of women suggests, in Philip's terms, that birth exists within the
context of descent from the status of work to the lower cultural position of labour as it exists within a historical sphere of non-productive
effort. As we shall see, one of the book's tasks is to recuperate pregnancy,
birth, and labour in all senses from expectations of diminished status and
from straight male control of labour, without at the same time reifying
it as definitive of a delimited womanhood. The spatial metaphor in these
epigraphs is suggestive of the book's structure of transformation: while
these descents—from the womb; into the mine—are analogous (part of
what the book will explore is a double bind in which women serve both
children and husbands) they are also the inverse of one another: the child
emerges from the birth canal into light while the miner passes from the
light along a birth canal-like passage into dark.

In tracing the complex intersections of historical precedent, lived
identities, and cultural expectations that govern the idea of "descent"
with the topography of Logan County, Hairston's book offers more than

a pessimistic trajectory in which women fall from work to labour. The opening poem's first stanza transforms the birthing-as-descent of the epigraph into a birthing-as-environment that alters human–natural relations and coal mining itself:

Pregnant belly of coneflower and larkspur. coalcaves of lupine and barberry. where shale grows up and bumps into the sun. breathes across the moon. lunar party. dream of history striated.

The first sentence's possessive "of" is bidirectional: the pregnant woman's body full of flowers; the flowers themselves pregnant bodies. As such, this sentence blurs the boundaries of what pregnancy might mean and where it might appear within *The Logan Topographies*. Mining is similarly transformed: just as "coalcaves" is a neologism that seeks to rearticulate mine space, the image of "lupine and barberry" disrupts the excavatory implications of "coalcaves." It does so by imagining a proliferation of wild flowers within that space. Amid a "dream of history" where geological striations call to mind the stratification of society through labour and work, pregnancy becomes shared with the natural world—"bumps into the sun" alluding to a pregnancy "bump"—and freed from the biological definition of childbearing named in descent through birth canal. One of the central tensions these poems explore is the female agency of birth versus societal control of women's bodies around childbearing. *The Logan Topographies* acknowledges a systemic cyclical experience of birthing. One page in its entirety reads "the undine gives birth to an undine who gives birth to an undine who gives birth to an undine who gives birth to an undine" (22). It avoids a portrayal of childbirth solely in terms of pain or trial, instead connecting the "spasm" and "jolt" of birth for a "first-mother" to the elemental, natural power of "a river" and to the promise of "iron and protein and summer" (24). The term "undine" was coined by Paracelsus in *Liber de Nymphis* (1566) to name a river or water spirit. The inclusion of the undine within the human cycle of birth, like the inclusion of the "coneflower and larkspur," reorients birth from only human contexts and towards environmental ones—a reorientation that bears fruit in the book's final image, discussed below.

If we read an optimism into the narrative of the place of women within a repetitive cycle of human history—"people come here.

people left here. / people return here. people stay here" (3)—"22 Mountain" as a sequence depicts a problematic tension between the roles and labour of women within a male world. As we head into Logan itself, we go "past Chafin Bar and Hatfield Liquors, brief homes to aged middlemen waiting on time" (4). In contrast to the leisure time the "waiting" men enjoy in coal mining West Virginia, women feature only as the relations of male figures. Past "the policied homes," we find

the owners: early men with trucks
and limited speech; their wives, all, itinerant mothers looking for water;
the sons: pig boys raging in the bougainvillaea.

Men within the community own homes and vehicles, possessing both status and freedom of movement. Women, by contrast, are "wives" and "itinerant mothers," uprootable. The action of "looking for water" does not parallel "early men with trucks" despite the syntactical equality of the categories "men," "women," and "children" each having their own independent clause, despite their shared position at the end of lines. Indeed, the women are enclosed between "men" and "sons" responsible to both and never existing as women; they are defined by their roles as wives and mothers, in relation to male power. These women engage in an effort-oriented activity that is not seen as producing anything despite being vital to the life of the men and sons who surround them: water-gathering. This instances Philip's claims about theft and about labour-as-poverty. Water-gathering is an uncompensated labour. Like pregnancy, it contrasts the material work of the men with trucks who become "owners" and then in time the drinkers in their "brief homes," the bar and liquor store; the women's water-gathering translates into this liquor, and the women remain outside the narrative.

The first sequence of *The Logan Topographies* identifies not a simple, homogeneous group of African-American coal miners facing oppression within majority white society in the United States of America, but a fractured group containing its own social discords, a fraught "their" with a problematic "ethos of only we belong here" (5), problematic because the "we" so often excludes along class and gender lines, as well as within race lines. The town's "policied homes" references the "company homes" of the coal mining towns[13] while invoking the policing of African-American life within twentieth-century America.[14] Rice and Brown note that "Logan and Mingo [coal] operators [...] paid hundreds of thousands of dollars to county sheriffs, who employed antiunion deputies" in order to restrict workers' attempts to mobilize.[15] (Logan is infamous as the site of the "largest armed uprising in American labor history," [Vardamann, 2008, 12][16]). *The Logan Topographies* acknowledges the complex intersectional space articulated by Kimberlé Crenshaw in her article "Mapping the Margins: Intersectionality, Identity Politics, and Violence Against Women of Color" (1993): the way "the future is a fist of coal" (5) evidently registers very differently for men and women within the topography of Logan.

Though women as wives and mothers experience a lower status than the men who can and do drive away, women remain tied to the wider community, of which the poems declare "They know their poverty only when the wood of those who have crossed / shine a deepening brown" (5). In ritual terms, this moment invokes both Christ on the cross and the coffins of dead citizens of Logan, but the "deepening brown" presents a shifting image of the way colour signifies in this community. "Shine" suggests an upward mobility, crossings (or coffins) that are ever glossier and more attractive; one narrative traced by this collection is the possibility of class aspirations made tangible through work: "The DeBarnes win every time [...] they get their access roads paved" (33). Yet "deepening brown" also invokes cultural prejudices about shades of black skin, within and outside

---

[13] Rice and Brown, *West Virginia: A History*, 188.

[14] Hazel Carby traces the way "a rural black folk without the necessary industrial skills, untutored in the ways of the city" were exploited in "the streets of New York, Chicago" and other urban spaces in twentieth century American, yet managed to transform the stakes of the way others degradingly mythologized them. Detroit, Cleveland, Philadelphia, and Pittsburgh" (739). Carby notes now both individuals and institutions labelled "the behavior of these migrating women as a social and political problem" (740), and such ideas have shaped my own reading of Hairston's book, featuring as it does mobile, rural Black women who turn to song.

[15] Rice and Brown, *West Virginia: A History*, 228.

[16] Vardamann notes "that event does not figure in the poems" (12)—which is literally true, although the book's working through of violence not only gestures to the Battle of Blair Mountain, but the effect of not naming singular instances of events is to allow for a reading of their replication or reoccurrence—a central realization of the later Black Lives Matter movement—rather than to focus on one particular instance.

African-American communities. These cultural prejudices have fatal consequences in "22 Mountain," especially when combined with male control of female sexual agency. In one poem, a "one-eyed / woman hunched in hemlock [...] was to give birth to a child who would not maintain her skin" (8). This unnamed "she" is caught between the past of "was" and the future of "to give birth" and "maintain," indicating the generational pressures put on female labour, and the concomitant male anxiety over control of the future.

The consequence of this prohibited crossing of skin colour lines is male violence against women:

her poppa snatched away, threw into the galaxy of forest, dared
her to find it in the matching peat and wet, this rifle
eating her breast

They say you can hear her only after midnight and only with your ear

to the ground

This fatal labour takes the form of a cautionary fable whose murdered protagonist exists as a mythic, warning figure; the recasting of transitive verbs as intransitive (snatched, threw) serves to remove "her" from the poem. What is thrown into the "galaxy of forest" might be the woman or her newborn child, leaving her not to gather water but to find her own offspring. While "galaxy" offers an extra-terrestrial glimmer of escape, "the matching peat and wet" of the next line drags it back to earth. Likewise, the sustenance of breast-feeding is replaced by the "rifle," connoting both an actual weapon injuring the female breast and the figurative notion of a baby plundering or thieving from its mother. Here, the woman's place is twice inscribed as in and of the earth: "matching peat" and "ear // to the ground" imagine an elemental connection between female identity and earth spaces, yet also cast these spaces as sites of loss, harm, and exile—descent, in the book's epigraphic terms.

This policing of female sexuality and black skin is part of what the third sequence, "The Hill," terms the "contests, generational" of class aspiration. Upward mobility involves a troubling norming of black identity: "always, the hair: only one way to win: straight" (33); "the children of right skin" (34); "mother stayed to keep up the fields. And appearances" (36). Only passivity seems communally acceptable as a form of black female identity: the acceptance of (white) hairstyles; remaining in place. By contrast, male sexuality is marked by freedom, by an elective choice on which women are dependent: "the father chose another woman closer to the clouds and so they fell," one poem remarks about a woman and her children after her husband has moved on (35). Left behind, the children "imagined him cutting into a bleeding steak / at a cherry table," his choice allowing him to enjoy the trappings of his higher class. His absent presence manifests in the way the children "stood before a rented mirror and scrubbed at his eyes and noses with their toothbrushes" (35). The self-harm here is twofold: the act of erasing the memory of the father echoes the lightening and whitening desired by what "The Hill" elsewhere terms "cashew, almond, milk," a trajectory of acceptable black skin colour that echoes white supremacist and colonialist narratives, articulated for example in the infamous 1899 Pears' Soap advertisement in *McClure's Magazine* which linked "cleanliness" to "the white man's burden," as "a potent factor in brightening the dark corners of the earth as civilization advances."[17]

What if, though, the act of staying is precisely that: an act, a creative engagement with space rather than a passive adherence to it? What if the murdered mother heard in the night manifests both the results of male violence and the possibility of female improvisation and productive itineracy—"the ground" an elemental connection to earth, not a desultory base? After all, the woman who can be heard after her murder speaks out, across time, bearing witness to male violence. Similarly, the placement of the period in the idea that "mother stayed to keep up the fields. And appearances" allows for a reading in which an outside community is concerned with "appearances"—the way a black woman is "meant" to look and be—while the mother herself engages, by staying, in labour that ensures the earth is productive. Such a reading would indicate that "The Hill" is offering a turn from the enclosure of women-as-wives-and-mothers seen within the opening pages of *The Logan Topographies*.

At the heart of this third sequence is a spread with a poem titled "The Mother" page left and one titled "The Father" page right; this spread directly follows the departure of the father figure who "chose another" wife. While the fatherless household depicted in "The Mother" offers a scene of potentially passive fragmentation—"We keep our televisions

---

[17] Anne McClintock discusses this advertisement in *Imperial Leather*, pp. 32ff.

turned down low. We each have our own set. I watch / the beautiful people living the beautiful lives boxed nicely before me" (36)—this space also offers a chance for the reclamation of identity: "There is nothing / wrong with a glimmering life. We do like the sheen. Our skin wears it well." In her removal from the male economy of wife-trading, the female figure of "The Mother" is able to both engage in work and to reclaim her own skin. While the women of this house contend with outside criticism—"I know what they think about us at the bottom of the hill"— they are able to invoke their own labour as the means by which they have "bought" this "company house." The poem's conclusion, "We bled / for our money. We earned our hill" indicates that the attainment of property does not come solely from capitalist practice but from a wider range of possibilities of "earning," including watching television, valuing one's own skin, and imagining alternative lives beyond patriarchal family structures. Indeed, the line break after "bled" seems to invite a recognition of menstruation as constituent of female value, though not definitive of it; the shift marked in "The Hill" is not from labour to work but a redefinition of the division between the two spheres.

"The Father," by contrast, is a poem marked by negatives: "Not your niggers. Not theirs" (37). The violence of the poem—"they fought in any season. Any cracker who came or left" (37)—is not only racial in nature but conditioned by masculinity, by "generations of being men […] Even after the Mingo War." "The Father" laments that "my wife […] did not have any boys," the narrative of male anxiety about inheritance resurfacing again. At the same time, the generational cycle of "fathers, great and grand" is presented in diminishing terms: "men who crawled in lime, mouths harvesting coal dust, the air tightening night / as black as their lungs." The fate of men is black lung, a blackness that recalls the racial injustices of coal mining practice as a second slavery in the United States, a contrast to the bleeding and earning of the women.[18] This reversal of fortunes from the home-owning and liquor-drinking men of the book's opening derives not from any biological essentialism but from the different kinds of activity that "the mother" and "the father" are seen as engaging in from the ways women within

---

[18] *The Logan Topographies* uses as an epigraph for its second section, "Devil's Tea Table," two paragraphs from Ronald L. Lewis's *Black Coal Miners in America: Race, Class, and Community Conflict, 1780–1980*, which focus on "slave miners."

the book transform or provide alternatives to male conceptions of work as "fight and crawl" versus labour as simply "the forward look," the procurement of male progeny.

Where once the mother was enclosed by sons and a husband, the father in "The Father" is surrounded by the women of the left page and a daughter who ends his own narrative, presented by him as deviant: "Now this daughter how dares to be in *that* way. My daughter of right skin who wants to be wrong" (37). Whereas once the focus on daughters was on "maintain[ing]" skin colour, here control manifests in terms of same-sex intercourse: "in *that* way." This moment of *The Logan Topographies* imagines the possibility of queer black womanhood as an alternative to existing social scripts and notions of citizenship, with the next poems bringing in the figure of "a sable girl, / in church" who can "play, too, and crash into womanhood, wide-hipped and mouthy" (38, 39). The description of the "wide-hipped" girl riffs on the idea of "child-bearing hips" but refuses to impose that expectation on girls and women, instead offering ideas of creative play and unrepentant expression, of being "mouthy" in ways that might imply sexual prowess, verbal dexterity, and wilful insubordination alike. These, I argue, are the conditions that allow for a reimagination of the terms of labour, work, and citizenship within *The Logan Topographies*. One of the sable girl's concerns is with membership: "belonging requires membership and membership is its own house. / In the house of membership, the owner stands firm on price" (39). The double chiasmus here indicates that "belonging" is dependent on ownership and price, and therefore access to capital. Yet, because the communal "we" remains desirable, because the sable girl wants to belong, albeit on her own terms, "membership" remains desirable, even as the compromised membership terms women experience need renegotiating. Faced with a situation in which "the owner stands firm"—the market setting the piece–the solution "The Hill" offers for this predicament is creative at core: "Breaking away, instead of breaking even, is not choice, is imagination: a dare" (39). The prior "ethos of we belong here" is redefined, the traditional acceptance of status quo yielding to the activity and creativity of "imagination" as it allows for a rupture that, as the suggestive colon indicates, remains unpredictable: "a dare."

What I would like to note here is the way this narrative of reclamation and transformation offers an instance of what Charles T. Lee terms "ingenious citizenship"; that is, "creative resistance at the individual level" in which "the abject, who are remaindered by the [citizenship] script, and lack status, power, and resources [...] come up with original and creative ways to reinsert themselves into the script" while also performing an "appropriation and disruption" of that script.[19] Lee's contention is that "the more inventive we are in disrupting and appropriating the script, the more transformative the effects will be"[20]; among his examples, taken from an ethnography by Christine Chin, is the case of Lita, a foreign domestic worker from the Philippines serving as a live-in housekeeper in Malaysia. Denied worker's rights by her employer, Lita opted to forgo sanitary pads during menstruation, trailing blood around the house as she completed her cleaning duties. Rather than adopt familiar forms of citizenship script—tribunals, protests, strikes—to which she had tenuous access as a "foreign" worker, Lita adopts the unpredictable, "a dare" which succeeds in transforming her working conditions: she is given time off, something previously denied.

This situation surfaces in a number of ways within *The Logan Topographies*. Leaving the "house of membership," the sable girl finds membership with "the gooddaughter": "they find their way in a way that only girls can" (40). Riffing off the protective, norming criticism from "the father" that his daughter is in "*that* way," the female-centred method of looking forward imagines an inventive, improvised "way," a "breaking away" that is both geographic—"the campion opening for them" and sexual—"They kiss their sweaty parts and laugh" (40). Yet while this transformation is sexual, it consists ultimately in the way a linguistic act might bring about a sense of both self- and community identity: "No one ever calls us beautiful or sharp. You are beautiful. You are sharp. / Do you believe me?" (40). The terms of female identity are being recognized and altered here, but crucially the form of their inclusion is too: a question which invites an answer (receiving its affirmation, "Yes," at the end of the poem). The implication is that, while queer identity offers one means to break with citizenship scripts, the breaking is not dependent on nor definitive of queer identity—note

[19] Charles T. Lee, *Ingenious Citizenship: Recrafting Democracy for Social Change* (2016), 27–28. In addition to Lee's notion of "ingenious citizenship," my argument here develops from Melanie White's 2008 essay "Can an Act of Citizenship be Creative?" (in Isin and Nielsen, eds. *Acts of Citizenship*); I discuss her ideas in more details in "The Bewilderment of Peter Gizzi's 'Plural Noises,'" in Anthony Caleshu, ed. *In The Air* (2017).

[20] Charles T. Lee, *Ingenious Citizenship*, 48.

that queer and its synonyms feature nowhere in the text, and instead the actions of speaking, hand holding, and sexual acts are celebrated, instances of "imagination" and "dare" that become foundational for the new community.[21]

The Logan Topographies presents a series of women who are threatened with abject status and ultimately imagines their transformation of status not through legal means or changes in cultural mores but through the creativity of unanticipated acts—acts which at times are as familiar as staying, as watching television. The figure of the abject surfaces most fully in the final section, "The Bottom," in the form of the only named woman in the collection, a woman whose name has notably been used to diminish her identity rather than secure it: "A woman: formerly known as Coca Col on account of her shape" and "Just Candy now. The good shit in her nose and arms" (49). [Candy's] abject status emerges in her drug addiction—"eyes now slanted in chemical glee"—and in others' acts of gazing and naming and possessing: "sex slanted and shaded her eyes." She appears over two pages, and as the leaf turns towards her second scene, the drug-addled image of [Candy] is revised into a version where she reclaims the ways she moves through the topography of Logan. We see her "naked and barefoot" as she "dances onto the unpaved road" and heads "toward the cutting water" (50). What unfolds is somewhere between suicide and homecoming: "knowing and unafraid she lets the waves take her, / for there is permanence in the flowing and fleeting." Rather than present Candy's entry into the water as an absence or removal, "The Bottom" imagines it as a "collapse of memory" in which "there is calm."

In entering the water, Candy is associating herself with the undines and with the river that was connected to childbirth. Candy has seemingly served as a wet nurse: "her unkissed flowerfolds where babies have not played [...] her pillfilled stomach, up and up the toosuckled breasts."

---

[21] Through reading works by U.S. and Cuban poets (Wallace Stevens, José Lezama Lima, Robert Duncan, and Severo Sarduy) Eric Keenaghan argues, in *Queering Cold War Poetics* (2009), that poetic disclosure, particularly through lyric, was a means of developing a "queer ethic of vulnerability" that could reveal "the fullness of citizens' otherwise censored interior lives" (27). For Keenaghan, poetry has a role in resisting state definitions of the citizen: he opposes this "queer ethic" to contemporary Homeland Security slogans such as "Our Free Society Is Inherently Vulnerable" (13), underlining instead the value of poetic expressions of vulnerability.

But her actions subvert expectations of the imagery of what women, and in particular mothers, should look like and what actions they should engage in. While Candy's story asks for a form of pathos, and recognizes the role of male violence in her suicide, it does not invite pity: the water manages to "glitter her tiptoes now lifting / towards flight." This scene is echoed in the book's final spread, where the "descent" of the opening epigraphs get reimagined as "the descant of departure" in which "any arrival is an aria" (56). Like Candy's dance, the "descant" of song and the singing of "arias" (metathetically related to the "air" of flight) allow for the expression of something alternative to what the antepenultimate poem calls "the dream / of a belonging place" (55), that "ethos of we belong here" which promised solidarity but offered norming and control. The "breaking away" that the book imagines instead is fundamentally reciprocal in nature:

> Beyond the hawthorn, a vibrant loneliness:
> Unsteady bridge, love
> is afferent,
> returns itself. (56)

To affirm "love" as a citizenly activity might seem to introduce a romanticized and impractical element to the script of citizenship. But in the context of a world in which "because we love wrong we are no-one's daughter" (27), it should be clear that love has *always already* been part of citizenship scripts, both legally and culturally. The iconography of place in this image—bridge, hawthorn—blurs into the expression of a relationship between two or more people across the uncertain pause of the comma: "bridge, love." The use of "afferent" takes us into the body—the term is associated with the movement of the central nervous system—and so recalls the birth canal of the opening epigraphs. Afference, however, is not limited to childbirth. It is therefore recast as just *one* of the creative, female-centred actions women, queer and otherwise, might engage in. The book's final image "of a thousand stillborns, luminous, / lonewalking" (57) is itself a transformation of the terms of female citizenship: the stillborn is not failure or absence but multiplicity and light; from and among the stillborns comes the free activity of travel, "lonewalking." Such itinerancy does not require heteronormative definitions of social happiness yet also suggests the potential for discovery and connection: for afference.

If topography is at heart the writing of place, it is most accurate to describe the disruptive topography of *The Logan Topographies* as a writing out of place. It is a "breaking away" that blurs and dismantles both the culturally dependent, political boundaries of a township like Logan and the ideological expectations that delimit approved ways to behave within a given geographic space. As the female characters of the book engage in journeys that take them from the landscape of Logan and the other coal mining communities for which Logan is a placeholder, they are not simply preforming a form of emancipatory peregrination, a rejection of exile through the assertion of a freedom of movement. They are instead going further. They are responding to the normative script of citizenship by reimagining the terms and contract of belonging itself. Where at the start citizenship depended on loyalty to place, and to one's place in social strata, by the end it depends on something more fluid, amorphous, and ecological. The citizenship of afference that emerges within *The Logan Topographies* takes expectations of the division between labour and work and reconfigures their relationship to create an ingenious new script, one able to sustain both solitude and belonging, staying and travelling, life and death. The allegiance these characters have is to each other, rather than to nation, government, or patriarchy. Their labour is water-gathering; it is also the gathering together of those who are open to a flexible, improvisational song of citizenship.

WORKS CITED

Arendt, Hannah. *The Human Condition* (2nd ed.). Chicago: University of Chicago Press, 2013 [1958].

Carby, Hazel. "Policing the Black Woman's Body in an Urban Context." *Critical Inquiry*, vol. 18, no. 4, Identities (Summer, 1992), 738–755.

Carson, Warren. "Review." *Appalachian Heritage*, vol. 36, no. 3 (Summer 2008), 104.

Crenshaw, Kimberlé. "Mapping the Margins: Intersectionality, Identity Politics, and Violence Against Women of Color." *Stanford Law Review*, vol. 43, no. 6 (July 1991), 1241–1299.

Gay, Ross. "Review." *Postnoills,* August 2008. www.postnoills.com/main/?p=63. Accessed 21 April 2017. 2:13 pm.

Green, Chris. "Review." *Journal of Appalachian Studies*, vol. 13, no. 1 and 2 (2008), 255–257.

Hairston, Alena. *The Logan Topographies.* New York City: Persea Books, 2007.

Keenaghan, Eric. *Queering Cold War Poetry: Ethics of Vulnerability in Cuba and the United States*. Columbus: Ohio State University Press, 2009.

Lee, Charles. T. *Ingenious Citizenship: Recrafting Democracy for Social Change*. Durham: Duke University Press, 2016.

Logan, WV History and Nostalgia: Preserving Logan County history. https://loganwv.us/. Accessed 29 April 2017.

McClintok, Anne. *Imperial Leather: Race, Gender, and Sexuality in the Colonial Contest*. New York: Routledge, 1995.

McCoy, Beth. "Race and the (Para)Textual Condition." *PMLA*, vol. 21, no. 1, Special Topic: The History of the Book and the Idea of Literature (January 2006), 156–169.

Munshi, Sherally. The Archivist of Affronts: Immigration, Representation, and Legal Personality in Early Twentieth Century America. Columbia University Academic Commons. dx.doi.org/10.7916/D8639MV0.

Philip, M. NourbeSe. "Women and Theft." In *Frontiers: Selected Essays and Writings on Racism and Culture, 1984–1992*, 72–77. Toronto: Mercury Press, 1992.

Rice, Otis, and Stephen Brown. *West Virginia: A History* (2nd ed.). Lexington: University of Kentucky Press, 2010.

Smith, Lytton, "The Bewilderment of Peter Gizzi's 'Plural Noises'." In *In the Air: Essays on the Poetry of Peter Gizzi*, edited by Anthony Caleshu, 151–165. Wesleyan: Wesleyan University Press, 2017.

Vardamann, Wendy, "Poems including History—And More." *Women's Review of Books*, vol. 25, no. 2 (March/April 2008), 11–13.

Welch, Milton. "A Review of *the Logan Topographies* by Alena Hairston." In *The Believer*, vol. 5, no. 8 (October 2007), 38.

White, Melanie. "Can an Act of Citizenship be Creative?" In *Acts of Citizenship*, edited by Engin Isin and Greg Nielsen, 44–56. London: Zed Books, 2008.

Wright, Joanne Harriet. *Origin Stories in Political Thought: Discourses on Gender, Power, and Citizenship*. Toronto: University of Toronto Press, 2004.

CHAPTER 11

"What Gives Pause or Impetus": The Double Bind of Labor in Rodrigo Toscano's Poetics

Jose-Luis Moctezuma

I

Rodrigo Toscano explains that his poem "May Be!" grew out of a "poetic-critical *double bind*" in response to the Occupy movement. The Occupy movement arose in 2011 as counteraction to economic recession—occasioned by unregulated financial speculation by the banking industry—and a slew of other toxic depoliticizations. Occupy's key tactic was the mass occupation of public space, a tactic influenced by the Arab Spring, the Indignados, as well as various peace camps and climate camps within the broad global justice movement. In themselves, these mass occupations were sites of multiple modalities of labor, including the labor of constructing and maintaining counterpublics. Their existence must also have generated ripples, mostly invisible, through the structures of labor beyond their immediate geographies. At the same time, in their carnivalesque dimension, the Occupation spectacles intersected with a long history of radical work refusal. Kathy Weeks invokes this

J.-L. Moctezuma (✉)
City Colleges of Chicago, Wilbur Wright, Chicago, IL, USA

© The Author(s) 2019
J. L. Walton and E. Luker (eds.), *Poetry and Work*,
Modern and Contemporary Poetry and Poetics,
https://doi.org/10.1007/978-3-030-26125-2_11

kind of a history "of disidentification with the work ethic" which might include "various youth subcultures, from the beatniks to hippies, punks, and slackers" as well as Black working class "zoot suiters and hipsters" and "those second-wave feminists [...] who insisted that work—whether waged work or unwaged domestic labor—was not something to which women should aspire but rather something they should try to escape."[1]

How does a poet, or a poetry community, respond to these various affordances for work and nonwork? For Toscano, they present a double bind. On the one hand, Toscano says, he felt the instinctive urgency to "*go! go! go!*" as the occasion for political action required. On the other, he also sensed that the movement would "quickly run into a stone cold, mute-media surround, a hegemonic push back on the surge."[2] This bind was tightened by yet another bind: Toscano witnessed "poetic communities from multiple locations tipping freely into the movement, all generously offering up their energies," yet Toscano's "gut feeling [...] was that even the 'best' political poets with the 'best' of intentions" would, after the heartiest cultural productivity and poem-making and poem-delivering, remain frivolous or woefully behind the corporeal immediacy and policy-oriented politics the Occupy movement fiercely needed.[3]

At some level, the impending failure of the Occupy movement to move past the temporal and structural limitations of what Nick Srnicek and Alex Williams call "folk politics" would be exacerbated by a similar double bind, situated in-between the paucity of clearly articulated demands and the perceptible force of Occupy's highly visible communal form.[4] Toscano's poem expresses this hesitancy outright:

---

[1] Kathy Weeks, *The Problem with Work: Feminism, Marxism, Antiwork Politics, and Postwork Imaginaries* (Durham and London: Duke University Press, 2011), 79–80.

[2] Rodrigo Toscano, "Rodrigo Toscano on 'May Be!'" from the In Their Own Words Series, Poetry Society of America, www.poetrysociety.org/psa/poetry/crossroads/own_ words/Rodrigo_Toscano, accessed 15 April 2018, n.p.

[3] Toscano, "Rodrigo Toscano on 'May Be!'", n.p.

[4] Srnicek and Williams write, for instance, that "[u]nder the sway of folk-political thinking, the most recent cycle of struggles—from anti-globalization to anti-war to Occupy Wall Street—has involved the fetishisation of local spaces, immediate actions, transient gestures, and particularisms of all kinds" and that "things like protest camps tend to remain ephemeral, small-scale and ultimately unable to challenge the larger structures of the neoliberal economic system. This is politics transmuted into pastime." Nick Srnicek and Alex Williams, *Inventing the Future: Postcapitalism and a World Without Work* (Verso: London and Brooklyn, 2005), 3, 7.

Were there poetic acts that came *before* Occupy that were mainly *of* Occupy?

Are there now poetic acts or critical projects about Occupy that contain nothing of the *stuff* of Occupy?

Will there be poetic acts that fall between the cracks of Occupy, De–Occupy, and Re-Occupy, but that are still Occupational?[5]

Toscano's emphases illustrate a possible skepticism regarding the historical power of what I plan to call 'presencing' in the Occupy movement. On the one hand, to occupy a site or situation—perhaps the emergence of an 'event' in the sense Alain Badiou gives it—is to fill it with the "*stuff*" of history. It is to fill it with bodies that generate, interrogate, remix, and rewrite the functions of history. Such presencing is more than just the presence or coming-into-presence of a body politic; it is the intensification of a platform and its simultaneous transmission across diverse human and more-than-human bodies. In the spectacle of New York's Zuccotti Park, the continuous succession of speech-acts, habitations, and the presencing of bodies sought to respond to a mass-distributed sense of exclusion from the stage of history by oppressive corporate "persons." Even rhetorically, the spectacle insisted above all on its mass: 'We are the 99%!' The spectacle relied on an immediate concrescence of visible bodies and voices in a space of relations that aggressively excludes them from the 'global work' of Wall Street, an occupation of a space of occupations abstracted from any real sense of actual "occupation."

But on the other hand, such a spectacle, lacking a direct and finite articulation of what the occupation is meant to enact, would be reduced to the filament of brief incandescence on the global stage. It might be insubstantial, without "*stuff*." This is because to *occupy* a site or situation falls short of its projections if the other meaning of *occupation* (labor, work, vocation, activity) isn't sufficiently defined, demarcated, and distributed across a feasible plan of longevity that transcends the basic requirements of visible action and enunciation.

---

[5] Rodrigo Toscano, "MAY BE!: Chorus for Inquisitive Occupiers," 4 April 2012. www.poetryfoundation.org/harriet/2012/04/may-be-chorus-for-inquisitive-occupiers, accessed 15 April 2018.

Toscano's poem asked whether Occupy might, in some sense, be found in poetic acts which pre-dated the movement, poetic acts which occurred before Occupy became the "*stuff*" it now was. It also asked, now that Occupy had appeared as shared struggle, whether there were certain poetic acts that did contribute representationally to Occupy—perhaps by "the 'best' political poets with the 'best' of intentions" (q.v.)—but that didn't really contain any of its "*stuff.*" And he asked, conversely, whether there were certain poetic acts that *were not* about Occupy, and nevertheless part of it. I read these queries as formulations surrounding the conflicting definitions of occupation in regard to poetry as *representation* and poetry as *praxis*. Poetry occupies the space of relations (in Zuccotti Park or in a live reading) by articulating that very space in the presencing of bodies—this is the representative power of poetry. Just as well, poetry does the work of providing occupation—whether in the brief space of an event, or in the long durée of a poetic career—to the poet who politicizes the space of relations with a sustained labor of generating meaningfulness in a shared struggle with others. This is poetry as an occupation, the work of inclusion contra the capitalist forms of exclusion. It is in this register that Toscano raises the question of the "occupational"—the occupational hazards of precarity and precarious economics, as well as the occupational hazards of working outside and against the posthuman climate of Wall Street's fiduciary abstractions—whether in "poetic acts" (q.v.) or in the occupation of zones of displaced labor.

It is notable that poetry, the most unobvious of occupations, the most intangible and seemingly inconsequential, is what Toscano narrates and openly puts forward as an object of inquiry. Does poetry, as W.H. Auden once provocatively asserted, really "mak[e] nothing happen," particularly at historical junctures of high relevance and affective reach?[6] What sort of work does poetry do—what is its labor in the face of the neoliberalist erosion of traditional models of occupation and labor practices? Toscano calls this a double bind because there is a conflict between representation and praxis, between occupation (of space) and occupation (as labor). The double bind of poetry might

---

[6]W. H. Auden, "In Memory of W.B. Yeats," in *The English Auden: Poems, Essays, and Dramatic Writings 1927–1999*, ed. E. Mendelson (London: Faber and Faber), 242.

approximate to the double bind of labor in the accelerationist age of capital. On the one hand, poetry makes *nothing* happen, and the event of poetry is seemingly restricted to a localized duration, a spectacle that dissolves in the act of reading and performance; on the other hand, poetry makes *everything* happen, since it redistributes psychic energy and propels minds to affective forms of labor, resistance, and communal solidarity.

It is important to consider here that Toscano's double bind is distinct from the usage of the term as originally given it by British anthropologist Gregory Bateson. Bateson's double bind conceptualized a theory of schizophrenia that cohered within the larger apparatus of systems theory and the human production of meaning and social value. The "schizophrenogenic" moment (as Bateson terms it) occurs when a child is caught between two conflicting signals, customarily from a parent or adult authority, in which the parent extends a condition for love that is simultaneously contradicted by the capacity of the child to fulfill such a condition.[7]

The parent-child model is useful to Bateson as an encapsulating cybernetics for the family dynamic in which schizophrenia takes root. But we might extend the parent–child model to allegorize the whole of global capitalism's psychical entrainment of subjects and their relationship to labor, one in which capitalist society acts as the parent who gives contradictory signals (you are *free to labor* as you wish; on the other hand, you must labor *as the market demands* if you wish to be free) which lead toward schizophrenogenic behaviors in subjects within workplace situations. Indeed, Gilles Deleuze and Felix Guattari would later comment on Bateson's theory of schizophrenia by questioning

---

[7] For instance, a condition for love might be an instruction or a prohibition—"Do x!" or "Don't do x!"—and the conflicting secondary injunction, perhaps communicated through tone, body language, implicature, etc. might be, "'Do not see this as punishment'; 'Do not see me as the punishing agent'; 'Do not submit to my prohibitions'; 'Do not think of what you must not do'; 'Do not question my love of which the primary prohibition is (or is not) an example.'" Gregory Bateson, Don D. Jackson, Jay Haley, and John H. Weakland, "Toward a Theory of Schizophrenia" (1956), in Gregory Bateson, *Steps to an Ecology of Mind: Collected Essays in Anthropology, Psychiatry, Evolution, and Epistemology* (San Francisco: Chandler 1987 [1972]), 210.

its narrowness and by extending it to the whole of capitalist psychical entrainment, and particularly to the rituals of Oedipalization:

> [...] where is there a father who doesn't simultaneously transmit the two contradictory injunctions—'Let's be friends, son, I'm the best friend you've got,' and 'Watch out, son, don't treat me like one of your buddies'? There is nothing there with which to make a schizophrenic. We have seen in this sense that the double impasse in no way defined a specific schizo-phrenogenic mechanism, but merely characterized Oedipus in the whole of its extension.[8]

Oedipus is the whole of capitalist entrainment, in the sense that schizophrenia is merely an intensification of the double impasses that block the labor of poetic acts, and block the representations these acts are continuously in the process of articulating. Toscano assigns to his 'double bind' an appropriately dual meaning: there are two distinct binds, two dilemmas, as opposed to Bateson's single binding situation, orchestrated by conflicting signals at different levels of abstraction. Toscano's "poetic-critical *double bind*" can be understood as the simultaneous expression of two conflicting directives: yes, poetry is an occupation that can and must speak for other occupations (representation); and yes, poetry is without occupation because it presumably does nothing practical or efficient (praxis) and elaborates space in a nondirective ways. Poetry is simultaneously caught in the reverse dilemma: it cannot sufficiently represent the unrepresentable qualities and stages of labor, but poetry is an occupation that can and must, at least, enact forms of practice that resonate at some level with those who labor, even if particular laborers do not really compute the 'difficult' vernaculars of poetic form.

Toscano's doubts regarding the occupational powers of poetry may have some answer in another poem of his, "12 riddles of spirit, crook in hand":

> A clear stream of *libertas*
> clarion tenor
> MACHINE'S REVELATION
> is not enough

---

[8] Gilles Deleuze and Felix Guattari, *Anti-Oedipus* (1972), translated (1977) by Robert Hurley, Mark Seem, and Helen R. Lane (London: Continuum, 2004), 394.

What gives pause
or impetus
to my hand or mouth
in culture
interests me

The double bind is re-echoed here in "What gives pause / or impetus / to my hand or mouth." Does one automatically "*go! go! go!*," as Toscano felt during the first waves of Occupy Wall Street? Or does one pause at such a notion of action, skeptical at the acceleration that blurs rather than clarifies labor and occupation? I interpret "MACHINE'S REVELATION" as the marker for not merely the practices of industrialization and post-Fordism, automation, and outsourcing (the abstract machine of capital, the actual mechanics of production), but also as the trace of a recontextualization of the human organism at work. Is the laborer in the age of capital a programmable automaton or a self-regulating agent of "*libertas*"? Are not perhaps these two characterizations one and the same? For instance, the self-regulating or *automatic* machine, well-built or well-trained, organic or inorganic, seems to function seamlessly once inserted into the site of operations: this might describe labor at its finest or highest intensity. Toscano grounds his image in the corporeal equipment and micropolitics of labor: the hand works, the mouth desires. It is not enough to question the organic value of the human laborer, there must be an idiomatic repurposing of the human laborer as a body that activates other bodies, instructs them, engages with them, propels them into flights of immanence. Presumably, the Wall Street Occupiers were on this plane of cognition.

In the remainder of this chapter I track what Toscano's "poetic-critical *double bind*" in the spaces of labor (by definition the public sphere) that poetry is often striving to populate with bodies, energies, and "occupations." I read across Toscano's early work (*The Disparities* [2002], *Platform* [2003], and *To Leveling Swerve* [2004]), and bring to the surface various pressures Toscano makes on the machinic potential of the body to enjamb with what Antonio Negri, Michael Hardt, and Paolo Virno have each theorized as "the multitude." In what ways does Toscano's praxis of enjambment/disenjambment (in his lyric and in his performances) echo the double bind of enchantment/disenchantment, typifying the reduction of labor practices to guttural, often voiceless, and necessarily physicalized existence?

II

The Disparities (2002), Toscano's second book, confronts the shape of the disaster in the language of a difference engine. "Circular No. 6," for instance, glances at the corrosive velocities of capital in the dissembling of functions and qualities within financial transactions: "Cashspeak. A card recut before nine months / In the instance of [...] after two frames—stopped."[9] Here the "MACHINE'S REVELATION" (q.v.) is disguised in the cinematic whirr of trading and speculation. The cutting and recutting of the "card" figures not only the credit card or the punched card, but also the playing card, the tarot card—a metaphysics of speculation that butts against the dark magic of the circulation of financial instruments.

The titular poem, "The Disparities," ranges its effects along an accretion of rhythmic units and clauses that play upon the splits and seizures of a post-capitalist identity: "*Mine, ours, theirs, yours:* possessive's spell still lingering / When this next morning, not so strong, post-person, worlds / Collide, tremulously explore last night's dreamscapes. / (what?) Recall a pre-citizen existence, speak—".[10] The question of personhood dwells over the phantasmagoria of "post-person" politics: What is possession in the age of capital? Can one possess oneself, or *a* self, in the fragmented designer worlds of consumerist identity formation? The invocation to "speak" rings out, anachronically, over the notion of a "pre-citizen existence," presumably an existence predating the fiber optic mechanisms of surveillance states, the datafication of society, and the aggressive financialization of everyday life.

Toscano envisions the formation of a public, and the constitution of various polities, in the poetic act. In the poetic act, the possession of self is dissolved in the occupation of "uninhabitabilities": "Biographical. To be spoken for. To know / This much, this long: new uninhabitabilities – / Generational? not entirely, but parts / On the way (encountered / re-combining)—hopes, fears—".[11] The question of occupation returns to the fold; what cannot be inhabited is precisely the beginning of an inhabitation (the voice to the body, the echo to the call, the oracular

---

[9] Rodrigo Toscano, *The Disparities* (Los Angeles: Green Integer, 2002), 9.

[10] Toscano, *The Disparities*, 19.

[11] Toscano, *The Disparities*, 48.

poem to the printed text). Similarly, what cannot serve as an occupation gestures toward the structuration of occupational forms. Toscano quickly glances at such a public, the Tzotzil of the Chiapas region in Mexico, whose orality presupposes the "biographical," the moment of generationally being spoken for in the combinatory power of a people: "When having faced the front page (them) re-shaping 'I' / *Tzotzil*, the name of a people—that mean it."[12] This disparity stares down the shapelessness of post-person politics confronted by the disintegrated / re-integrated "I" of the Tzotzil people. Labor is not explicitly thematized in *The Disparities*. But there are relational schema drawn over its map of calculable ruptures that hint at the noxious causes of the schizophrenogenic capitalized "I" seeking to be spoken for, or be intuited by, a certain kind of public. That is, a public like the one embodied by, more frenetically, the Occupy Wall Street movement or, less paradigmatically, by the multiple pueblos of the Tzotzil or the Zapatistas. There are symptomatic readings of the non-lyric "I" within the crevices of (inevitable, inescapable) disparity. No commune, only disparities, in the plural. Under such conditions, the question of labor remains a question of redefining the self in its relation to the public, to work, and to the cultural apparatus.

This question materializes in more specific modalities in Toscano's next book, *Platform* (2003). The first poem of the collection, "Early Morning Prompts for Late Evening Takes Or, Roll 'em!,'" is a hesitant yet relentless work, constructed mostly of oblique, restless questions, which the title frames as "Prompts." It holds open question of who or what is being prompted, and the kinds of activity to which they might be stimulated. There is a concern, clearly, with the temporality of these activities. Whatever they are, they mature between sun-up and sundown. Specifically, there is a probable allusion to the news cycle, with "Late Evening Takes" suggesting punditry and opinion-formation, and "Roll 'em!" suggesting cameras and perhaps also newspaper presses. "Roll 'em" may have other connotations: showing one's cards in Poker when all the bets are in, or, more faintly, it may suggest bodily violence of some kind, a chance for things to be seized. At the same time, the last of the poem's "Prompts" seems to figure praxis as something distant and inaccessible; in its final lines, it openly asks if there is "a realization of

---

[12] Toscano, *The Disparities*, 49.

what's yet unrealized— / postscript or / preamble / to praxis?"[13] This can be understood as a question about whether what remains "unrealized" is permanently unrealizable—is there even *in principle* a realization of what's yet unrealized? But it can also be understood as a question about, roughly speaking, whether praxis is blocked by *known unknowns* or by *unknown unknowns*—have the contents of "what's yet unrealized" even been provisionally and conjecturally represented yet? Through such equivocations, the poem returns us to the double bind of the poetic act. Is the poem representative of what it builds up and gives voice to, bringing diverse publics into view? Or do the poem's representational powers fall short of actual praxis because they cannot measure up to the scale of such a public? In this way, the poetic act's "unrealized" public is held in vibrant suspension, neither the "postscript" that is preceded by praxis, nor the "preamble" that makes praxis possible. It is not surprising to find the notions of praxis and of labor tightly connected, but in Toscano's work it seems to be the poetic act, or the lyric vision generated by the poetic act, that could make these linkages possible.

In "Piece Beginning with Some Haunting Lines from Bertolt Brecht's 'The Doubter,'" Toscano slyly mixes allusions to Ezra Pound's "A Few Don'ts by an Imagiste" and the poststructuralist meta-fictions of Miguel de Unamuno and Luigi Pirandello to accommodate the poem's sudden awakening to consciousness and ensuing search for its author. Like Pirandello's self-aware meta-characters, the poem accesses its own subjectification and asks its author, "*don't* de-materialize me, author," along with a plea that the author "*gotta* re-materialize me."[14] The key to the materialization of the dematerialized acts of poetry is labor—or at least, something like labor. Toscano constructs a new verb form: "I / labor-ite."[15] The conventional infinitive, *to labor*, turns out to be insufficient, and perhaps too overdetermined, to cover the range of "overlays" that poetic labor socially reconstitutes in its multiple "occupations" of presencing; hence, *to labor-ite* transcends the static qualities of labor as toil and striving, and describes a transitive force that might possibly unify the laboring body across mediums, publics, and spectacles "in a clear stream of *libertas*."[16]

---

[13] Rodrigo Toscano, *Platform* (Atelos, 2003), 19.

[14] Toscano, *Platform*, 23.

[15] Toscano, *Platform*, 24.

[16] Toscano, *Platform*, 24.

At the same time, Toscano's precise positioning toward labor as praxis and/or as representation is complicated by the satiric mode that informs much of his poetic force. In "A Brief Retrospective of Chump De Ville's Poetic Oeuvre over the Last Decade (Satire No. 2)," praxis returns as a "'provisional' term" that calls into question the commitment of the careerist poet:

> [...] term, so bleached of its original color–so cleaved of its urgent
>   pairing, praxis
>   (an organizational *praxis*).[17]

The cleavage is indicative of a larger split between representation and praxis, particularly in a hypothetical poet whose initials seem to suggest a pecuniary interest in the furthering of his CV, a careerism which is only "strategic along / *representational* lines."[18] In some Hegelian perversion, poetry is representative here only of itself—as *geist* or a 'spirit of the laws'—rather than serving as a voice for the people and communities it means to embody and marshal. In "My Target Audience, As It *Is* an Issue... (Satire No. 3)," the vocality of the CV-padding poet is dispersed in "people's pep talk / poetics / phrenologizing / 'depth' / of engagement / 'aaah ... there's a doozy!'"[19] Toscano satirizes the cosmetic tissue of poetry that feigns at political engagement whose depth is only as far as "the edge / of the platform,"[20] afraid at plunging into the realism of activist involvement. The resonance of the book's title emerges here: what *platform* does the poet speak from? Is a platform a space of occupation, or is "having a platform" the labor of occupation?

The historical context surrounding Toscano's *Platform* is significant here. Antedating, but creating the conditions for, the Occupy Wall Street event, the anti-globalization protests that disrupted the 2001 G8 Summit in Genoa, Italy set the stage for the poem "In-Formational Forum Rousers—Arcing (Satire No. 4)." Toscano interweaves headlines from international newsfeeds in Norwegian with a fractured nonlinear narrative on the slow violence of financial markets and the immediate

---

[17] Toscano, *Platform*, 38.

[18] Toscano, *Platform*, 40.

[19] Toscano, *Platform*, 45, 51.

[20] Toscano, *Platform*, 52.

violence of protest. Juxtaposed to the manifestation of the anti-globalist protesters, poetic force becomes satirized here as the abstracted product of failed producer-production relations. The reclusion of poetry into self-aware Hegelian subject finds some part of its cause in the high modern-ism of Anglo-American poetics which effects this kind of relationality and finds its analogue in both L=A=N=G=U=A=G=E avant-garde poetry and the banking industry: "Amalgamated Langpo Support Plank–Bank / in order to make first payment on Chase / Global Goblins."[21] Toscano's satirical mode vents its spleen in paying its share to "that time of the year when my Anglo-American High / Modernist Dues / are due."[22]

Toscano's place as a bilingual Chicano poet who emerged after the L=A=N=G=U=A=G=E generation of poets gives him a privileged lens into the contradictions of a school of poetry that was simultane-ously elitist and politicized, ostensibly white and yet aware of vanguard Anglo-American poetry's failure to adequately represent POC commu-nities and the laborers of the margins. The conceptual abstractions of L=A=N=G=U=A=G=E poetry and its consequent inability to stand in for or give voice to the "unskilled" (often undocumented) workers work-ing outside of the elite culture of New York City and its cosmopolitan satellites are partially dramatized in Toscano's "Ideo-Degradable Verses from Immokalee," where undocumented tomato workers are picked up in trucks and taken "to the performance site" of cheap exploitative labor. Working for "*Taco Hell*," the laborers are paid only "*one-tenth of one cent*." The laborers bemoan that "We can't participate / more openly / in politics," adding that "—we're workers too! With special problems and solutions to / those problems."[23] The irony in being "undocumented" (or what Jacques Derrida remarked about the "*sans papiers*") even as they are being "documented" by poetry's spiritualizing labor returns us to the double bind of poetry. Poetry documents the struggles of laborers who are undocumented on two levels: as laborers and as subjects of representation.

Indeed, working and living in New York City at the time, Toscano was shrewdly aware of the gulf that lay between his work as an organ-izer at the Labor Institute and as an experimental POC poet in concert with the New York avant-garde scene. Perhaps in this division between

---

[21] Toscano, *Platform*, 132.

[22] Toscano, *Platform*, 131.

[23] Toscano, *Platform*, 180.

poetry as labor and poetry as representation, the schizophreno-genic "post-person" self of *The Disparities* re-emerges (in the poem "A Postscript") as that which "[on] related plane" contrasts "previous oppositional formation's / *specificity*." I read this *specificity* as that of corporate personhood, the post-Fordist *principium individuationis* man-ufactured by global capitalism's vision of a "Maximalist [...] expansion of horizon of self-representation" (208). This is at once a blessing and a curse, insofar as what Franco Berardi calls "the soul at work" has to make a Mephistophelean deal with "Semiocapitalism['s]" reduction of person-hood to the automatisms of cognitive labor. Berardi's "soul at work" is a materialist one predicated on Epicurean and Lucretian metaphysics: "what the body can do, that is its soul."[24] In the fiber optic "cogwheels" of cognitive capitalism, human labor is indeed "spiritualized" into pure bio-informatics, but it comes at the cost of the extremest assimilation of personhood (human and otherwise) by corporate personhood, in which "Workers self-representation" stands "in relation to immediate employers' / 'needs'."[25] The double bind of labor seems unsurpassable within this relationality, which insists on the corporatization of unions, movements, and peoples within the meticulously graphic-designed "one-for-all" template of cognitive capitalism.

And yet Berardi's curious appeal to a politicized Lucretianism is met by Toscano's insistence on the "potentiality" of the "Working atoms of socialism," a phrase of promise that would be re-echoed in his next book, *To Leveling Swerve* (2004), whose very title, indeed, channels Epicurus and the Lucretian clinamen. At some level, *To Leveling Swerve* functions as a direct response to the very notion of "having a plat-form" in *Platform*: the platform of poetry and politics is ruptured by the swerve, even as the swerve institutes a new "leveled" space of rela-tions. Much of the architecture of *To Leveling Swerve* is based upon the paradox of "leveling" a "swerve," which means to either neutralize a permutation in the structure of things, or to regularize the infinite per-mutation of things to such an extent that the swerve is everywhere, and in everything, constant. In "Arms Akimbo, Scolding Plekhanovin," the

[24] Spinoza, quoted in Franco 'Bifo' Berardi, *The Soul at Work: From Alienation to Autonomy*, translated by Francesca Cadel and Giuseppina Mecchia (Los Angeles: Semiotext(e), 2007), 21.

[25] Toscano, *Platform*, 207.

double bind of poetry is staged as the Marxian problematic of "uneven development":

> Those of you unfamiliar with the terms 'MLA'
> 'Zukovsky' 'art-object' (its current status)
> —You don't belong at this reading!
> And the fault is all mine
> —Uneven Development.[26]

The secondary meaning given to "uneven development" resonates in the double bind: in "Relay Alpha, Bravo, Charlie," the "enormous gaps in [...] education" simultaneously encountered by poetry's occupation-less subjects and by its occupied spaces render the platform lopsided and irregular, even if such unevenness constitutes the essential aesthetic or vanguard qualities of the work of poetry.[27] Zukofksy's difficulty, MLA's academic insularity, and the fetish character of the art-object provoke boredom, disaffection, and rootlessness for those who lie outside the ambit of global capitalism's elite class. Poetry cannot speak within these ever-tightening crevices, which tighten the bind of meaning into single-axis structures accessible only to the few.

The relative failures of the protests and strikes dramatized in *Platform* to permanently disrupt global capitalism's reach are re-staged throughout *To Leveling Swerve* as conditions of depression or "illness" that produce verse lines in punctuation-phobic passages. In "62 Prose-Units Written in Illness," Toscano raises the question of class difference while evoking the Lucretian image of ceaseless flows and waterfalls:

> Can't imagine how much bullshit affect bucketfulls class differences in motion having to swim the river swirling currents odd flotsam in a torrent same direction waterfall called earth itself.[28]

The torrent of class struggle is aligned with the "laminar flows" of Michel Serres' vortices, declinations, and swerves in the latter's discussion of Lucretian physics as the source of all material processes that

---

[26] Rodrigo Toscano, *To Leveling Swerve* (San Francisco: Krupskaya, 2004), 18.

[27] Toscano, *To Leveling Swerve*, 13.

[28] Toscano, *To Leveling Swerve*, 33.

undergird socio-political, economic, and aesthetic compounds.[29] In a later passage Toscano references Lucretius quite directly:

> Lucretius a fanatic lunatic peacenik materialist who had no model as to how to do that in poetry implore through Memmius upper-class bum-licker who's just as well off munching half-rotted herring than tapping out L's Hexameters as to what a geo-distant class's aspirations were some 2,000 years before but meant for the now as legacy to be tapped into at some unspecified time.[30]

Toscano figures in Lucretius an unevenness in methodology that approximates to a poetics of uncertainty which has "no model as to how to do that in poetry" (q.v.) whether as praxis or as representation. Indeed, the representational strata of poetry is upset by the lack of traction the liberal spatial distribution of verse units enforces. Clauses run into and out of each other with little traffic control, and "L's Hexameters" are somehow lost in the mire (or double bind) of poetry's failure to withstand cognitive capitalism's crushing hold on labor. The future-perfect of Lucretian revolutionary time is promising only in that it is "unspecified," provisional, and ever-distant. Meanwhile, in the age of accelerated politics and abstracted labor, the labor of poetry falls exhausted in "illness" or listlessly channels the various automatisms of language flows that bear little relation to communal forms and the politics of the present.

Toscano's block format recalls Keston Sutherland's reflections on the ubiquity of prose "blocks" as a regular feature of anglophone anti-capitalist poetry after the financial crisis of 2007–2008. Sutherland relates the compressed form of these block poems to a "poetic subjectivity under duress" schizophrenogenically split between "private interiorized histories of trauma" and the "destructive force of capital."[31] In Serres' reading of Lucretius, such a split finds its analogue in the split between *euenta* and

[29] Michel Serres, *The Birth of Physics*, translated by David Webb and William Ross (London and New York: Rowman & Littlefield, 2018 [1977]).

[30] Toscano, *To Leveling Swerve*, 40.

[31] Keston Sutherland, "Blocks: Form Since the Crash," lecture at the Organism for Poetic Research, New York University, http://archive.org/details/BlocksSeminar AtNYU13November2015, 13 November 2015.

coniuncta, violence and alliance, event and conjunction. Toscano weaves these strands together in another "block" poem, "POSTCARD TO LUCRETIUS," part of a series of "postcard" poems, each typed in ALL CAPS, which play at macro- and micro-cosmic gesturalism:

AND SO BRIEFLY AND IN THE RUSH OF THINGS INDEED MEET US THE SOCIAL MOVEMENTS THE COUNTER MOVEMENTS THE AESTHETIC COMPACTS WHAT THEY SAY SEEM TO SAY OR THE ODD SUM THEIR COMBINATION THE RATIO NAY HEAT OF SUCH APPELLATIONS FULMINATE PARSING EVERYTHING TIME AND TIME AGAIN SIREN DOLOR IN DALLYING SUCH DREAD SUCH PEOPLE PULSING OF PALLID WONDROUS EYES THAT TO THEM I SUBMIT AND REBEL OF ME SOME PORTION YEARNING TO MOVE ON PASSED THOSE WATERS TO BONE'S-ASHES BOUND INEVITABLY SO NECESSARY HAZY FEARFUL THIS CROSSING.[32]

Toscano's postcard fashions a simulation of Lucretian clinamen that aspires to weave together the antinomies of micro and macro substances, most significantly that of praxis and representation. It is, indeed, in the figure of Lucretian physics, that Toscano visualizes a version of Paolo Virno's grammar of the multitude, quite literally, this time in the sentence-level laminar flow of declamations, yearnings, and declinations.[33] The movement toward a submission to the "SOCIAL MOVEMENTS" which swerve into "COUNTER MOVEMENTS" effects a kind of anti-personhood which rejects both corporatization and individuation. When Toscano writes that "TO THEM I SUBMIT AND REBEL OF ME," we are reminded of the primary double bind with which we began: the "clear stream of *libertas*," itself a Lucretian laminar flow, juxtaposed with the "MACHINE'S REVELATION," or what I identify as the learned and inherited automatisms of corporate personhood. There is at once a submission to corporatization (the automated nature of machinic revelation) and a counter-resistance which resembles a submission to the multitude or what Eugene Thacker calls "the swarm." In both cases, the "YEARNING TO MOVE ON" leads to a death "SO NECESSARY HAZY FEARFUL."

[32] Toscano, *To Leveling Swerve*, 55.

[33] Cf. Paolo Virno, *A Grammar of the Multitude: For an Analysis of Contemporary Forms of Life* (New York and Los Angeles: Semiotext(e), 2004).

I wager that this death is the annulment or nullification of the double bind. As Nick Srnicek, Alex Williams, and other accelerationists have argued, automation is not only the way of the future, but the possible liberation of labor from its own entrapment and capitalist entrainment. Labor freed from labor may well be "a clear stream of *libertas*"; equally so, the return to a Lucretian politics, evidenced by Toscano's lyric mode, may accept the terms and conditions of machinic revelation, of a learned and controlled automatism, provided that "what gives pause or impetus" emerges from a recalibration of the body's centrality to the forces of praxis and (self-)representation.

The "MACHINE'S REVELATION" re-emerges in another post-card poem, "POSTCARD TO HORACE," in which the genre of the *ars poetica* is revisited and recontextualized as the deskilling of human endeavor and its rescaling to automatic labor rituals:

MONUMENTS TO MACHINE'S EGO BUILD BY CERTAIN METHODS CERTAIN TECHNIQUES LABOR DEPLOYED ARRANGED CONDUCTED THAT AT A CROSSROADS FEEDS TO RUN IT OR CAN WE STARVE IT A PLAN THE HOT END IDLING DOWN.[34]

We cannot interpret this as an embrace of the machine's ego, but perhaps it can be read as the reframing of the double bind as one which envisions a *leveling* of human labor alongside an automatism which transcends mere class struggle or class divisions. That is, 'to leveling swerve' may be read as the convergence of praxis and representation in the leveling of human endeavor with machinic representation. Both are to be considered a 'poethics' of the everyday, a new *ars poetica* which signals the emergence of 'spiritualized automata' who go beyond the double bind within the embrace of total automation and a submission to (or melting into) the multitude.[35]

Toscano indicates as much in the titular poem: "Gotta love the tools; we seek breaks or voluminous strength from such toil."[36] The embrace of total automation, supplemented by Lucretian clinamen and chance

---

[34] Toscano, *To Leveling Swerve*, 51.

[35] Cf. Joan Retallack, *The Poethical Wager* (Berkeley: University of California Press, 2003).

[36] Toscano, *To Leveling Swerve*, 75.

operations, would be later investigated in Toscano's later work (in *Deck of Deeds* and *Collapsible Poetics Theater*). But for now, the artisanal "love of tools" provides a welcome conclusion to the cultural impasse which the double bind of poetry had formerly represented for Toscano in his early work.

WORKS CITED

Auden, W. H. "In Memory of W.B. Yeats." In *The English Auden: Poems, Essays, and Dramatic Writings 1927–1999*, edited by E. Mendelson. London: Faber and Faber.

Bateson, Gregory, Don D. Jackson, Jay Haley, and John H. Weakland. "Toward a Theory of Schizophrenia" (1956). In Gregory Bateson, *Steps to an Ecology of Mind: Collected Essays in Anthropology, Psychiatry, Evolution, and Epistemology*. San Francisco: Chandler, 1987 [1972].

Berardi, Franco 'Bifo.' *The Soul at Work: From Alienation to Autonomy*. Translated by Francesca Cadel and Giuseppina Mecchia. Los Angeles: Semiotext(e), 2007.

Deleuze, Gilles, and Felix Guattari. *Anti-Oedipus* (1972). Translated (1977) by Robert Hurley, Mark Seem, and Helen R. Lane. London: Continuum, 2004.

Retallack, Joan. *The Poethical Wager*. Berkeley: University of California Press, 2003.

Serres, Michel. *The Birth of Physics*. Translated by David Webb and William Ross. London and New York: Rowman & Littlefield, 2018 [1977].

Srinicek, Nick, and Alex Williams. *Inventing the Future: Postcapitalism and a World Without Work*. Verso: London and Brooklyn, 2005.

Sutherland, Keston. "Blocks: Form Since the Crash." Lecture at the Organism for Poetic Research. New York University, 13 November 2015. http://archive.org/details/BlocksSeminarAtNYU13November2015. Accessed 15 April 2018.

Toscano, Rodrigo. "MAY BE!: Chorus for Inquisitive Occupiers." *Poetry Foundation*, 4 April 2012. www.poetryfoundation.org/harriet/2012/04/may-be-chorus-for-inquisitive-occupiers. Accessed 15 April 2018.

———. "Rodrigo Toscano on 'May Be!'" From the In Their Own Words Series. *Poetry Society of America*. www.poetrysociety.org/psa/poetry/crossroads/own_words/Rodrigo_Toscano. Accessed 15 April 2018.

———. *Platform*. Berkeley: Atelos, 2003.

———. *The Disparities*. Los Angeles: Green Integer, 2002.

———. *To Leveling Swerve*. San Francisco: Krupskaya, 2004.

Virno, Paolo. *A Grammar of the Multitude: For an Analysis of Contemporary Forms of Life*. New York and Los Angeles: Semiotext(e), 2004.

CHAPTER 12

Distributed and Entangled Posture in Catherine Wagner's *My New Job* and *Nervous Device*

Holly Pester

THE RHYTHMIC INQUIRY OF POSTURE

Catherine Wagner's *My New Job* (2009) and *Nervous Device* (2012) are intimately concerned with the embodied nature of work, across the material-immaterial distinction, and intimately concerned with the processes that discipline the body into a form of labouring subject. This chapter will closely consider how Wagner's poetry addresses the physical activity of work and the polyvalence of interpellative materials that discipline the body as subject. In particular, it will explore the embodied thresholds that emerge in Wagner's work, thresholds which suggest shapes prior to, and in antagonism with, their articulations within patriarchal capitalist categories. In line with my interest in embodying thresholds, the key figure of my interpretative methodology will be—not structure, network, or assemblage, but rather—*posture*.

Posture, a term we often use in reference to symptomatic and idiomatic characteristics of the labouring body, means both the attitude and

H. Pester (✉)
University of Essex, Colchester, UK

© The Author(s) 2019
J. L. Walton and E. Luker (eds.), *Poetry and Work*,
Modern and Contemporary Poetry and Poetics,
https://doi.org/10.1007/978-3-030-26125-2_12

alignment of a thing's physical components. While 'posture' describes the shape of a body, a body's posture is itself descriptive of a body's bearing of mass in relation to time. The shape held by a human body's posture, the signifying line of neck, shoulders and spine, is a material positionality held contingently in place. This continuously adjusting order of interrelations, which sees "a thing and that which stands around it [...] bound together," is a gerundial mix of subject-object, passive-active formations.[1] As a verb, *posturing* suggests how a body is wielded; posturing is the act of adopting a set of gestures through stance and performative acts. Like the meaning-making, montage process of actions in Bertolt Brecht's *gestus*, which are always at once individually and socially figuring, posture congeals distinct forms of the individual with dialectical historicity.[2] With posture something (time plus gravity for instance) is being imposed on the body as it acts, making posture generative of meaning of the explicit and detailed continuum of material conditions. This fact of historical situations being manifest in posture likewise links it to Judith Butler's phenomenological account of a body *becoming* its gender through "a series of acts which are renewed, revised, and consolidated through time."[3] In this chapter I will incorporate such theories of performative transformations of the body to re-consider the way we get stuck in certain alignments as an effect of work we have done and shapes we have made with our bodies, as historically situated yet potentially innovating of certain orientations. Sara Ahmed describes how bodily orientations and social practices are histories repeated in the situated body; our movements are "shaped by what is behind us" creating "a loop between what is toward and behind."[4] This looping, as manifest in physical and metaphysical orientations, is what I hope to reveal as the rhythmic potential of posture.

Interpreted in relation to work, posture is a continuous action (sitting or standing, bending or kneeling, lying down or running, et cetera).

---

[1] John A. Schumacher, *Human Posture: The Nature of Inquiry* (New York: SUNY Press, 1989), 19.

[2] Walter Benjamin, *Understanding Brecht* (New ed.) (London: Verso, 2003), 3.

[3] Judith Butler, "Performative Acts and Gender Constitution: An Essay in Phenomenology and Feminist Theory," *Theatre Journal*, vol. 40, no. 4 (1988), 523, https://doi.org/10.2307/3207893.

[4] Sara Ahmed, *New Materialisms: Ontology, Agency, and Politics*, edited by Diana Coole and Samantha Frost (Duke University Press, 2010), 247.

It is also an accumulation of attributes implicated in rendering the body as utility. As such, as a formation of body matter, posture is indivisible from market economy. The effects on the body of prolonged physical work, or of prolonged acts of non–work, or indeed of any prolonged occupancy of some particular labour-oriented apparatus—for instance, desk, chair, computer, or anywhere you put a laptop—layer up in the worker's bodily horizons as sedimented histories in correlation to labour time. This is to say that a body's orientation is a temporal and dialectical interplay between the immediate, present body and its habits.[5] In this phenomenological sense, posture is a knotting of agented and repeated gesture, embodying work after the particular tasks of work have ended. Work—including work which is not done, work which is partly deflected or evaded—becomes sedimented somatically as posture.

We could stop there and say posture is therefore an indexical figuring of institutions of work and leisure. Yet if we were to use posture, as Lisa Robertson has with prosody[6] and John Wilkinson with cadence,[7] as a spatial politics, where the past and future are in erotic and syntactic tension as historicity, then the potential co-transformation of worker-subjects and labour milieu through posture is opened up. In other words, we can read with the performativity of posture to specifically review a poetics of work continuums in the body. In the body's acts of posturing, we can trace the performic citizen, the continuously emergent and rhythmic subject, whose posture does not only elaborate market imperatives, but also kicks back as an obtuse object. When Catherine Wagner says in her poem, "I made no money from my poems but they statused me," we think first of the stature and standing of the professional behind that statement.[8] We think of the albeit limited capital and measures of employability and social reputation that recompense for the poem's production. We also hear "status" in terms of the statuesque. The poem gives the poet both alignment and orientation with which to perform the poem, and to perform themselves through it. It gives the poet an apparatus to be in rhythmical relation to, which sees adaptions

---

[5] Maurice Merleau-Ponty, *Phenomenology of Perception*, translated by Donald A. Andes (New York: Routledge, 2012 [1945]).

[6] Lisa Robertson, *Nilling: Prose* (Toronto: Book Thug, 2012).

[7] John Wilkinson, "Cadence," *Reality Studios*, vol. 9, nos. 1–4 (1987), 81–87.

[8] Catherine Wagner, *Nervous Device* (San Francisco: City Lights Books, 2012), 1.

and elaborations of the self, based on the poet's orientation around it, thus producing meaning and economic value that is interruptive on its own industry.

Wagner's assertion of "status" reveals the poem to be an act of posturing, and also a co-movement with postured formations from acts of labour and related acts of consumption. We can extend this to say that the poem as a co-movement with posture has the potential to be critical, interrupting and resilient to the dominant structures of capitalist labour and patriarchal inscriptions on the body. I will explore this in further readings of Wagner's poetry where configurations of limbs and orientations of subject identities are brought to bear against apexes of economic time: "I paid to be / directed rectangularly and down a hall."[9]

Posture therefore is potentially both embodied subjectivity and an *innovation* of work-time and affects of the temporal matrix of the worker's body. Here too performativity in relation to posture becomes plain. That is, posture is in part a work of citation, driven by the compulsion to be self-identical within interlocking matrices of institutional (and other) demands for legibility. Performance—to be figured in this chapter in reference to *gestus*, to the affective surplus of the poetry reading, and to socially performed gestures of identity legibility—shows how body matter corresponds to efforts and environment, labouring activity and subject capture.

In this chapter, I aim to consider the body in relation to work—and more specifically as I go on, postures of a contemporary 'female body' in relation to twenty-first-century neoliberal labour economies—by drawing out the *entanglement* of a body and worker subjectivity as is seen in Wagner's *My New Job* (2009) and *Nervous Device* (2012). In both books Wagner stages the subjectification of a worker-consciousness in its interactions with the biological, anatomical practices of wage-work as well as the work, more numinous but perhaps no less threatening, of composing poetry in a neoliberal environment. In the final part of this chapter I explore whether there might be a way of approaching the particularity of the worker-consciousness in resistance to its environment by invoking (as Wagner does in her *Nervous Device*) the posturing stance of William Blake's 'bounding line.'

---

[9] Catherine Wagner, *Macular Hole* (Albany: Fence Books, 2004), 55.

EXERCISES

"Exercises," a sequence of twenty-two short poems in Wagner's collection *My New Job*, offers a vibrant discourse on the embodied labouring subject and how a poetic critique of work can emerge from critically harnessing the performances and postures of physical exertion. According to the notes and acknowledgements each poem in the sequence was written between sets of physical therapy exercises, and written "one line per set." Each line of poetry is thus framed as a consequence of a discrete physical activity that has motivated and shaped its particular production, something we are prompted to think about in the specific context of their labour economies and social dynamics. In other words, the somatic descriptions within the poems are contextualized within the poet's experiences of productive and reproductive labour, both in the home and the workplace, in such a way that politicizes the body matter in acts of effort. In the poems there is often a strange de-centring of the connection between the subject, or lyric 'I,' the body, and the *producer* of the movements:

> I lean forward on the nerve ebullient
> my sweet alive and roasting in a current
> sciatica verboten clockwork nerve
> precinctual. Slip off.[10]

The discrete anatomies and the lyric subject are out of sync and variously related. The enthusiastic move to bear weight on the body's own sensitivity is ensnared in a love-and-death tempo,[11] one of a prohibiting ("verboten") system ("clockwork") that situates the "nerve" (the sciatic nerve, the body's biggest) as machine-like, separate from the 'I' and weirdly distinct from the action. While this might seem to present a disembodied agency that precedes and directs, embodied exterior, an 'I' that *does* the body as Butler has warned against,[12] I would argue that the disarticulation offers a more radical substantiating of embodied possibilities, where the 'I' is divided and embodied and the body is neither singular nor stable. However, this elaboration is conditioned

---

[10] Catherine Wagner, *My New Job* (Albany: Fence Books, 2009), 6.

[11] Wilkinson, "Cadence," 81.

[12] Butler, "Performative Acts and Gender Constitution," 521.

and circumscribed by "precinctual" routines and conventions. Here the word "precinctual" means "divided into precincts," but also suggests 'pre-instinctive.' Here the body encounters its own moves as a constraining environment into which its agency does not extend, but rather in which its agency must play out. The "Slip off" might suggest aborting the act, leaving work early, or a fault in the motion such as an injury (a slipped disk even). The phrase also poses a slippage between worker as a construct and worker as worn and torn body, coming in and out of correlation with the forces and results of the movements; "Muscle under collarbone hurt today / from fooling around with computer. / Look left and up pulls like a bitch."[13]

The poems are numbered and labelled with the time at which the set of exercises (presumably) took place, for example, "EXERCISE 3 (11/20/00 PM)."[14] The suggestion of routine signals (rather than illustrates) an inscripted and constitutive body, operating under Michel Foucault's notion of disciplinary power.[15] According to Foucault's influential historical study, within hierarchical and close surveillance institutions, norms and regulatory ideals are internalised into a subject's self-monitoring behaviour and habits. However, Wagner arguably aligns here with critiques of Foucault's theory as rendering the body inert and separate from experience.[16] Instead, Wagner is pushing physical experience and institutional discourse into a flesh bond with lyric subjectivity. Such lyric subjectivity rejects any central location of power, which Foucault—despite his insistence on the ubiquitous and dynamic character of power—associates with the brain. We read this bonding through a mix of perspectives on the body and various causes for its actions. We find interiors where body matter is specimen-like ("the pudding inside lanced with yards of net") and exterior glances towards a designated figure ("your limp and slowy back").[17]

Another element, again signalling to a Foucauldian 'docile body' but with a counter-twist, is the aforementioned dating of the exercises. These

---

[13] Wagner, *My New Job*, 16.

[14] Wagner, *My New Job*, 3.

[15] Michel Foucault, *Discipline and Punish: The Birth of the Prison*, translated by Alan Sheridan (Vintage Books, 1977).

[16] Lisa Blackman, *The Body: The Key Concepts* (New York: Berg, 2008).

[17] Wagner, *My New Job*, 6.

are, significantly, not in chronological order. So while there is a presiding sense of obedience to the task there is also a limited sense of aspiration or progression toward an optimum physical status. While the exercises correspond to conditioning tasks where "By bending behaviour towards a terminal state, exercise makes possible a perpetual characterization of the individual,"[18] Wagner's bends and derangements of teleological 'training' bring lived practices and permutations of vital, inarticulate, experience of a body, or what Lisa Blackman calls a "somatically felt body," into play.[19] What we might take from this process is that the performing of exercises, as posed in poetic frames, leads to a varying constitution of a body from discursive organism, material relations and accumulating affects. Posture, therefore, is both the contextual scene of this process— that includes the situation of commodified labour and the idea of self— and the muscular time the exercises signify.

> the nerves treed into my skull
> lit up & whamming
>
> Where are you, muscle relaxer.
> Vague dirtying round the edges & a thoughtfulness[20]

Within this context of materially-felt economic time we might ask, what values are being produced in inverse or direct correlation to the substance of effort? The title of the sequence itself, a kind of play on words, weaves the procedures of physical therapy with those of constrained writing. The exercises supposed to strengthen, heal, and compose the body are woven together with exercises which writers undertake in self-conscious indifference to producing literary value, and/or the prompts imposed on students in creative writing workshops, with the expectation that they can't then fail to produce a little literary value.

This play on the word *exercises* exemplifies the sequence's *situatedness*, a term I take from Donna Haraway's epistemological notion of situated knowledge, meaning a speaker's limited and embodied objectivity that

---

[18] Foucault, *Discipline and Punish*, 161.
[19] Blackman, *The Body*, 30.
[20] Wagner, *My New Job*, 18.

is knowingly constituted from material locations.[21] In this case the situatedness of the act—and the corresponding translation into meaningful material comes from local, particular feelings and movements—speak out to various social realities, politics and knowledge. The minute bodily configurations, stresses and affordances which fill up the sequence, although they remain rooted in the scene of domestic physical therapy, become portable across many contexts. The somatic descriptions within the poems are on a plane with the poet's experiences in the home and workplace: "Haven't cleaned the house since Martin left, and living out of the freezer, [...] To reward me my email is up."[22] At no point does the text let go of the poet's social and domestic roles, including the university workplace and its strange parity with the industries of contemporary poetry. We hear about the lateness of a "book review"; we hear about the social interactions and specific culture of being a poet ("'Super reading' I said" and "I'd never buy the book").[23]

In this way, certain postures of the body as they relate to forms of work indicate a shapely demonstration of material entanglement of the embodied subject with the market-economy, even in supposed states of immaterial labour. At our desks, as we hunch and lurch forward towards the screen, we are in a continuous state of producing data and value. This also true while we perform acts of leisure, timewasting, creative practice, or therapeutic exercise. This is a situation well understood as a facet of economic neoliberalism, where the body is a configuration of entangled acts of work and productivity within effaced boundaries between work and life, biology and market economy.[24]

The exercises release a kind of citational performativity: "I do 'em so they get easier so at the end I'm just lying here / Quoting myself,"[25] as well as inarticulate impulses and expressions. These responses to the work of therapeutic exercise, and its contextualization within the ever

---

[21] Donna Haraway, "Situated Knowledges: The Science Question in Feminism and the Privilege of Partial Perspective," *Feminist Studies*, vol. 14, no. 3 (1 October 1988), 575–599, https://doi.org/10.2307/3178066.

[22] Wagner, *My New Job*, 16.

[23] Wagner, *My New Job*, 7.

[24] Melinda Cooper, *Life as Surplus: Biotechnology and Capitalism in the Neoliberal Era* (Seattle: University of Washington Press, 2008).

[25] Wagner, *My New Job*, 14.

pervasive continuum of waged work, are sometimes flat introspective reportage, sometimes analytic, sometimes complaint, sometimes wry or scatological, and sometimes eager celebration of the body's spontaneous *expressions* of substances, fluids and kick-backs: "Breathed and ovulated, breathed & blood fanned out."[26] Additionally, sometimes the subject regards the body as non-human or slapstick substance: "Raise up your back like an insect on the face of a nation."[27] Such hybridizing of physical description with social relations—the moving patterns of stress and flesh against the subject's self-knowledge—sees the embodied subject in its material and immaterial entanglements. This entanglement of systems of capital and technologies of labour result in an alienated character of the post-human body that is co-extensive with its environment.[28]

Wagner's figuring of the portions of forces forming a partial worker, a human-ish organism, agitate such questions as: is it possible for this body to express itself outside the currency of work? And, in posing the abstract machine, social form, and sensuous body as being simultaneously constituted by the exercises, is there an emergent posturing resistance to those enframings of the subject by and through capital? The answer to these questions is what's at stake in the *compositions* that make up the sequence. With many of the gestures and details of the exercises being met by references to worker- or consumer-subjectivities, we see that every transaction of energy insists on analogous transactions of value.[29] The last line of the first set is, "A long number quoted and a check will be sent."[30] Here the suggestion may be that the default space in which our bodies live is economically structured, and that pushing our bodies into various other states means metonymically negotiating other (abstract, i.e. economic) boundaries. However, the postures at work in this sequence, and the composition of their expression as an extension of the effort in the poems, reveal an innovation on forms of participation and involuntary tensions with the stresses of work and social

[26]Wagner, *My New Job*, 26.

[27]Wagner, *My New Job*, 5.

[28]Rosi Braidotti, *Metamorphoses: Towards a Materialist Theory of Becoming* (Cambridge: Polity Press, 2002), 227.

[29]Kathi Weeks, *The Problem with Work* (Durham and London: Duke University Press, 2011).

[30]Wagner, *My New Job*, 3.

reproduction. In this verse there is a strange obedience being played out alongside a turbulence remodelling:

> I politely rise to meet
>   my knee
> As I get sore in the belly
> I hate the knee
> am however diligent and strict[31]

The lines break to bend and meet each other at counterpoints; the knee is twice a join and line-break that is first property of the subject (my knee) despite being radically distinct to the 'I,' and then an idea *of* the body (the knee). The body's encounter with itself, eroticizing itself even, is situated within a social formation that stops us from reading it as a singular discrete unit, rather as a composition of joins, breaks and gestures. It points to other bodies and portions of bodies in a way that is both sensual and political. As the subject "politely" rises to meet her knee, importing the relations of the public sphere and the *polis*, it becomes an experimental citizen's body that can modulate and transform through extension into other bodies and forms: "Each body, each birth, each coming into speech, bears the radically unquantifiable potential of co-transformation."[32]

If the body, as it enacts and is subjected to the exercises, reveals glimpses of the ecologies and economies that occur by way of effort and as the intellectual byproducts of effort, then the compositions (the poems) as fragments of somatic description can be recognized as ubiquitous way beyond the specific exercise routines. That is to say, the work of the exercises—the physical therapeutic ones and their extension into writing—is to become a lens onto the work of capital and other forms of domination and disciplinarity. To put it differently, the composition of the texts, and the corresponding composition of body in various postures and poses, is a meditation on the accrued and displaced forms of value that are compositely formed by quotidian posture as a congealing of body matter, work-time and subject capture.

The hybridizing that Wagner creates in these compositions can be seen in the line "Push to the night a tender sacrum," where we are

---

[31] Wagner, *My New Job*, 12.
[32] Robertson, *Nilling*, 75.

pointed to a triangular bone in the lower back, the *sacred* bone, that connects to meanings and significances beyond the body.[33] The word "sacrum" creates a fusion of anatomy and theology, thus what we witness is a kind of cleaving, a simultaneous splitting and coupling of discourse and body, as well as the inscriptions on the body and the body's responses to its inscription. The move described (pushing the sacrum to the night) again suggests an arched back, on all fours; an insect or animal pose that postures what's left in the human skeleton of our tail. The sacred bone, so called because it may have been the part of the animal offered in sacrifice, becomes cosmic and tender, animal and mechanic. In other words, the incongruously named bone reveals a body composed of hybrid forms and texts. The body as a closed, discrete whole is therefore problematised, and instead a composite of extensions and transactions emerges.[34]

My New Job

My New Job is a collection bookended by two sequences that render forms of work, effort and labour on a micro-material level improbably legible through poetic metrics. The first is the sequence "Exercises," which, as discussed, situates the body as a composition of bio-political mechanisms and extensions, transactions of energies and affects. The book's final poem, "My New Job," as the title suggests, wryly sites the subject in becoming at a beginning of work: a new role and a new self within the conditions of wage-labour. From the title we might ask, how might self-knowledge emerge through the situatedness of employment, and how might a body be constructed by institutional apparatus? The answer is given somewhat by the unyielding nature of the poem. Through the text the subject is metrically laid out, self-reflective as a worker and as a minor function of a system, yet incongruously composed and without coherent substance of voice or body. Fragmented

---

[33]Wagner, *My New Job*, 3.

[34]Luciana Parisi and Tiziana Terranova, "Heat-Death: Emergence and Control in Genetic Engineering and Artificial Life," *CTheory* (10 May 2000), 5–10.

by dramatic caesura and gaps, the voice of the poem performs a kind of resistant formation to the comprehensible objective of the job:

> I am Invested in
> by a Huge Fund
> Heavy   highquality
> furniture[35]

Being in conflict and complicity with capital is a recurrent theme throughout the collection *My New Job*, in which Wagner critiques the conflict between forms of wage labour within the academic institution and the poet's own (re)productions within this context. The conflict is, in simplified terms, that the poet is often engaged in critiquing the mechanisms of the institution whilst relying materially on its resources. Elsewhere Wagner has commented on the precarity of fellow workers in her institution, reflecting on the entrapments of a neoliberal system, and specifically, on the renewed predatory activity of neoliberal capitalism within the university following the 2008 economic crash including the ongoing brutal and creative erosion of university workers' rights and privileges within academia.[36]

In the title poem of *My New Job* we again see somatic and affective entanglement with labour apparatus, as well as drifting material from utterances and encounters radically other to this environment: obscure matter, comedic suggestions and odd narratives ("Meanwhile My toad / absorbed / pollution").[37] Knowing what we know about the author and her writing on the politics of contemporary academic employment, we might assume that the 'new job' is within the academy, the "Huge Fund" suggesting some sort of monolithic institution that fills its employees with validity. However, with opaque material such as "I was trying My lizard turd / was trying to join the other / Mud," it is far from a straightforward critique.[38] Instead the speaking subject recounts,

---

[35] Wagner, *My New Job*, 107.

[36] Catherine Wagner, "Poetic Labor Project: Catherine Wagner," Labor Day 2010, labday2010.blogspot.co.uk/2012/07/catherine-wagner.html, accessed 27 November 2015. See also Wagner's chapter in this collection.

[37] Wagner, *My New Job*, 112.

[38] Wagner, *My New Job*, 112.

ambiguously, staged movements through—or otherwise recognizes themselves in relation to—a series of "walk-throughs" and articulated spaces, "wires" and "plugs." The subject is sometimes deftly roaming, sneaking in and out of these spaces, and sometimes disarticulated by them:

> I know my fluorescent doorway
> A rectangle Among the ceiling tiles
>
> Ordinarily flecked coated 1) foam rectangles
>
> and one hard white light rectangularly rubbled
> 2) glass rectangle
>
> ......
>
> Ugly lattice to the Duct area
> Unscrew the grille Smallen myself
> Into the dark cold Square pipe[39]

The worker, the one identified as such by their new job, is operating quite weirdly in the office building and its uncomfortable, un-ergonomic routines.

Interspersed into this formative pressure of employment on the subject, we are transposed to the yoga mat, where practices of bodily poses and breathing again serve to fashion a self at odds with pleasures and awkward economies of this practice. With, "I was lying Down on the yoga mat / My bones / basketing air,"[40] the self is cultivated through industries of health and luxury, "Highquality scented / humid air."[41] A more optimistic reading would see the yoga mat as dialogically opposed to the work space, offering a contrasting kind of breathing that offsets the exhaustions of work, but as we have seen in "Exercises," the entangled connections of productivity and leisure are what compose the subject in this poetics.

For Luce Irigaray, within one breath are held two kinds of breath, *natural* and *cultural*, and a self is shored up through a cultivation of

---

[39] Wagner, *My New Job*, 108.
[40] Wagner, *My New Job*, 107.
[41] Wagner, *My New Job*, 107.

breathing that ideally brings the two together as an autonomous subject.[42] What Wagner gives us are the systems and affects of labour that demand two other kinds of breath, the biological and the economic. The figured subject is reproducing itself as productive and excessive, coming into contact with the apparatus of capital and functioning as an embodied yet often refractory device of it.

The body is more than once described as "Bone-basket": "To share My cold What is in / My basket Bone-basket / With the other breathers / Workers."[43] From this there is a hint of a kind of class consciousness, as unity of the working class is figured as the solidarity of breath with itself, as in-breath gives way to out-breath, to form unity with other breathers/workers. We see this offset formally on the page with lines in isolating space, regimented and often curtailed. A voice is speaking from within a system, as we repeatedly see now in this collection. Hierarchies are not torn down, but by the particularity of voice and acts of the body, rehearsals for more revolutionary, or at least disruptive, modes of being are sedimenting too. This embodied subject is at work, in its corridors and angles, but is aware of these orientations and speaking back to them: "I will re-orient now I will claymation."[44]

The speaker of the poem makes her body re-form and hide in strange places in the workplace, a kind of resistance which is not organized around revolutionary possibilities, but which is rather a somatic awareness of becoming shaped by work. The disciplinary folding still takes hold of the body, and yet in the final stages, with a Freudian return to the womb with, "I was bornt / I stood on the street / With the hookers / Who were selling/ Disappear into a hole/ Into Mama/ but come back out. / Go in, boys. / Go in and stay there," we see that the body, with its embodied possibilities, is the ultimate hiding place for problems with work.[45] What's more, by extending these crafted scenes of wage work into a political currency with sex work, which all disappears into "a"

---

[42] Luce Irigaray, *Between East and West: From Singularity to Community* (New York: Columbia University Press, 2002).

[43] Wagner, *My New Job*, 108.

[44] Wagner, *My New Job*, 112.

[45] Wagner, *My New Job*, 114. "With the hookers": Were it not for the various mentions of 'hooks' pulling the speaker or being effused by them in the poem, this term for sex worker would grate. Instead this form of labour is homophonically brought into the context of erroneous organs and appliances of the workplace.

hole, Wagner makes the embodied knowledge of work, and the somatically felt corruptions of value and exchange of labour time, relevant to
the feminist issue of what Kathi Weeks calls "gynocentric ethic of care"
and caring labour.[46] This playing out of work ethics and labour politics
on various components of the feminized body—especially as connected
to ethics of sex work and sex *as* work—is something we see more of in
Wagner's next collection, which I will attend to now, while continuing to
elaborate the framing device of posture.

NERVOUS DEVICE, THE BOUNDING LINE AND THE AFFECTIVE SURPLUS OF POETRY PERFORMANCE

So far Wagner's poetics has offered a means of tracing the postures of
a human body in relation to acts of work, or as figured by work, that
shows how biopolitical traffic continues flesh into capital and labour back
into flesh. It has transpired that paradoxically, the more specifically the
body is defined, the more vulnerable it appears to manipulation as mere
value, and therefore the more de-specified and ill-defined it becomes.
Or paradoxically, the more specifically the body is defined, the more
exquisitely sensitized it appears to the disciplinarity of neoliberal labour
economies, a disciplinarity which de–specifies, disrupts, de–locates and
distributes the subject. Yet through posture, I read in Wagner's work
peculiar alignments that make this entrapment of the body apparent, and
potentially resistant.

In the rest of this chapter, I will interrogate this tendency of 'peculiar alignments' in Wagner's work, and read the 'bounding lines' within
and around the lines of definition that are drawn around an embodied
subject from gathered meaning rather than prescribed categories. In
doing so I hope to develop what posture offers as a line of definition
that figures an embodied subject as a radical mediator of work-time.
I want to suggest that Wagner's poetics, and in particular her later collection, *Nervous Device* shores up a special kind of *bounding line* for the
body, one which cannot be resolved as an effect of value. The poems in
Nervous Device, I will argue, push us to consider embodied thresholds
of persona and gesture which exist prior to and in antagonism with their
various articulations as commodifiable and socially coded. In the poem

[46]Weeks, *The Problem with Work*, 66.

"Another Human Made Me Come," for example, there is a pleasure being created at specific, sensuous contact points that define one body from another; indeed, taking the title one way, it is the contact with one body that 'makes' the other body. Erotic arousal creates an innovative knowledge of the body: "postdimensional, where I contacted you / unprepare yourself."[47] What we can take from this might be that the sense that the matter of our bodies is what enables us to comprehend environments. Our bodies, rather than formless pieces of matter, are sensitive interfaces with multifarious means of knowledge-making in collaboration with the world.[48]

> In other time I slept backwards
> swam quiet having my clit provoked
> and fingers inside doing what
> what, I could not attend the ballet
> time befriends horned
> fog to leave her workings agitate
> inside whorl room upon room.[49]

Here the subject is being drawn by sexual pleasure as a set of environments and interfaces, with some self-composition. The body shares lines and angles with exterior and interior architectures while sexual encounter is the processes of assimilating to and interacting with these boundaries. For Wagner, throughout this collection, sex, as an autoerotic, penetrative and more discursive set of practices, brings much of the political questions of affective labour, the economic value of wage labour, as well as the phenomenological orientation of the body in relation to other bodies and substances, plus poetic intimacy, into one complex concern. What is more, what particularizes one thing from another in *Nervous Device* is not *just* the texturing of social reality, nor the discretisation of resources for market forces to evaluate and optimize; that is, Wagner's poetry proposes thresholds which are not only a function of social construction or markets. Wagner investigates thresholds that are material and embodied, erotic and sensual, and which are never resistless to the ordering power of capital.

---

[47]Wagner, *Nervous Device*, 51.

[48]Karen Barad, *Meeting the Universe Halfway: Quantum Physics and the Entanglement of Matter and Meaning* (Durham: Duke University Press, 2007).

[49]Wagner, *Nervous Device*, 51.

The first section of the "Notes and Acknowledgements" for *Nervous Device* features a particularly arresting invocation of such embodied thresholds.[50] In this text gender distinctions, populations, and temporalities through linguistic pronouns are interchanged, showing fluidity but also distinguishable relations.

> The book's working title, "The Bounding Line," quotes the catalogue essay for William Blake's only exhibition, a failure staged above his brother's hosiery show in Golden Square. In the essay, Blake defends the importance of the bounding line for differentiating figures. When Jem Sportsman interviewed me and asked me about audience and what is the bounding line, at some point I discussed my tilted cervix and said that "if you" – if she – "put in" his "finger just a few inches" she would "feel it – here –" and then I stuck out my fist and had him put her finger inside it which freaked him out though not as much as if I'd offered her my vagina to put his finger in. Later in the interview we referred back to that moment – when I wanted (and she went along) to imply to the audience that we was putting his finger in my vagina and touching my cervix – we said "for the sake of the interview of course" "yes of course, for the sake of the interview, heh heh," to imply boundary.[51]

The text brings into agitated interplay the boundary between cultural producer and cultural consumer ("asked me about audience"); the boundary between the inside and the outside of bodies (so that both a "cervix" and part of a "fist" may be "inside"); the fixity ("tilted") and the fluidity ("putting his finger in my vagina") of genital embodiment; the production and policing of gender ("had him put her figure inside of it"); the ecstatic conflation of agencies in action ("we were"); and the testing and crossing of social boundaries ("freaked him out") and the reiteration of taboo where transgressions have occurred ("heh heh").

The scenario described above is a telling framing device for Wagner's poetics in that there is a scene of encounter and interaction. Using Blake's critical concepts relating to the "bounding line," which Wagner

---

[50]The text has elsewhere appeared as a poem. See Catherine Wagner, "The Bounding Line," 22 September 2010, electiveaffinitiesusa.blogspot.co.uk/2010/09/catherine-wagner.html, accessed 15 April 2018.

[51]Wagner, *Nervous Device*, IX.

offers as a model, there are two bodies fielding their differentiations and navigating as a means to be in common through their particularity (finger, cervix, humour, misunderstanding). Boundaries of physical interfaces and of social negotiation are *felt* if not breached. Boundaries are problematized, not blurred, while a shared agency sporadically becomes possible ("we was"). In the scene overall we have a metonymic shift between figures, metaphors and their interactions. The fist is a metaphor for the vagina, signalling a transference between public and private, between acceptable and taboo. The fist becomes the vagina, and the vagina is thereby a metaphor and proxy for the fist: an image of militant feminist empowerment; its penetration is a metaphor for the activity of the audience becoming a force and a feeling in the poem/poet; this itself is a figurative construct of the bounding line, which is coenesthetically the defining shape of a form.

The social site of poetry here is viewed as a meeting point with a given eroticism; the schema of audience and poet is a bodily interaction that produces new specific forms, and new meanings. Through this scene, as well as being situated in Wagner's poetics of bodies being-in-relation, to use Irigaray's term, we are also introduced to the economy of affective labour in the (poetry) performance.[52] We also see how Wagner *postures* the extended politics that forms between performance and the mechanisms by which gender is produced, and reproduced, in domestic and wage-labour, as well as in the affective labour of sexual relations.

One way of thinking this out is to say that the poet's body *hosts* the audience's perception and presence. There are many examples in the text of analogues between poem and a portion of the body as it becomes an 'accommodating' shape. For example this from "Make a Machine for Mastering Self":

> You know how to make an asshole
> With your fingers touching?
> That's cherry-picking stance[53]

---

[52] Irigaray, *Between East and West*, 100.
[53] Wagner, *Nervous Device*, 37.

And this from "Regarding the Use-Value and Exchange Value of Orgasms, with a List of Orgasm Analogues":

> If this poem is not desirable
> But you've made yourself read it
>
> ......
>
> Dear friend, that's a condom, you've
> Inoculated your cock against insanity
> (I'm figuring the reader as male, why'd
> I do that)—friend, there's a reason
> (Really have to pee now)
> To let pleasure be.[54]

Here we see gestures pointing towards the affective labour of sex being put into a continuum with, and as a condition of, the poem's productivity. In other words, sex, which in its many facets is accounted for by feminist critique to be a form of work and social reproduction,[55] is metaphorically interchangeable with the function of the poem, in that it becomes a space of encounter where genders, bodies and subject positions orientate and sedimentally form. Similarly, as with the "Notes and Acknowledgements," the environment of the poem becomes a space of both sexual encounter and of theatrically-based acts of gender production. (What's more, the irresistible image of cherry-picker and the frame of mechanic the crane suggests the shape of a pointing arm or a bent body.)

Overall what is building in this reading of Wagner's work is a critique of how women's bodies are constituted in relation to patriarchal capitalism as commodities of exchange and circulation, that sees the body as portions of affects and matter in cycles of value with micro-macro interfaces. As Irigaray describes, "Women-as-commodities are thus subject to a schism that divides them into the categories of usefulness and exchange value; into matter-body and an envelope that is precious but impenetrable, ungraspable, and not susceptible to appropriation by women

---

[54]Wagner, *Nervous Device*, 45.

[55]Silvia Federici, "On Sexuality as Work," *The Commoner*, 2012, www.commoner.org.uk/wp-content/uploads/2012/02/05-federici.pdf.

themselves; into private use and social use."[56] In Wagner's poetics the body that is formed through sexual encounter, at work in the office, on the yoga mat, or at the point of composing and performing poetry, are all in multiple entanglements with capital, which can be traced in my reading, through posture, and it is posture that makes the historicity of these politics apparent and therefore potentially resisted.

In the poem "Innocent Money" we see performance figured through a metonymic scenario of both the work of love and sex, and the affective labour of performance; the audience is a lover and the lover is an audience. Here the performative aspects of poetry, the poetry reading, and the work *of* the poem are figured as a theatre of exchange and encounter:

> Your lover is beyond
> the proscenium arch
> (you are audience
>   and play in your own play).
> She is performing,
> She is/I am handling
> my carcass
> with strings.
> We seek admiration.[57]

This feels like a wry or even cynical point of making social performance and sexual performance interchangeable with the economic currency of women's discursive flesh and labour. But this illustration of the turbulent flows of feminized capital brings much of the politics of performance (for instance the poetry reading) and the performance of gender into dialogue with feminist critiques of wage work. In other words, it is a sort of posturing meta-criticism. It ends with, "Actually you are / controlling my carcass," suggesting that the reader/audience, as a point of interaction and subversive-conviviality, provides the vitalism necessary for the poet/poem to exist, not without insinuating that women's bodies are in a struggle to be self-defining outside patriarchal needs and desires.[58]

---

[56] Luce Irigaray, *This Sex Which Is Not One*, translated by Catherine Porter and Carolyn Burke (Ithaca, NY: Cornell University Press, 1985), 176.

[57] Wagner, *Nervous Device*, 12.

[58] Wagner, *Nervous Device*, 13.

While *Nervous Device* often probes the biological and social interactions that produce meanings via their relations, in "Innocent Money" social performance and sexual performance are explicitly interchangeable, reminding us that scenes of reproduction have mutual counterparts in public and private, workplace and domestic contexts.

> At some point
>   early in the playing
> I enter my carcass
>   to embrace you
>   – Our proscenium[59]

The use of the word *carcass* as opposed to *body* suggests that what animates it is not herself; this is not, at this moment, an autonomous body. The audience, the lover and the activity of performance are what animate it in a gesture that sites the performance close to the role of a stripper or other forms of sex work:

> I must maintain
>   our separation, boys
> so that you will continue
>   to invest.[60]

The verb "to invest" is used to describe relationship of the audience, or "boys," to the performer. The assertion of innocence in the title "Innocent Money" must be taken ironically (there is no such thing as innocent money) but the economic exchange is being figured as sex work in a move that once again insists a relation of capital to erotic encounter and exchange. Yet in the embodied knowledges of performance and exchange, a self-knowledge outside patriarcho-capital is gestured towards.

What's crucial here is the realized title for the collection, *Nervous Device*, in comparison to the Blakean working title, *The Bounding Line*. The nervous device, we might imagine, is both the poem and the body of the performer. Both are nerve-filled environments, loaded with meeting points and portals of re/orientation; communicative, affective, and a dynamic between audience, poet and text. A 'device' is functional, but its

[59]Wagner, *Nervous Device*, 13.
[60]Wagner, *Nervous Device*, 12.

nervousness makes it *adaptive* in accordance with its environment. This a sequence of possibilities I have described in Wagner's poetry where the 'worker' is redetermined as a set of fleshy nodes and socially descriptive gestures within the workplace, yet with transformative potential via its mattering. Within the history of nervousness presented here then, there is the concept of the bounding line, which offers more meaning to the sense of potential adaptiveness through particular and peculiar nerves, or in other words, through affects and connected energies of the orientating body.

Simply put, the bounding line is a graphic line, or the nature of a figure's drawn outline, that defines a shape. The term has a greater complexity in that the line also provides an ontic relationality between forms and the phenomenological event of forms. In other words, it is the fact of the *line* that distinguishes between forms, yet it is *bounding* in that it is a communicative border that creates meditative temporal and material milieu between forms and formations. The line needs to be explicit in order for it to transmit potential connections. This stylistic methodology for mark-making is part of the expanded aesthetics surrounding Blake's art, poetry and philosophy. The bounding line is not only what maps out the various forms on the page, but also a metaphysical principle. The bounding line is what works within the world to crucially discriminate one thing from another:

> How do we distinguish the oak from the beech, the horse from the ox, but by the bounding line? How do we distinguish one face or countenance from another, but by the bounding line and its infinite inflexions and movements? [...] What is it that distinguishes honesty from knavery, but the hard wiry line of rectitude and certainty in the actions and intentions. Leave out this line and you leave out life itself.[61]

Blake's "definite and the determinate" form is a differential state that means virtual realities and actual worlds can communicate, making it possible for new realities to emerge. As in *The Book of Los*, such lines distinguish past and future, actual and possible, human and god, with both being alive and active to each other.[62] The political aesthetics of the

---

[61] Philadelphia Museum of Art, *William Blake: A Descriptive Catalogue of an Exhibition of the Works of William Blake Selected from Collections in the United States* (Philadelphia: Philadelphia Museum of Art, 1939), archive.org/details/williamblakedesc00phil, accessed 15 April 2018.

[62] Peter Otto, "Politics, Aesthetics, and Blake's 'Bounding Line,'" *Word & Image*, vol. 26, no. 2 (26 March 2010), 172–185, https://doi.org/10.1080/02666280902944528.

bounding line therefore translate as clarity of differentiation; it is creative in that it produces *particularities*. For Blake it is through particularity of body and being that things can relate to each other and be in common, as is explained by Saree Makdisi:

> The freedom offered by our being in common, is an infinite capacity for particularity — not individuality, which for Blake is a form of confinement and limitation, but particularity, always becoming anew, tracing and retracing different trajectories of actualisation.[63]

How does this particularity relate to posture as I have been figuring it here? Posture is a sedimented manifestation of labour and particular, repeated experiences, while posturing has been understood as the performative acts that dramatize, subvert and cite social expression, and that orientate a body to its habits, gender and sexuality. Both notions of posture play out in the poetics of Wagner as gender epistemes that relate to acts of material and immaterial labour. Therefore, on one hand we can say that, in view of patriarchal capitalism's assimilating power over subjects and docile bodies, there is a bounding line around the worker, which I have called posture, and even if capital is capable of dissolving the worker into just a bundle of values, posture is in a continuum with every other posture and backbone. This continuum then is also: historical and future figures of work; virtual and symbolic, physical and material forms; particular and collective; and loaded with potential for the individual to rhythmically redescribe themselves.

CONCLUSION

In this chapter I have attempted to figure posture as meaningful signification of a body, which is a combination of matter and form, and through which we can read a politics of work-time in correlation with performances of gendered subjectivity. By interpreting a body as a historical situation within which efforts, identities, gestures and affects have sedimented, I have located in Wagner's poetics the particularities of a descriptive body in various forms of work that unfolds loops of

---

[63] Saree Makdisi, *William Blake and the Impossible History of the 1790s* (Chicago: University of Chicago Press, 2003), 320.

orientation and makes its peculiar acts of work and performance excessively meaningful.

With Blake's bounding line, the actual and the virtual can communicate, as can the infinite and the particular, and in the resonance between them a possibility emerges which exceeds the social imaginary and its regimentation by capital. Lines of bodies and lines of poetry in Wagner's two collections systematically become environmental, breathing into each other and distinguishing each other. A line of poetry, as a gesture of differentiation, builds the form of the poem overall. The poem, in its nervousness, aligns and orientates the poet into conditions and positions, making them ornate or roughly unfinished. Posture is the line that the body is being shaped into by mannerisms, behaviour and the time-actions of work, and Blake's image-making is analogous with posture in that it shows a political conversion of effort into form.

The "minute particularity" of the bounding line, revealed in pictured forms, translates to the points of matter that mark the figure of the worker in space and time. What Wagner's work draws is the determinate line of this figure, a wriggling, dense darkness that contains all the actual disintegration, dislocation and indeterminacy suffered by this figure, yet embodies them as infinite possibilities to resist capital and orders of patriarchy as systems of domination, which offer destructive ways for things to be in common where everything is related primarily by value. A body's expressive and dynamic matter, as well as its corporeal form as orientated posture, is not only an index of historical formations, but a responsive, nervous and bounding, set of perceptions that are capable of infinite relations and reorientations. Wagner describes this perfectly in 'Rain Cog':

> Someone whose symbolic
> Presence makes the
> Liquid flush from pores in
> My vaginal skin.   There.
>
> ......
>
> A nervous device, a communicator
> The juice waits stupidly.[64]

---

[64]Wagner, *Nervous Device*, 9.

WORKS CITED

Ahmed, Sara. "Orientations Matter." In *New Materialisms: Ontology, Agency, and Politics*, edited by Diana Coole and Samantha Frost. Durham: Duke University Press, 2010.

Barad, Karen. *Meeting the Universe Halfway: Quantum Physics and the Entanglement of Matter and Meaning*. Durham: Duke University Press, 2007.

Benjamin, Walter. *Understanding Brecht* (New ed.). London: Verso, 2003.

Blackman, Lisa. *The Body: The Key Concepts*. Oxford and New York: Berg, 2008.

Braidotti, Rosi. *Metamorphoses: Towards a Materialist Theory of Becoming*. Cambridge: Polity Press, 2002.

Butler, Judith. "Performative Acts and Gender Constitution: An Essay in Phenomenology and Feminist Theory." *Theatre Journal*, vol. 40, no. 4 (1988). https://doi.org/10.2307/3207893.

Cooper, Melinda. *Life as Surplus: Biotechnology and Capitalism in the Neoliberal Era*. Seattle: University of Washington Press, 2008.

Federici, Silvia. "On Sexuality as Work." *The Commoner*, 2012. www.commoner. org.uk/wp-content/uploads/2012/02/05-federici.pdf. Accessed 15 April 2018.

Foucault, Michel. *Discipline and Punish: The Birth of the Prison* (1975). Translated by Alan Sheridan (1977). New York: Vintage Books, 1977.

Haraway, Donna. "Situated Knowledges: The Science Question in Feminism and the Privilege of Partial Perspective." *Feminist Studies*, vol. 14, no. 3 (1 October 1988), 575–599. https://doi.org/10.2307/3178066.

Irigaray, Luce. *Between East and West: From Singularity to Community* (1999). Translated by Stephen Pluhácek (2002). New York: Columbia University Press, 2002.

———. *This Sex Which Is Not One* (1977). Translated by Catherine Porter and Carolyn Burke (1985). Ithaca: Cornell University Press, 1985.

Makdisi, Saree. *William Blake and the Impossible History of the 1790s*. Chicago: University of Chicago Press, 2003.

Merleau-Ponty, Maurice. *Phenomenology of Perception* (1945). Translated by Donald A. Andes (2012). New York: Routledge, 2012.

Otto, Peter. "Politics, Aesthetics, and Blake's 'Bounding Line.'" *Word & Image*, vol. 26, no. 2 (26 March 2010), 172–185. https://doi.org/10.1080/02666280902944528.

Parisi, Luciana, and Tiziana Terranova. "Heat-Death: Emergence and Control in Genetic Engineering and Artificial Life." *CTheory* (10 May 2000): 5–10.

Philadelphia Museum of Art. *William Blake: A Descriptive Catalogue of an Exhibition f the Works of William Blake Selected from Collections in the United States*. Philadelphia: Philadelphia Museum of Art, 1939. archive.org/details/williamblakedesc00phil. Accessed 15 April 2018.

Robertson, Lisa. *Nilling: Prose*. Toronto: Book Thug, 2012.

Schumacher, John A. *Human Posture: The Nature of Inquiry*. New York: SUNY Press, 1989.

Wagner, Catherine. *Nervous Device*. San Francisco: City Lights Books, 2012.

———. *Macular Hole*. Albany: Fence Books, 2004.

———. *My New Job*. Albany: Fence Books, 2009.

———. "Poetic Labor Project: Catherine Wagner." 17 July 2012. labday2010. blogspot.co.uk/2012/07/catherine-wagner.html. Accessed 27 November 2015.

Weeks, Kathi. *The Problem with Work*. Durham and London: Duke University Press, 2011.

Wilkinson, John. "Cadence." *Reality Studios*, vol. 9, nos. 1–4 (1987).

PART II

Reflections

CHAPTER 13

The Exploit:
Affective Labor and Poetry at the University

Catherine Wagner with David Boeving, Sylvia Chan, Alex Cintron, Emily Corwin, Rachel Galvin, Courtney Kalmbach, Jessica Lowenthal, Jessica Marshall, rob mclennan, Ian Schoultz, Chelsea Tadeyeske, Alison Thompson, Amy Toland, Rodrigo Toscano, Jo Lindsay Walton, and Others

The word-bank I was working with felt very restrictive.
> Emily Corwin, student in my graduate poetry workshop

I love poetry, but why doesn't reading, thinking, and writing about poetry in this context feel good?
> Fred Moten, *The Undercommons*

No world is intact / and no one cares about you.
> Alice Notley, "No World Is Intact," *Grave of Light*

C. Wagner (✉)
Miami University, Oxford, OH, USA

© The Author(s) 2019
J. L. Walton and E. Luker (eds.), *Poetry and Work*,
Modern and Contemporary Poetry and Poetics,
https://doi.org/10.1007/978-3-030-26125-2_13

The Exploit is a collaborative project about poetry and labor in the academy. I framed the project to myself as a didactic joke, though not a very funny one. Poetry-making in the academy may, under the right conditions, provide a haven for modeling less-alienated forms of affective labor.[1] But The Exploit produced a poetry-making zone that emphasized alienating hierarchies. It tried to align creative production with the imperatives that drive the contemporary university: productivity and return on investment. To increase participants' efficiency, poetic labor performed for the Exploit project was to be integrated or fused with the labor we were already performing for our jobs and classes. At different stages, the Exploit has involved a contingent part-time faculty member, various editors and readers, and students in my graduate poetry workshop. As an instance of affective labor—as an example, in Hardt and Negri's terms, of the production or modification of affective experience—this project succeeded in making all of us feel bad.[2]

LABOR IN THE CORPORATE UNIVERSITY

The context for the project is the corporatization of the contemporary university. Like many universities, my workplace, Miami University, has moved to an RCM (Responsibility-Centered or Resource-Centered Management) model, a budget system in which individual units are directly responsible for the revenues and costs generated within their operation.[3] It is incumbent on each unit to find ways to cut costs and increase revenue. The implicit assumption that every sector of the contemporary university should be 'financially viable' can have a range of negative effects on the core mission of education and research, perhaps

---

[1] "Every day that you go into your classroom, you have a chance not to issue the call to order, and then to see what happens." Fred Moten and Stefano Harney, *The Undercommons: Fugitive Planning and Black Study* (Wivenhoe, New York, and Port Watson: Minor Compositions, 2013), 127, www.minorcompositions.info/wp-content/uploads/2013/04/undercommons-web.pdf.

[2] Michael Hardt and Antonio Negri, *Multitude: War and Democracy in the Age of Empire* (New York: Penguin, 2004), 108.

[3] Jennifer Cohen, Theresa Kulbaga, and Cathy Wagner, "Imperial Partitioning in the Neoliberal University," *World Social and Economic Review of Contemporary Policy Issues*, no. 8 (April 2017), 60–77, wer.worldeconomicsassociation.org/papers/imperial-partitioning-in-the-neoliberal-university/.

especially in humanities departments. The percentage of the Miami budget spent on instruction is only about 26%—a surprisingly low figure, given the tendency of administrators and state legislators to point to faculty salaries as significant cost drivers—and about average for public universities. State funding cuts, administrative bloat, student recruitment, construction, and athletics divert funding from universities' core mission of education and research. Faculty do their own marketing to keep programs afloat and are encouraged to create revenue-seeking programs. At Miami, faculty were encouraged to create a new revenue-generating Low-Residency MFA, which we are marketing and advertising ourselves, and because all programs are funded according to enrollment, we market all of our degrees, maintaining an active social media presence. As Katie J. Hogan and Michelle A. Massé explain in a book on the gendered "servicification" of the contemporary university, new budget models require faculty to find "not only one's inner secretary but one's inner accountant, one's inner fund-raiser, one's inner IT specialist, and one's inner travel agent."[4]

Alongside the marketing and other service activities, faculty still do a lot of teaching. But the bulk of teaching labor these days has been pushed onto graduate students and contingent faculty. "Students and contingent faculty serve as cheap sources of campus labor so that colleges and universities can direct funds toward improving campus facilities and sports complexes, all in the name of recruitment, retention, and marketing," Hogan and Massé explain.[5] Tenure-line faculty positions have shrunk by almost half at Miami since the 2008 crash, though the English department serves just as many majors. Because lower-paid contingent faculty should not be expected to do service (though at some institutions they do), tenure-line faculty are responsible for much more administrative work than formerly. New assessment and marketing initiatives add to the advising, curricular revision, and governance work formerly done by twice the number of full-time faculty. Faculty in my department, short on time to spend on new marketing imperatives, hire unpaid interns to do publicity work—an ethically sketchy situation in

---

[4] Katie J. Hogan and Michelle A. Massé, *Over Ten Million Served: Gendered Service in Language and Literature Workplaces* (Albany, NY: State University of New York Press, 2010), 10.

[5] Hogan and Massé, *Over Ten Million*, 11.

which students use student loan money to pay for the opportunity to provide free labor. Many students apply for these internships, hoping to gain experience that will give them a leg up on the job market. Similarly, graduate students apply for the opportunity to be exploited as underpaid "teaching assistants." They do it to find community and mentorship, to learn the ropes about networking and publishing, and to find a haven for writing, And teaching, of course, is a calling; to ask to be paid decently for it might seem tacky. A manifesto written for the MLA Subconference on Pedagogy in 2014 claimed that "adjuncts and especially graduate students are frequently told that what we do is not 'work'— not a job but a vocation, not a task but a project, not a wage relation but a labor of love."[6] Per-credit-hour faculty and graduate students in creative writing put up with low wages because, like their employers, they believe that "occupational commitment [...] in the arts cannot be matched to the monetary considerations of a market economy of exchange."[7]

Employers also benefit from "the promotion of the collaborative classroom," which, as Sarah Brouillette explains, "has tended to delink research expertise from teaching. The collaborative or 'decentered' classroom can be run by the students themselves, or managed by adjunct workers with little capacity to conduct research and bring it to bear on their teaching [...] Though the decentered classroom-cum-network may be premised upon a democratic desire to unsettle the presumption of the individual's singular authority, this unsettling poses no real threat."[8] No real threat to institutional inequalities that exploit a vulnerable population, paying poverty wages for labor that is, more and more often, characterized as facilitation of learning rather than as teaching. The labor of education is displaced onto easily substitutable facilitators, and from there, onto the student who is now deemed to have ownership over their own learning process—an ownership that requires them to take out

---

[6] Bennett Carpenter, Laura Goldblatt, Lenora Hanson, Anna Vitale, Karim Wissa, and Andrew Yale, "Feces on the Philosophy of History! A Manifesto of the MLA Subconference," *Pedagogy*, no. 3 (10 October 2014), 386.

[7] Pierre-Michel Menger, "Artistic Labor Markets: Contingent Work, Excess Supply and Occupational Risk Management," in *Handbook of the Economics of Art and Culture, Volume 1*, ed. Victor A. Ginsburgh and David Throsby (Amsterdam: Elsevier, 2006), 776.

[8] Sarah Brouillette, "Academic Labor, the Aesthetics of Management, and the Promise of Autonomous Work," *Nonsite*, no. 9 (1 May 2013), nonsite.org/article/academic-labor-the-aesthetics-of-management-and-the-promise-of-autonomous-work.

student loans to pay the highest tuitions in history, not for being taught by decently paid experts, but for having their learning facilitated by an underclass making poverty wages.

FIRST HACK

Systemic changes in academe formed the background for the Exploit, but the project was also selfishly personal. I found myself, even before becoming director of creative writing, spending minimal time on teaching and writing in comparison to time spent on public relations and marketing, filling out spreadsheets, and doing various assessments and metrics tasks to help administrators figure out how to reallocate resources. I got burned out. I needed to do some reallocating myself. How could I increase my efficiency? The project's title plays on the sense of an *exploit* as a *hack*, in the sense used by IT workers—taking advantage of a flaw in a system, or using something in a way that its designers never anticipated.[9] Could I combine resources to achieve the teaching and research outcomes expected of me? Could I win/win? Where was the low-hanging fruit? Was it in the classroom?

The first iteration of the Exploit, the first 'hack' attempt, was a collaboration with a contingent faculty member who was teaching the Introduction to Creative Writing class I normally taught—I was on leave. I hoped to exploit vulnerable points in the system to accomplish three goals. First, selfishly, to conserve the energy and labor I would spend generating the publications that I could use to justify the slightly reduced teaching load reserved for research-active tenure-line faculty and allowing me eventually to seek promotion. Second, I hoped that the project might somehow benefit my colleague. And third, in a culture in which hierarchies are usually only acknowledged silently, I wanted us to openly assess the ways that our positionality inflected our relationship.

While cost-cutting and academic entrepreneurialism have pushed new types of labor such as marketing onto faculty, the labor of teaching and research has increasingly been pushed onto underpaid

[9] See Hackers Online Club, en.wikipedia.org/wiki/Exploit_(computer_security), hackersonlineclub.com/exploits/; and Anonymous, "Hackers & Crackers," *Maximum Security*, 4th ed. (Indianapolis: Que, 18 November 2002), www.informit.com/articles/article.aspx?p=30048&seqNum=3.

or unpaid contingent faculty, interns, and assistant researchers. Acknowledging this shift in labor practices, I set out to do poetic 'research' with a model partially borrowed from the sciences, in which parties of lower status work for less compensation and credit than the higher-status collaborator receives. The hack was intended to underline the absurdity of being paid my associate-professor salary of $66,000 to be on research leave while someone else taught my classes for $2400 each (without the medical insurance, pension benefits, or job security I continued to enjoy).

I invited the poet Amy Toland, a former graduate student who was teaching my Introduction to Creative Writing class, to work with me on a dialogue, in part poetic, about compensation: what did we owe to one another? What kind of compensation was appropriate to our relationship and our project? Could the Exploit serve us both? Amy would contribute research and writing to the project, and I could offer Amy work experience (of a sort) and cultural capital (to the extent that I have some—that is, the piece might eventually be published and Amy could put it on her CV). I wanted to pay Amy in addition, but Amy refused. She objected to the project's underlining of the exploitative terms of its context. As she wrote to me: "We've agreed about the […] overarching economic hierarchies that surround our relationship and impact the way we approach this project. Why then, introduce an additional hierarchy? […] This type of gesture only serves to emphasize the inequality that we're questioning."[10] Amy also did not feel 'exploited' by me or by Miami because she believed she had made an informed choice. I came to understand that I had built the first iteration of the Exploit on the rather insulting assumption that Amy was not aware of her situation, that she had chosen it because she was not fully an agent in her working life. The project's terms cast her as an abject partner. Our collaboration soon trailed off, strained by our busy schedules and mutual affective discomfort. Amy did help me to produce some material for the project: we debated our positions via poems constructed out of materials we sent one another. Here's a collaborative poem made using a description of an automaton, a psalm translation by Thomas Wyatt, and a technical description of a cam:

---

[10] Amy Toland, email to author, 16 July 2014.

Autobiography of Meg Brandish (deceased)

As a device/toy/model relying on
the use of a snail/drop cam,
my rise slow, my drop or fall sudden,
I worked efficiently in one direction only
whereof plenteous ransom would come.
My voice was my borrow.
I, an eccentric, heartshaped character
lifting a forkful of food to my mouth—
the cam rotates my will
to rise, connected to my arm
by a wire link. When I fall
in cave of deep repair,
the cam rotates
a follower to rise. Watchman,
explain how the device raised
my desirous fork.

In lieu of compensation, I fed Amy's cats.

Second Hack

One morning in early spring of 2014, burnt out, I received a solicitation for work. In a grump about lacking time to write, I created a poem-template that could be adapted for submission to any magazine. I decided to try to use it to enroll editors and readers into the Exploit, and for the rest of the year sent out only the template poem, and only when I received a solicitation:

Notice

Catherine Wagner is a content provider who has been requested by David Boeving to deliver a work of poetry to be published in Bathhouse. While Bathhouse and David Boeving are not expected to compensate Wagner monetarily for her labor, it is possible to estimate that she will be paid $31.00 by Miami University for writing the present text, as poetry production is assessed as 'research' at the institution where she works and 33.3% of her time on the job is meant to be spent on research. Of the various solicits for content provision she has received in recent years, only the Poetry Foundation, an organization endowed by the Lilly pharmaceutical fortune, has offered monetary compensation for content generated by Wagner. Most arts-media organizations, lacking or rejecting

similar resources, process content through a set of vectors that is sometimes described as a gift economy, sometimes as a source of symbolic capital. These vectors move through the bodies of content providers, editors,
interns, and other workers, through the paper-producing trees, money
jobs, living rooms, office photocopiers, government agencies, inherited
funds and power plants that enable the processing of poetry in the marketplace. In a bid to use the percentage of her body and time occupied by
these vectors more efficiently, and to buff their surface areas to an agree-
able or disagreeable shine, Wagner is currently responding to solicits for
work with this text being processed by you. Wagner would like to express
gratitude here and now for your time and for the work you do.

The poem was an attempt to hack my publishing practice, exploiting
a weakness in the system in order to save time and to add line-items
(notated as duplicates) to my university Annual Activities Report. If
count mattered more than content, I'd make a show of switching my
focus to the count; more bang for my buck. Meanwhile, the poem tried
to draw attention to the material underpinnings of the 'gift economy'
poetry is often understood to be. Poems I send in response to solic-
itations are often taken, but this one was rejected by multiple places
(it did get taken by a few). *Touch the Donkey* editor rob mclennan told
me he "wondered whether the piece was meant as a slight to the edi-
tor/journal that had requested it"—perhaps I was complaining about
not being paid.[11] Rob's response resembles many collaborators' affective responses to the Exploit project: hot feelings unexpectedly emerged
around what I thought of as coldly ironic efforts to draw attention
to material systems of poetic production and distribution. Part of the
problem was that I'm not always affectively highly tuned, but I'll speculate on another reason: poetry-lovers love poetry in part because it
represents alternatives to the system on which our material existence
depends. Because poetry "has no remunerative value" it is, the claim
goes, "liberated from the orthodoxies that constrain just about every
other art form."[12] A focus on the economic underpinnings of the

---

[11] rob mcclennan, email to author.

[12] Kenneth Goldsmith, "I Look to Theory Only When I Realize That Somebody Has
Dedicated Their Entire Life to a Question I Have Only Fleetingly Considered: The
Purposes of Repurposing," Poetry Foundation, 1 April 2015, www.poetryfoundation.
org/poetrymagazine/articles/70209/i-look-to-theory-only-when-i-realize-that-some-
body-has-dedicated-their-entire-life-to-a-question-i-have-only-fleetingly-considered.

poetic 'gift economy' might, then, appear to be a devaluing or dismissal of the radical volunteerism that the production and distribution of poetry depends on. But the notion that, as Robert Graves said, "there's no money in poetry," is of use to capital: it sanctions the exploitation of workers' commitments to poetry, undervaluing them in ways that have material consequences.[13] At any rate, given that "Notice" was an attempt to take advantage of editors by encouraging them to use their time and material resources to publish the same poem that was appearing elsewhere, it's not surprising that the gratitude I tried to express was perceived as ironic.

THIRD HACK

Planning my spring 2015 graduate poetry workshop, I decided to retrofit for the Exploit project the semester-long collaborative assignment I often give to creative writing classes. Usually students develop the collaboration from the ground up with my help, but, recalling that I would be presenting a paper at an AWP panel on poetic labor in early April, I decided to make the collaboration part of the Exploit. I'd pass the buck to my class, asking students to collaborate with me on developing and presenting the paper, thus hacking the class and the panel at the same time. The students would research labor practices at the university and find ways to present the material; create poems, some of them collaborative; and present their work at AWP as my contribution to the panel. Their work toward the collaboration would do double-duty by earning them part of their grade for the class, and my teaching would merge with the work I would normally have spent outside of class writing a panel presentation. We agreed that any poems students produced as part of the project could be sent out for publication under the student's name as long as all parties involved in that particular collaboration agreed. Also, if students wanted to, they were free to use my name as collaborator regardless of the level of my participation in the making of the poem. Finally, I would approve the final version of material produced for the Exploit, though collaborators were free to revise their contributions for their own purposes afterward.

---

[13] Robert Graves interviewed by Kenneth Allsop, in Kenneth Allsop, *Scan* (London: Hodder and Stoughton, 1965), 32.

The affective tensions involved in the classroom iteration of the project were what finally led me to understand that The Exploit project's affective charge was not a side-effect, but a central component of it. The project's design derailed affective channels associated with the production of poetry. In the case of my class's Exploit, the fact that credit for the work would go to me even if my students' names and contributions were prominently featured meant that the students were being instrumentalized. The implicit endgame of a university creative writing class is the reverse of instrumentalization—or rather, students are encouraged to instrumentalize *themselves* by transforming their writing selves into author-selves. The goal is to help each student develop toward producing 'work of publishable quality,' and more broadly, developing their individual brand as a writer, so the creative writing instructor's affective labor tends to be geared toward promoting the individual self-actualization of the student. The creative writing classroom thus needs to be a "safe environment" in which the instructor is responsible for creating an "atmosphere of trust," a "less stressful writing environment" that "lower[s] students' anxiety" so that they build up "confidence in their own abilities."[14] Though I spent a good deal of time articulating project goals with the students, I struggled to create an atmosphere of trust. My collaborators were for the most part willing but unenthusiastic participants. They had good reason to be willing: my status in the setting was higher than theirs and they might stand to benefit if they pleased me. They also had good reason to be unenthusiastic, because although I let them know that they would be co-authors with me on the project, they were unable to view their participation as autonomously collaborative. Many of the poems the students produced for The Exploit project were overdetermined, ventriloquizing our theoretical readings, respectably but dispassionately fulfilling the prompts. I had unintentionally emphasized the poems' market value as exchange chips, the result of labor exchanged for grade. A surprising number of the students' poems were interesting, but mostly because they departed from assignment directives.[15]

[14] Liz Almond, "The Workshop Way," in *The Creative Writing Handbook: Techniques for New Writers*, ed. John Singleton and Mary Luckhurst (London: Macmillan, 1999), 18, 19.

[15] A poem the students wrote collaboratively and performed as part of the AWP presentation is attached as an appendix.

The Exploit project, because it highlighted students' lack of agency in a major part of the creative production the class required, foreclosed a convincing performance of affective labor on my part.[16] Eventually I realized that despite some attempts to mitigate the exploitation it enacted, The Exploit, in a small way, mimicked contemporary conceptualist projects that "outsource" the labor of participants of lower status.[17] Although the point of such projects might be to draw an audience's attention to discomfiting inequities, the social or economic credit accumulated redounds to the name of the artist while the inequity is reproduced. Like any good "American neo-liberal," I was using The Exploit to expand market-oriented thinking into "domains of behavior or conduct which were not market forms of behavior or conduct."[18]

The realms where poetry is produced and circulated, though influenced by market forces, are not necessarily dominated by them. Reflecting on the Exploit may help me move toward what Kathi Weeks describes as "a vision of what subjects in relation could become in contrast to what they are" in the university environment.[19] An exploit has at least three potential modes: *exploitation* (benefitting unfairly from someone else's work), *hack* (in the sense used by IT workers—taking advantage of a flaw in a system), and *adventure* (a bold or daring act; a lark or escapade). The project's first iterations have explored only the first two modes. Reimagining it as adventure for a future version will help me find ways to redeploy the affective circuits that flash alongside the production

---

[16] Because negative course evaluations can result in job loss, contingent faculty may be especially motivated to engineer a "safe," low-stress classroom atmosphere—thus participating in an affective circuit that is a far cry from the "autonomous circuits of valorization" Michael Hardt has described as liberatory. Faculty with more security may be able to take more pedagogical risks. See "Contingent Appointments and the Academic Profession," American Association of University Professors (2014), 175.

[17] Kristian von Hornsleth's "Homeless Tracker" project, for example: hornslethhomelesstracker.com/.

[18] Michel Foucault, *The Birth of Biopolitics: Lectures at the Collège de France, 1978–1979*, translated by Graham Burchell (New York: Picador, 2010), 267; www.aaup.org/file/Contingent%20Appointment.pdf; and Michael Hardt, "Affective Labor," *boundary 2*, vol. 26, no. 2 (Summer 1999), 100.

[19] Kathi Weeks, *The Problem with Work: Feminism, Marxism, Antiwork Politics, and Postwork Imaginaries* (Durham, NC: Duke University Press, 2011), 247.

and distribution of poetry in the academy toward "new forms of cooperation [...] outside the logic of capital and the market."[20]

THE EXPLOIT

(By ENG 651 graduate students Alex Cintron, Emily Corwin, Courtney Kalmbach, Jessica Marshall, Ian Schoultz, Chelsea Tadeyeske, and Alison Thompson).

I forgave
We for
We are my
We are Miami
Mes amis
I'm going to use
Hey, olvidado
My body remembers
I'm going to crack the joint open
I'm going to rub the sore eye out
I'm going to slurp down some cheap wine then grade five more essays
I'm going to burn my killed trees
I'm going to use students to use you
I'm going to use poems to whoa me
I'm going to be useful to whoa me
I'm going back to work hunchbacked
I'm going to eat drugs for maintenance
I'm going to spill into this lumbering form
Add junk
Part-time
Full
Assist
Full of going up up up
Hey, olvidado
We will sleep for three hours then teach composition
I will be newfangled and ugly
I will be former

---

[20] Silvia Federici, *Revolution at Point Zero: Housework, Reproduction, and the Feminist Struggle* (Oakland: PM Press, 2012), 111.

I will be fog
I carry yellow legal pads, battery cord, office keys, smelly little places
the armpit the
    tongue, whiteboard markers, chapstick, tension in my shoulders
I carry tic tacs, aspirin, kleenex, black coffee, clenched belly, zantac,
paper clips, ten
    hours stuck on to gleaming cyber world
We forgive the math department for switching rooms without
informing proper channels
We forget to eat lunch or breakfast we forget to pick up a protein for
dinner
We forget what the weather is doing in windowless offices
We add junk
We part
We full profess
We assist
I add junk to my resume
I adjunct after my master's
I contract no light at the bottom of higher ed
I contract a windowless whiteness
I contract an office of always winter mostly whiteness
I contract whiteness
My contract is mostly whiteness with signatures that look like graffiti
in a bar's
    bathroom stall—drawing of a collapsed heart filled in with YOU
SUCK AT
    DRAWING HEARTS
Add junk to the prosperous collision
Add junk to the well adjusted well spoken well to do
Add junk and spit it out
Hey, olvidado
Assist
You forgive fully part-time
You forgive your well-being for not being
You realize that sadness is not like a dark ominous cloud and it is
silly to utilize this
    metaphor
Realize that it is instead rather small but plenty and like a swarm of
tiny spores
Realize the roadkill you pass on the way to class is your mascot
Realize that at least your face is not contorted and frozen in horror
unattractively

Realize that at least your guts are held in
Realize that in class you cannot stop thinking about roadkill and this
is distracting
Realize that whatever you are talking about to your class is actually
in no way more
    important than roadkill
Forget that staring into the mirror until you disappear takes a long
time
Forget that you don't have the time for this
Remember to adjunct as the means to an end
Realize that adjunct is only an extension of the means
Remember caring about our students
Consider administration
To add junk
To part
To fill
To assist
Remember creativity
I forgot to learn
I go to class to learn
I go to class to be creative
Go to class to class
Go to class to learn how to be creative
Go to class to learn about class
Go to class to rip creativity out through my pores and never speak to
it again
We apologize for our disheveled state
We apologize for running late
We intended to be on time this time
We give the world beauty one line at a time
In class you are
A part
Assist

WORKS CITED

Almond, Liz. "The Workshop Way." In *The Creative Writing Handbook: Techniques for New Writers*, edited by John Singleton and Mary Luckhurst, 18–40. London: Macmillan, 1999.
American Association of University Professors. "Contingent Appointments and the Academic Profession." www.aaup.org/report/contingent-appointments-and-academic-profession. Accessed 27 May 2018.

Brouillette, Sarah. "Academic Labor, the Aesthetics of Management, and the Promise of Autonomous Work." *Nonsite*, no. 9 (1 May 2013). nonsite.org/article/academic-labor-the-aesthetics-of-management-and-the-promise-of-autonomous-work.

Carpenter, Bennett, Laura Goldblatt, Lenora Hanson, Anna Vitale, Karim Wissa, and Andrew Yale. "Feces on the Philosophy of History! A Manifesto of the MLA Subconference." *Pedagogy*, vol. 14, no. 3 (10 October 2014): 381–393.

Cohen, Jennifer, Theresa Kulbaga, and Cathy Wagner. "Imperial Partitioning in the Neoliberal University." *World Social and Economic Review of Contemporary Policy Issues*, no. 8 (April 2017): 60–77. wer.worldeconomicsassociation.org/papers/imperial-partitioning-in-the-neoliberal-university/.

Foucault, Michel. *The Birth of Biopolitics: Lectures at the Collège de France, 1978–1979*. Translated by Graham Burchell. New York: Picador, 2010.

Graves, Robert. Interviewed by Kenneth Allsop, in Kenneth Allsop, *Scan*. London: Hodder and Stoughton, 1965. 29–33.

Goldsmith, Kenneth. "I Look to Theory Only When I Realize That Somebody Has Dedicated Their Entire Life to a Question I Have Only Fleetingly Considered: The Purposes of Repurposing." Poetry Foundation, 1 April 2015. www.poetryfoundation.org/poetrymagazine/articles/70209/i-look-to-theory-only-when-i-realize-that-somebody-has-dedicated-their-entire-life-to-a-question-i-have-only-fleetingly-considered.

Hardt, Michael. "Affective Labor." *boundary 2*, vol. 26, no. 2 (Summer 1999): 89–100.

Hardt, Michael, and Antonio Negri. *Multitude: War and Democracy in the Age of Empire*. New York: Penguin, 2004.

Hogan, Katie J., and Michelle A. Massé. *Over Ten Million Served: Gendered Service in Language and Literature Workplaces*. Albany: State University of New York Press, 2010.

Menger, Pierre-Michel. "Artistic Labor Markets: Contingent Work, Excess Supply and Occupational Risk Management." In *Handbook of the Economics of Art and Culture, Volume 1*, edited by Victor A. Ginsburgh and David Throsby, 765–811. Amsterdam: Elsevier, 2006.

Moten, Fred, and Stefano Harney. *The Undercommons: Fugitive Planning and Black Study*. Wivenhoe, New York, and Port Watson: Minor Compositions, 2013. www.minorcompositions.info/wp-content/uploads/2013/04/undercommons-web.pdf.

Weeks, Kathi. *The Problem with Work: Feminism, Marxism, Antiwork Politics, and Postwork Imaginaries*. Durham, NC: Duke University Press, 2011.

CHAPTER 14

Floating On—If Not Up—Ward

Tyrone Williams

for my father, Eddie Lee Williams

In early 1977 I completed a song I'd been working on with a pianist. It was worth the investment since the song, having been showcased through a Detroit recording and songwriting outfit called Groovesville Productions (headed by Brian Spears), was going to get placed on the debut album by a new R&B group from Detroit called The Floaters. However, between the time we started working on the song and the phone call I got from Brian informing me that the group really liked the finished product, the composer had moved to New Hampshire, disillusioned after three years of having our songs rejected. By the time we got the contracts to him in Nashua, New Hampshire and back—this was pre-fax, pre-email—ABC, the group's label, had decided to go with a different song. I was crushed by the news, but my disappointment was compounded when the Floaters' single from the album, "Float On," roared to Number One on the Billboard charts and gave the Detroit group its first—and only—smash hit. Above all else, I'd lost my dream of trying to repay my father back for all the long hard years he had toiled in

T. Williams (✉)
Xavier University, Cincinnati, OH, USA

© The Author(s) 2019
J. L. Walton and E. Luker (eds.), *Poetry and Work*,
Modern and Contemporary Poetry and Poetics,
https://doi.org/10.1007/978-3-030-26125-2_14

the automobile plants around Detroit and for all the years he had driven a truck delivering distilled water. I stopped writing songs and turned my full attention to poetry.

When I was trying to write rhythm and blues songs in the mid-seventies, my main motivation—aside from the adventure I was having pursuing fame—was repaying my father back for the sacrifices I had read into or projected onto his life. When I was small, not even ten, my father worked during the day at a sporting goods store in downtown Detroit called Griswold's. At night he attended some vocational school or college (I don't recall which), taking classes in design and architecture. He was always building and installing birdhouses in the backyard and crafting little knick-knacks for the house. It was, I'm sure, a source of shame (perhaps "just" disappointment) to him when it became apparent to both of us I had neither the interest in nor the inclination for things mechanical or crafts forged in woodshops. He was always working on our cars and often tried to teach me how to change the oil or do a tune up; his words went in one ear and out the other. However, I was fascinated by his architectural sketches and drawings and long after he'd gone to bed after a day of work and night of class I pored over them, absorbing the curves, lines and diagrams as though they were the secret language of worlds as alien as those conjured up in the science fiction novels I regularly devoured. So it isn't surprising that my first interest in the arts was in illustration and drawing—I even got invited out for a look-see at the prestigious Cranbrook Art Academy (located just north of Detroit) on the basis of one of my early sketches.

Eventually, for no reason I could fathom at the time, my father stopped attending night school; my well of drawings and diagrams dried up. A few months later my second sister came into the household, my mother took a job at a nursing home, and me and my eldest sister found ourselves saddled with baby-sitting duties, including feedings and changing diapers. This newfangled responsibility cut deeply into my reading regimen and my baseball playing. I was so resentful of the 'sacrifice' I was being forced to make that I scarcely noticed my father had switched jobs and was working at the Chrysler automobile plant in Highland Park. Eventually, over the next ten years, he would wind up working at the plants of General Motors and Ford before settling into the job he learned to love best of all, one he still loves today—driving a semi. I did not know it then, of course, but when our family doubled (a third sister followed the second two years later) my father gave up his dreams of being an architect and settled into a series of working-class jobs. He quit the sporting goods store he enjoyed (he was a baseball and football fan) to make more money on the assembly line.

I never forgot the lesson I drew from his experiences (rightly or wrongly) and when my songwriting career came to a sudden halt after the pianist I was working with became disillusioned and moved to New Hampshire I was devastated because I knew I'd never make enough money for him and my mother to retire on with ease. At the same time I hated the idea of sacrifice, the narrowing of choices, and I'm certain that watching my father's career options dwindle as our family grew had its deleterious effects on me—I did not marry until I was well into my forties. Yet, when I look at the lives of my sisters—all mothers, all with careers—I wonder if I have drawn the wrong lessons from the example of my father's sacrifice. Did he stop attending night school simply because he lost interest in architectural design? Was driving a truck—which he still does today even though he is 'officially' retired—his way to have a career he could prosper at and enjoy? And if so, then the sacrifices I have made—for example, I am not a father—cannot measure up against the ones he made for us. I will never be able to repay the debt I owe him, but I do hope that the choices I have made—I write and teach—are enough to qualify as minimal payments on the interest.

CHAPTER 15

Extract from the Poetic Labor Project

Amber DiPietra

The Poetic Labor Project (PLP)—organized by Brandon Brown, David Brazil, Steve Farmer, Sara Larsen, Lauren Levin, Suzanne Stein, and Alli Warren—began as a gathering in Oakland in 2010, where poets were invited to give short statements reflecting on how they earned a living. The convocation was partly a response to the form of the academic conference, wanting to create a space for poets who did not work in the academy to discuss poetry, poetics, labor, and social life. The PLP has continued to grow as a blog (labday2010.blogspot.com), with over eighty responses from poets (concentrated in the Bay Area of California but also across the US and internationally, with a substantial Chilean contingent). The text below was originally a podcast recorded for the project in 2011.

Since this piece was written in 2010, I have left San Francisco and moved back to Florida due to health issues and increasing pain. Public transit as well as disability services and community are fairly non-existent in Florida, so I am now a sex worker and body worker, which is labor I can do from home.

A. DiPietra (✉)
St. Petersburg, FL, USA

© The Author(s) 2019
J. L. Walton and E. Luker (eds.), *Poetry and Work*,
Modern and Contemporary Poetry and Poetics,
https://doi.org/10.1007/978-3-030-26125-2_15

WORK-WORK

The short answer to 'What do you do?' is 'disability advocate.' Though often it is easier to respond with 'disability service provider,' because people can interpret that as case manager or social worker, and that makes sense to them.

The longer, more accurate answer is that I work for the Independent Living Resource Center in San Francisco, where I am absolutely not a social worker (via the old model of managing someone else's choices and determining abilities based on bureaucratic qualifiers). Independent living centers exist nationally in most major cities. They are government-mandated, largely government-funded nonprofits that serve as places where people with disabilities can go to get information about resources, such as assistive technology, support groups, accessible arts programs, alerts about proposed legislation impacting disability issues. ILCs are where people can get help with navigating social services like personal or in-home care, low income housing options, employment accommodations, et cetera. My work also requires me to keep up with the politics around healthcare, genetic testing, civil rights and technological innovations.

It requires me to be a constant communicator—either via phone, in-person, or increasingly, via social networking—since one of the biggest issues facing people with disabilities is the divide that still exists in terms of social integration. But most of all, this work requires me to sit with people and envision outcomes. People come to me with a mass of reality and their language around it—a new diagnosis or years of living with nagging, stupid issues that crop up. Things like: 'the landlord won't let me have a ramp and now three steps keep me prisoner in my apartment,' or 'I need to take Goldie to class on my shoulder because she can talk to the voices while I take notes for my exam,' or 'I go to job interviews and as soon as I walk in the door with my white cane, the interviewer sounds plastic.' Primarily, mine is a job of collaborative making. A kind of peer-counseling poiesis. I listen, co-brainstorm, share stories about folks in similar situations. I take the language that is given to me and give it back to the person who has come to see me—either by offering a way to prioritize around the issue, by reframing options, or by simply emoting in a way that is authentic and carries new momentum.

FREELANCE-WORK

As a 'peer mentor' at my independent living center, it is hard to know how much or how little to do, how best to facilitate a space for the client's envisioning process. Especially when we are stand together against such gaping holes in community support systems. There are appeals to file, requests to fill out, bureaucratic languages that must be worked within. Then I go home and I swirl these interactions around in my head for days at a time, trying to hit upon some creative suggestion I can offer in each individual situation. This 'taking it home with me' is not really required as part of my paid work, but it is the part that makes me a poet within the context of the work. I have wanted to push that impulse further and I have wanted to combine my paid work as an independent living center worker with my work as one who writes poems. I have also wanted to bring in body-work, the hardest, most basic work. I wanted to create a single space to function as a poet, a body-worker and a disability advocate, so I have been experimenting with Write to Connect, a creative writing class for folks in the disability community.

BODY-WORK

I ran out of cartilage over twenty-five years ago and all of my bones, including the vertebrae in my neck, have been grinding to a halt since then. I am thirty-two years old. I have bone spurs, tendon impingements, and frozen joints. If I want to maintain any freedom of movement for the next, hopefully, several decades, I must work every day, slowly, tediously, to keep some modicum of space between my internal moving parts. This means undoing the time spent working by swimming, sitting in warm waters, lying down, making dull circles with ankles, shoulders, wrists, et cetera. It also means massage, acupuncture, and energy work. And Art Workouts! (This embarrasses me, to go into all this, because I feel like I have said this stuff on the internets before. I am kind of phobic about being repetitive, because being repetitive in writing seems to mimic somatic constriction I experience all the time. However, it also tends to loosen gently, methodically, which is absolutely the point.)

All of this body-work requires a huge amount of money, time, and attention. I give far less of any of these resources to the body-work than I give to other types of work. That's because I get bored, because it is invisible, because it feels indulgent, because it leads me into claustrophobic self-narratives about the nature of how I do or do not move, because it seems simple and I haven't figured out how to plug my somatic machinations into my writing in a way that is totally interesting and accurate. I think a sure bet is to find a way to offer the body-work to others. For instance, to have an energy work practice I offer out of my apartment. Currently, I'm confused about the apprenticeship process for that—and how I really feel about it as a fair exchange. If you know of an energy worker/poet who could help me legitimize this for myself, please send me an email. Most days, I want to be a practitioner of some unquantifiable transformations for and with others, more than I want to be a poet.

Social- and Domestic-Work

Sicilian and Spanish immigrants by way of Cuba, people who are cigar rollers, nurses, hair dressers, musicians, waiters, bartenders, grounds keepers, actors, house painters, appliance repairers, and sales reps for cigarette vending machines, wine and beer—these are my family. Most of them with incredible genes that have them looking smooth, tan and athletic into their 70s. They've worked hard all their lives so I could stay home, in Florida, in their houses, and write poetry. If I had wanted, I could've done that. Or, my family cajoles, 'You could rent a little place in the cool neighborhood where the gays and the arty people are redoing the old shotgun houses.' And be my very own Ybor City Thoreau—with family to do the laundry and cooking.

But, I chose 'to haul ass outta Florida' as my grandfather Chino put it. And since I have asked so much of my family—it is a lot for them to have accepted, emotionally, culturally, me putting 3000 miles between us—the least I can do is fly across the country a few times a year. I don't make very much money working at a disability nonprofit (especially in a time when politicians want to cut funds that will allow people with disabilities the basic freedom of remaining in their own homes, outside of institutions). With the money I make, I save up to buy plane tickets home, to see my family. That's always my goal. Not money for writers' retreats or conferences or whatever. This is ironic for two reasons: (1) my family would buy my tickets and (2) I chose to spend an inordinate amount of money on academia which I then abandoned. That is to say, I used the excuse of 'needing to go to grad school for creative writing' in order to move out to San Francisco.

The riddle for both is as follows: I felt like my family (many of them did not finish high school) would never let me leave Florida if I didn't use grad school, an obscure and irrefutable idea, as an excuse. I also felt incapable of work; an MFA was an expensive way of stalling. Which actually feels like ultimate dumb-assery to me, the grad school thing (but it is also the way I met magical friends). To me, work was physical labor, which I always saw my family doing. Watched them doing when I, a fourteen-year-old with locked shoulders, had a hard time even dressing myself. I got an MFA, but then decided being a creative writing professor had not enough to do with the peer mentoring work that needed doing, the kind of work I now do at the independent living center. Because by the time I had finished my MFA, I had also discovered the disability community. As for using the majority of my tiny savings for tickets home, that's about emotional debt (how my family let go while remaining present to fall back on), and a sense of honoring their work, much of it blue collar, by trying to match it with my own.

I think of Chris Daniels, in his talk for Labor Day, saying:

I see labor as an attribute of human behavior which transforms reality. You make a chair, you've transformed reality. You work as a clerk, you take a pile of paper here and move it there, you transform reality. You teach for a living, hopefully, you want to transform a human mind, you want to help someone transform reality and in your work you are — hopefully — transforming reality.[1]

My little brothers are struggling, back in Florida, to figure out what kind of new experiences they want to have. They are doing badly in school because we don't come from a studious culture. It is no longer clear to me what to tell them. My experience—a disability advocate/poet that left for SF—is a total anomaly. I want to do more work for them, help them transform their reality, but I am not sure where to begin. Especially if transforming means discarding cultural foundations.

---

[1] Chris Daniels, Contribution to Poetic Labor Project, labday2010.blogspot.com/2010/09/chris-daniels.html, accessed 10 January 2019.

POETRY- AND SLEEP-WORK

In her Labor Day Project talk, Sara Larsen describes the time she spends under the San Francisco Bay, rapid transiting toward capitalism. I think about how much better I would be doing health-wise if I had stayed a small arthritic Hispanic girl in Florida, Thoreau style, soaking in the Gulf of Mexico with my abuela to help me out. In SF, I spend more time commuting, under the sea, than rehabilitating in it. It will always be too fucking cold for me to swim here.

I fantasize all the time about being able to have sex, conversations, swim/ambulate and connect people in my sleep. This is why I write poetry. It is a little like being able to do that. I love what Andrew Joron said during his Labor Day talk about being a surrealist, about dreaming while you are awake. It makes me understand how I could possibly join work and sleep. I need to sleep at least ten hours most nights to keep my joints from totally stiffening up. Sleep feels like productive work; my friend Lexi Brayton says 'sleep is emotional research.'

There is a desire for the continuous, to be a single fluid element. For there to be no mess. (There wasn't space to elaborate on domestic-work in this talk—the part of me that, as a disabled woman with a bit of the super crip syndrome, has a need to keep very clean floors. So that I know I can. Absurdly, with splintered ankles, four cats, and dwelling in close proximity to the Tenderloin. How DOES she do it?—do I do it?—they ask. A boyfriend that sweeps and mops! Love as economical exchange—a whole other subject on the spectrum of work. I should add that he is also not insulted by my longing to converse and have sex while staying asleep. And that he has recorded this podcast.)

Poetry is messy. It is filtering bits of mica or raking the flats for a resonant tone. It is Sisyphus stuff, as work-work is often compared to. The labor it takes for things to elapse in time. I move in small circles, trying to find clearings and new energies. Work-work, freelance-work, body-work, poetry- and sleep-work align in the moments outside time, real time. Which is not trying, but dreaming. Awake, together with great fervor and to much use.

WORK CITED

Daniels, Chris. Contribution to Poetic Labor Project. labday2010.blogspot. com/2010/09/chris-daniels.html. Accessed 10 January 2019.

Index

© The Editor(s) (if applicable) and The Author(s),
under exclusive license to Springer Nature Switzerland AG 2019
J. L. Walton and E. Luker (eds.), *Poetry and Work*,
Modern and Contemporary Poetry and Poetics,
https://doi.org/10.1007/978-3-030-26125-2

Printed by Printforce, the Netherlands